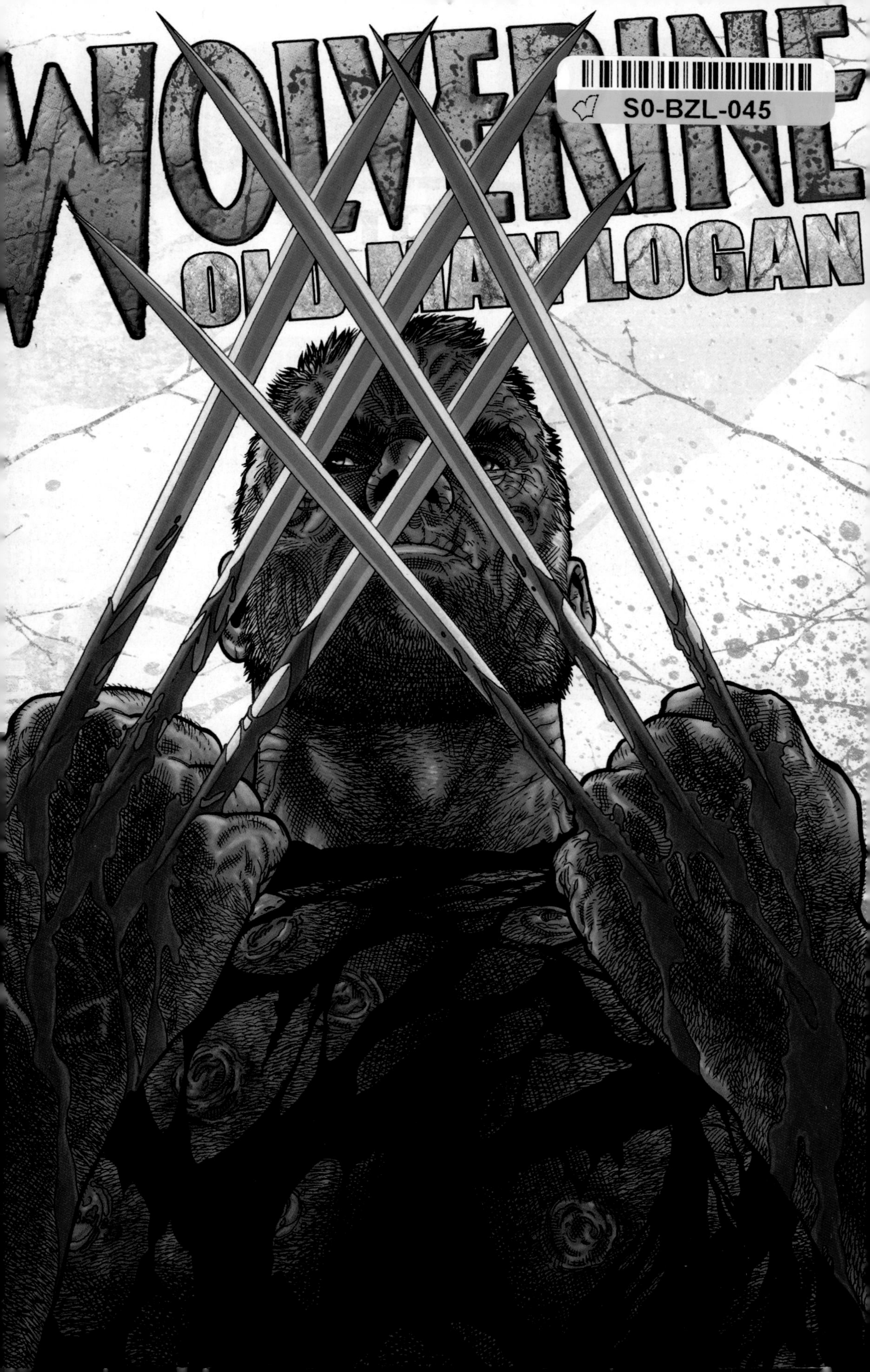
WOLVERINE
OLD MAN LOGAN

WOLVERINE
OLD MAN LOGAN

WRITER: MARK **MILLAR** • PENCILER: STEVE **McNIVEN**

INKERS: DEXTER **VINES** WITH MARK **MORALES** & JAY **LEISTE**

COLORISTS: MORRY **HOLLOWELL** WITH CHRISTINA **STRAIN**, JUSTIN **PONSO**

JASON **KEITH**, NATHAN **FAIRBAIRN** & PAUL **MOUNT**

LETTERER: VC'S **CORY PET**

ASSISTANT EDITORS: AUBREY **SITTERSON**, MICHAEL **HORWITZ** & JODY **LEHEU**

EDITORS: JOHN **BARBER** & JEANINE **SCHAEFE**

GROUP EDITOR: AXEL **ALONS**

COVER ARTISTS: STEVE **McNIVEN**, DEXTER **VINES** & MORRY **HOLLOWEI**

COLLECTION EDITOR: MARK D. **BEAZLE**

ASSISTANT MANAGING EDITOR: JOE **HOCHSTEI**

ASSOCIATE MANAGING EDITOR: ALEX **STARBUC**

EDITOR, SPECIAL PROJECTS: JENNIFER **GRÜNWAL**

SENIOR EDITOR, SPECIAL PROJECTS: JEFF **YOUNGQUIS**

PRODUCTION: JERRY **KALINOWSI**

BOOK DESIGNER: RODOLFO **MURAGUC**

SVP PRINT, SALES & MARKETING: DAVID **GABRIE**

EDITOR IN CHIEF: AXEL **ALONS**

CHIEF CREATIVE OFFICER: JOE **QUESAD**

PUBLISHER: DAN **BUCKLE**

EXECUTIVE PRODUCER: ALAN **FIN**

WOLVERINE: OLD MAN LOGAN. Contains material originally published in magazine form as WOLVERINE #66-72 and WOLVERINE: OLD MAN LOGAN GIANT-SIZE. Sixth printing 2015. ISBN# 978-0-7851-3172-4. Publis by MARVEL WORLDWIDE, INC., a subsidiary of MARVEL ENTERTAINMENT, LLC. OFFICE OF PUBLICATION: 135 West 50th Street, New York, NY 10020. Copyright © 2010 MARVEL No similarity between any of the nar characters, persons, and/or institutions in this magazine with those of any living or dead person or institution is intended, and any such similarity which may exist is purely coincidental. **Printed in the U.S.A.** A FINE, President, Marvel Entertainment; DAN BUCKLEY, President, TV, Publishing and Brand Management; JOE QUESADA, Chief Creative Officer; TOM BREVOORT, SVP of Publishing; DAVID BOGART, SVP of Operation Procurement, Publishing; C.B. CEBULSKI, VP of International Development & Brand Management; DAVID GABRIEL, SVP Print, Sales & Marketing; JIM O'KEEFE, VP of Operations & Logistics; DAN CARR, Executive Dire of Publishing Technology; SUSAN CRESPI, Editorial Operations Manager; ALEX MORALES, Publishing Operations Manager; STAN LEE, Chairman Emeritus. For information regarding advertising in Marvel Comics or Marvel.com, please contact Jonathan Rheingold, VP of Custom Solutions & Ad Sales, at jrheingold@marvel.com. For Marvel subscription inquiries, please call 800-217-9158. **Manufactured between** 4/1/2015 5/4/2015 by R.R. DONNELLEY, INC., SALEM, VA, USA.

1 0 9 8 7 6

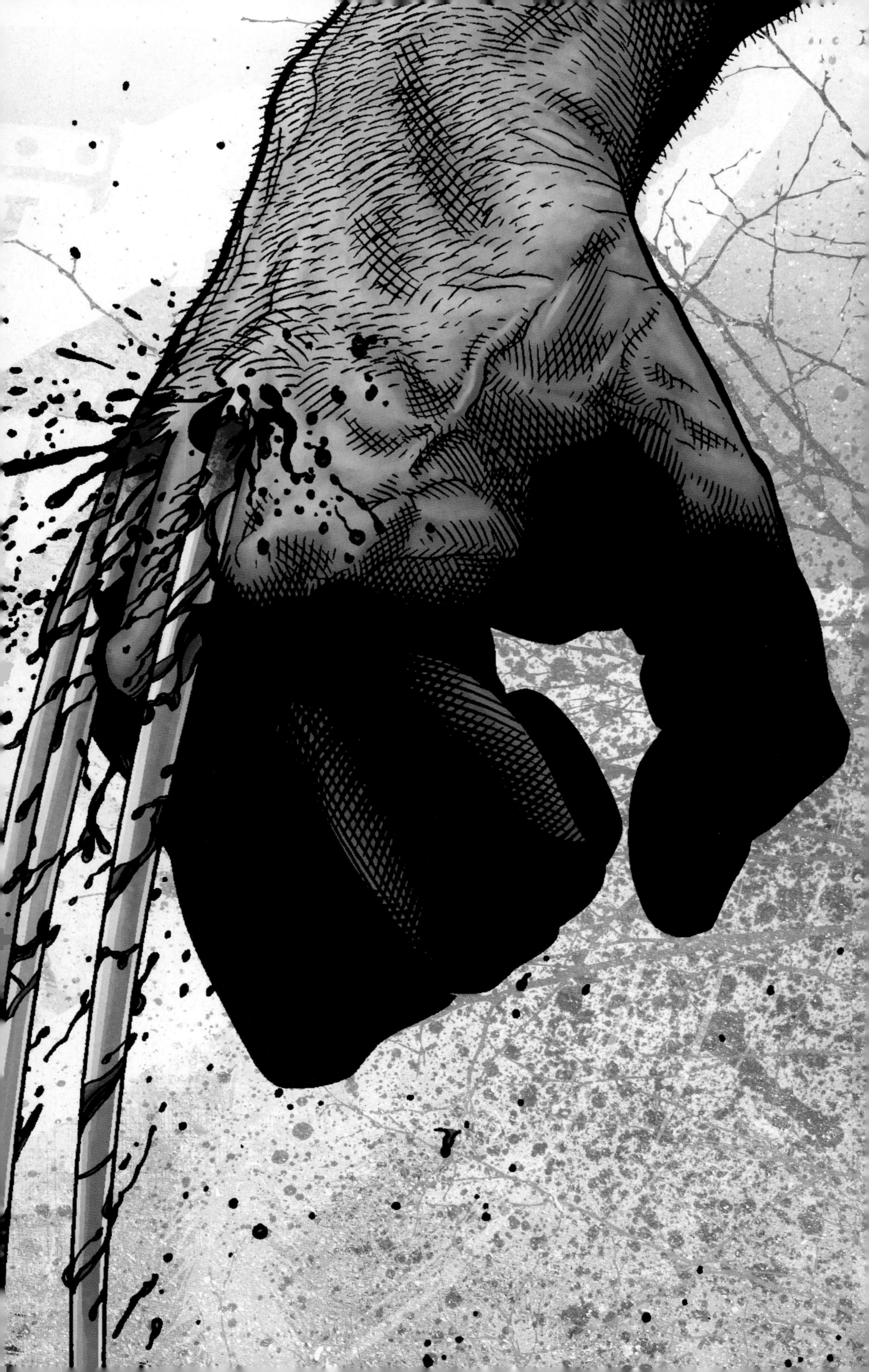

CHAPTER ONE

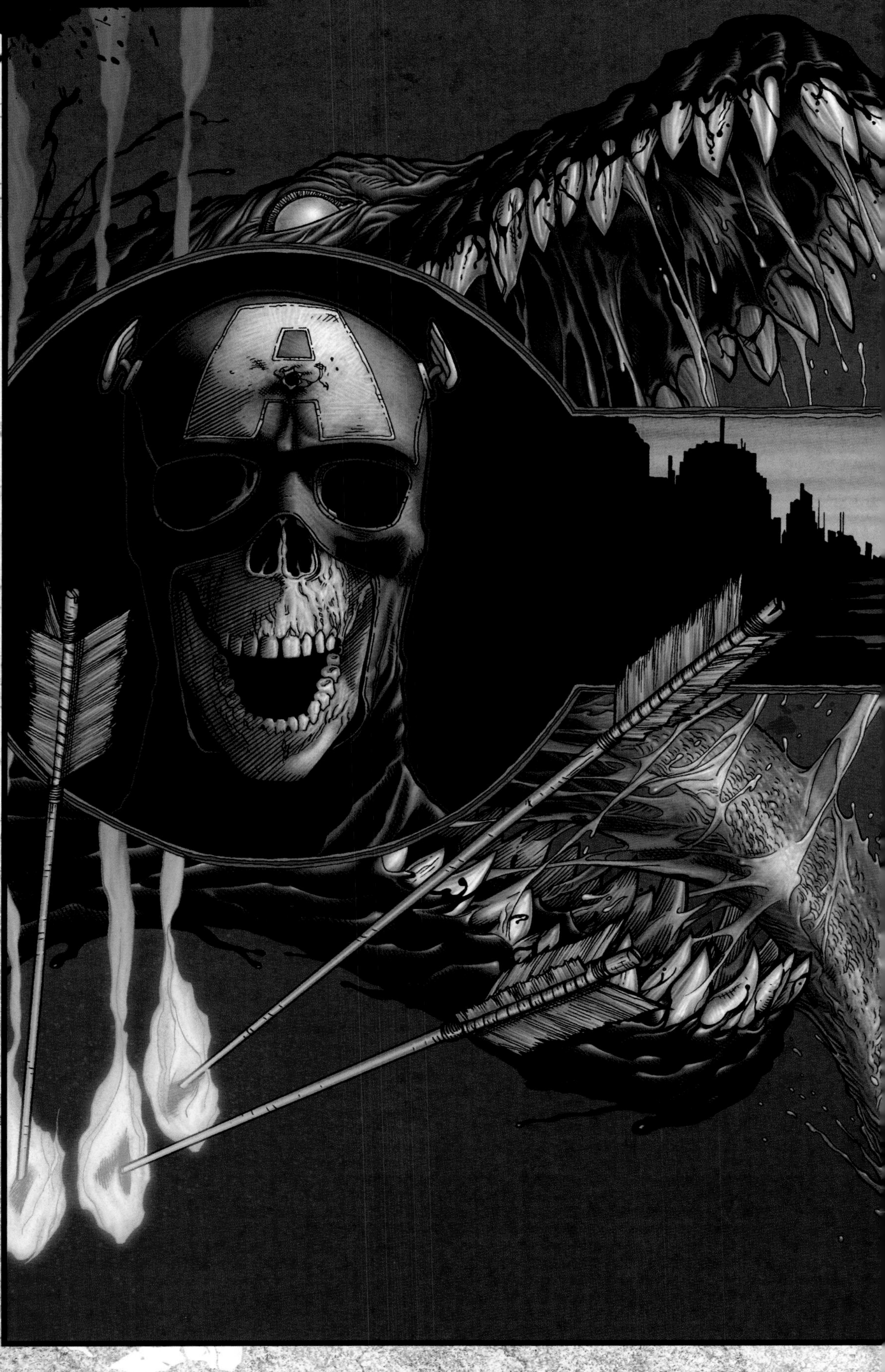

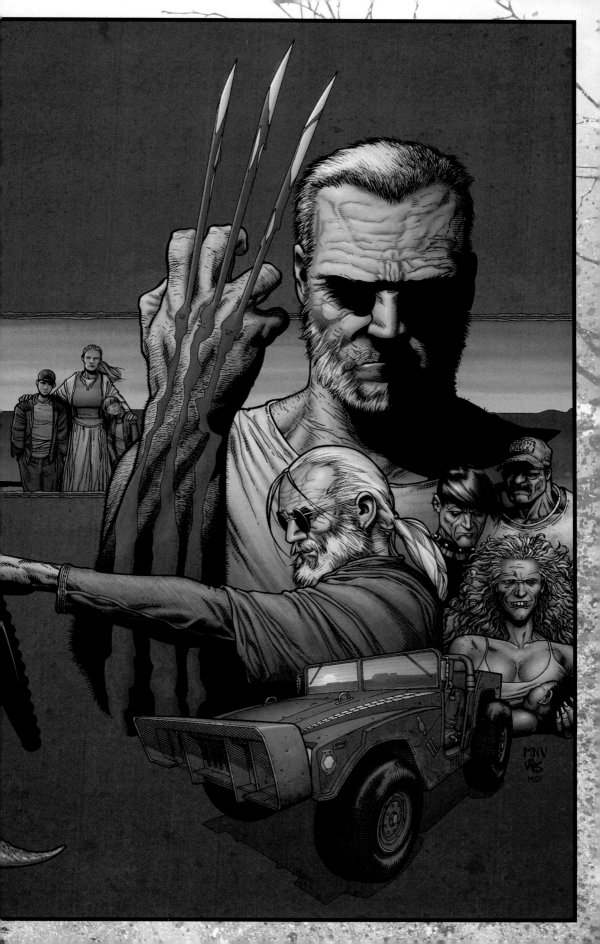

MICHAEL TURNER VARIANT COVER

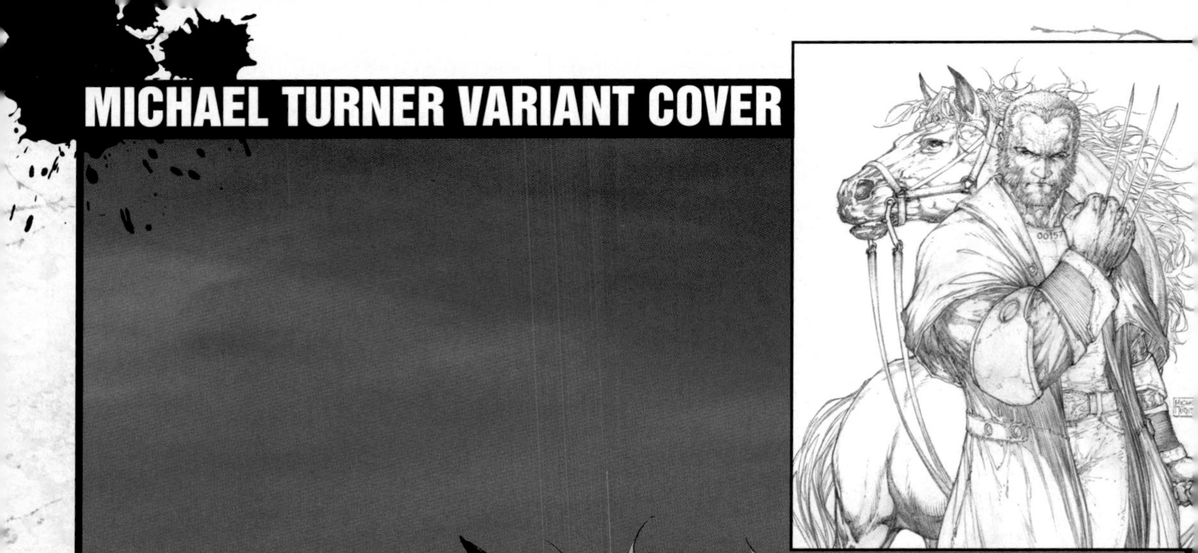
00157

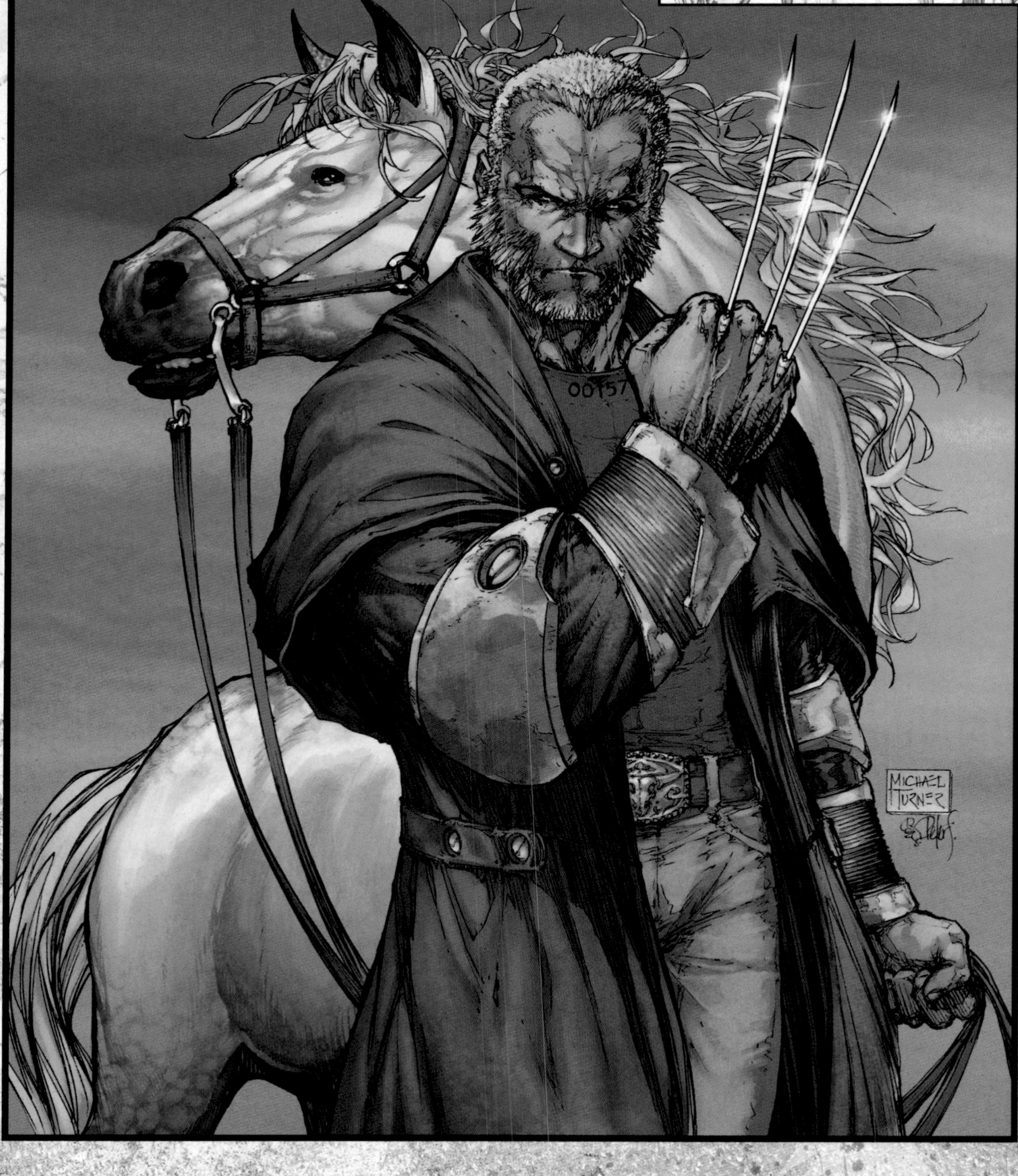
00157
MICHAEL TURNER

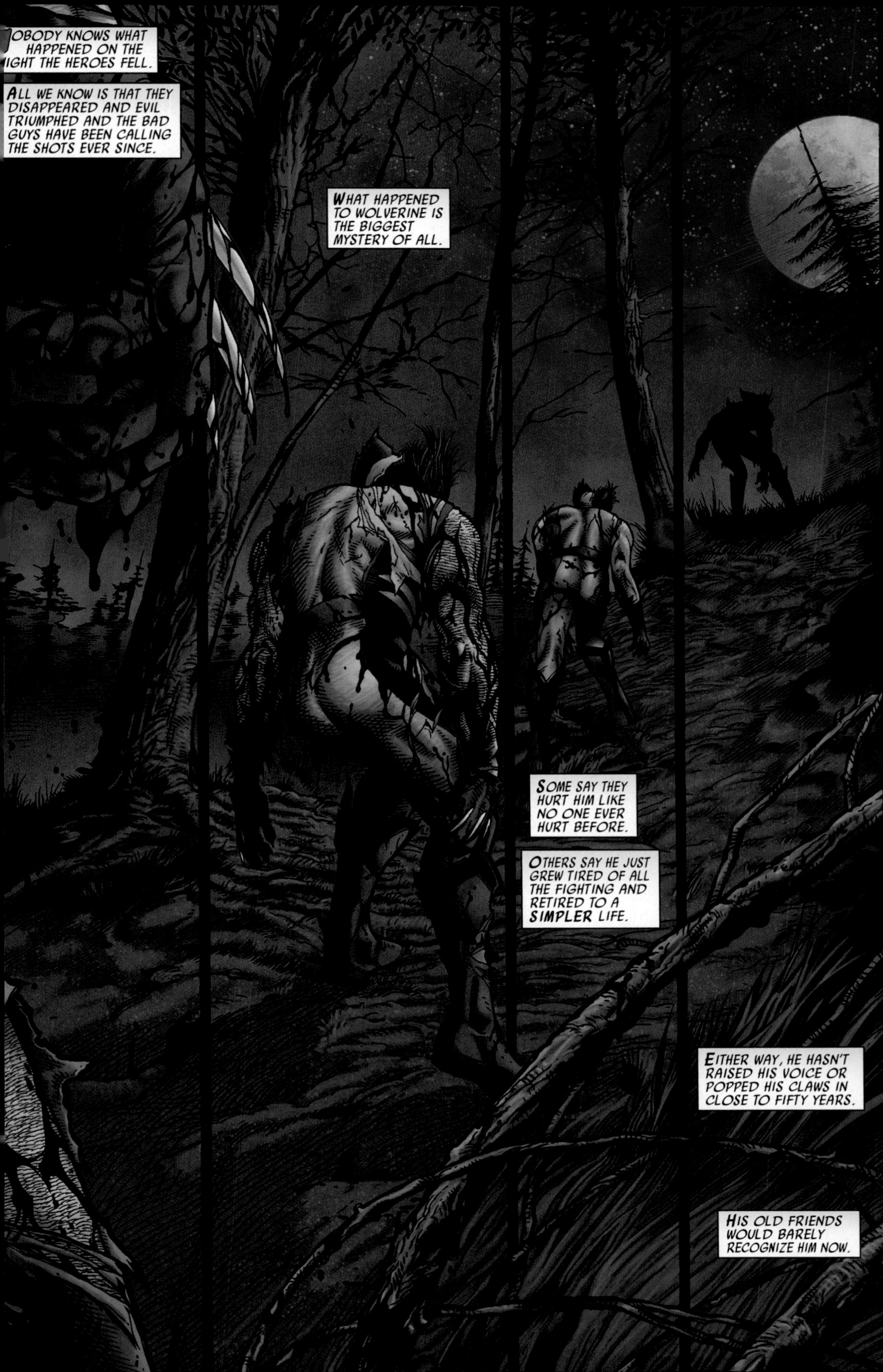
OBODY KNOWS WHAT HAPPENED ON THE IGHT THE HEROES FELL.
ALL WE KNOW IS THAT THEY DISAPPEARED AND EVIL TRIUMPHED AND THE BAD GUYS HAVE BEEN CALLING THE SHOTS EVER SINCE.
WHAT HAPPENED TO WOLVERINE IS THE BIGGEST MYSTERY OF ALL.
SOME SAY THEY HURT HIM LIKE NO ONE EVER HURT BEFORE.
OTHERS SAY HE JUST GREW TIRED OF ALL THE FIGHTING AND RETIRED TO A SIMPLER LIFE.
EITHER WAY, HE HASN'T RAISED HIS VOICE OR POPPED HIS CLAWS IN CLOSE TO FIFTY YEARS.
HIS OLD FRIENDS WOULD BARELY RECOGNIZE HIM NOW.

OLD MAN LOGAN
PART 1

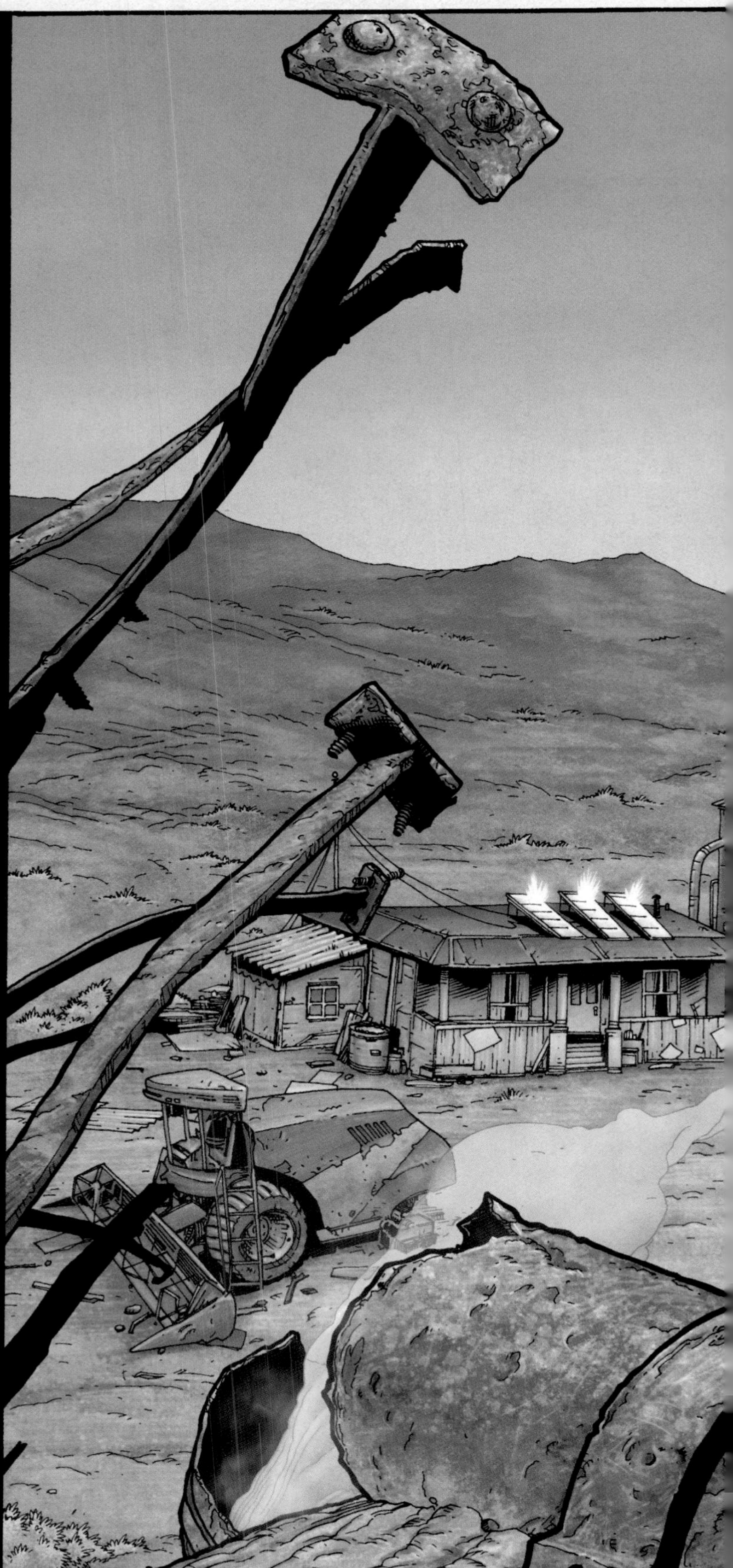

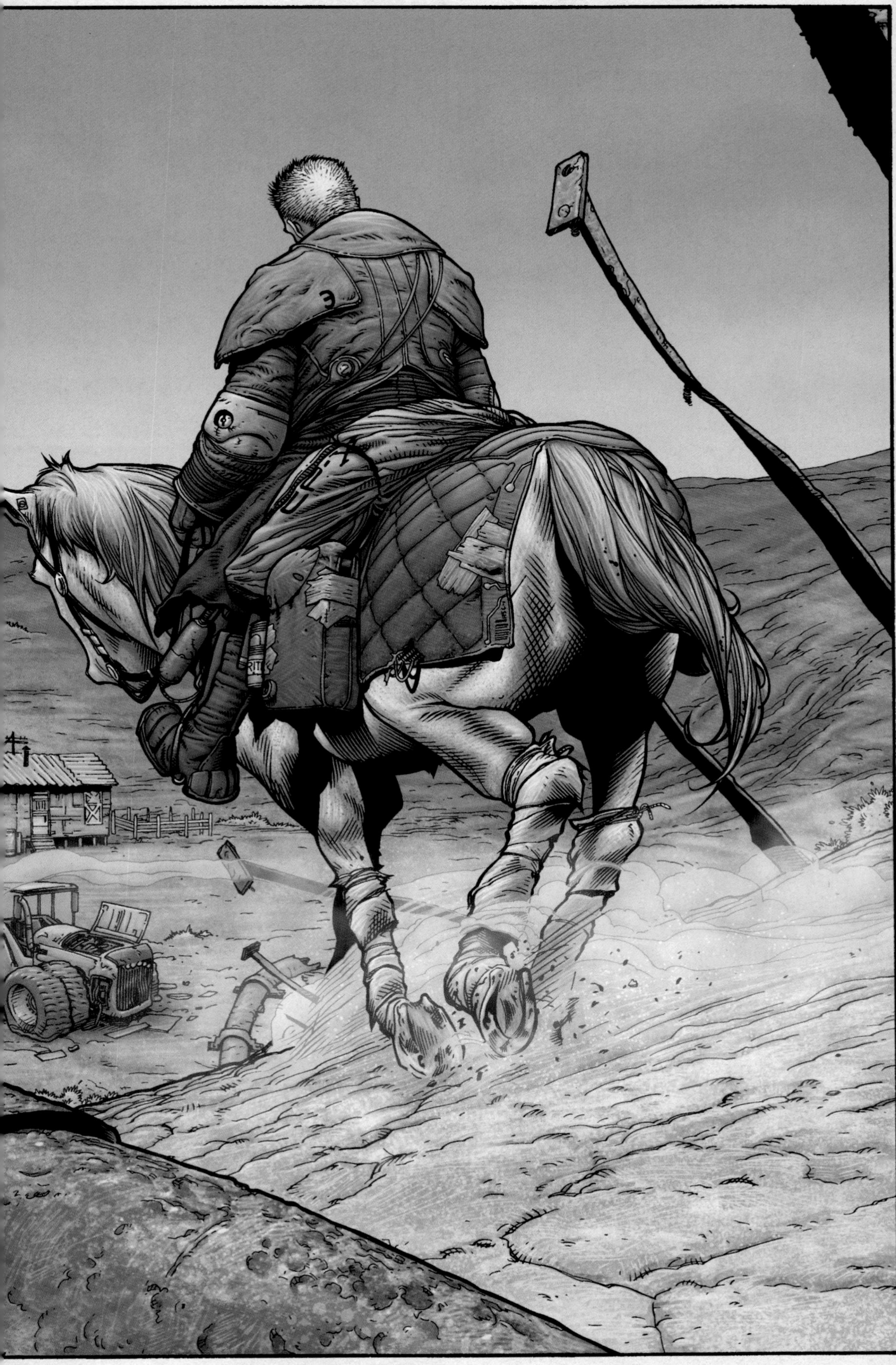

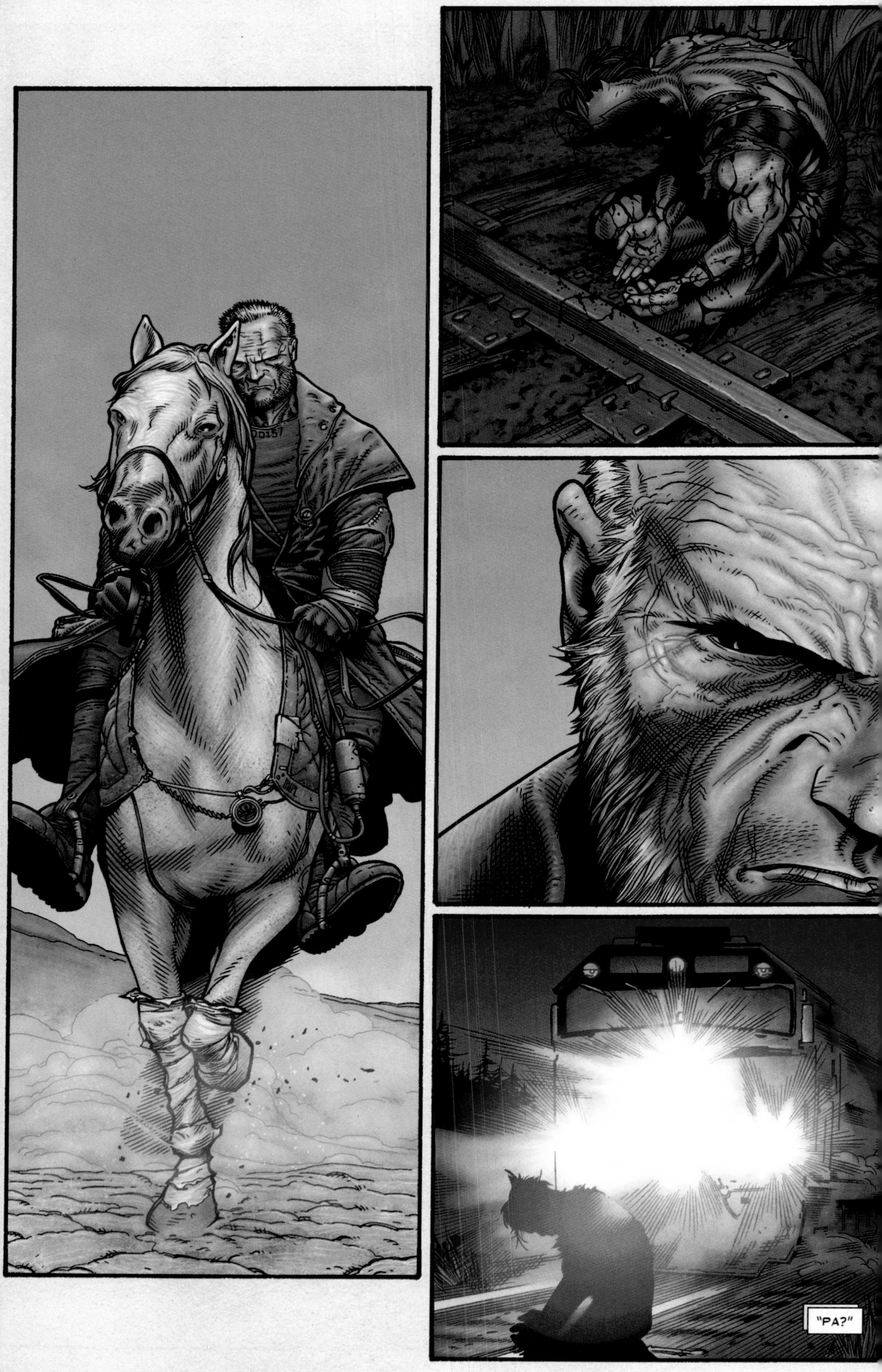
"PA?"

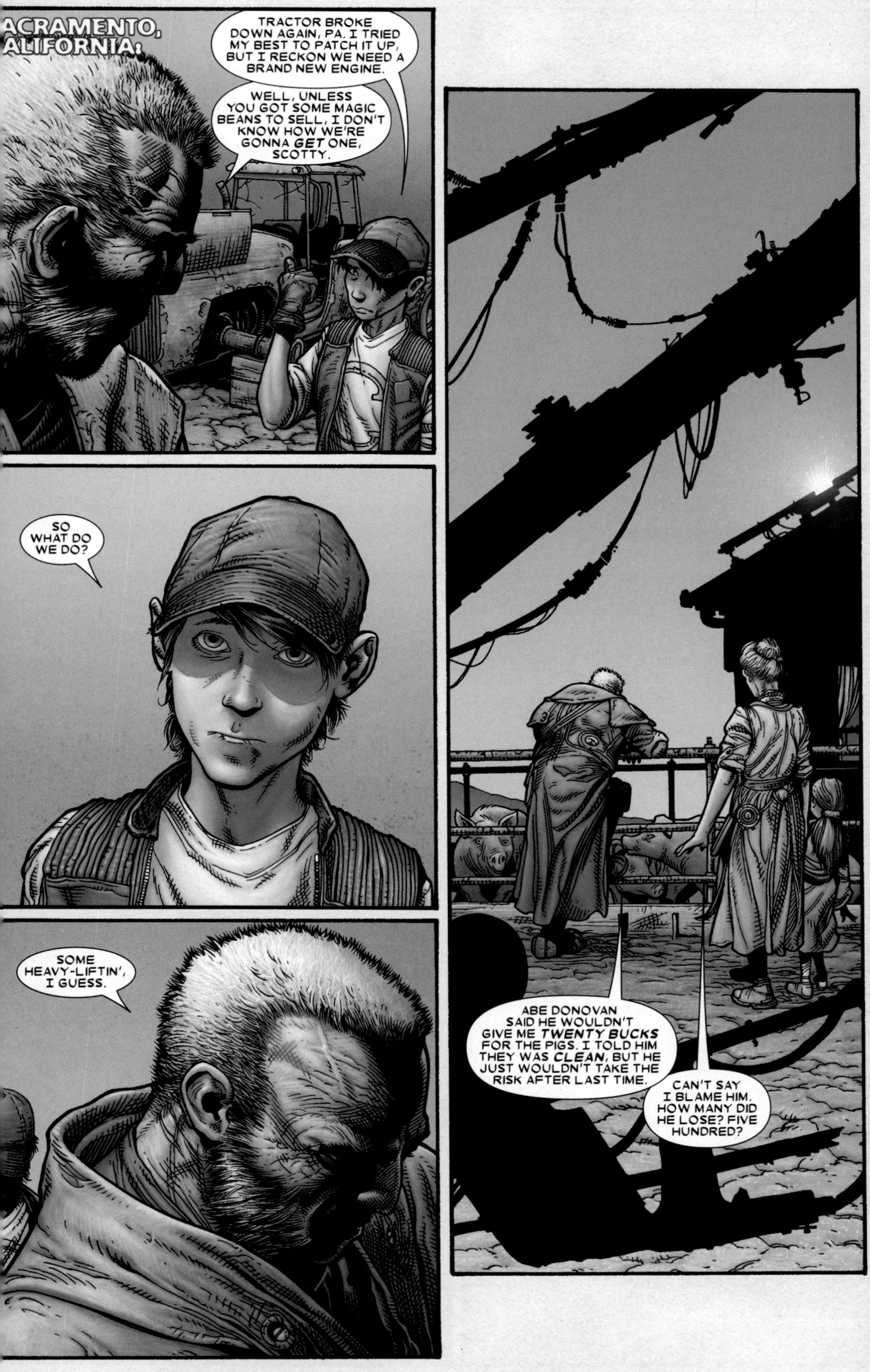
SACRAMENTO, CALIFORNIA:
TRACTOR BROKE DOWN AGAIN, PA. I TRIED MY BEST TO PATCH IT UP, BUT I RECKON WE NEED A BRAND NEW ENGINE.
WELL, UNLESS YOU GOT SOME MAGIC BEANS TO SELL, I DON'T KNOW HOW WE'RE GONNA GET ONE, SCOTTY.
SO WHAT DO WE DO?
SOME HEAVY-LIFTIN', I GUESS.
ABE DONOVAN SAID HE WOULDN'T GIVE ME TWENTY BUCKS FOR THE PIGS. I TOLD HIM THEY WAS CLEAN, BUT HE JUST WOULDN'T TAKE THE RISK AFTER LAST TIME.
CAN'T SAY I BLAME HIM. HOW MANY DID HE LOSE? FIVE HUNDRED?

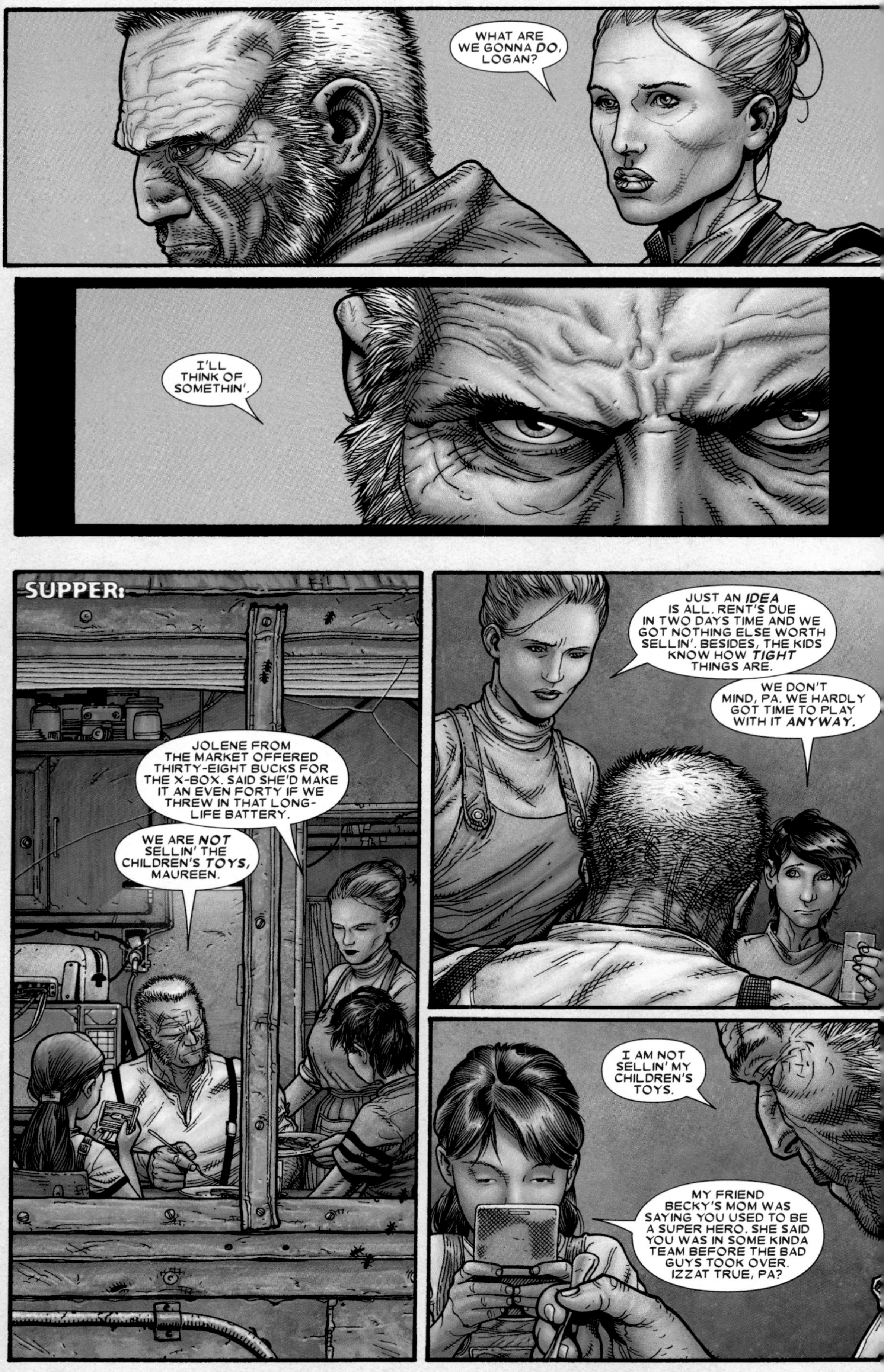
WHAT ARE WE GONNA DO, LOGAN?
I'LL THINK OF SOMETHIN'.
SUPPER:
JOLENE FROM THE MARKET OFFERED THIRTY-EIGHT BUCKS FOR THE X-BOX. SAID SHE'D MAKE IT AN EVEN FORTY IF WE THREW IN THAT LONG-LIFE BATTERY.
WE ARE NOT SELLIN' THE CHILDREN'S TOYS, MAUREEN.
JUST AN IDEA IS ALL. RENT'S DUE IN TWO DAYS TIME AND WE GOT NOTHING ELSE WORTH SELLIN'. BESIDES, THE KIDS KNOW HOW TIGHT THINGS ARE.
WE DON'T MIND, PA. WE HARDLY GOT TIME TO PLAY WITH IT ANYWAY.
I AM NOT SELLIN' MY CHILDREN'S TOYS.
MY FRIEND BECKY'S MOM WAS SAYING YOU USED TO BE A SUPER HERO. SHE SAID YOU WAS IN SOME KINDA TEAM BEFORE THE BAD GUYS TOOK OVER. IZZAT TRUE, PA?

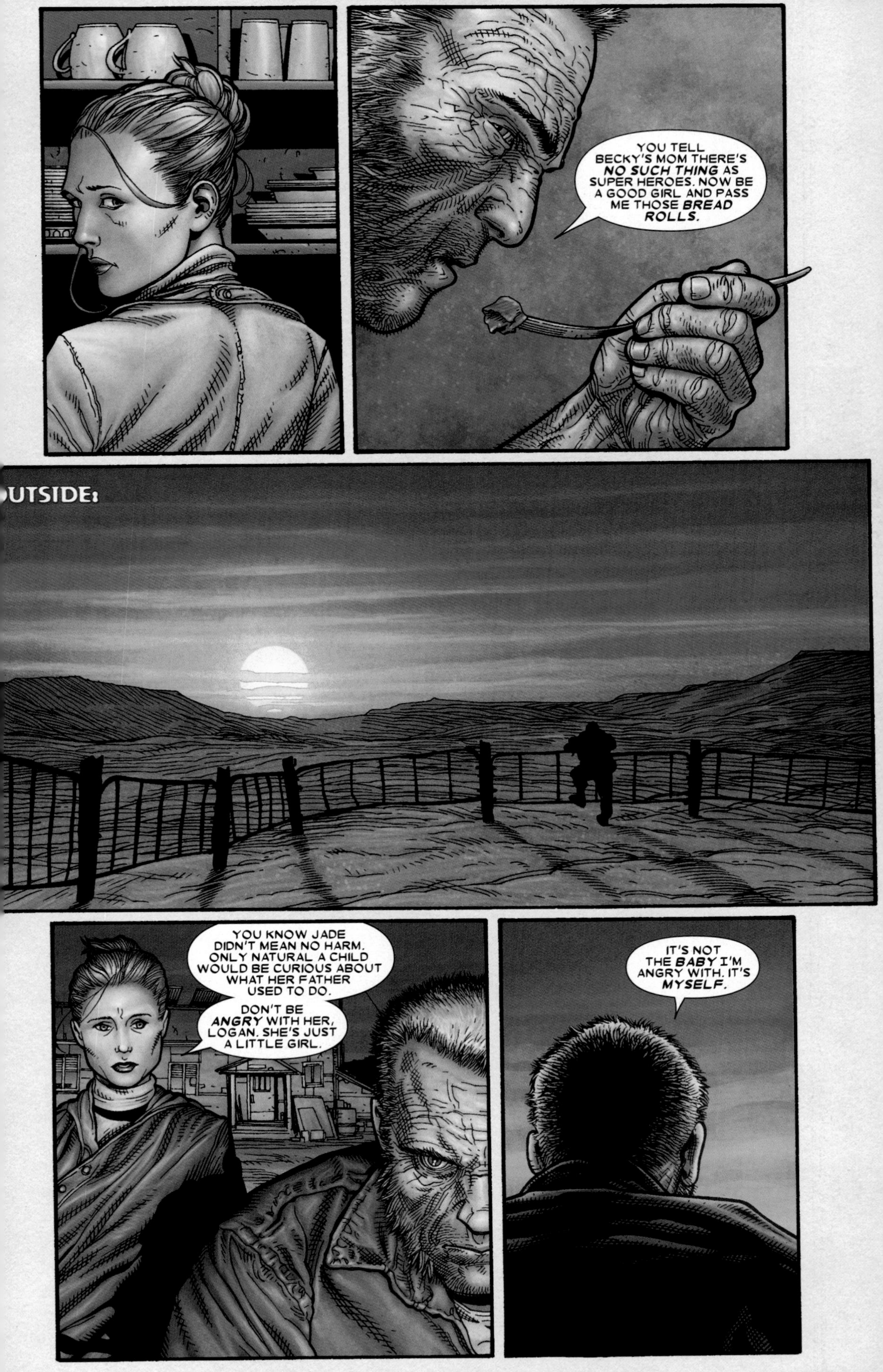
YOU TELL BECKY'S MOM THERE'S NO SUCH THING AS SUPER HEROES. NOW BE A GOOD GIRL AND PASS ME THOSE BREAD ROLLS.
UTSIDE:
YOU KNOW JADE DIDN'T MEAN NO HARM. ONLY NATURAL A CHILD WOULD BE CURIOUS ABOUT WHAT HER FATHER USED TO DO.
DON'T BE ANGRY WITH HER, LOGAN. SHE'S JUST A LITTLE GIRL.
IT'S NOT THE BABY I'M ANGRY WITH. IT'S MYSELF.

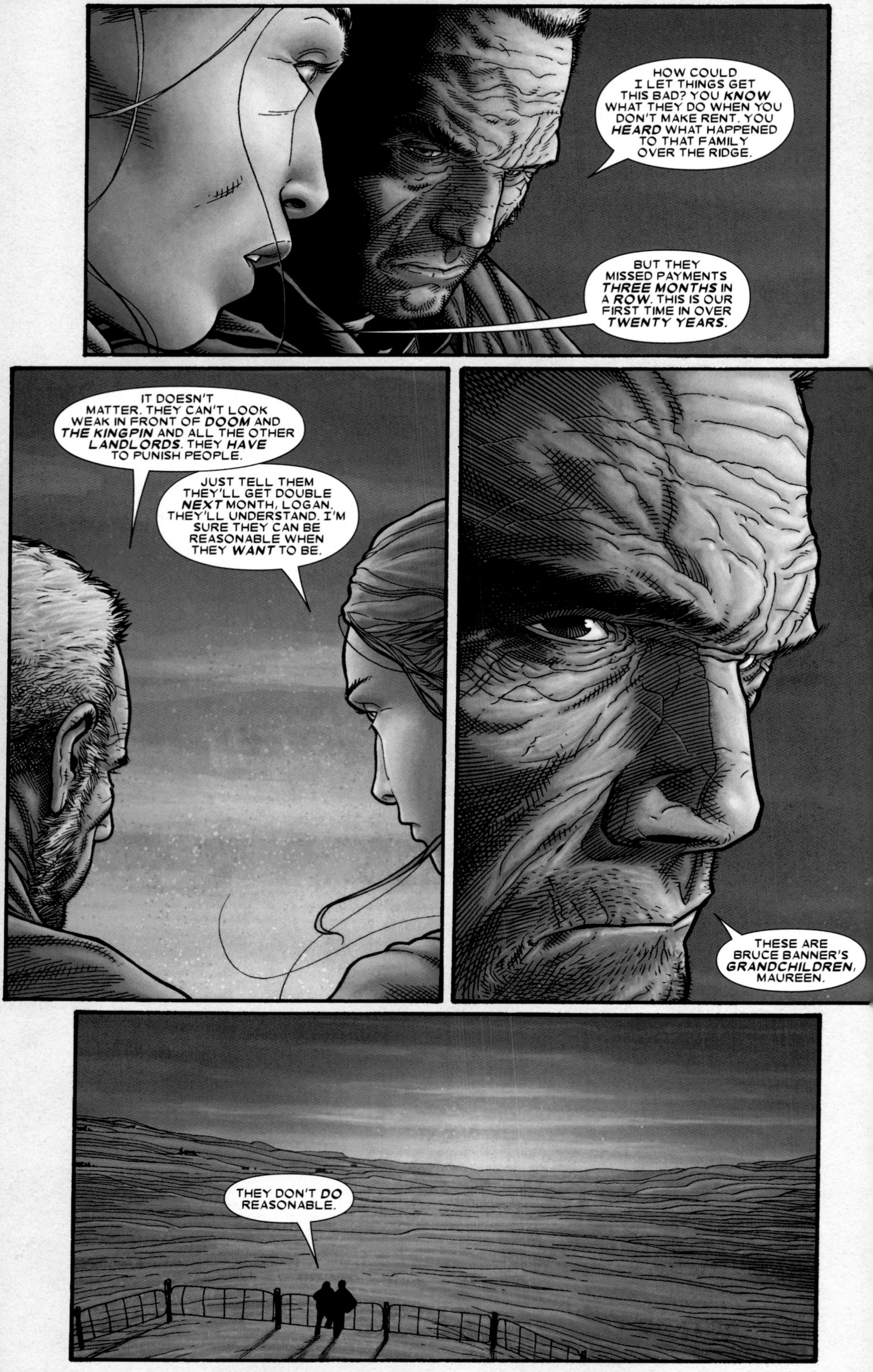
HOW COULD I LET THINGS GET THIS BAD? YOU KNOW WHAT THEY DO WHEN YOU DON'T MAKE RENT. YOU HEARD WHAT HAPPENED TO THAT FAMILY OVER THE RIDGE.
BUT THEY MISSED PAYMENTS THREE MONTHS IN A ROW. THIS IS OUR FIRST TIME IN OVER TWENTY YEARS.
IT DOESN'T MATTER. THEY CAN'T LOOK WEAK IN FRONT OF DOOM AND THE KINGPIN AND ALL THE OTHER LANDLORDS. THEY HAVE TO PUNISH PEOPLE.
JUST TELL THEM THEY'LL GET DOUBLE NEXT MONTH, LOGAN. THEY'LL UNDERSTAND. I'M SURE THEY CAN BE REASONABLE WHEN THEY WANT TO BE.
THESE ARE BRUCE BANNER'S GRANDCHILDREN, MAUREEN.
THEY DON'T DO REASONABLE.

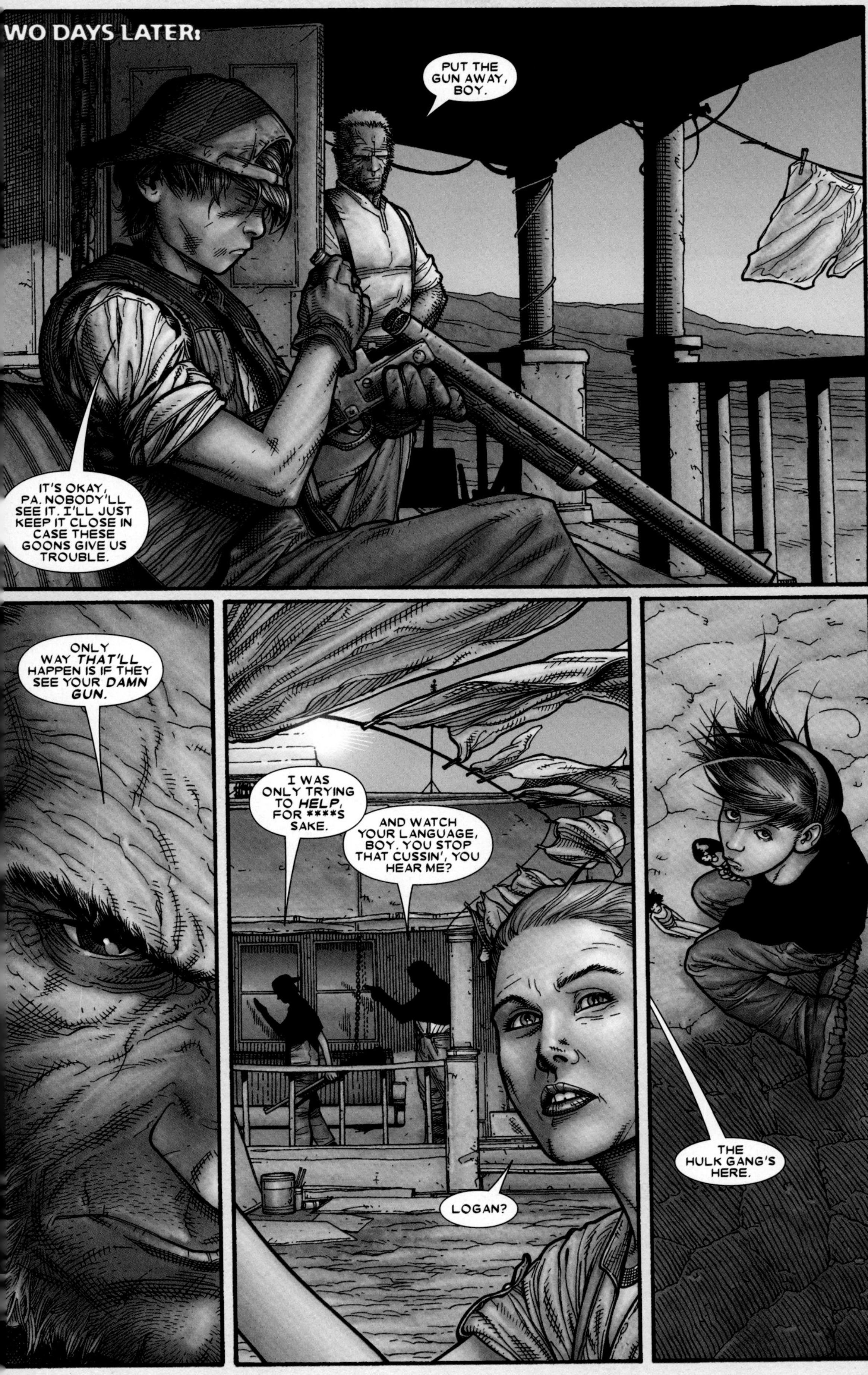
WO DAYS LATER:
PUT THE GUN AWAY, BOY.
IT'S OKAY, PA. NOBODY'LL SEE IT. I'LL JUST KEEP IT CLOSE IN CASE THESE GOONS GIVE US TROUBLE.
ONLY WAY THAT'LL HAPPEN IS IF THEY SEE YOUR DAMN GUN.
I WAS ONLY TRYING TO HELP, FOR ****S SAKE.
AND WATCH YOUR LANGUAGE, BOY. YOU STOP THAT CUSSIN', YOU HEAR ME?
LOGAN?
THE HULK GANG'S HERE.

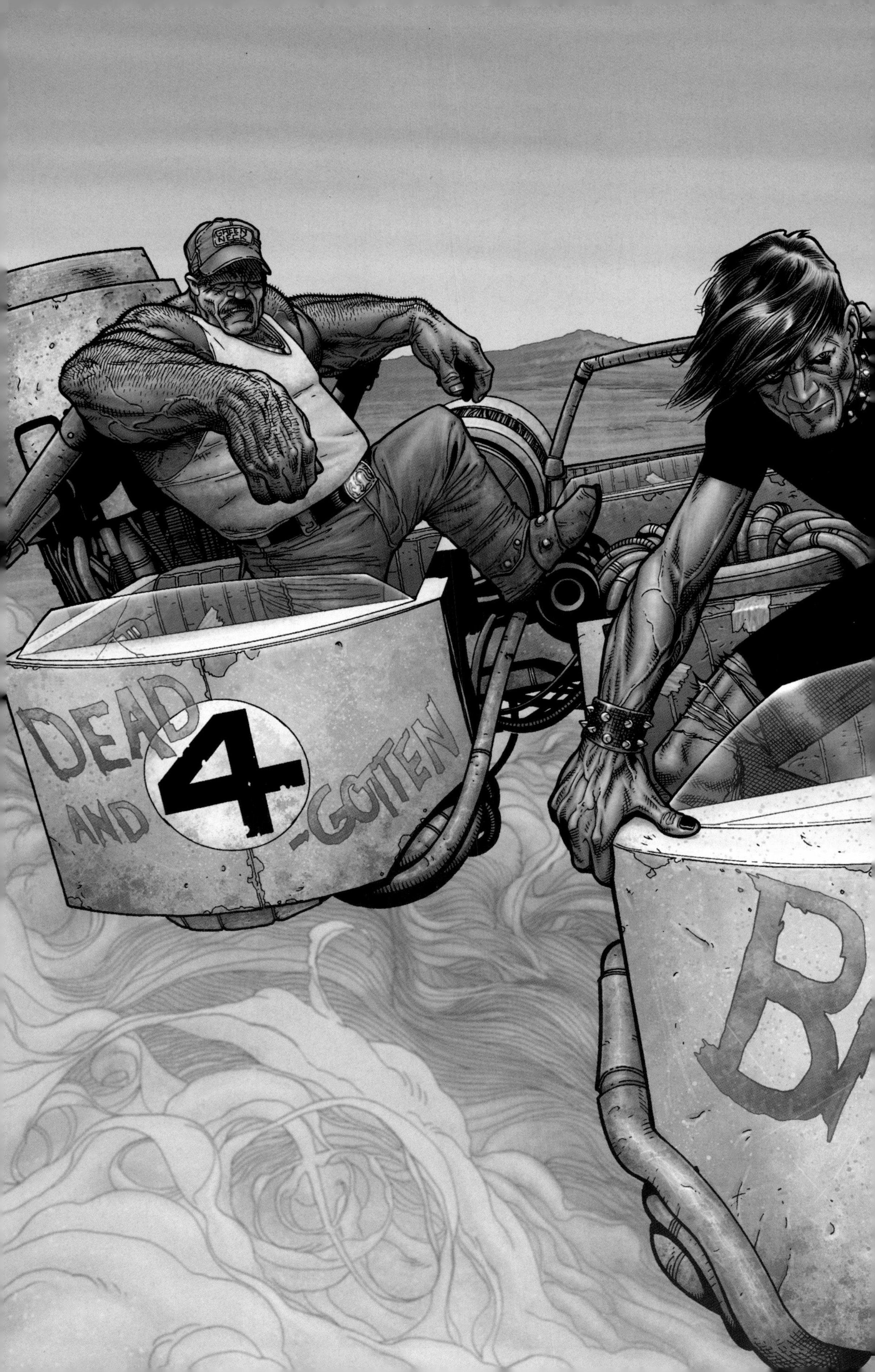
GREEN NECK
DEAD AND 4 -GOTTEN

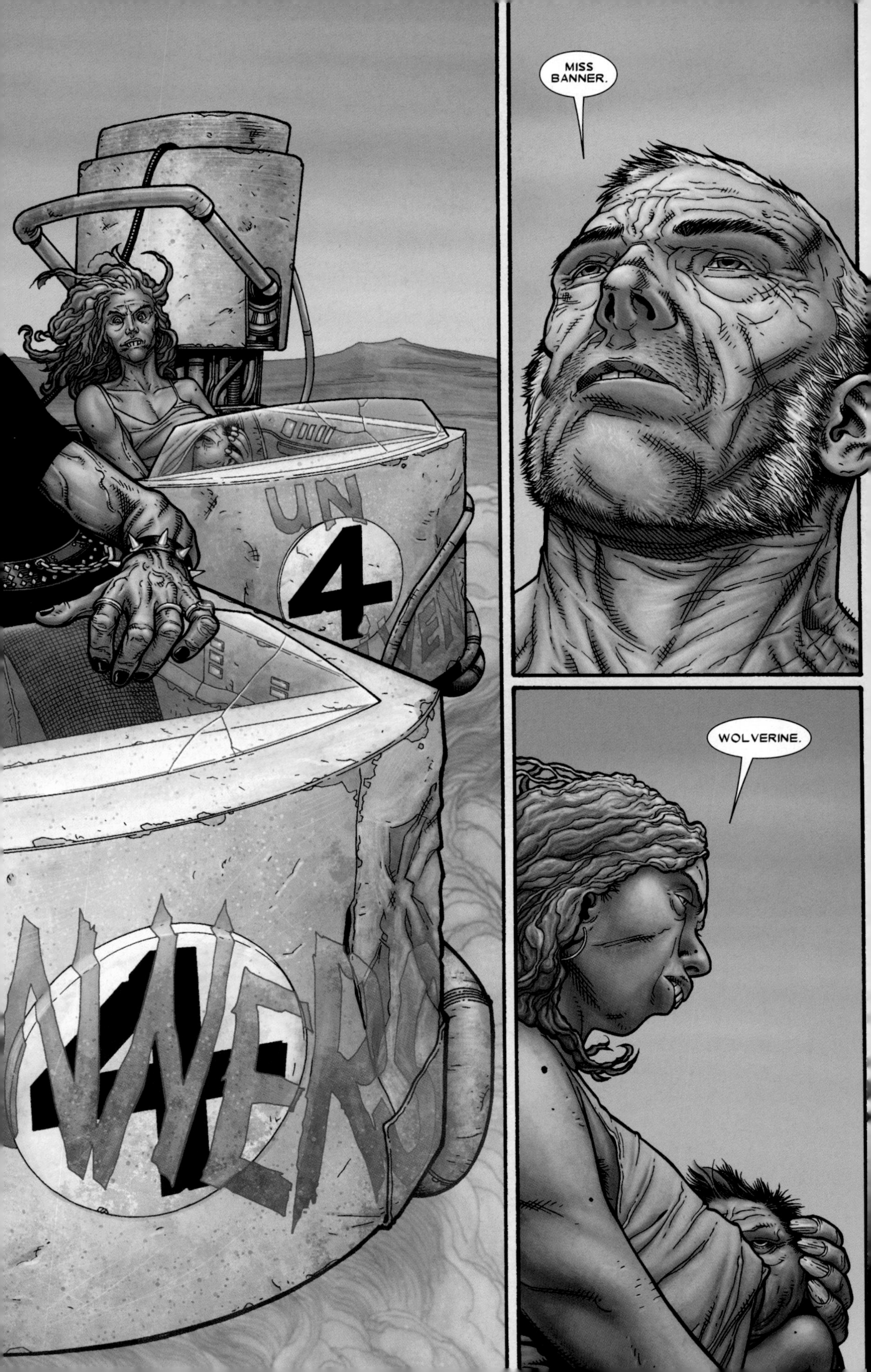
UN
4
MISS BANNER.
WOLVERINE.

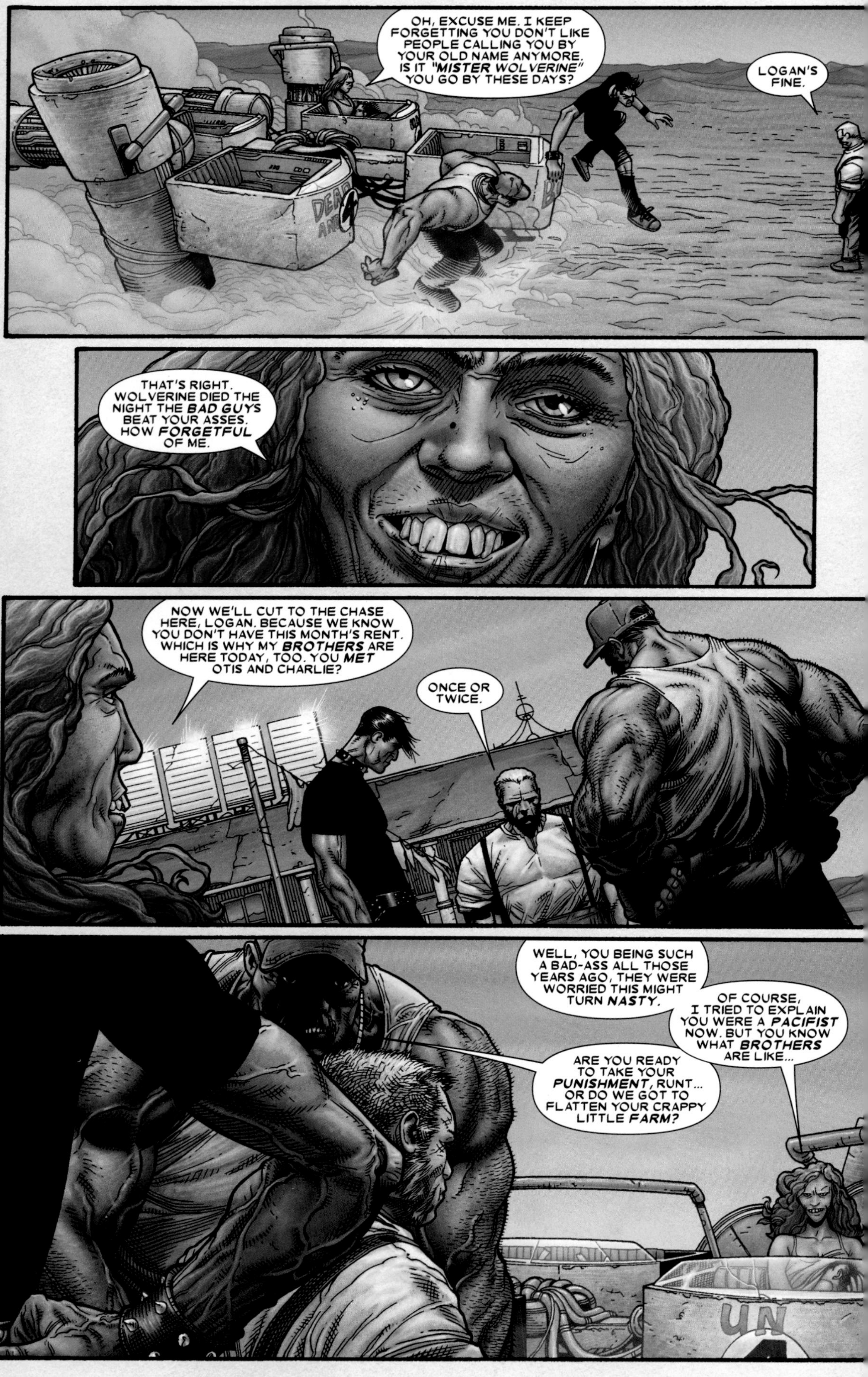
OH, EXCUSE ME. I KEEP FORGETTING YOU DON'T LIKE PEOPLE CALLING YOU BY YOUR OLD NAME ANYMORE. IS IT "MISTER WOLVERINE" YOU GO BY THESE DAYS?
LOGAN'S FINE.
THAT'S RIGHT. WOLVERINE DIED THE NIGHT THE BAD GUYS BEAT YOUR ASSES. HOW FORGETFUL OF ME.
NOW WE'LL CUT TO THE CHASE HERE, LOGAN. BECAUSE WE KNOW YOU DON'T HAVE THIS MONTH'S RENT. WHICH IS WHY MY BROTHERS ARE HERE TODAY, TOO. YOU MET OTIS AND CHARLIE?
ONCE OR TWICE.
WELL, YOU BEING SUCH A BAD-ASS ALL THOSE YEARS AGO, THEY WERE WORRIED THIS MIGHT TURN NASTY.
OF COURSE, I TRIED TO EXPLAIN YOU WERE A PACIFIST NOW. BUT YOU KNOW WHAT BROTHERS ARE LIKE...
ARE YOU READY TO TAKE YOUR PUNISHMENT, RUNT... OR DO WE GOT TO FLATTEN YOUR CRAPPY LITTLE FARM?

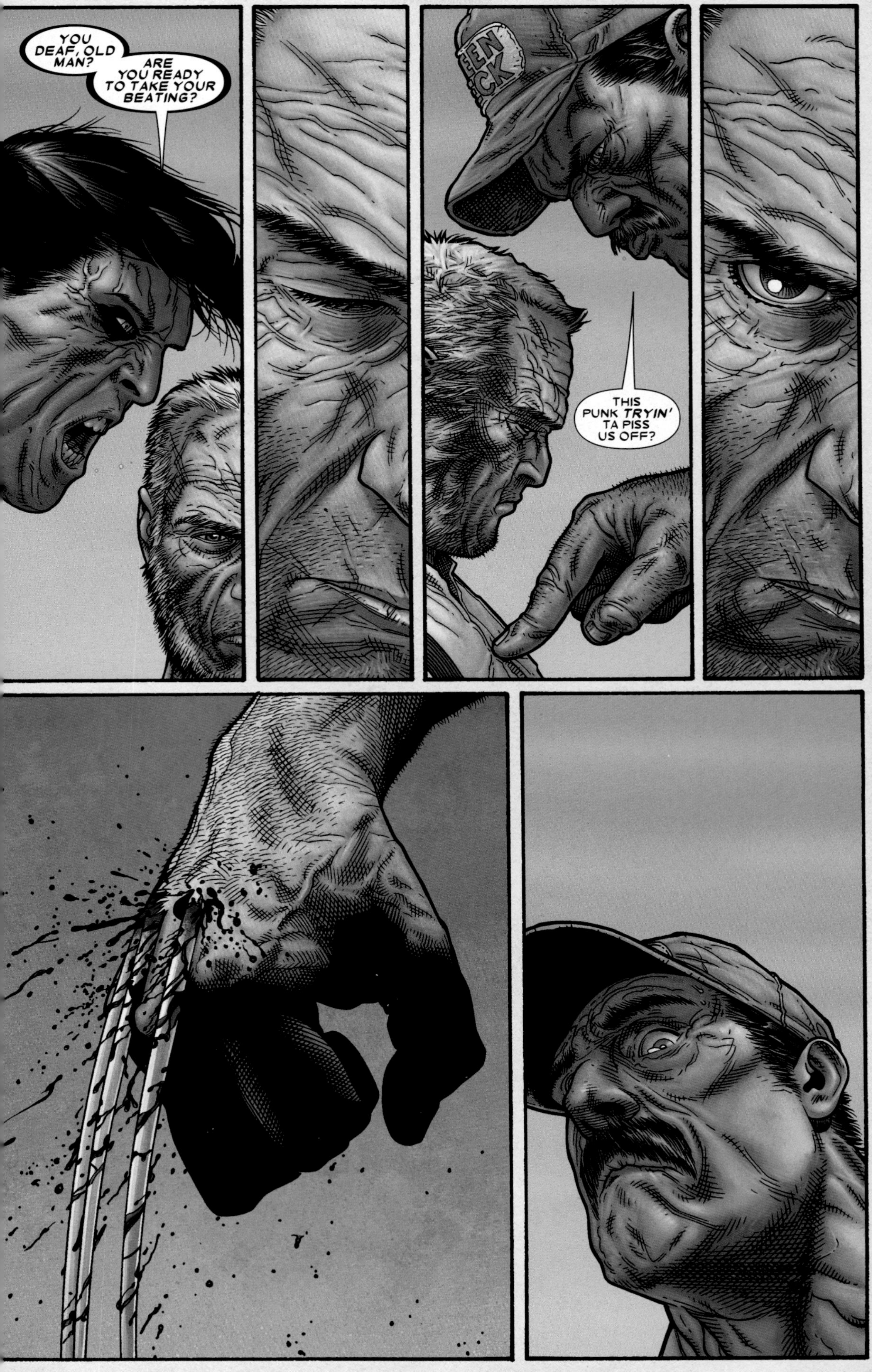

YOU DEAF, OLD MAN?
ARE YOU READY TO TAKE YOUR BEATING?
THIS PUNK TRYIN' TA PISS US OFF?

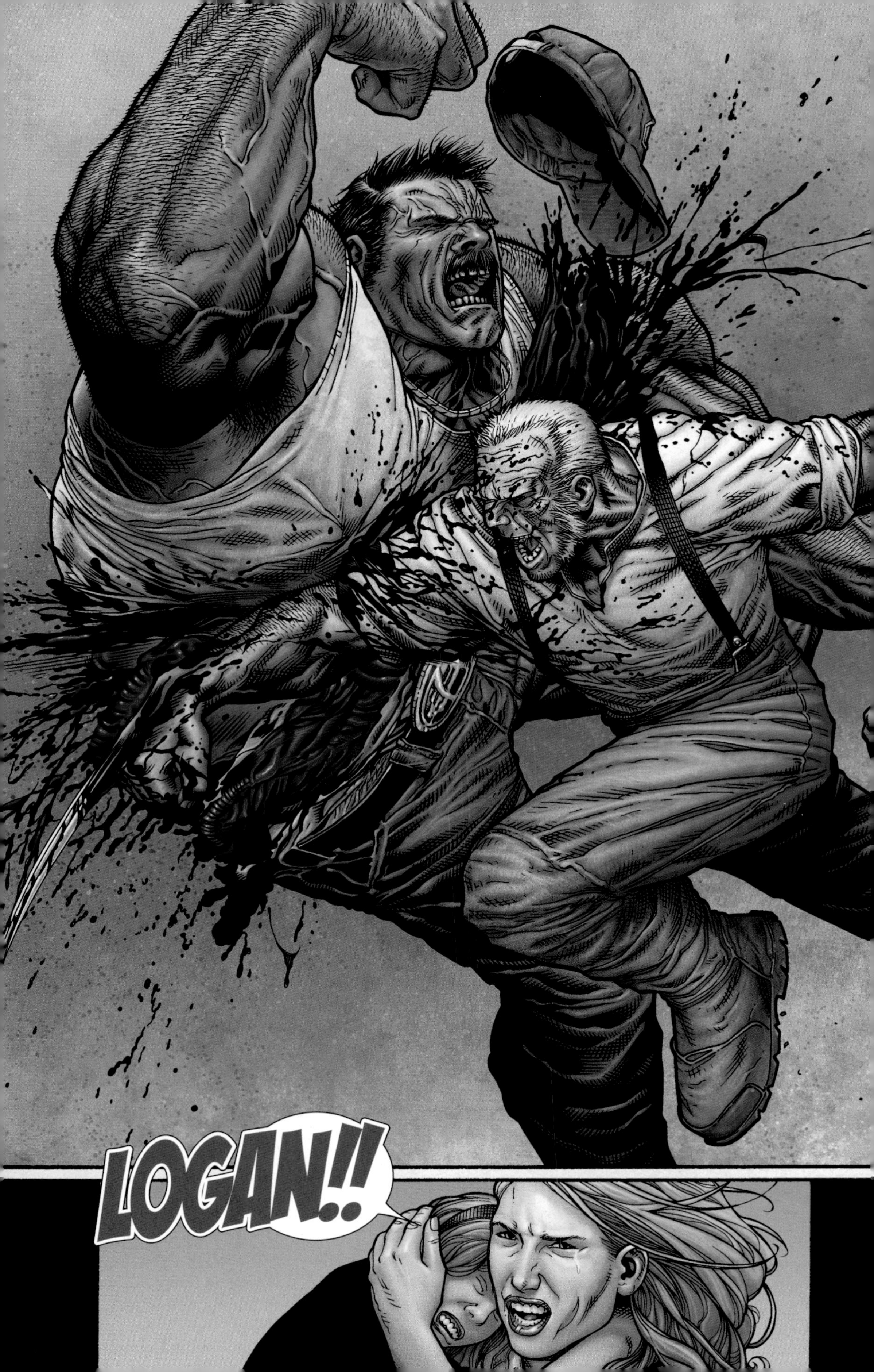
LOGAN!!

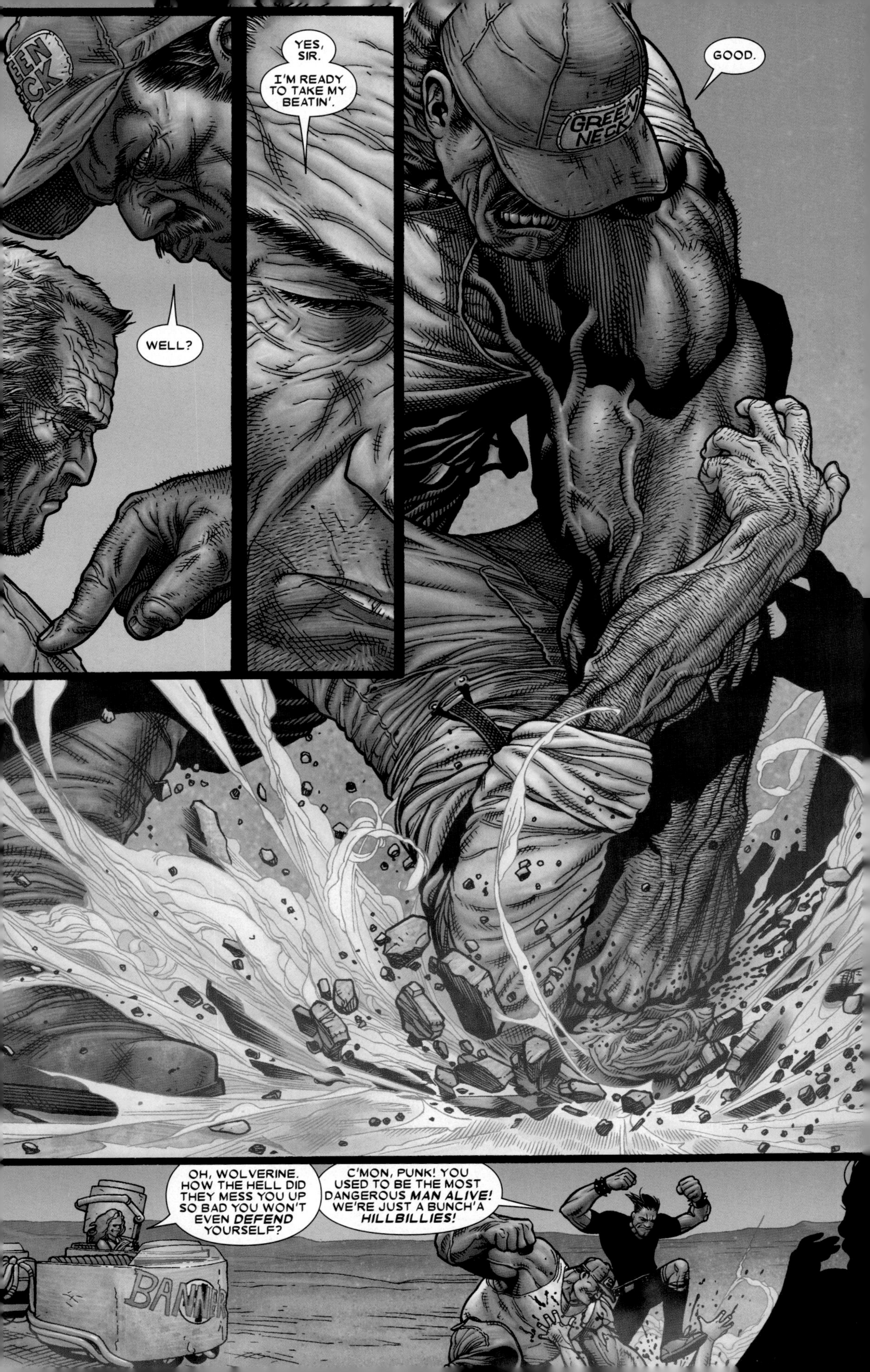
WELL?
YES, SIR.
I'M READY TO TAKE MY BEATIN'.
GOOD.
GREEN NECK
OH, WOLVERINE. HOW THE HELL DID THEY MESS YOU UP SO BAD YOU WON'T EVEN *DEFEND* YOURSELF?
C'MON, PUNK! YOU USED TO BE THE MOST DANGEROUS *MAN ALIVE!* WE'RE JUST A BUNCH'A *HILLBILLIES!*
BANNER

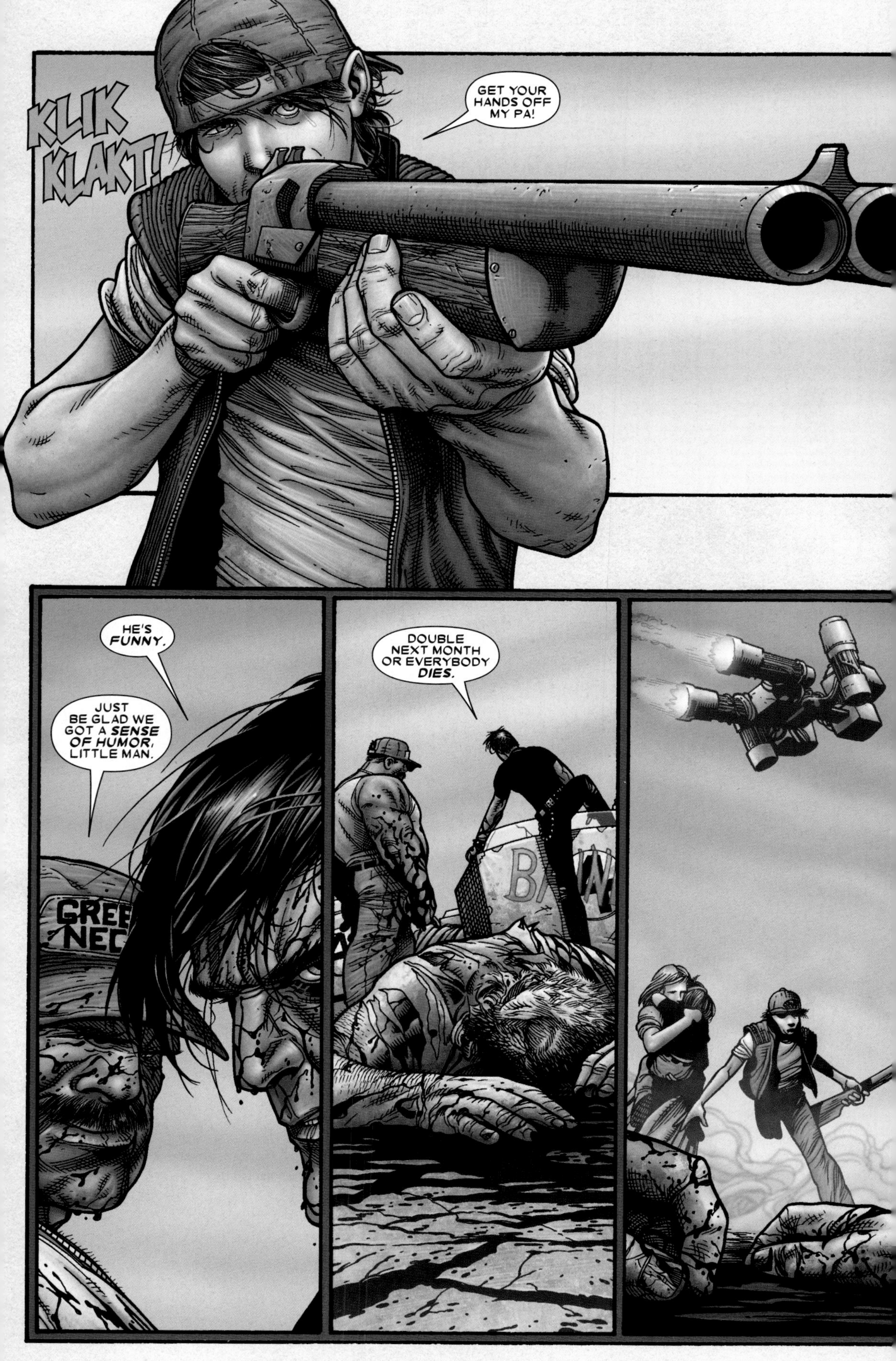
KLIK KLAKT!
GET YOUR HANDS OFF MY PA!
HE'S FUNNY.
JUST BE GLAD WE GOT A SENSE OF HUMOR, LITTLE MAN.
DOUBLE NEXT MONTH OR EVERYBODY DIES.

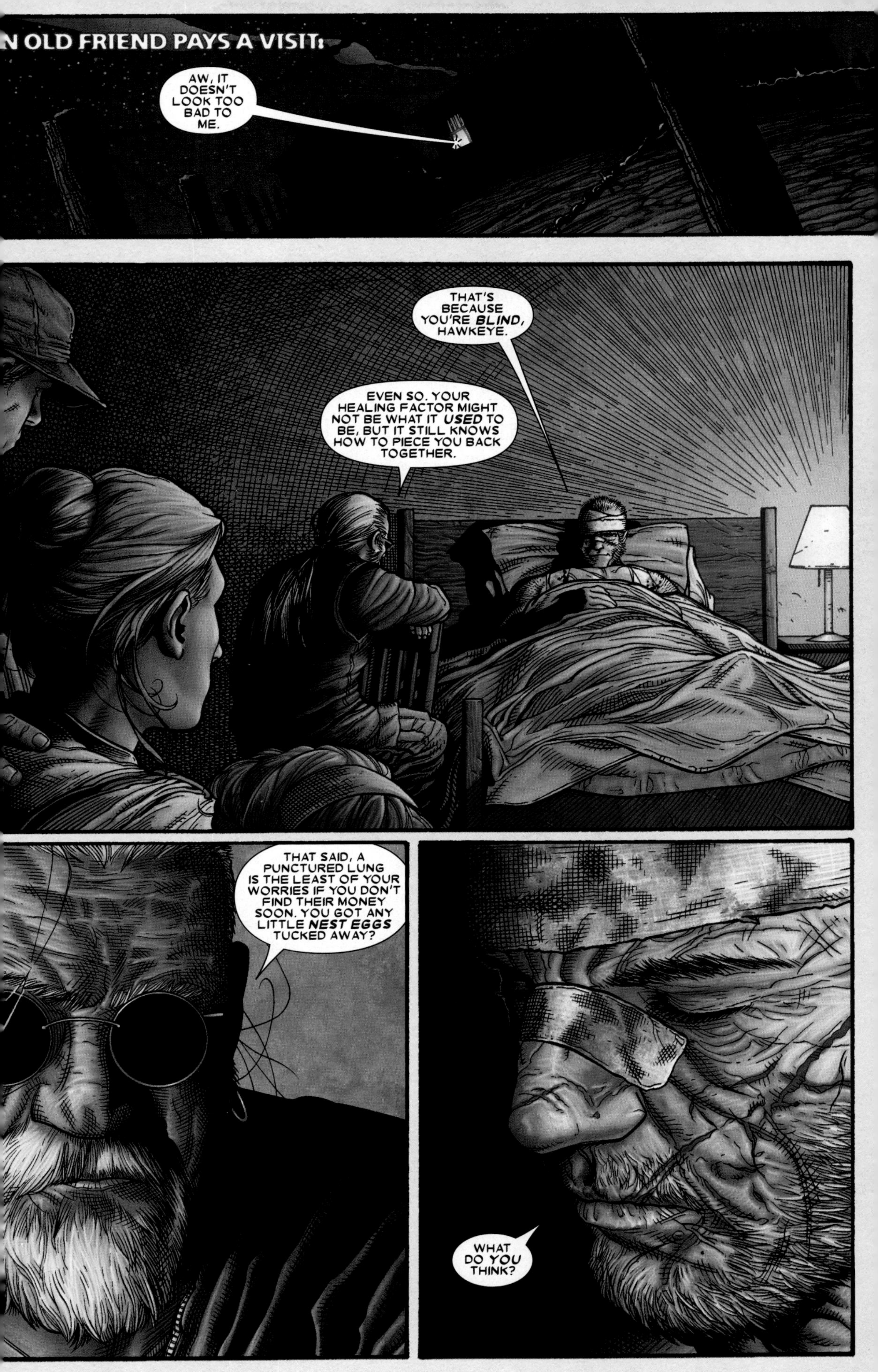
N OLD FRIEND PAYS A VISIT:
AW, IT DOESN'T LOOK TOO BAD TO ME.
THAT'S BECAUSE YOU'RE BLIND, HAWKEYE.
EVEN SO. YOUR HEALING FACTOR MIGHT NOT BE WHAT IT USED TO BE, BUT IT STILL KNOWS HOW TO PIECE YOU BACK TOGETHER.
THAT SAID, A PUNCTURED LUNG IS THE LEAST OF YOUR WORRIES IF YOU DON'T FIND THEIR MONEY SOON. YOU GOT ANY LITTLE NEST EGGS TUCKED AWAY?
WHAT DO YOU THINK?

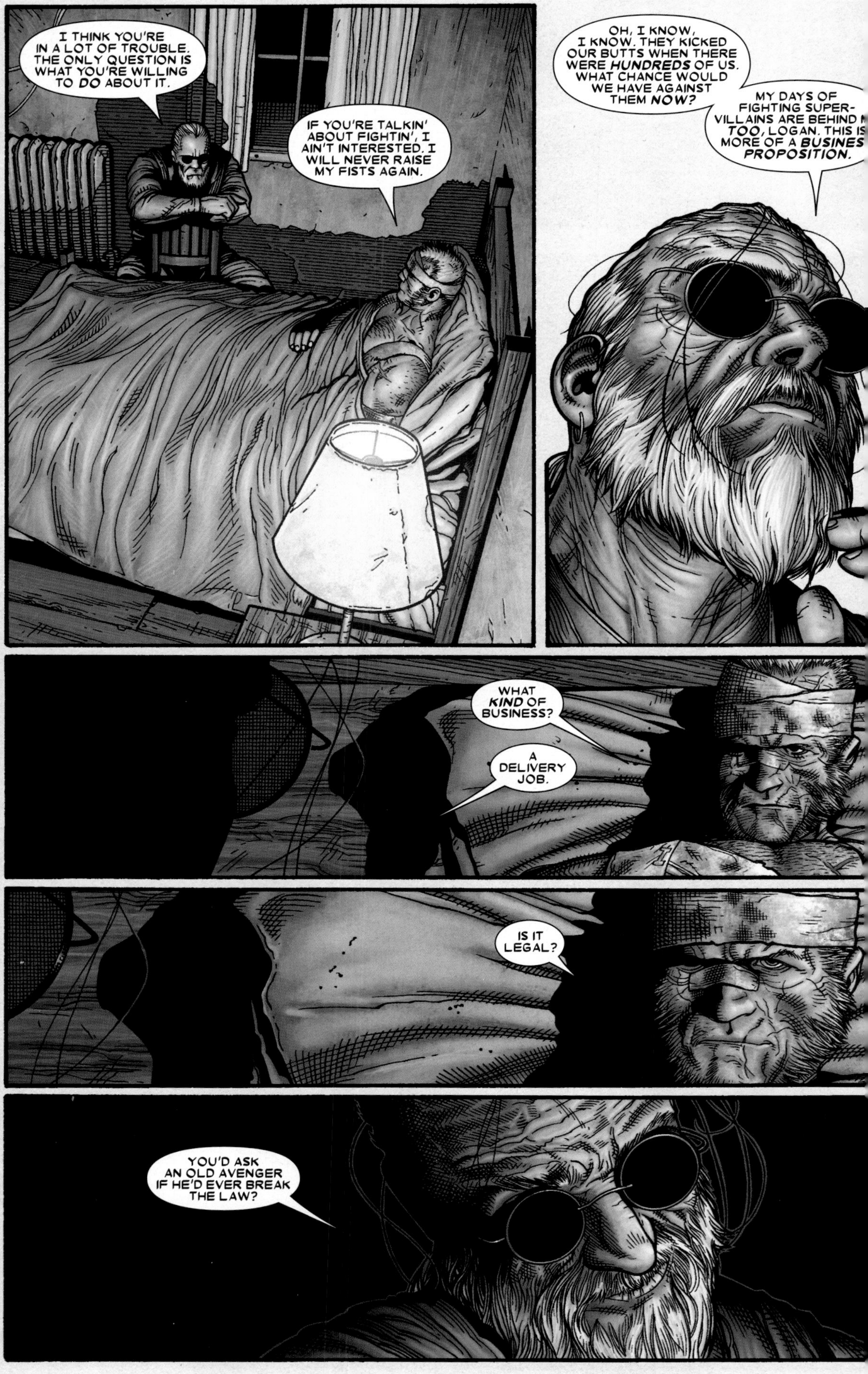
I THINK YOU'RE IN A LOT OF TROUBLE. THE ONLY QUESTION IS WHAT YOU'RE WILLING TO *DO* ABOUT IT.
IF YOU'RE TALKIN' ABOUT FIGHTIN', I AIN'T INTERESTED. I WILL NEVER RAISE MY FISTS AGAIN.
OH, I KNOW, I KNOW. THEY KICKED OUR BUTTS WHEN THERE WERE *HUNDREDS* OF US. WHAT CHANCE WOULD WE HAVE AGAINST THEM *NOW?*
MY DAYS OF FIGHTING SUPER-VILLAINS ARE BEHIND *TOO*, LOGAN. THIS IS MORE OF A *BUSINES* *PROPOSITION.*
WHAT *KIND* OF BUSINESS?
A DELIVERY JOB.
IS IT LEGAL?
YOU'D ASK AN OLD AVENGER IF HE'D EVER BREAK THE LAW?

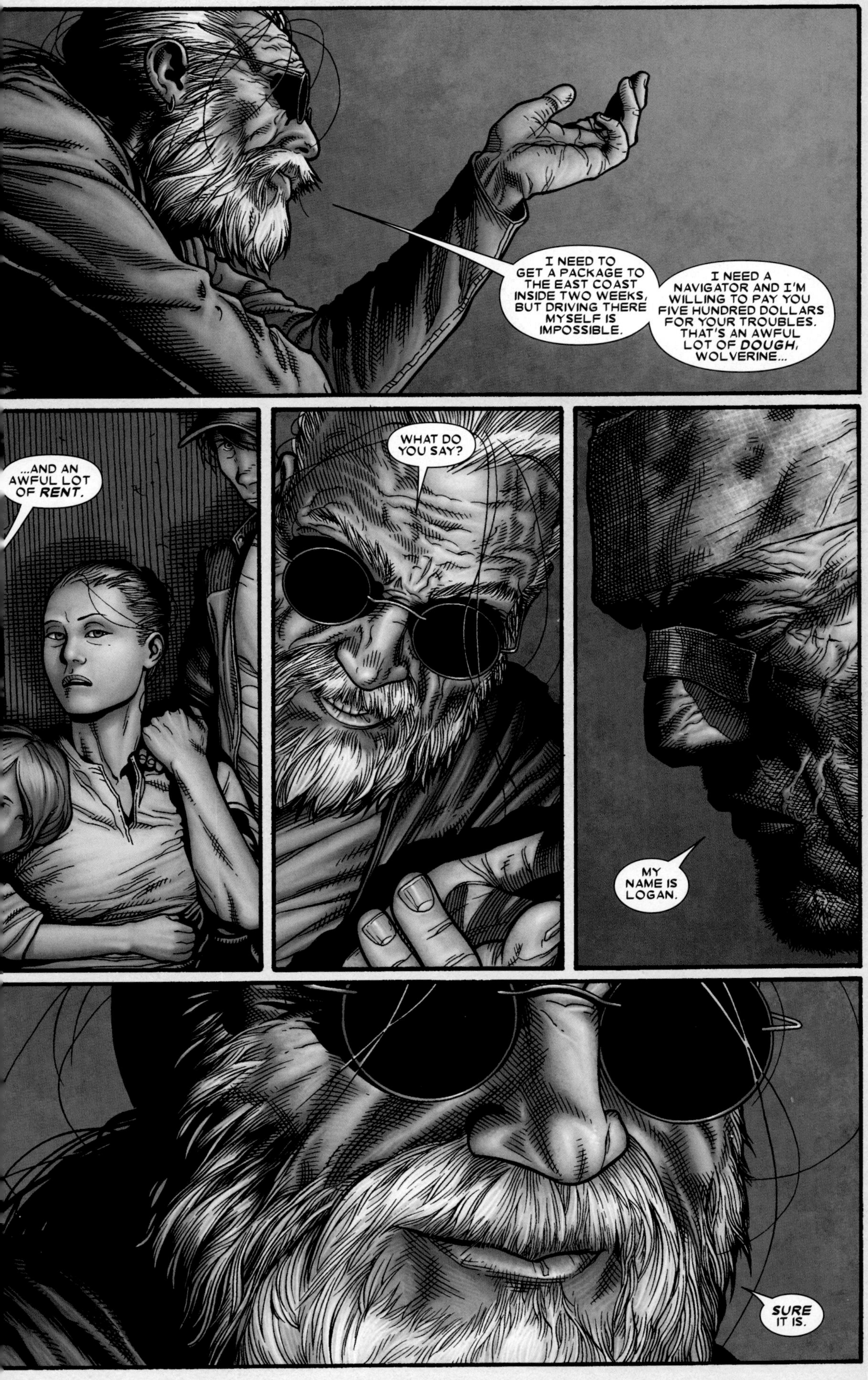
I NEED TO GET A PACKAGE TO THE EAST COAST INSIDE TWO WEEKS, BUT DRIVING THERE MYSELF IS IMPOSSIBLE.
I NEED A NAVIGATOR AND I'M WILLING TO PAY YOU FIVE HUNDRED DOLLARS FOR YOUR TROUBLES. THAT'S AN AWFUL LOT OF DOUGH, WOLVERINE...
...AND AN AWFUL LOT OF RENT.
WHAT DO YOU SAY?
MY NAME IS LOGAN.
SURE IT IS.

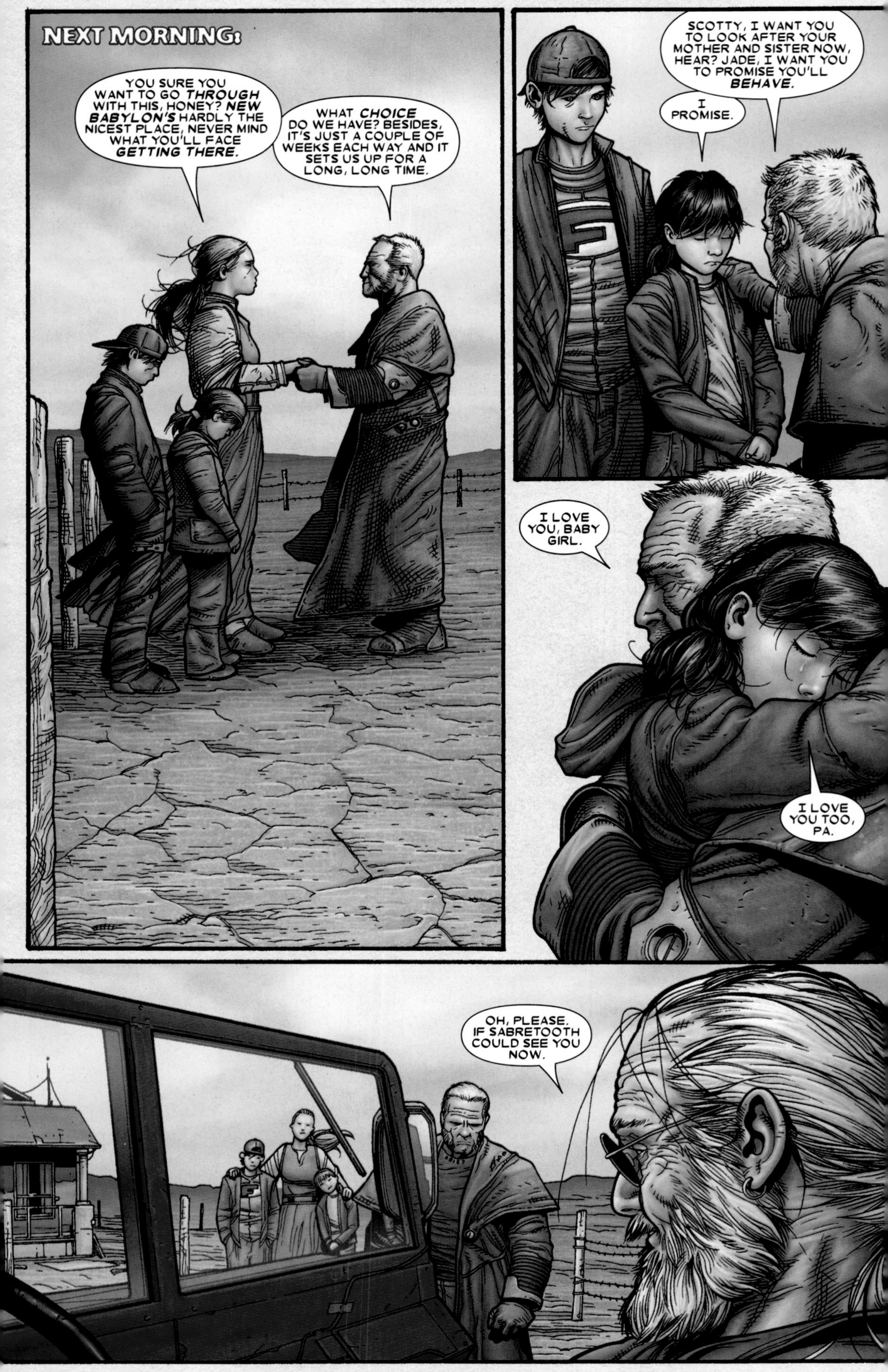
NEXT MORNING:
YOU SURE YOU WANT TO GO *THROUGH* WITH THIS, HONEY? *NEW BABYLON'S* HARDLY THE NICEST PLACE, NEVER MIND WHAT YOU'LL FACE *GETTING THERE.*
WHAT *CHOICE* DO WE HAVE? BESIDES, IT'S JUST A COUPLE OF WEEKS EACH WAY AND IT SETS US UP FOR A LONG, LONG TIME.
SCOTTY, I WANT YOU TO LOOK AFTER YOUR MOTHER AND SISTER NOW, HEAR? JADE, I WANT YOU TO PROMISE YOU'LL *BEHAVE.*
I PROMISE.
I LOVE YOU, BABY GIRL.
I LOVE YOU TOO, PA.
OH, PLEASE. IF SABRETOOTH COULD SEE YOU NOW.

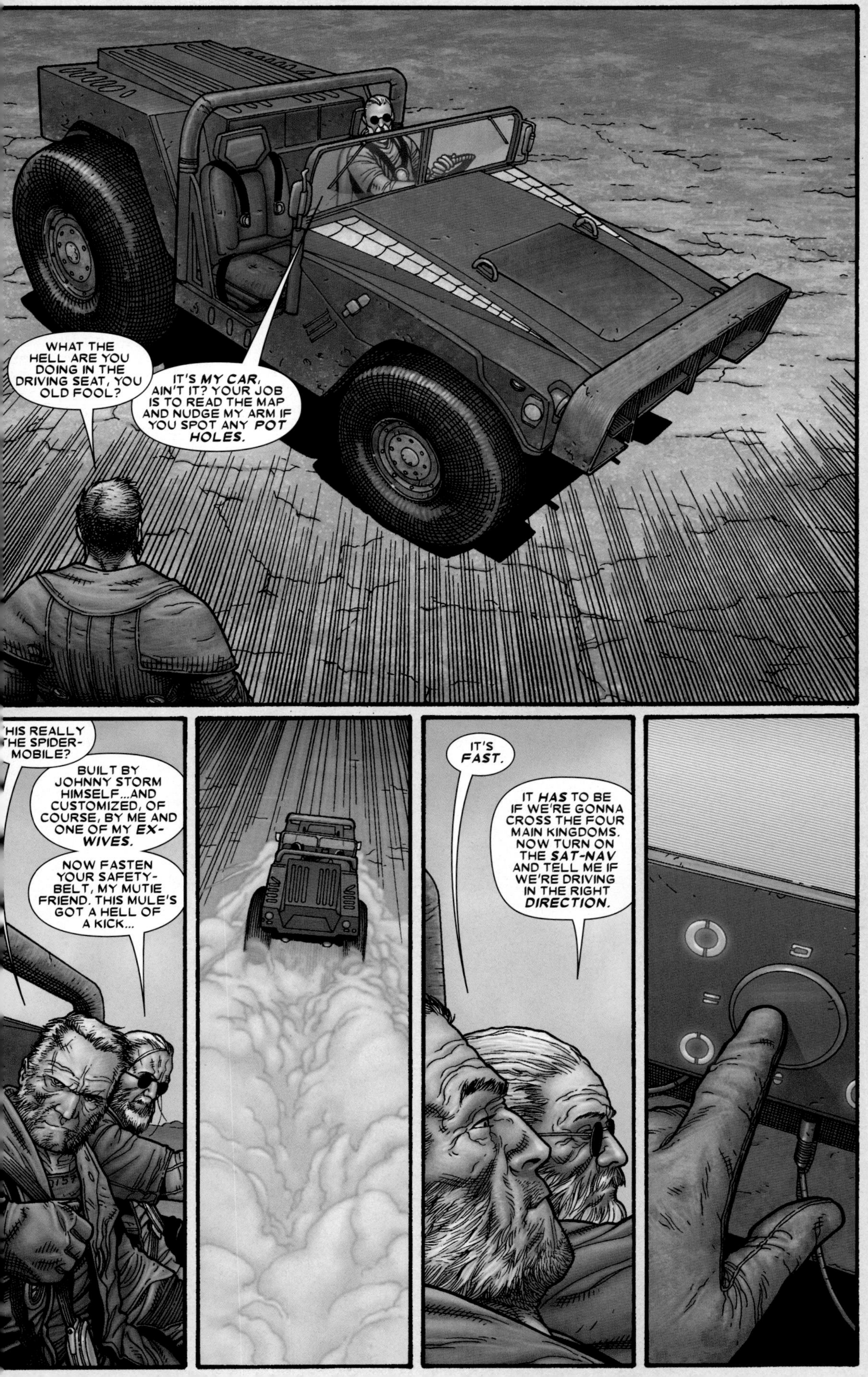
WHAT THE HELL ARE YOU DOING IN THE DRIVING SEAT, YOU OLD FOOL?
IT'S MY CAR, AIN'T IT? YOUR JOB IS TO READ THE MAP AND NUDGE MY ARM IF YOU SPOT ANY POT HOLES.
THIS REALLY THE SPIDER-MOBILE?
BUILT BY JOHNNY STORM HIMSELF...AND CUSTOMIZED, OF COURSE, BY ME AND ONE OF MY EX-WIVES.
NOW FASTEN YOUR SAFETY-BELT, MY MUTIE FRIEND. THIS MULE'S GOT A HELL OF A KICK...
IT'S FAST.
IT HAS TO BE IF WE'RE GONNA CROSS THE FOUR MAIN KINGDOMS. NOW TURN ON THE SAT-NAV AND TELL ME IF WE'RE DRIVING IN THE RIGHT DIRECTION.

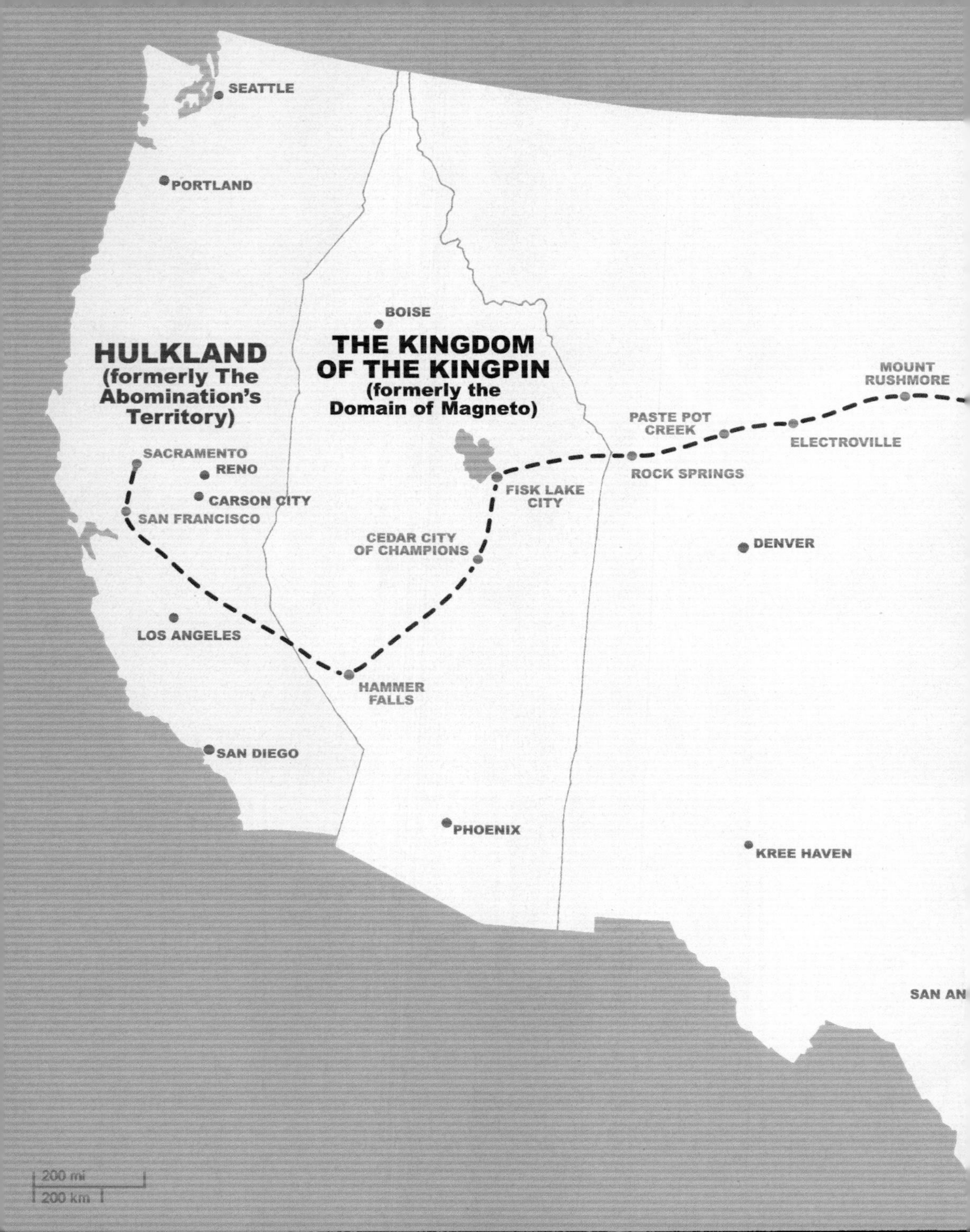
SEATTLE
PORTLAND
BOISE
HULKLAND
(formerly The Abomination's Territory)
THE KINGDOM OF THE KINGPIN
(formerly the Domain of Magneto)
MOUNT RUSHMORE
PASTE POT CREEK
ELECTROVILLE
ROCK SPRINGS
SACRAMENTO
RENO
CARSON CITY
SAN FRANCISCO
FISK LAKE CITY
CEDAR CITY OF CHAMPIONS
DENVER
LOS ANGELES
HAMMER FALLS
SAN DIEGO
PHOENIX
KREE HAVEN
SAN AN
200 mi
200 km

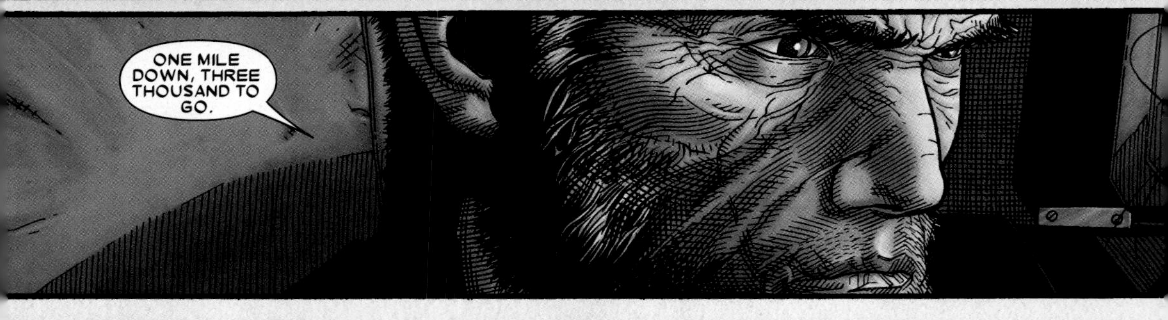
ONE MILE DOWN, THREE THOUSAND TO GO.

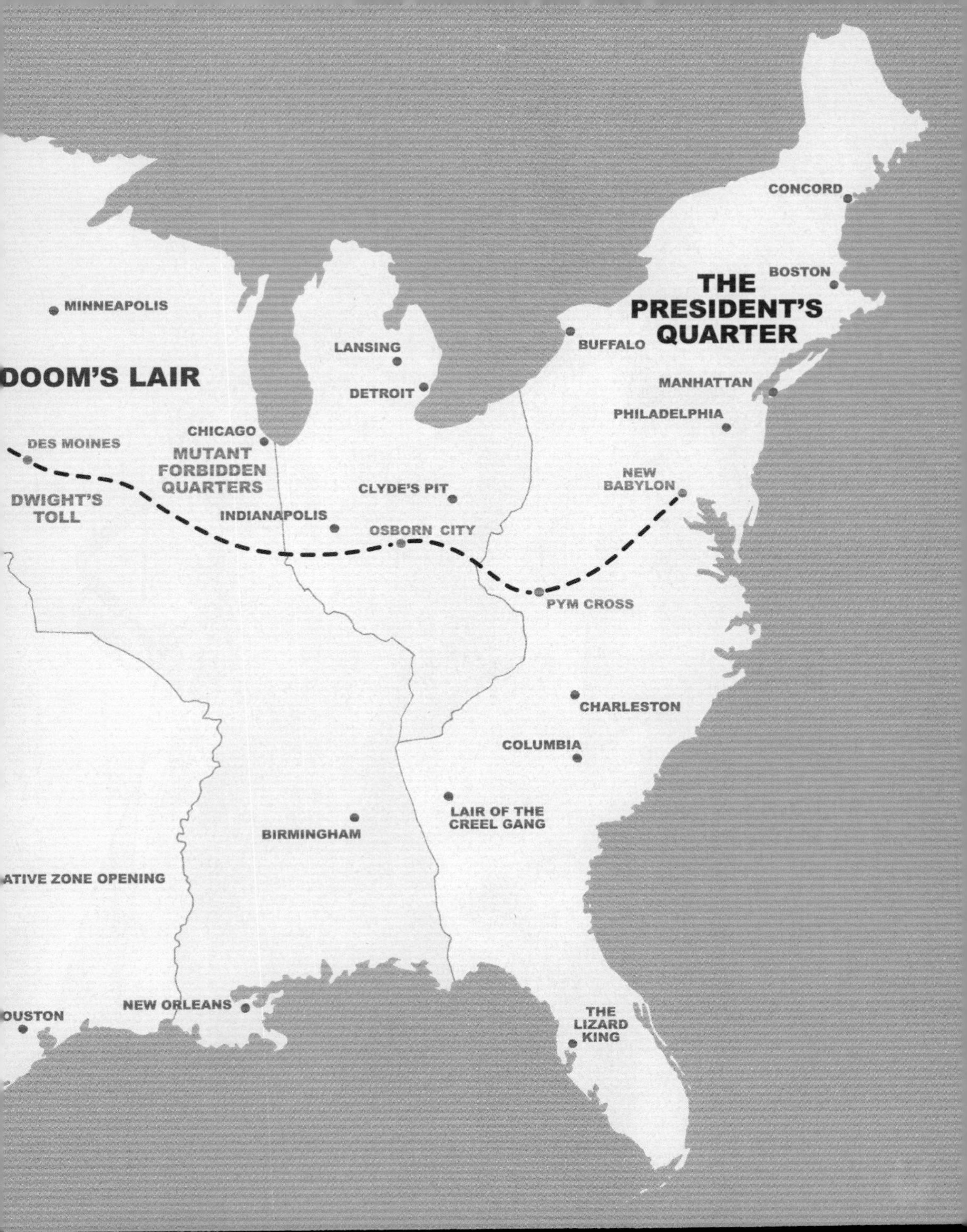
CONCORD
BOSTON
THE PRESIDENT'S QUARTER
MINNEAPOLIS
LANSING
BUFFALO
DOOM'S LAIR
DETROIT
MANHATTAN
PHILADELPHIA
CHICAGO
DES MOINES
MUTANT FORBIDDEN QUARTERS
NEW BABYLON
CLYDE'S PIT
DWIGHT'S TOLL
INDIANAPOLIS
OSBORN CITY
PYM CROSS
CHARLESTON
COLUMBIA
LAIR OF THE CREEL GANG
BIRMINGHAM
ATIVE ZONE OPENING
NEW ORLEANS
OUSTON
THE LIZARD KING

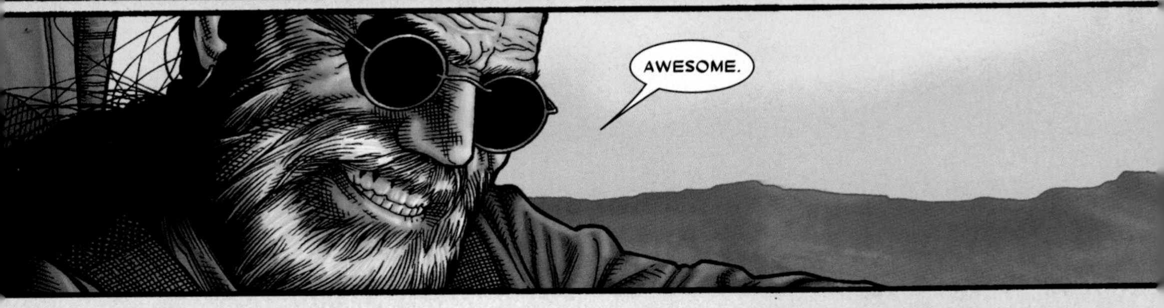
AWESOME.

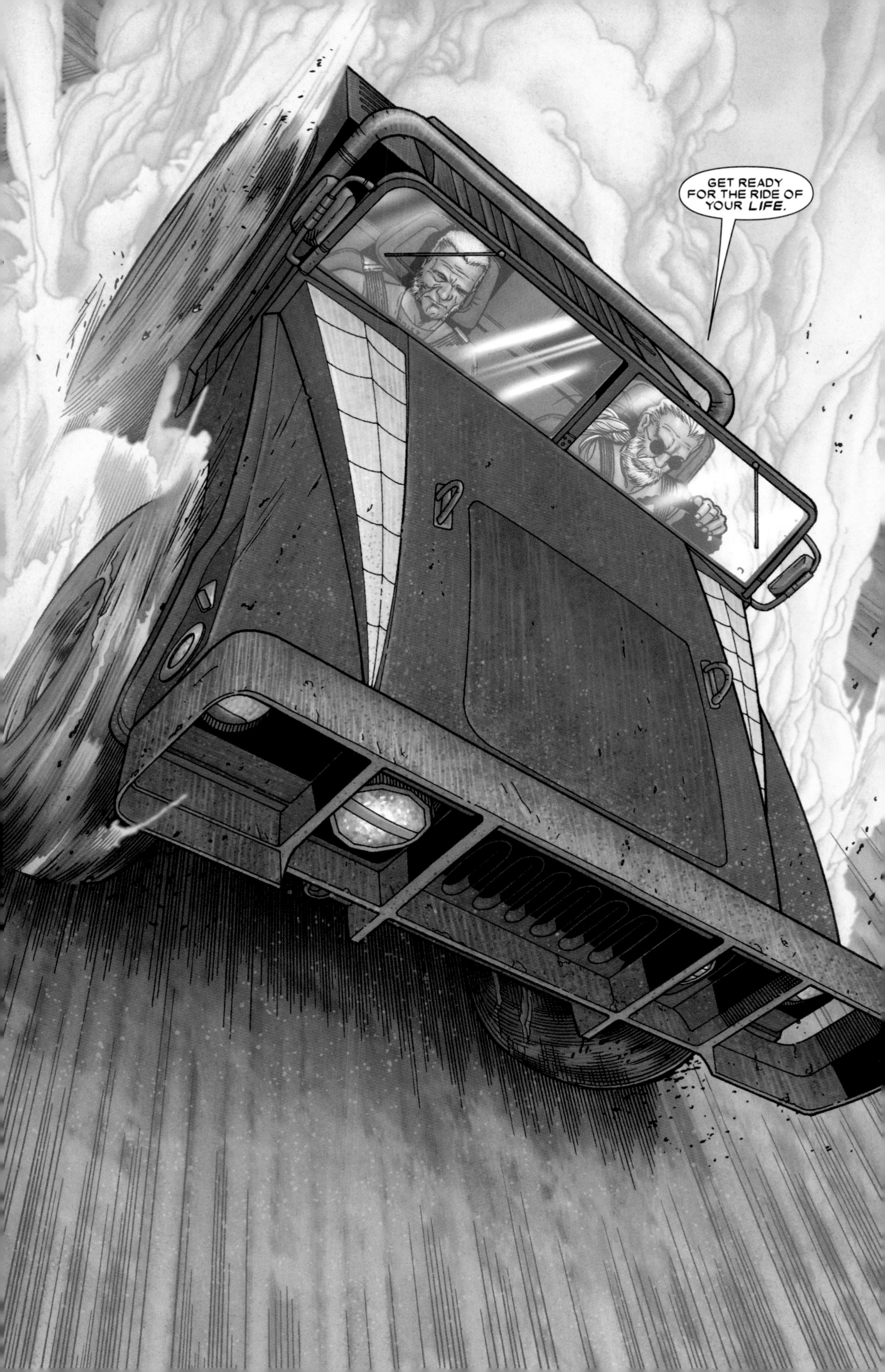
GET READY FOR THE RIDE OF YOUR *LIFE.*

CHAPTER TWO

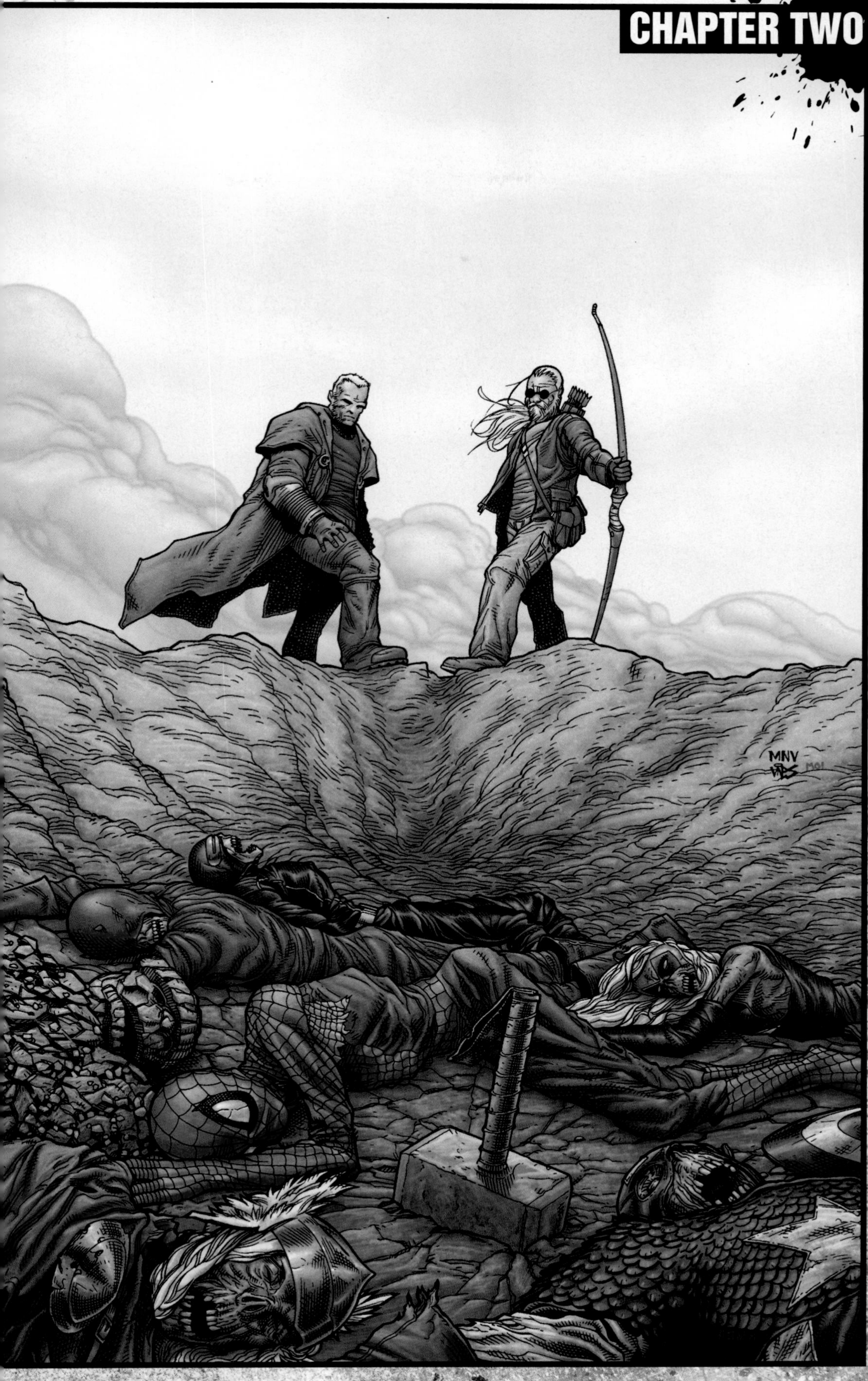

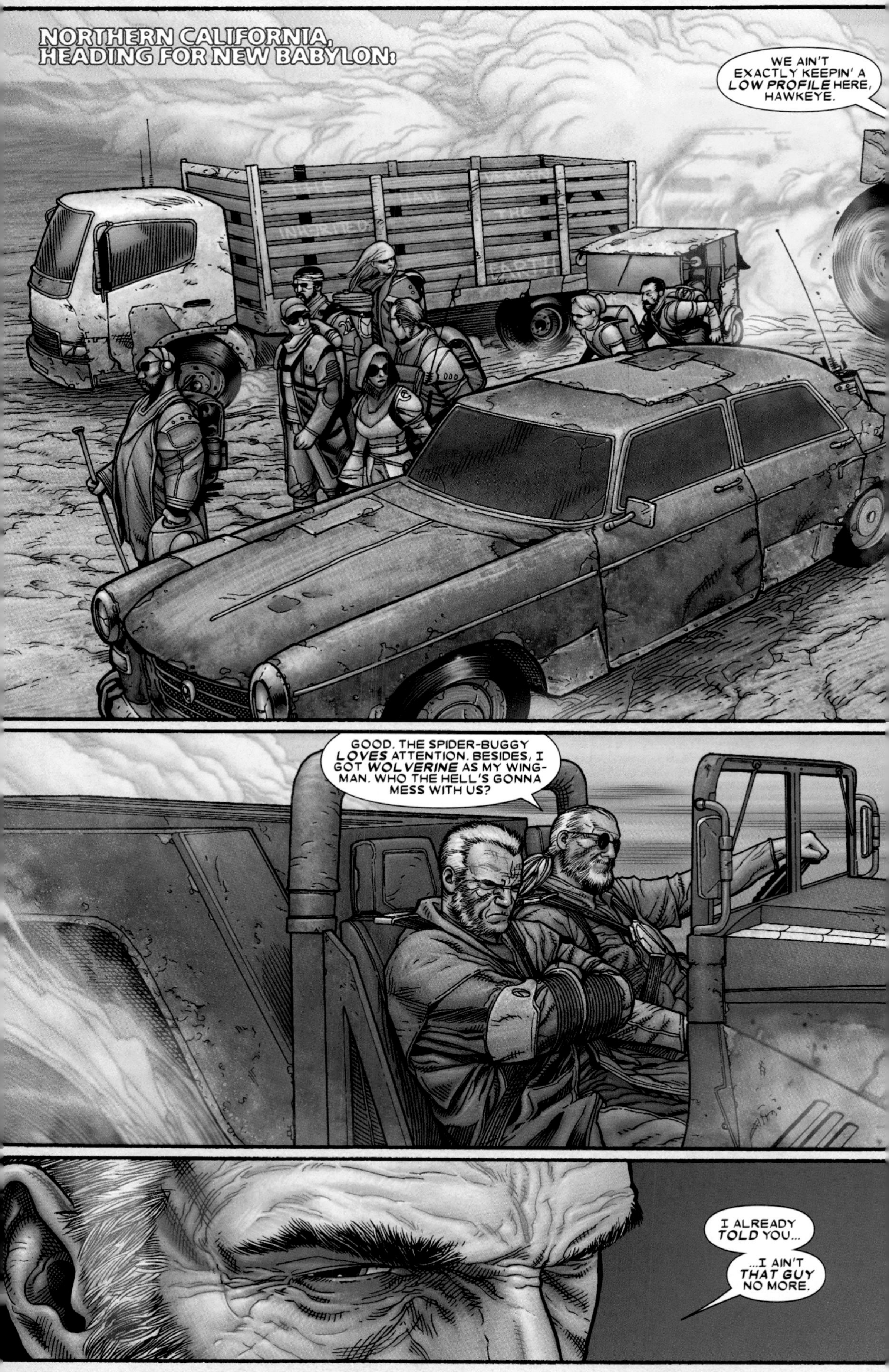
NORTHERN CALIFORNIA, HEADING FOR NEW BABYLON:
WE AIN'T EXACTLY KEEPIN' A LOW PROFILE HERE, HAWKEYE.
GOOD. THE SPIDER-BUGGY LOVES ATTENTION. BESIDES, I GOT WOLVERINE AS MY WING-MAN. WHO THE HELL'S GONNA MESS WITH US?
I ALREADY TOLD YOU...
...I AIN'T THAT GUY NO MORE.

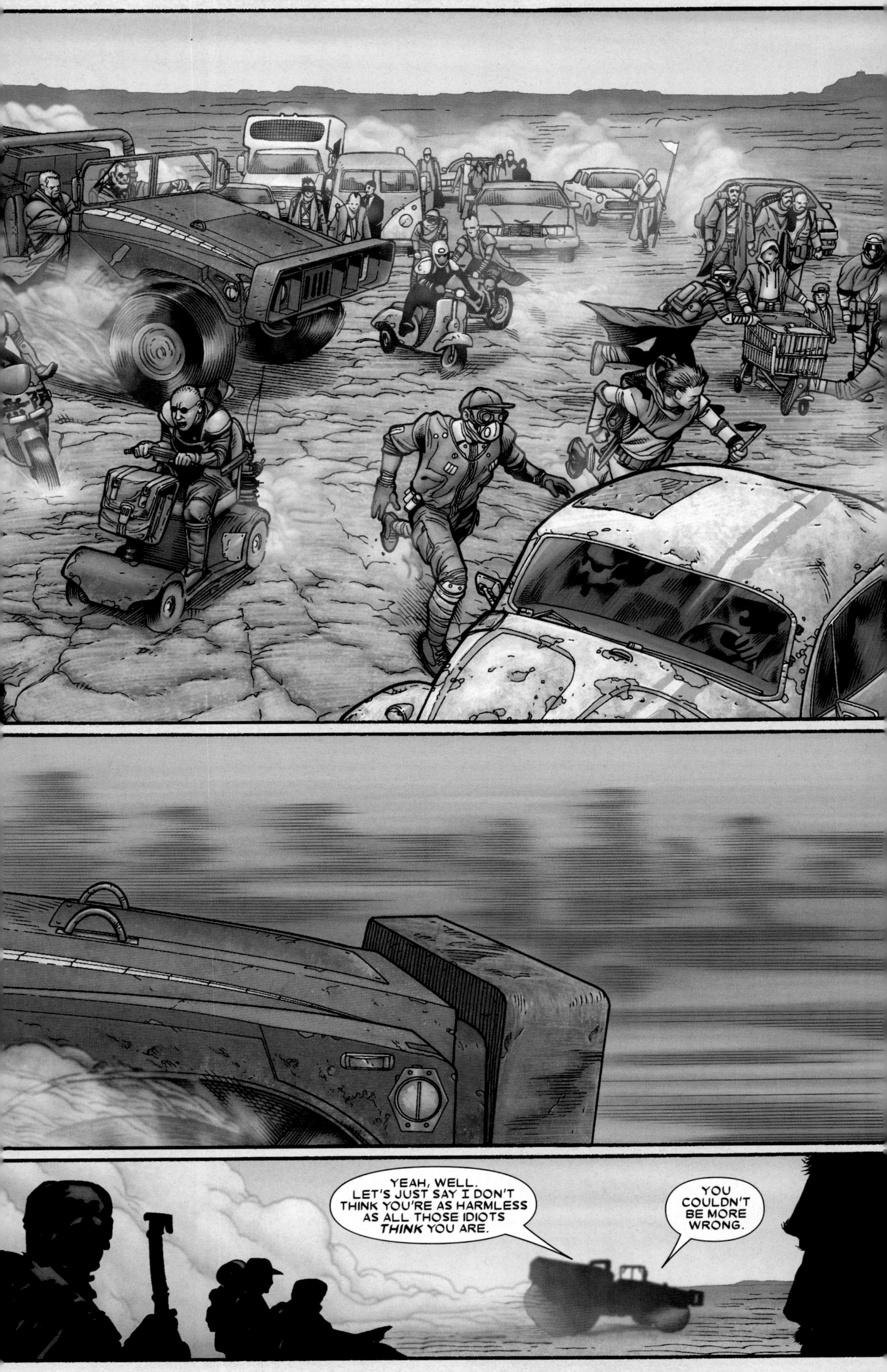
YEAH, WELL. LET'S JUST SAY I DON'T THINK YOU'RE AS HARMLESS AS ALL THOSE IDIOTS THINK YOU ARE.
YOU COULDN'T BE MORE WRONG.

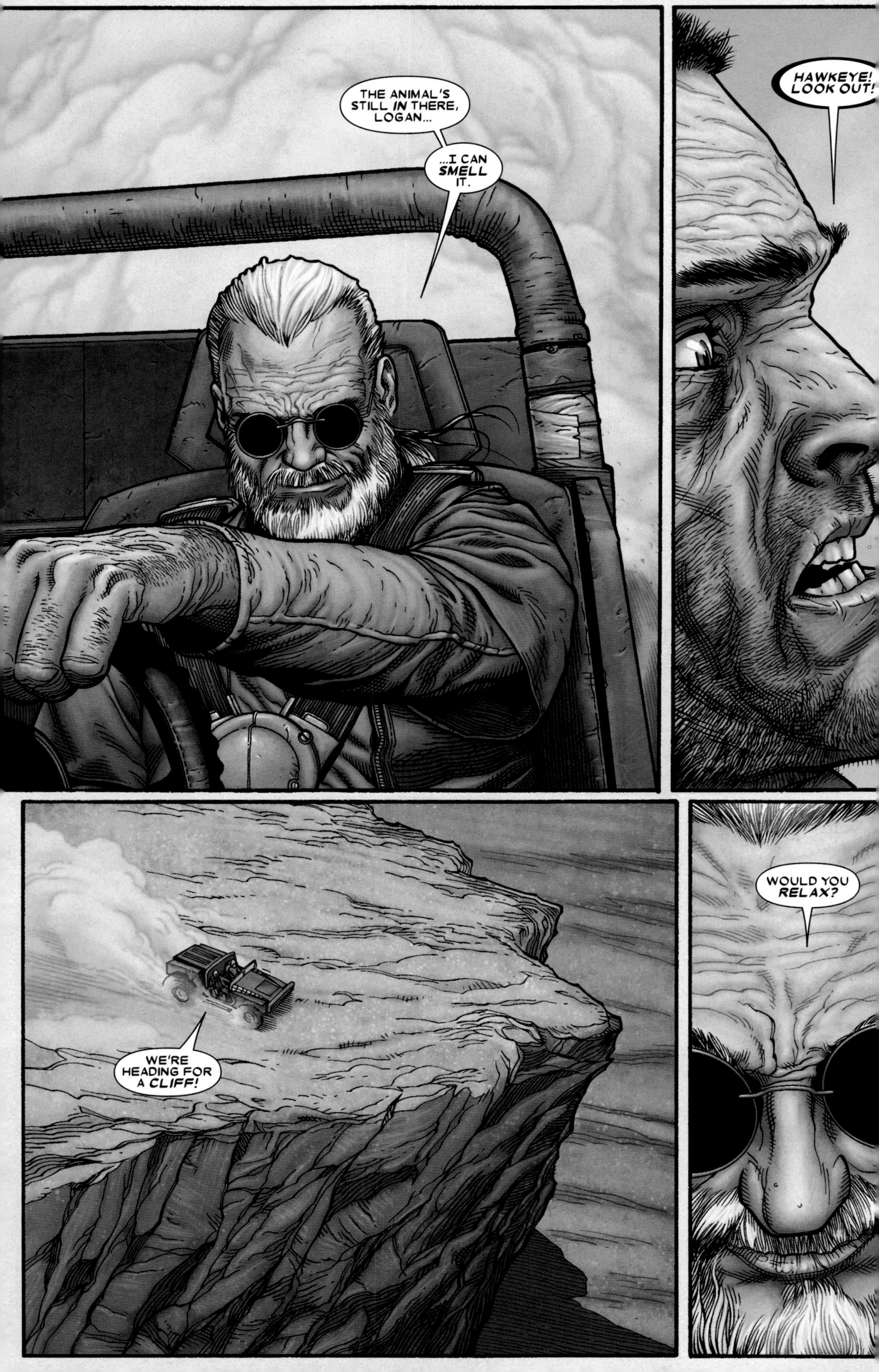
THE ANIMAL'S STILL *IN* THERE, LOGAN...
...I CAN *SMELL* IT.
HAWKEYE! LOOK OUT!
WE'RE HEADING FOR A *CLIFF!*
WOULD YOU *RELAX?*

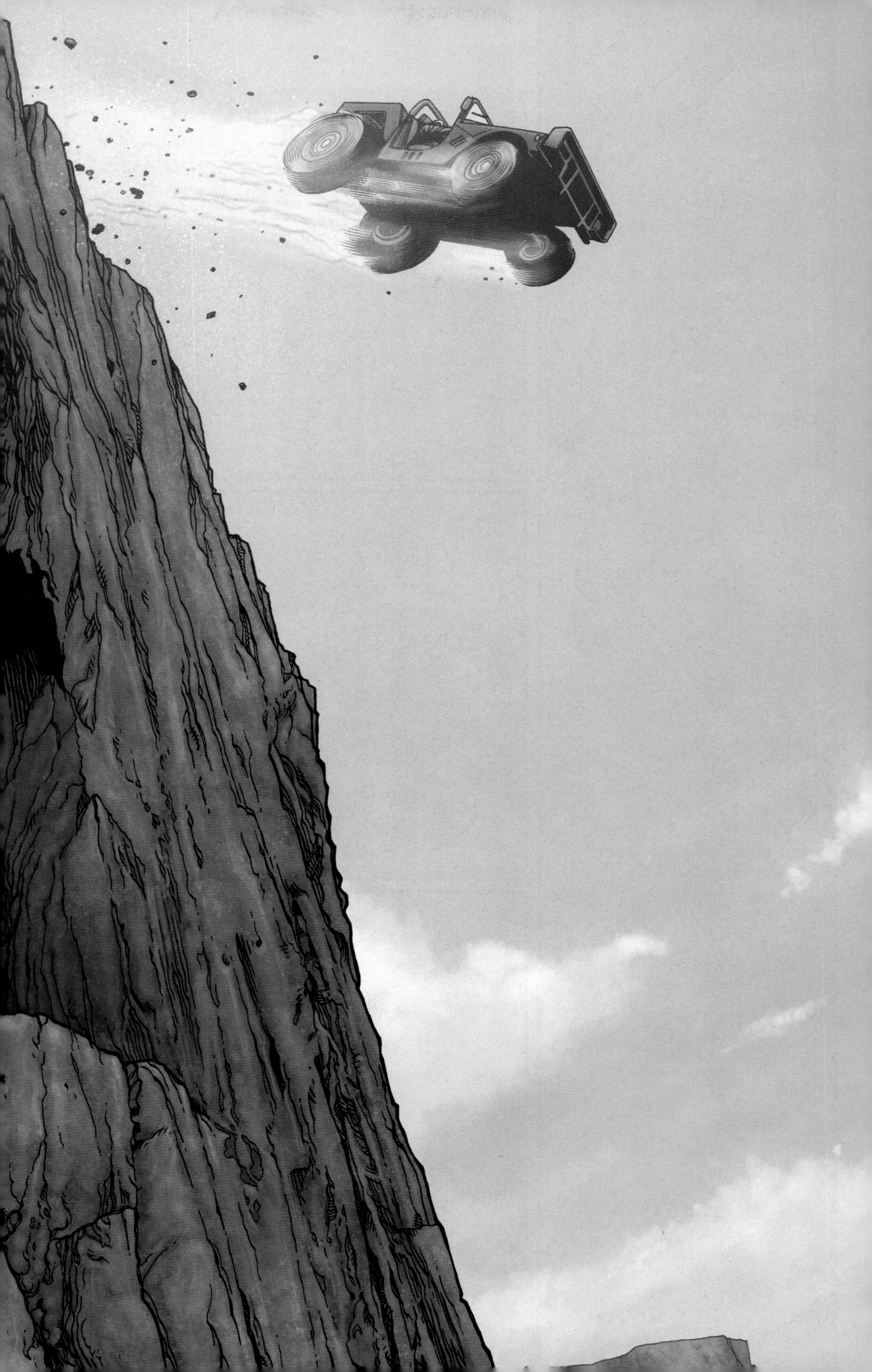

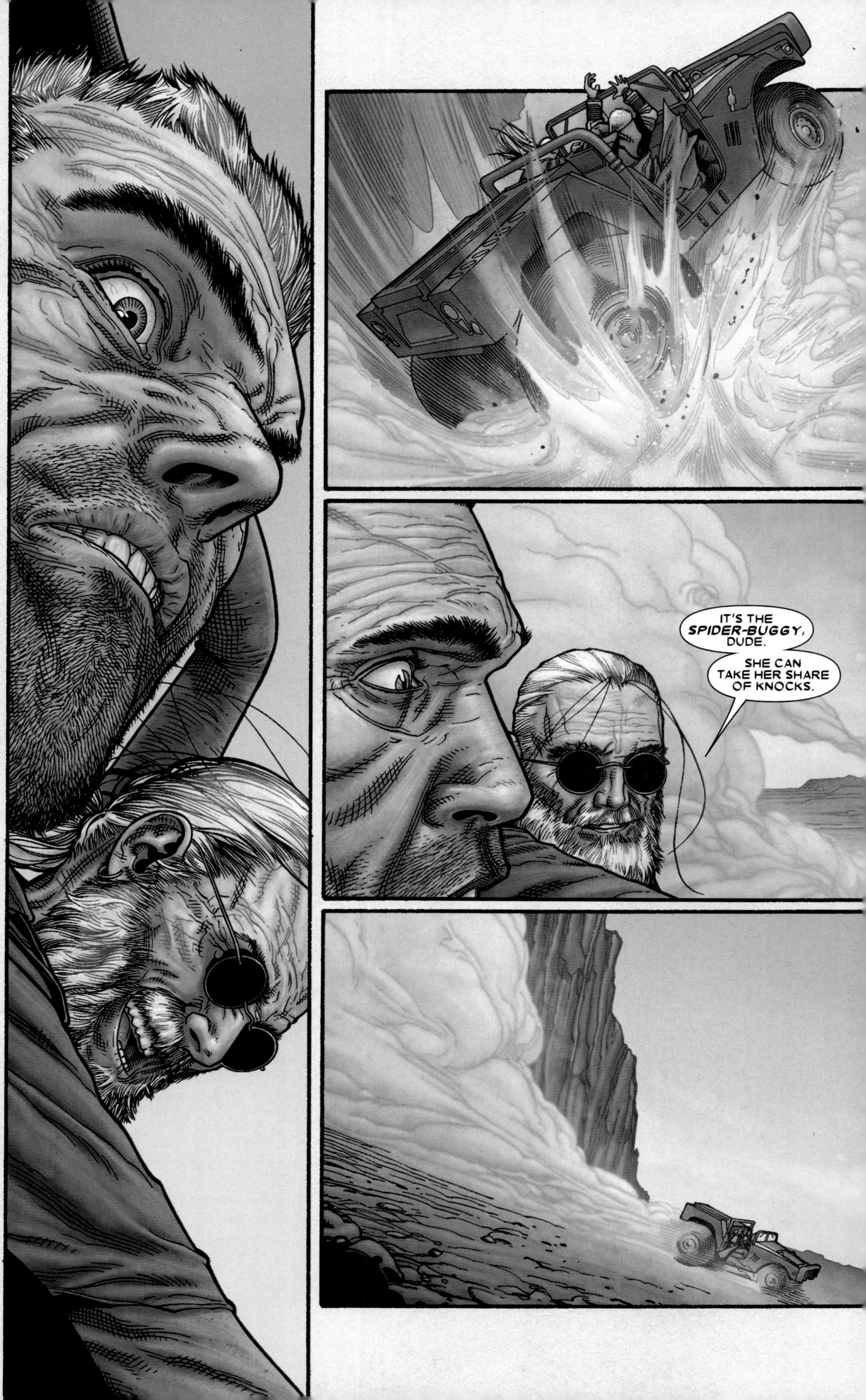
IT'S THE SPIDER-BUGGY, DUDE.
SHE CAN TAKE HER SHARE OF KNOCKS.

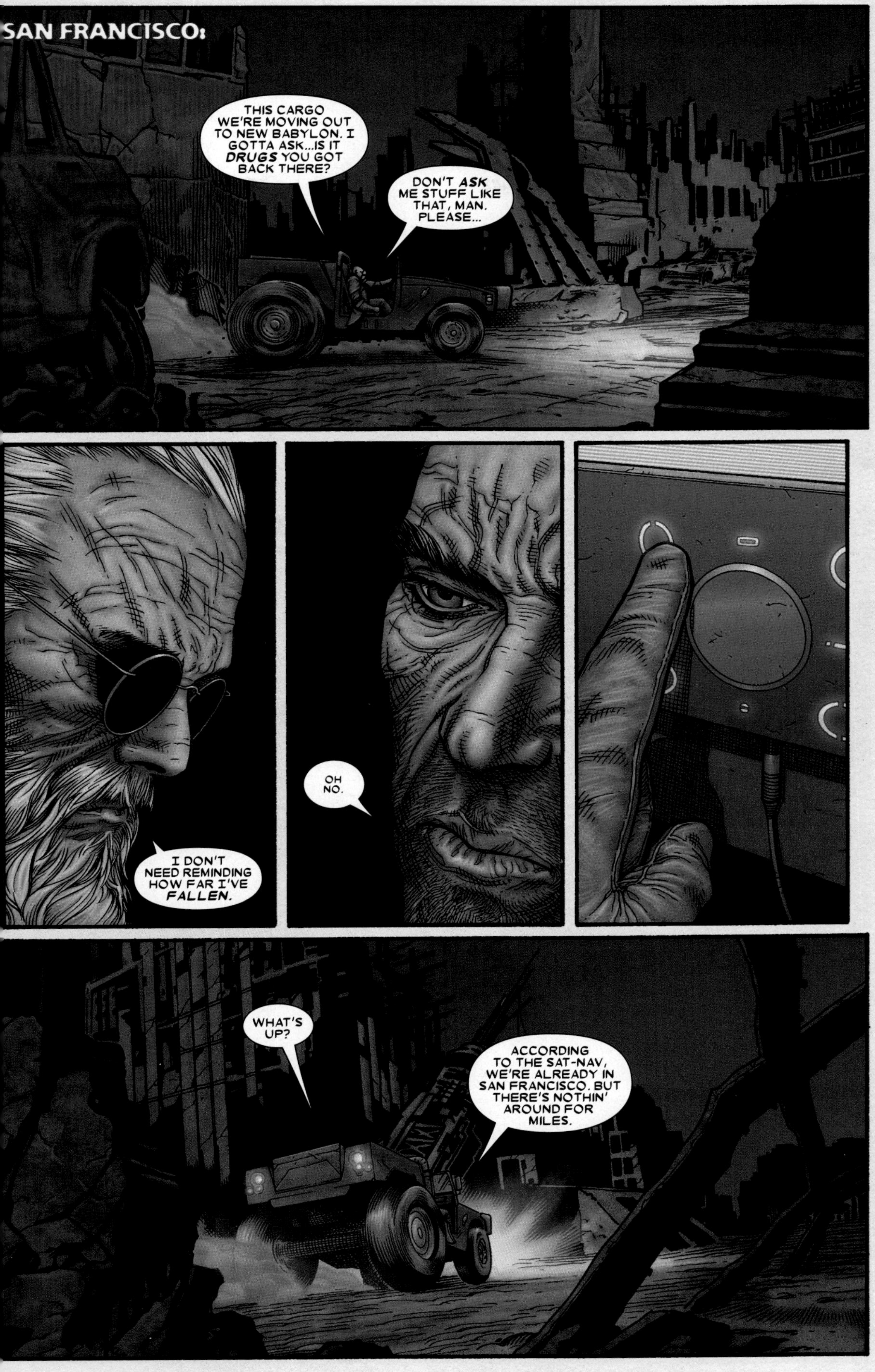
SAN FRANCISCO:
THIS CARGO WE'RE MOVING OUT TO NEW BABYLON. I GOTTA ASK...IS IT DRUGS YOU GOT BACK THERE?
DON'T ASK ME STUFF LIKE THAT, MAN. PLEASE...
I DON'T NEED REMINDING HOW FAR I'VE FALLEN.
OH NO.
WHAT'S UP?
ACCORDING TO THE SAT-NAV, WE'RE ALREADY IN SAN FRANCISCO. BUT THERE'S NOTHIN' AROUND FOR MILES.

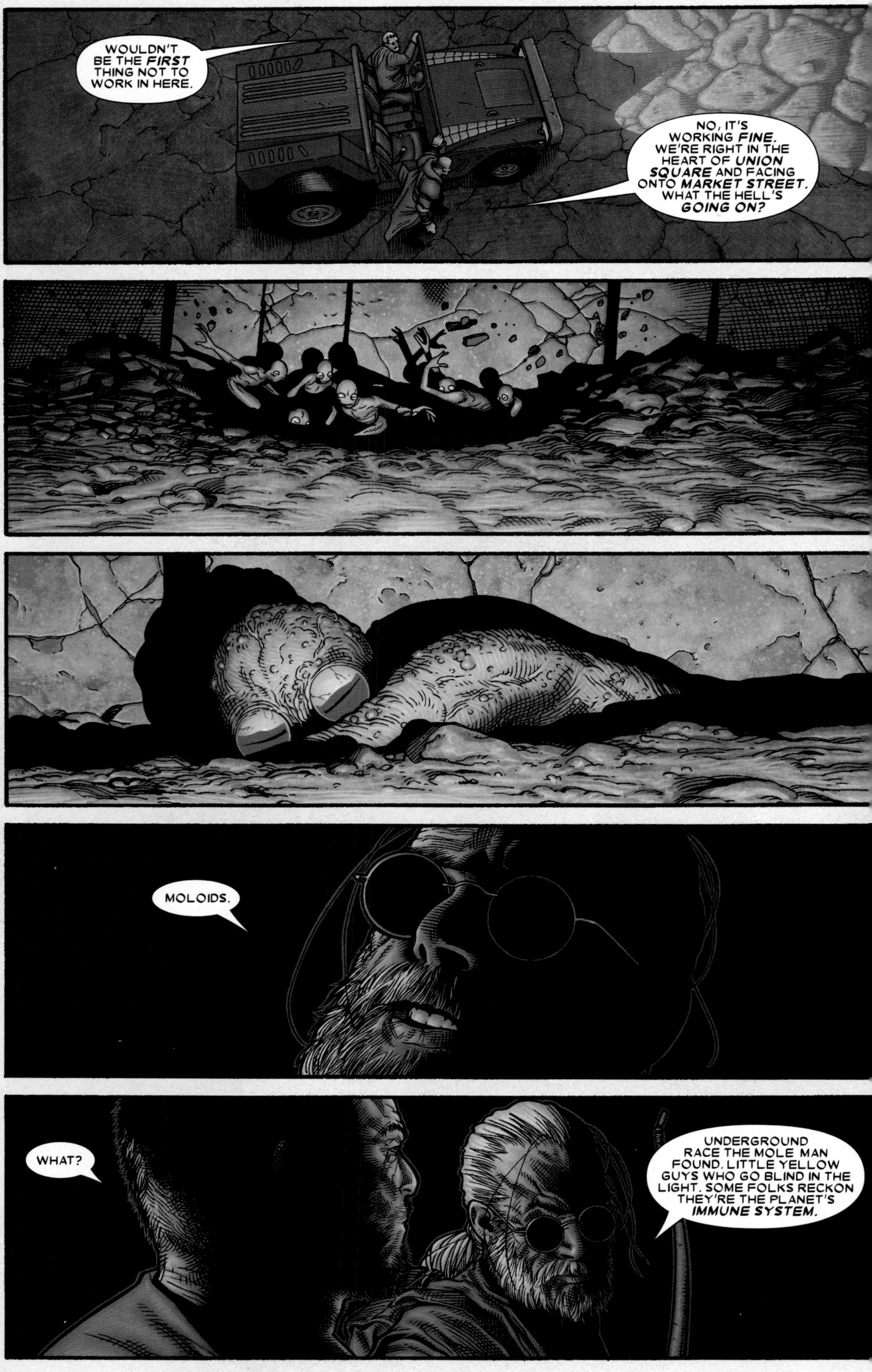
WOULDN'T BE THE FIRST THING NOT TO WORK IN HERE.
NO, IT'S WORKING FINE. WE'RE RIGHT IN THE HEART OF UNION SQUARE AND FACING ONTO MARKET STREET. WHAT THE HELL'S GOING ON?
MOLOIDS.
WHAT?
UNDERGROUND RACE THE MOLE MAN FOUND. LITTLE YELLOW GUYS WHO GO BLIND IN THE LIGHT. SOME FOLKS RECKON THEY'RE THE PLANET'S IMMUNE SYSTEM.

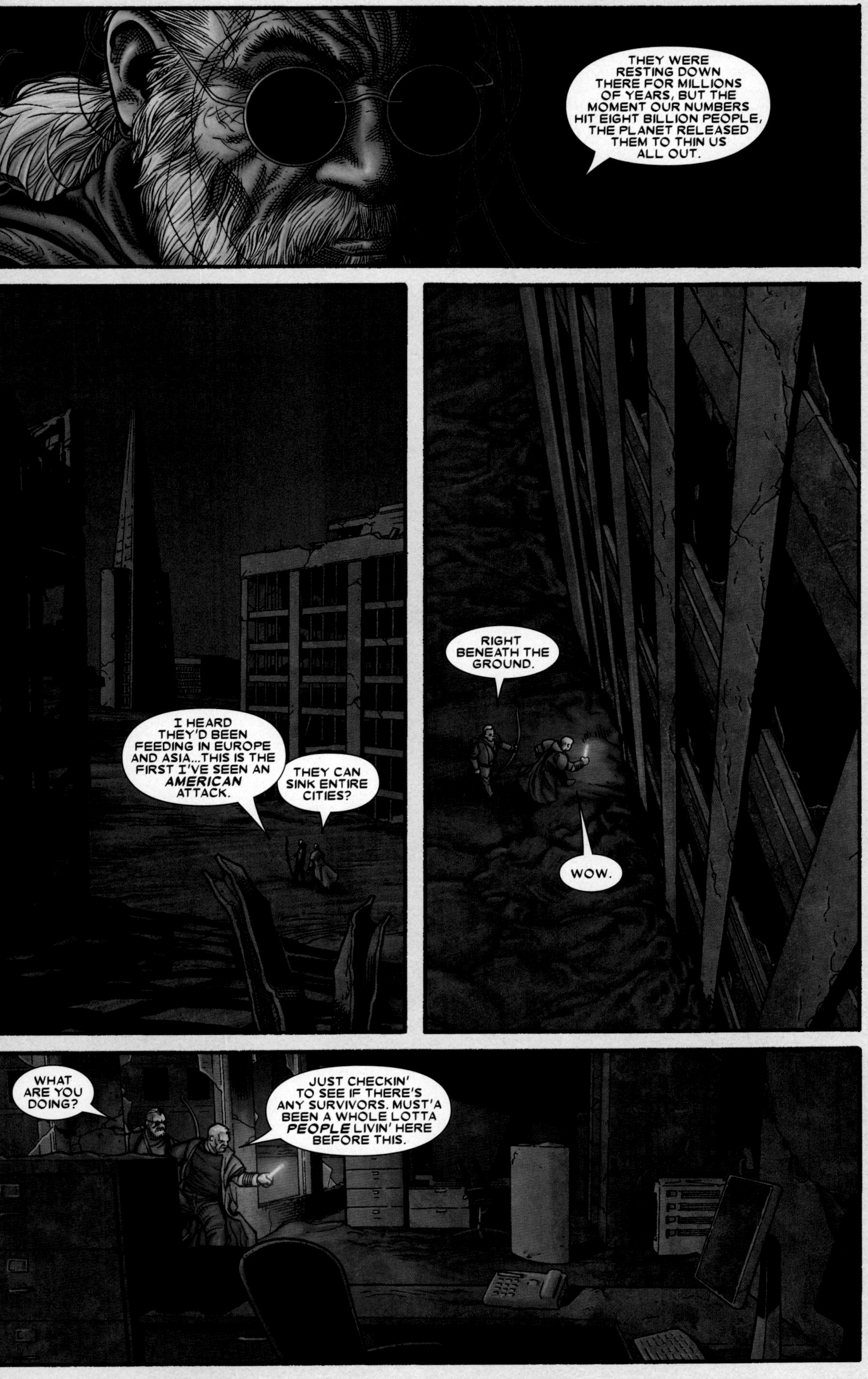
THEY WERE RESTING DOWN THERE FOR MILLIONS OF YEARS, BUT THE MOMENT OUR NUMBERS HIT EIGHT BILLION PEOPLE, THE PLANET RELEASED THEM TO THIN US ALL OUT.
I HEARD THEY'D BEEN FEEDING IN EUROPE AND ASIA...THIS IS THE FIRST I'VE SEEN AN AMERICAN ATTACK.
THEY CAN SINK ENTIRE CITIES?
RIGHT BENEATH THE GROUND.
WOW.
WHAT ARE YOU DOING?
JUST CHECKIN' TO SEE IF THERE'S ANY SURVIVORS. MUST'A BEEN A WHOLE LOTTA PEOPLE LIVIN' HERE BEFORE THIS.

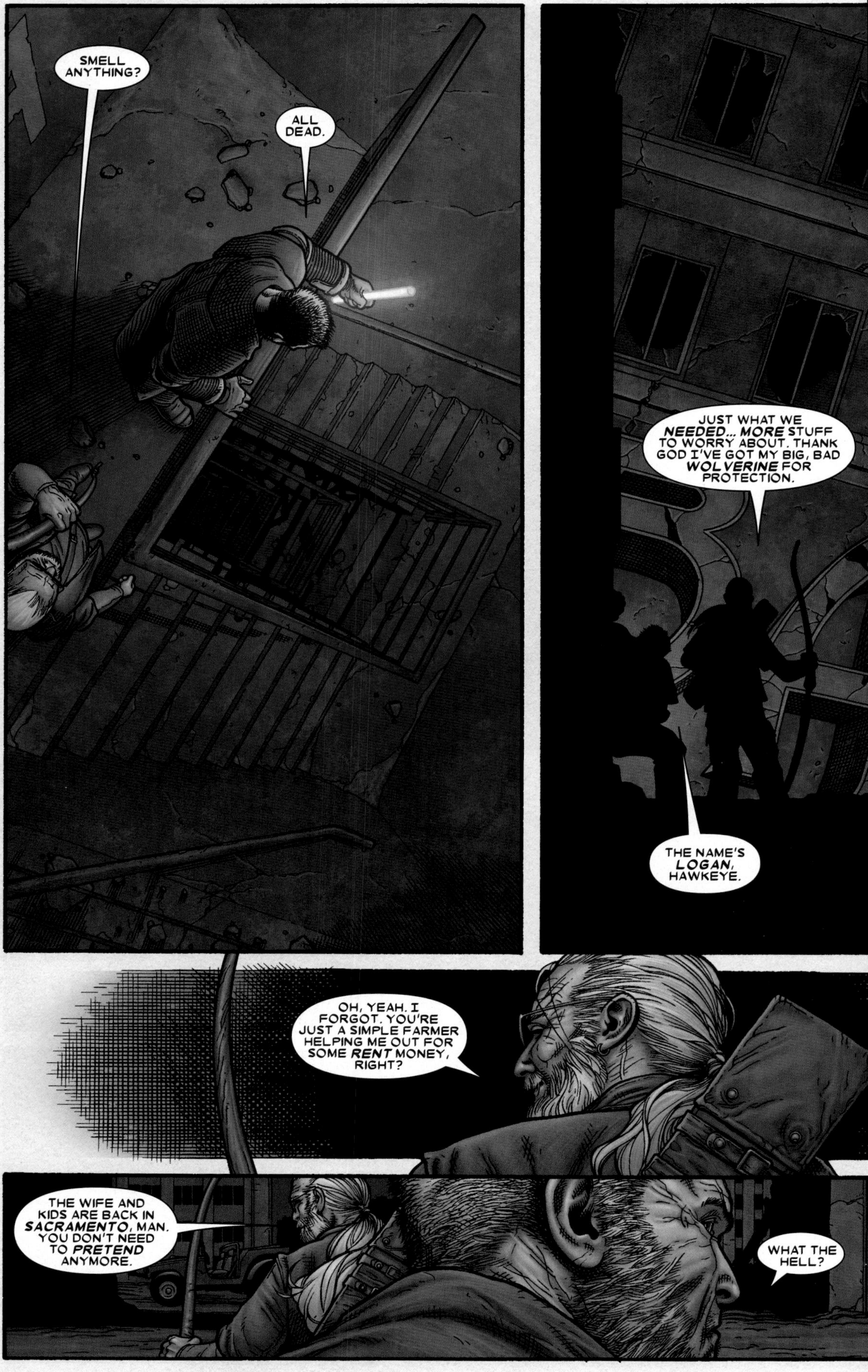
SMELL ANYTHING?
ALL DEAD.
JUST WHAT WE NEEDED... MORE STUFF TO WORRY ABOUT. THANK GOD I'VE GOT MY BIG, BAD WOLVERINE FOR PROTECTION.
THE NAME'S LOGAN, HAWKEYE.
OH, YEAH. I FORGOT. YOU'RE JUST A SIMPLE FARMER HELPING ME OUT FOR SOME RENT MONEY, RIGHT?
THE WIFE AND KIDS ARE BACK IN SACRAMENTO, MAN. YOU DON'T NEED TO PRETEND ANYMORE.
WHAT THE HELL?

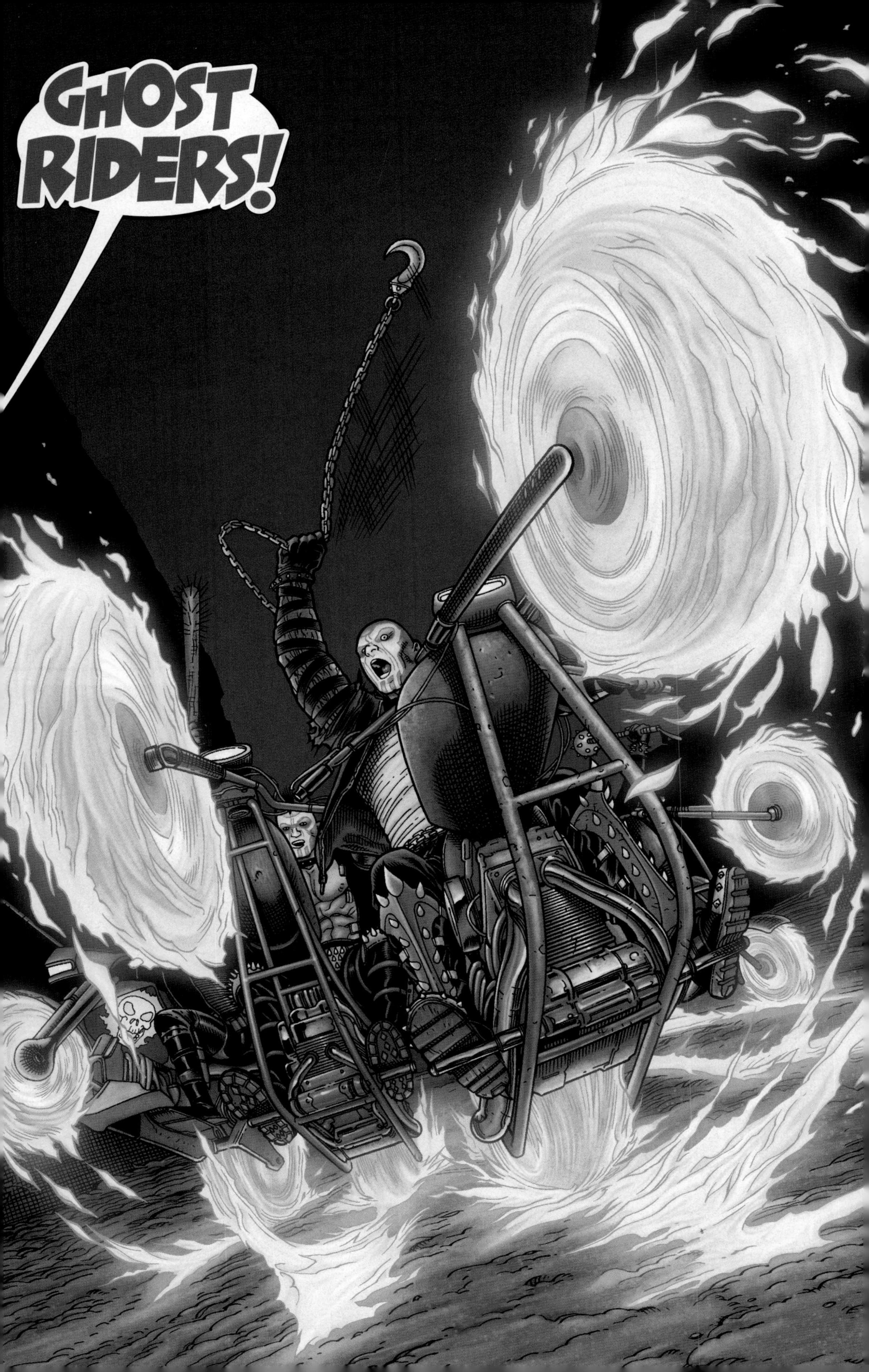
GHOST RIDERS!

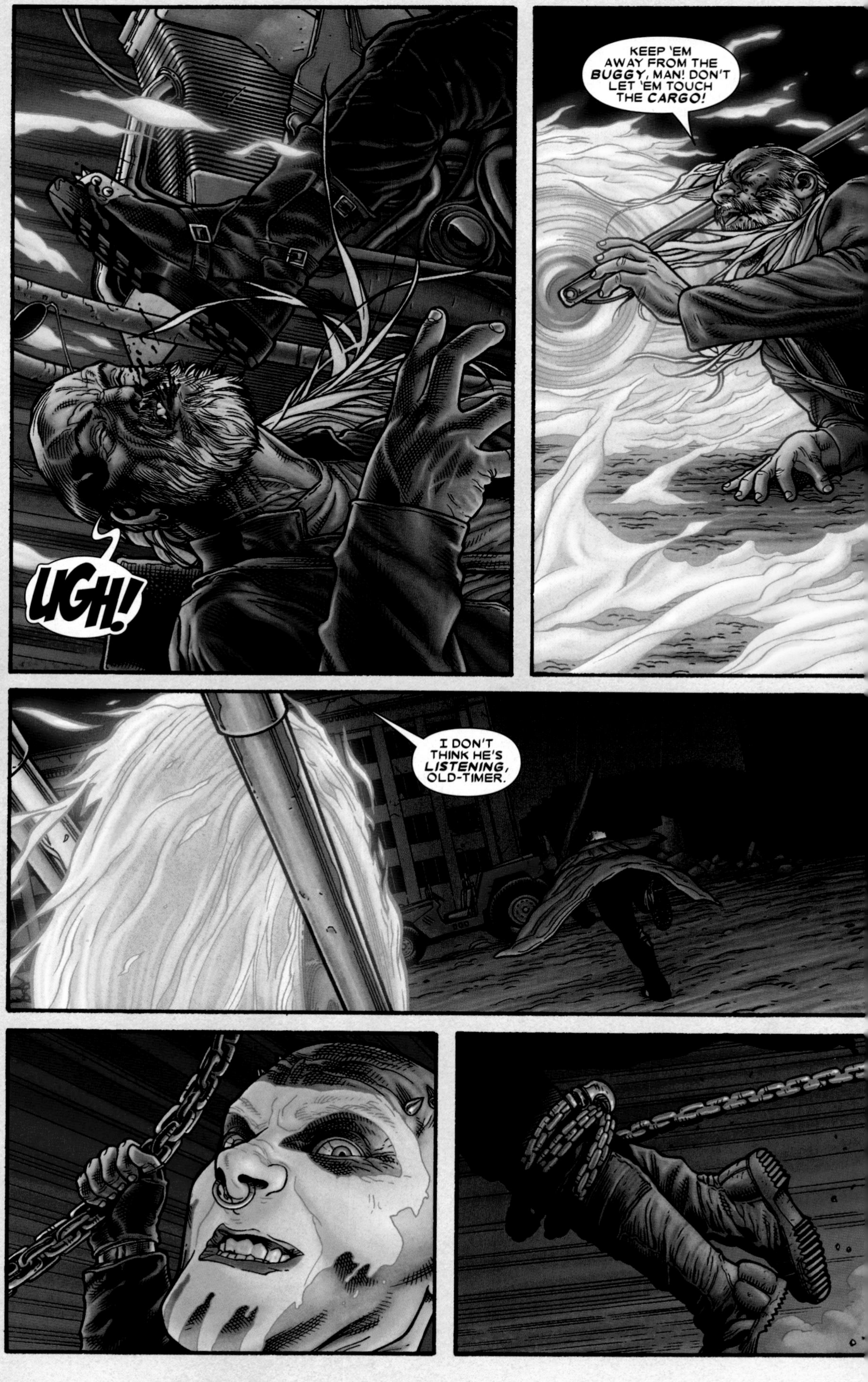
UGH!
KEEP 'EM AWAY FROM THE BUGGY, MAN! DON'T LET 'EM TOUCH THE CARGO!
I DON'T THINK HE'S LISTENING, OLD-TIMER.

UNGH!
WHAT'S THE MATTER, PIG?
STAND UP!
FIGHT BACK!
WHAT THE HELL'S WRONG WITH YOU, MAN?

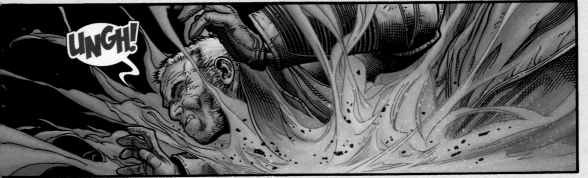

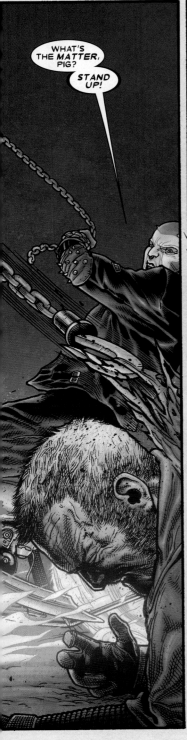

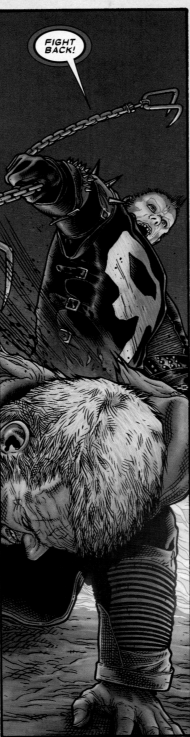

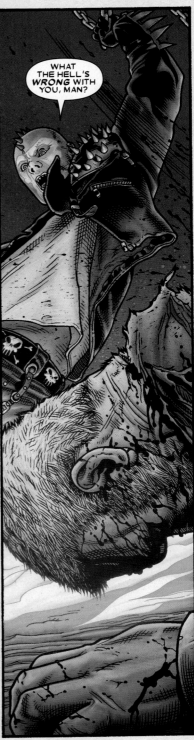

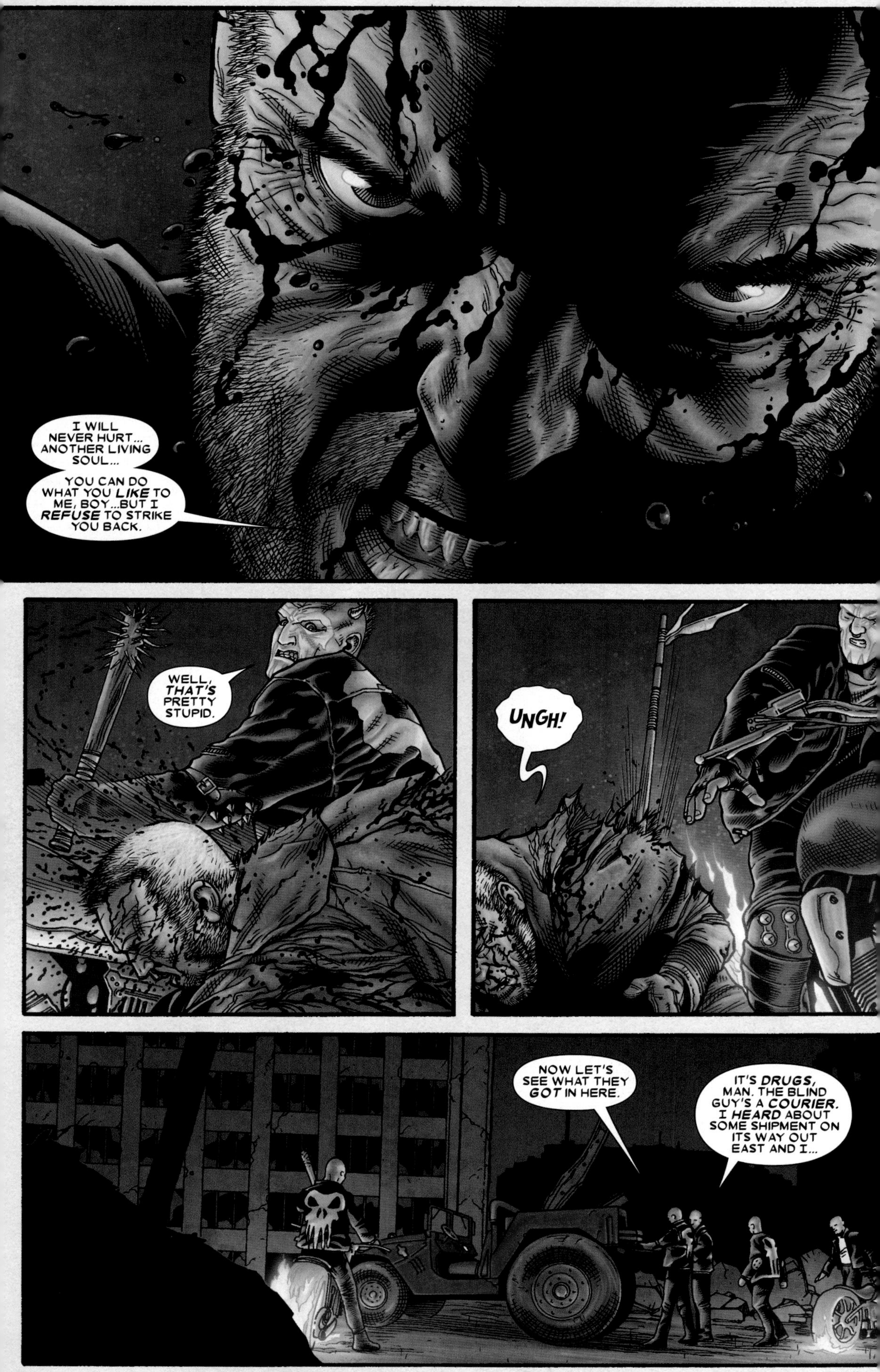
I WILL NEVER HURT... ANOTHER LIVING SOUL...
YOU CAN DO WHAT YOU *LIKE* TO ME, BOY...BUT I *REFUSE* TO STRIKE YOU BACK.
WELL, *THAT'S* PRETTY STUPID.
UNGH!
NOW LET'S SEE WHAT THEY *GOT* IN HERE.
IT'S *DRUGS*, MAN. THE BLIND GUY'S A *COURIER.* I *HEARD* ABOUT SOME SHIPMENT ON ITS WAY OUT EAST AND I...

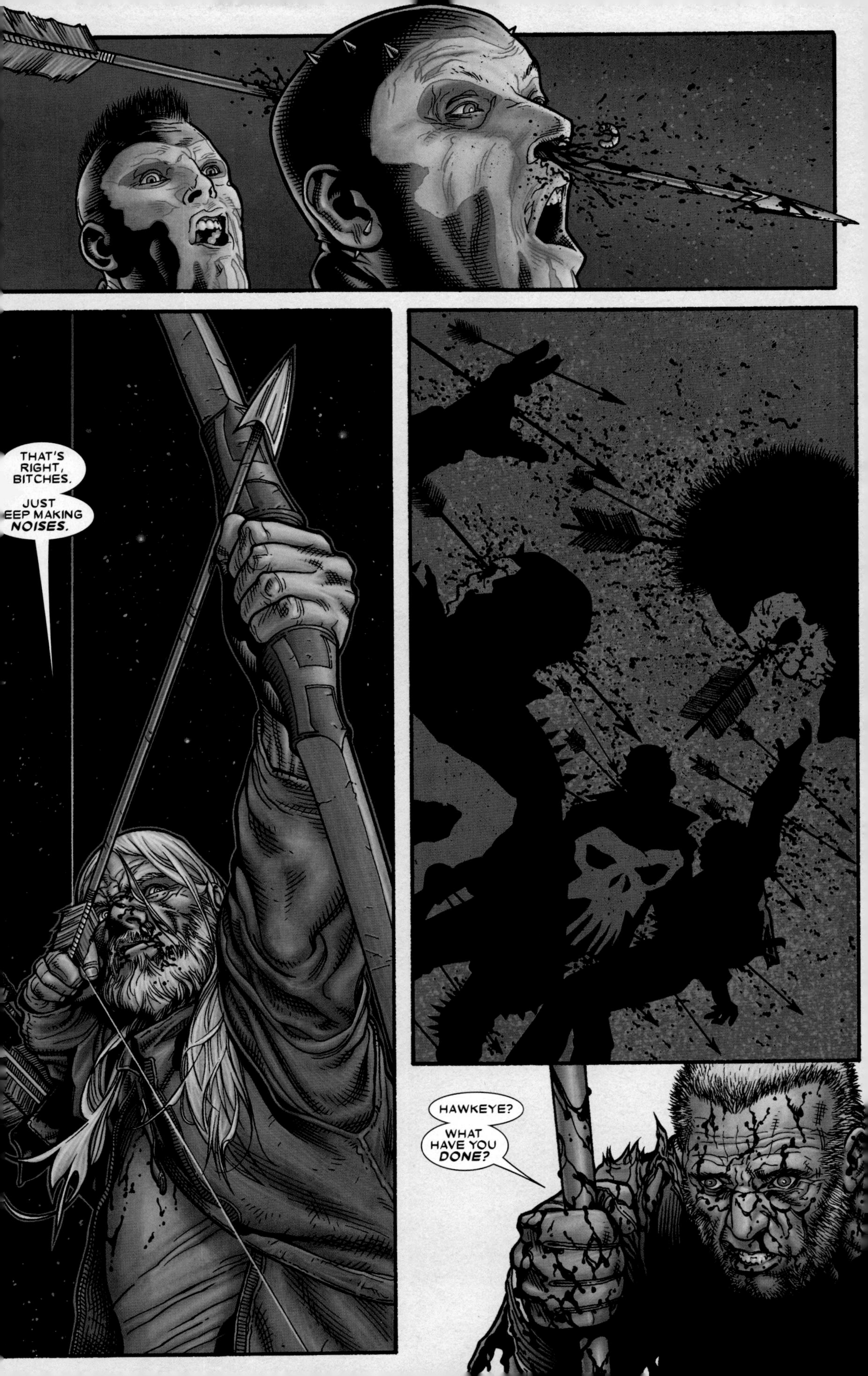
THAT'S RIGHT, BITCHES.
JUST EEP MAKING NOISES.
HAWKEYE?
WHAT HAVE YOU DONE?

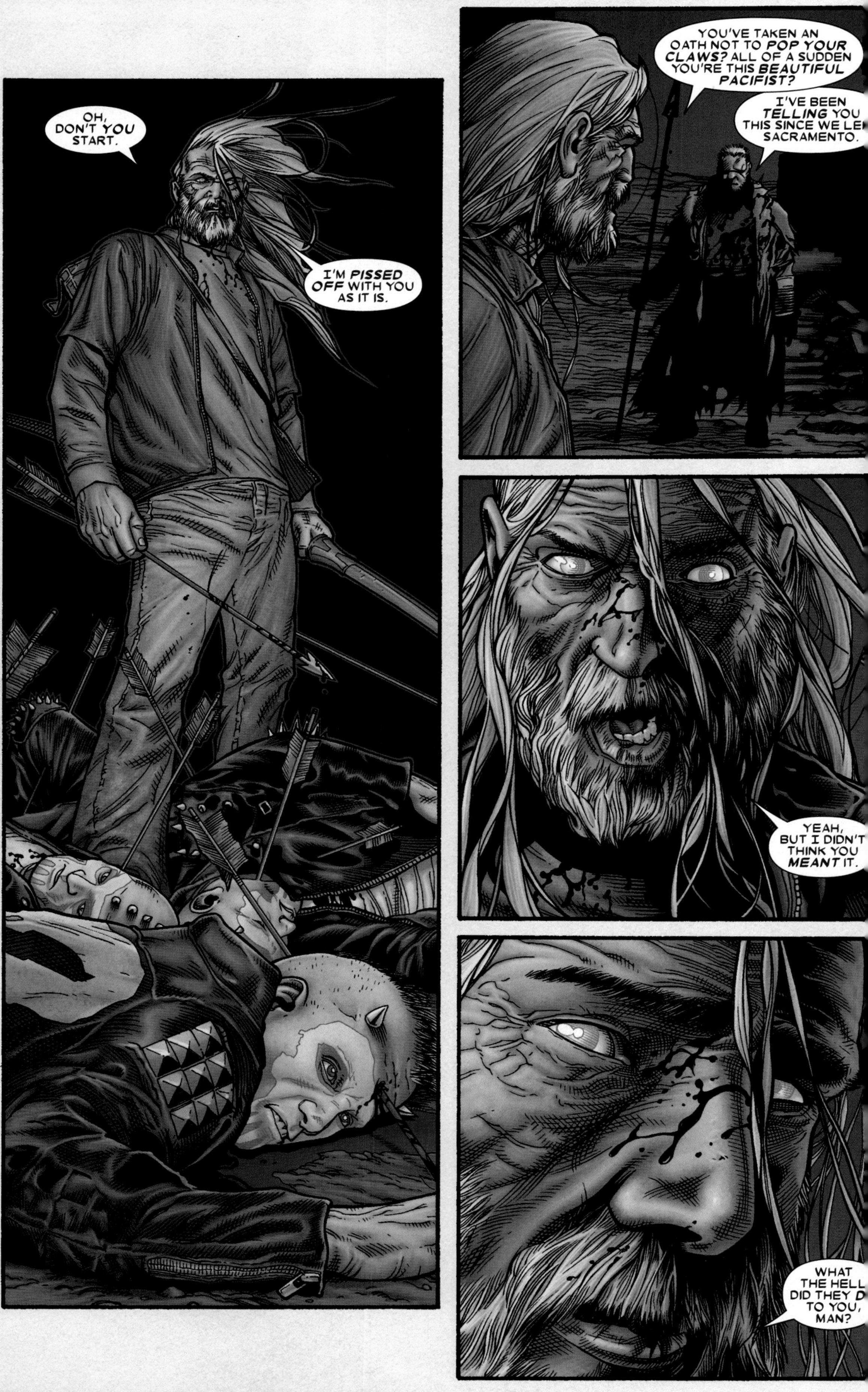

OH, DON'T YOU START.
I'M PISSED OFF WITH YOU AS IT IS.
YOU'VE TAKEN AN OATH NOT TO POP YOUR CLAWS? ALL OF A SUDDEN YOU'RE THIS BEAUTIFUL PACIFIST?
I'VE BEEN TELLING YOU THIS SINCE WE LE
SACRAMENTO.
YEAH, BUT I DIDN'T THINK YOU MEANT IT.
WHAT THE HELL DID THEY D
TO YOU, MAN?

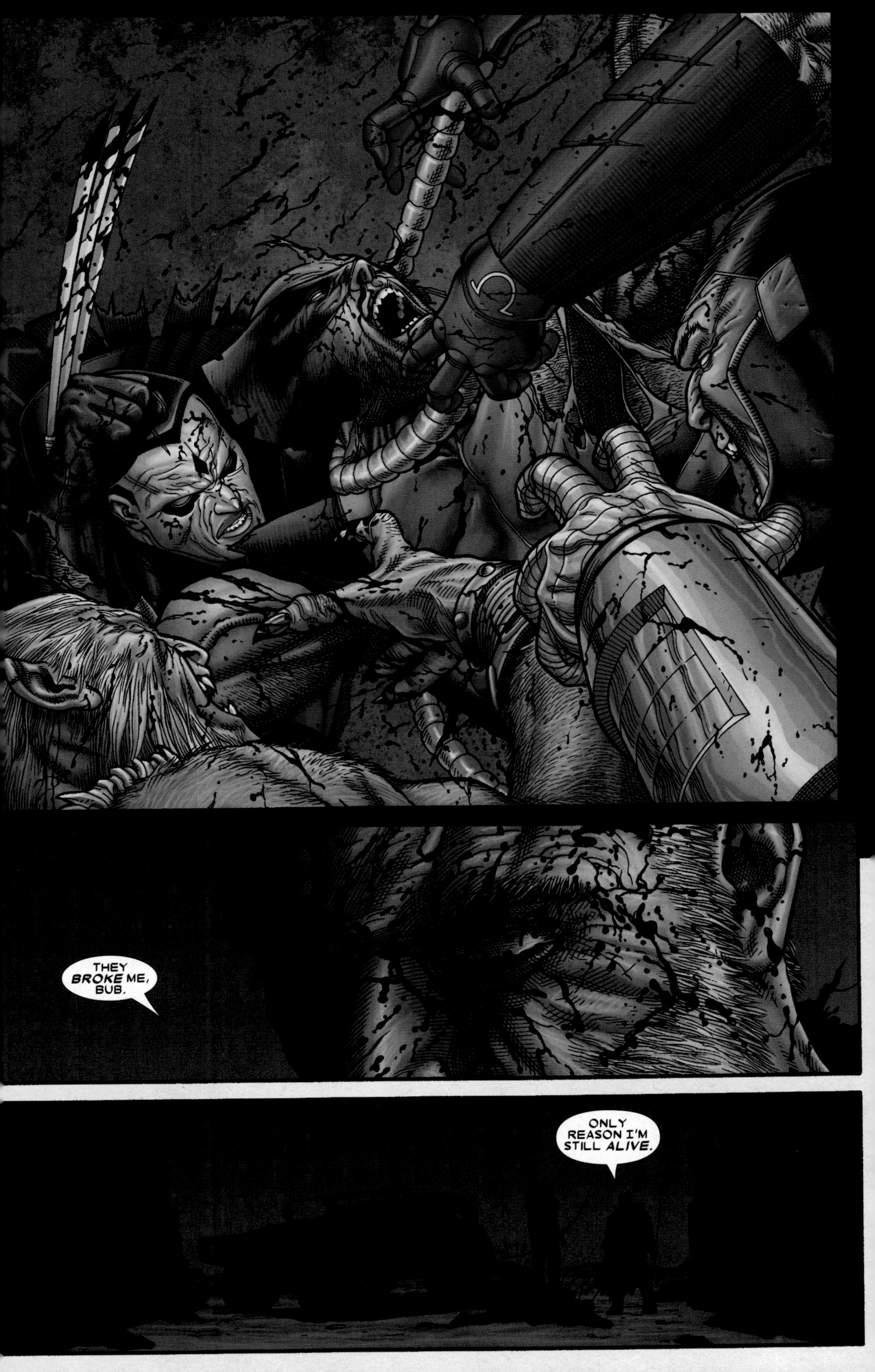
THEY BROKE ME, BUB.
ONLY REASON I'M STILL ALIVE.

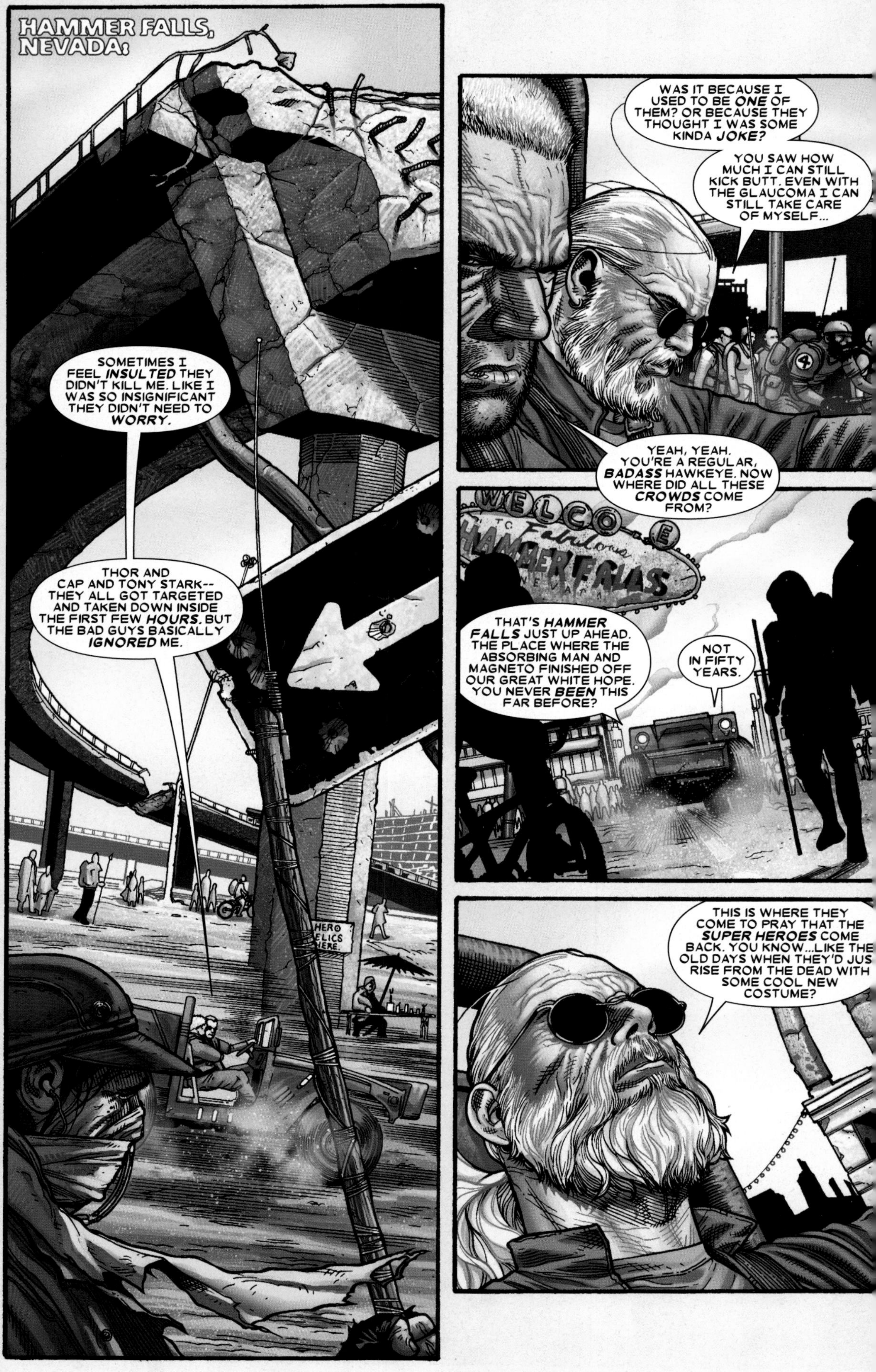
HAMMER FALLS, NEVADA:
SOMETIMES I FEEL INSULTED THEY DIDN'T KILL ME. LIKE I WAS SO INSIGNIFICANT THEY DIDN'T NEED TO WORRY.
THOR AND CAP AND TONY STARK-- THEY ALL GOT TARGETED AND TAKEN DOWN INSIDE THE FIRST FEW HOURS. BUT THE BAD GUYS BASICALLY IGNORED ME.
HERO ELICS HERE.
WAS IT BECAUSE I USED TO BE ONE OF THEM? OR BECAUSE THEY THOUGHT I WAS SOME KINDA JOKE?
YOU SAW HOW MUCH I CAN STILL KICK BUTT. EVEN WITH THE GLAUCOMA I CAN STILL TAKE CARE OF MYSELF...
YEAH, YEAH. YOU'RE A REGULAR, BADASS HAWKEYE. NOW WHERE DID ALL THESE CROWDS COME FROM?
WELCO E TO Fabulous HAMMER FALLS NEVADA
THAT'S HAMMER FALLS JUST UP AHEAD. THE PLACE WHERE THE ABSORBING MAN AND MAGNETO FINISHED OFF OUR GREAT WHITE HOPE. YOU NEVER BEEN THIS FAR BEFORE?
NOT IN FIFTY YEARS.
THIS IS WHERE THEY COME TO PRAY THAT THE SUPER HEROES COME BACK. YOU KNOW...LIKE THE OLD DAYS WHEN THEY'D JUS RISE FROM THE DEAD WITH SOME COOL NEW COSTUME?

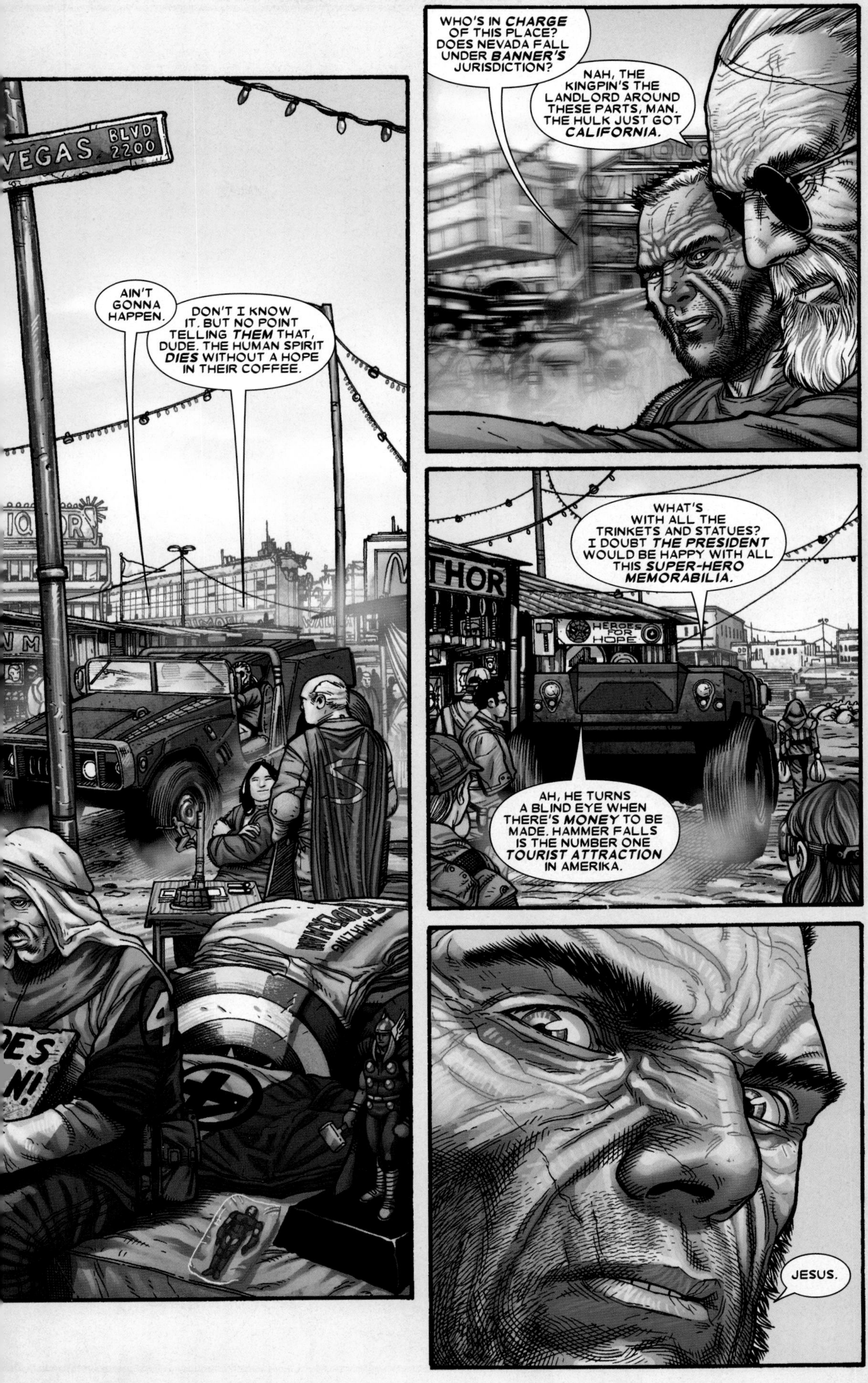
VEGAS BLVD 2200
AIN'T GONNA HAPPEN.
DON'T I KNOW IT. BUT NO POINT TELLING *THEM* THAT, DUDE. THE HUMAN SPIRIT *DIES* WITHOUT A HOPE IN THEIR COFFEE.
WHO'S IN *CHARGE* OF THIS PLACE? DOES NEVADA FALL UNDER *BANNER'S* JURISDICTION?
NAH, THE KINGPIN'S THE LANDLORD AROUND THESE PARTS, MAN. THE HULK JUST GOT *CALIFORNIA.*
THOR
HEROES FOR HOPE
WHAT'S WITH ALL THE TRINKETS AND STATUES? I DOUBT *THE PRESIDENT* WOULD BE HAPPY WITH ALL THIS *SUPER-HERO MEMORABILIA.*
AH, HE TURNS A BLIND EYE WHEN THERE'S *MONEY* TO BE MADE. HAMMER FALLS IS THE NUMBER ONE *TOURIST ATTRACTION* IN AMERIKA.
JESUS.

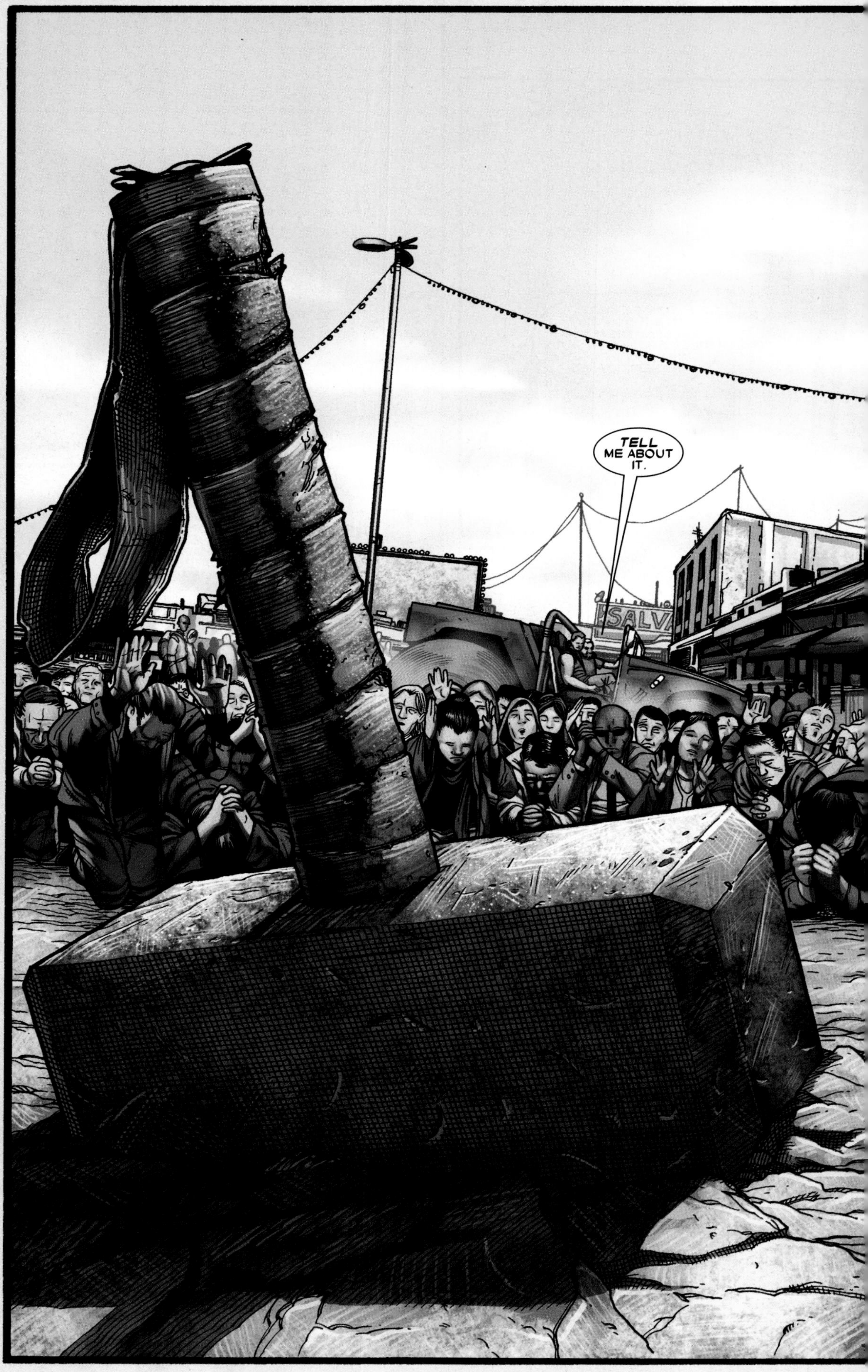
TELL ME ABOUT IT.
SALVA

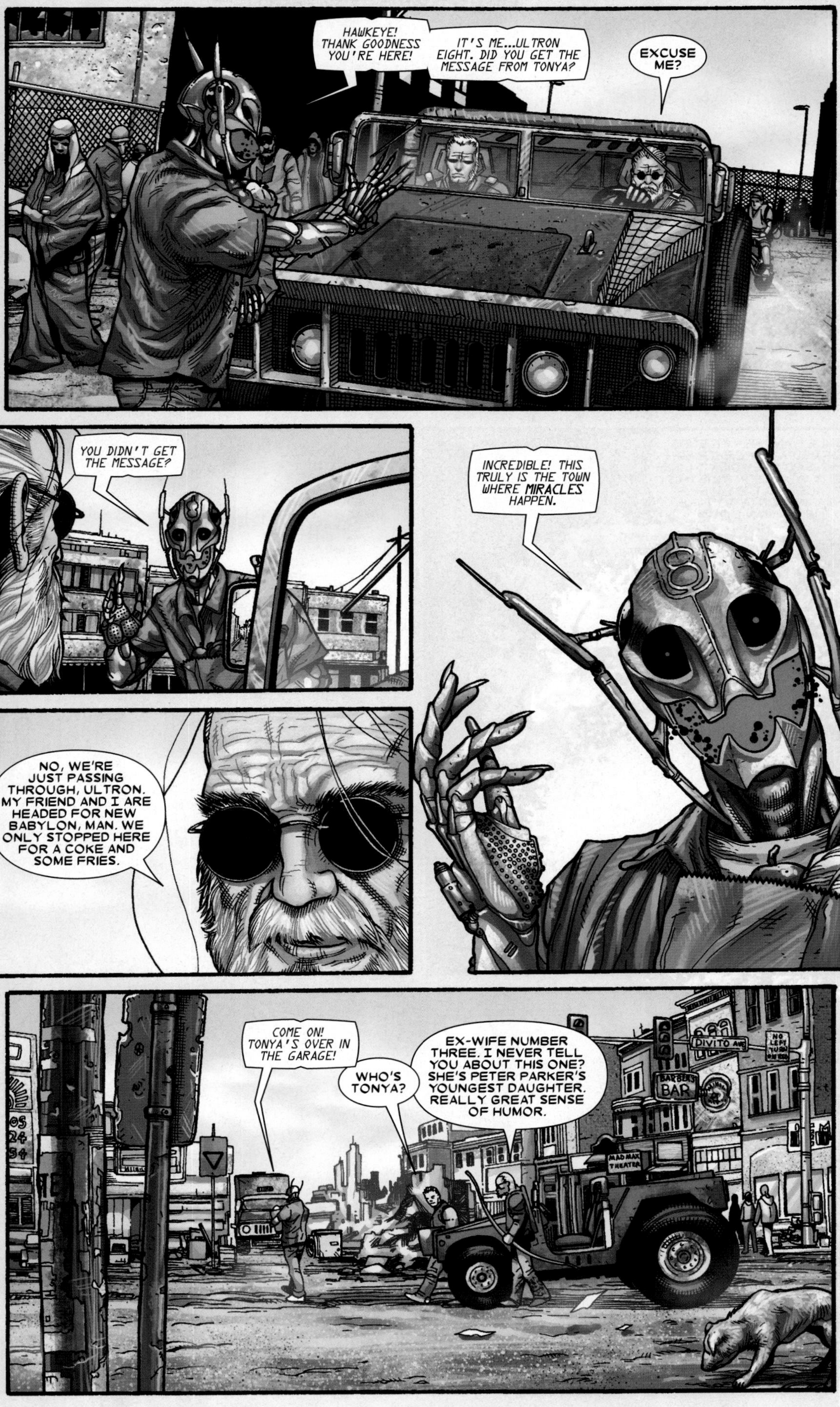
HAWKEYE! THANK GOODNESS YOU'RE HERE!
IT'S ME...ULTRON EIGHT. DID YOU GET THE MESSAGE FROM TONYA?
EXCUSE ME?
YOU DIDN'T GET THE MESSAGE?
INCREDIBLE! THIS TRULY IS THE TOWN WHERE MIRACLES HAPPEN.
NO, WE'RE JUST PASSING THROUGH, ULTRON. MY FRIEND AND I ARE HEADED FOR NEW BABYLON, MAN. WE ONLY STOPPED HERE FOR A COKE AND SOME FRIES.
COME ON! TONYA'S OVER IN THE GARAGE!
WHO'S TONYA?
EX-WIFE NUMBER THREE. I NEVER TELL YOU ABOUT THIS ONE? SHE'S PETER PARKER'S YOUNGEST DAUGHTER. REALLY GREAT SENSE OF HUMOR.

TONYA'S GARAGE:

WELL, IT WAS ONLY A MATTER OF *TIME*, WASN'T IT? FILLING HER HEAD WITH ALL YOUR *NONSENSE...*

EXCUSE ME?

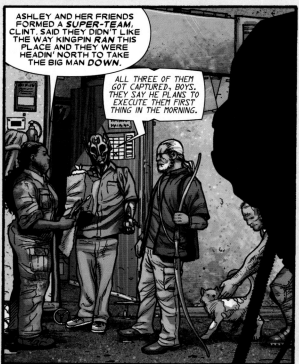

ASHLEY AND HER FRIENDS FORMED A *SUPER-TEAM*, CLINT. SAID THEY DIDN'T LIKE THE WAY KINGPIN *RAN* THIS PLACE AND THEY WERE HEADIN' NORTH TO TAKE THE BIG MAN *DOWN*.

ALL THREE OF THEM GOT CAPTURED, BOYS. THEY SAY HE PLANS TO EXECUTE THEM FIRST THING IN THE MORNING.

COULDN'T YOU TELL HER YOUR *DRUG-DEALER* STORIES? AT LEAST THAT WAY SHE'D BE EARNING A *LIVING...*

I DON'T UNDERSTAND. WHO ARE WE EVEN *TALKING* ABOUT HERE?

SHE'S TALKING ABOUT *ASHLEY*, MAN...

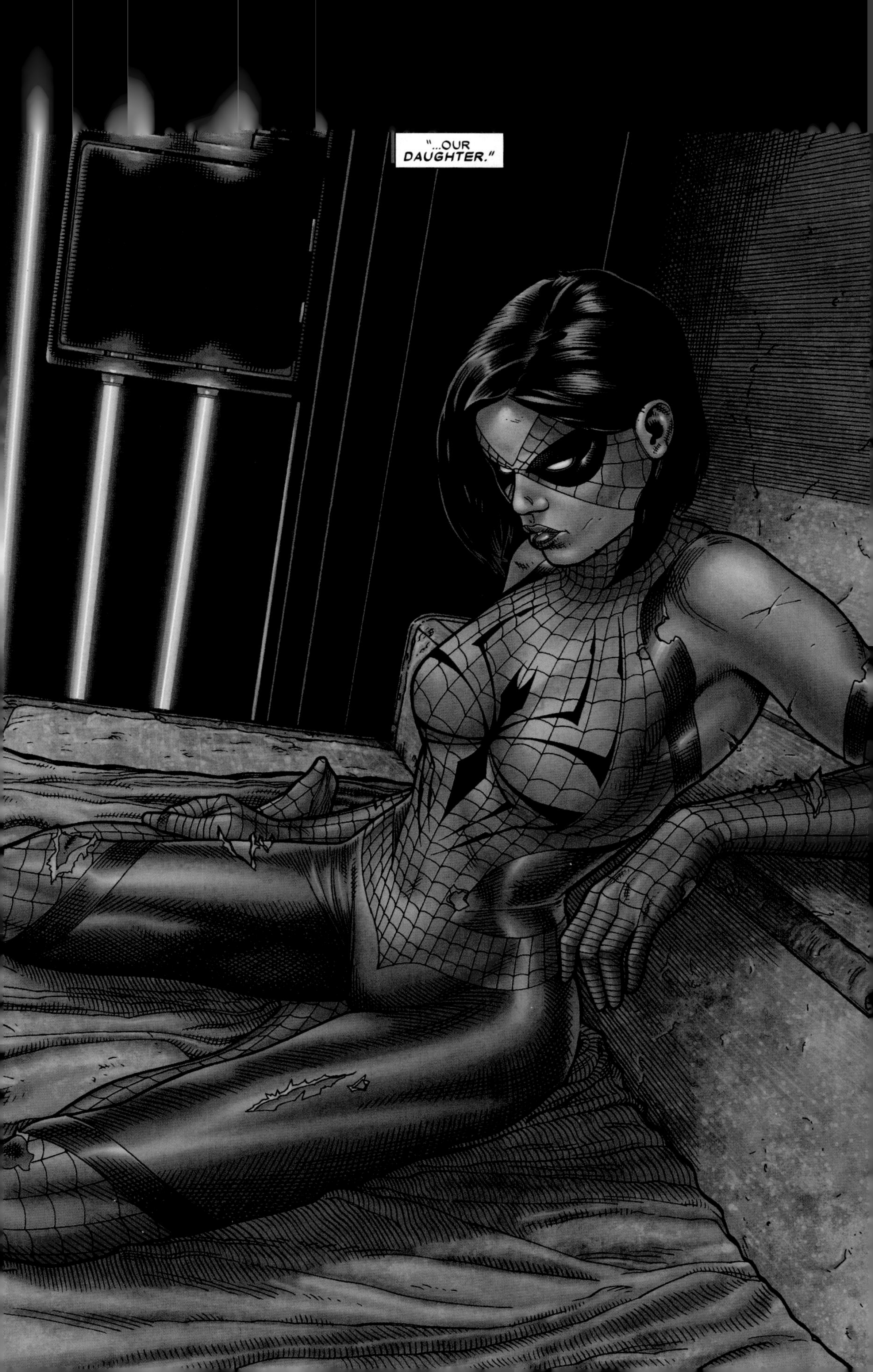
"...OUR DAUGHTER."

CHAPTER THREE

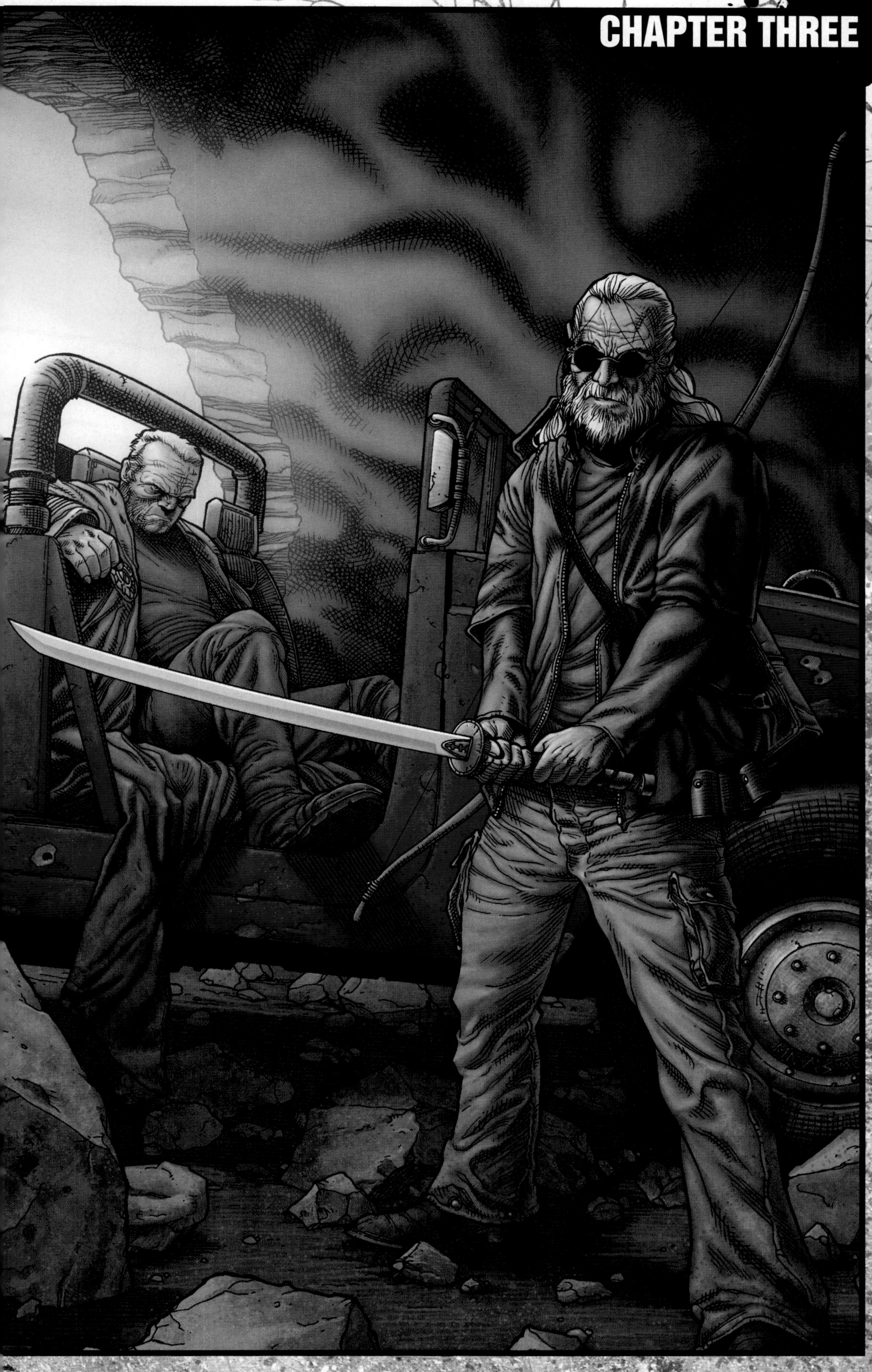

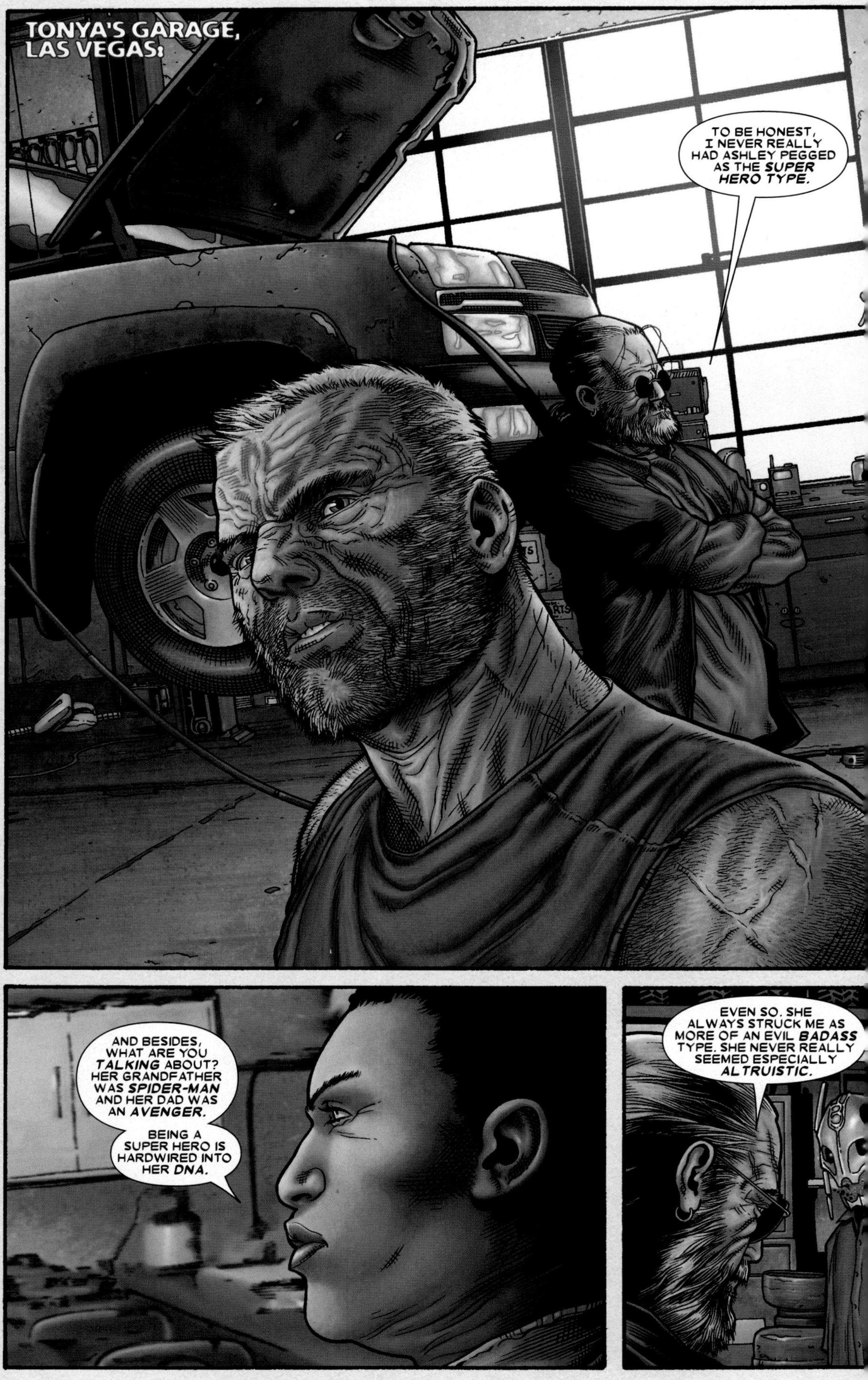
TONYA'S GARAGE, LAS VEGAS:
TO BE HONEST, I NEVER REALLY HAD ASHLEY PEGGED AS THE SUPER HERO TYPE.
AND BESIDES, WHAT ARE YOU TALKING ABOUT? HER GRANDFATHER WAS SPIDER-MAN AND HER DAD WAS AN AVENGER.
BEING A SUPER HERO IS HARDWIRED INTO HER DNA.
EVEN SO. SHE ALWAYS STRUCK ME AS MORE OF AN EVIL BADASS TYPE. SHE NEVER REALLY SEEMED ESPECIALLY ALTRUISTIC.

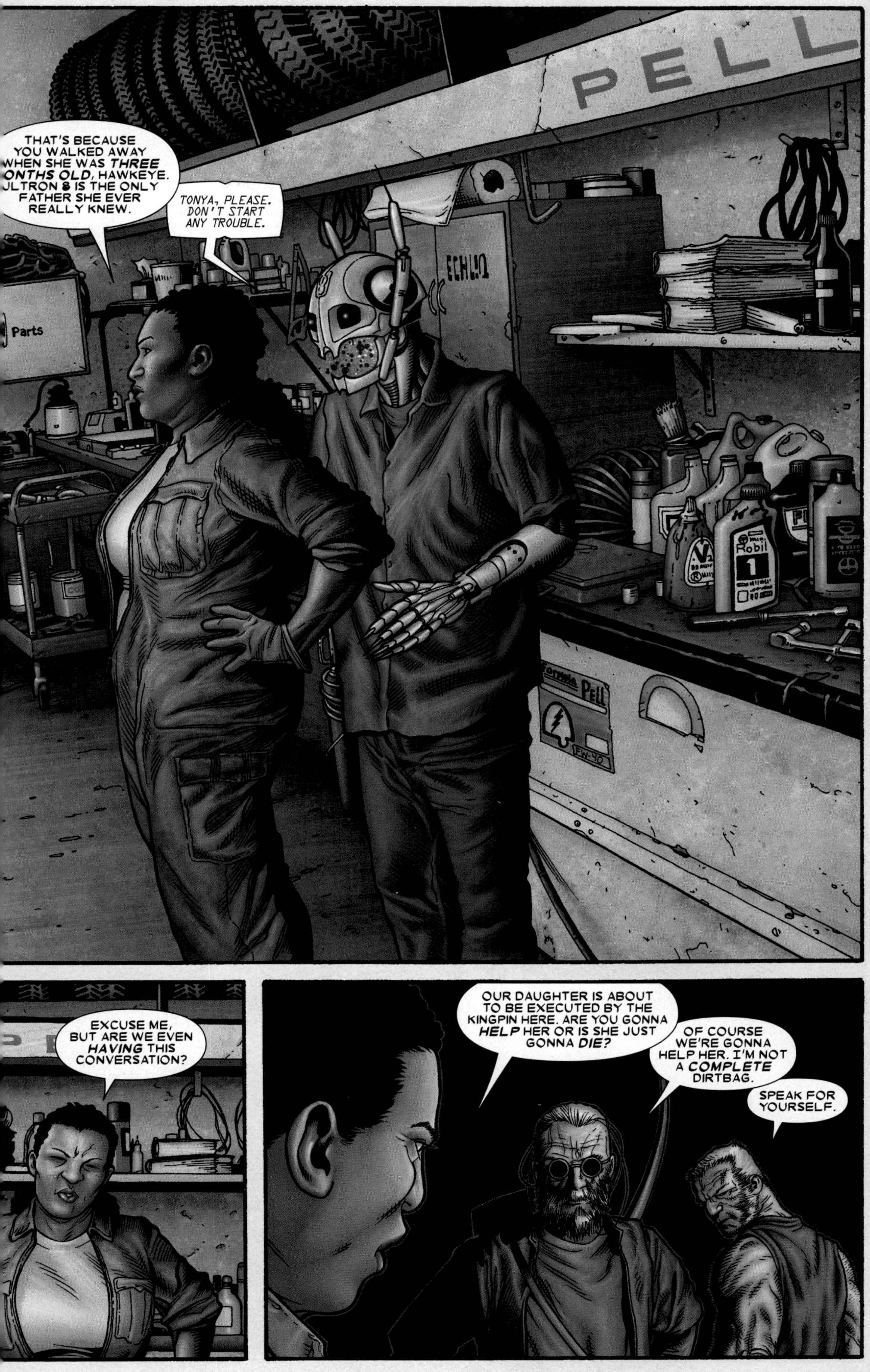
PELL
THAT'S BECAUSE YOU WALKED AWAY WHEN SHE WAS *THREE ONTHS OLD*, HAWKEYE. ULTRON 8 IS THE ONLY FATHER SHE EVER REALLY KNEW.
TONYA, PLEASE. DON'T START ANY TROUBLE.
Parts
EXCUSE ME, BUT ARE WE EVEN ***HAVING*** THIS CONVERSATION?
OUR DAUGHTER IS ABOUT TO BE EXECUTED BY THE KINGPIN HERE. ARE YOU GONNA ***HELP*** HER OR IS SHE JUST GONNA ***DIE?***
OF COURSE WE'RE GONNA HELP HER. I'M NOT A ***COMPLETE*** DIRTBAG.
SPEAK FOR YOURSELF.

WHAT?

I GOT HIRED AS YOUR *MAP READER,* BUB. I AIN'T GETTIN' DRAGGED INTO ONE OF YOUR *STUPID ADVENTURES.*

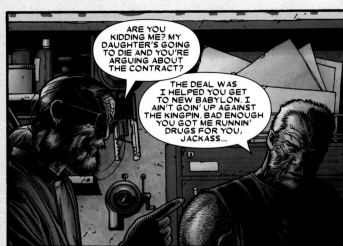

ARE YOU KIDDING ME? MY DAUGHTER'S GOING TO DIE AND YOU'RE ARGUING ABOUT THE CONTRACT?

THE DEAL WAS I HELPED YOU GET TO NEW BABYLON. I AIN'T GOIN' UP AGAINST THE KINGPIN. BAD ENOUGH YOU GOT ME RUNNIN' DRUGS FOR YOU, *JACKASS...*

I'LL PAY YOU *DOUBLE.*

WHAT?

YOU NEED TO CLEAR YOUR DEBTS WITH THE HULK GANG, RIGHT? YOU HELP ME SAVE MY DAUGHTER AND I'LL DOUBLE YOUR *MONEY.*

I STILL AIN'T FIGHTIN'.

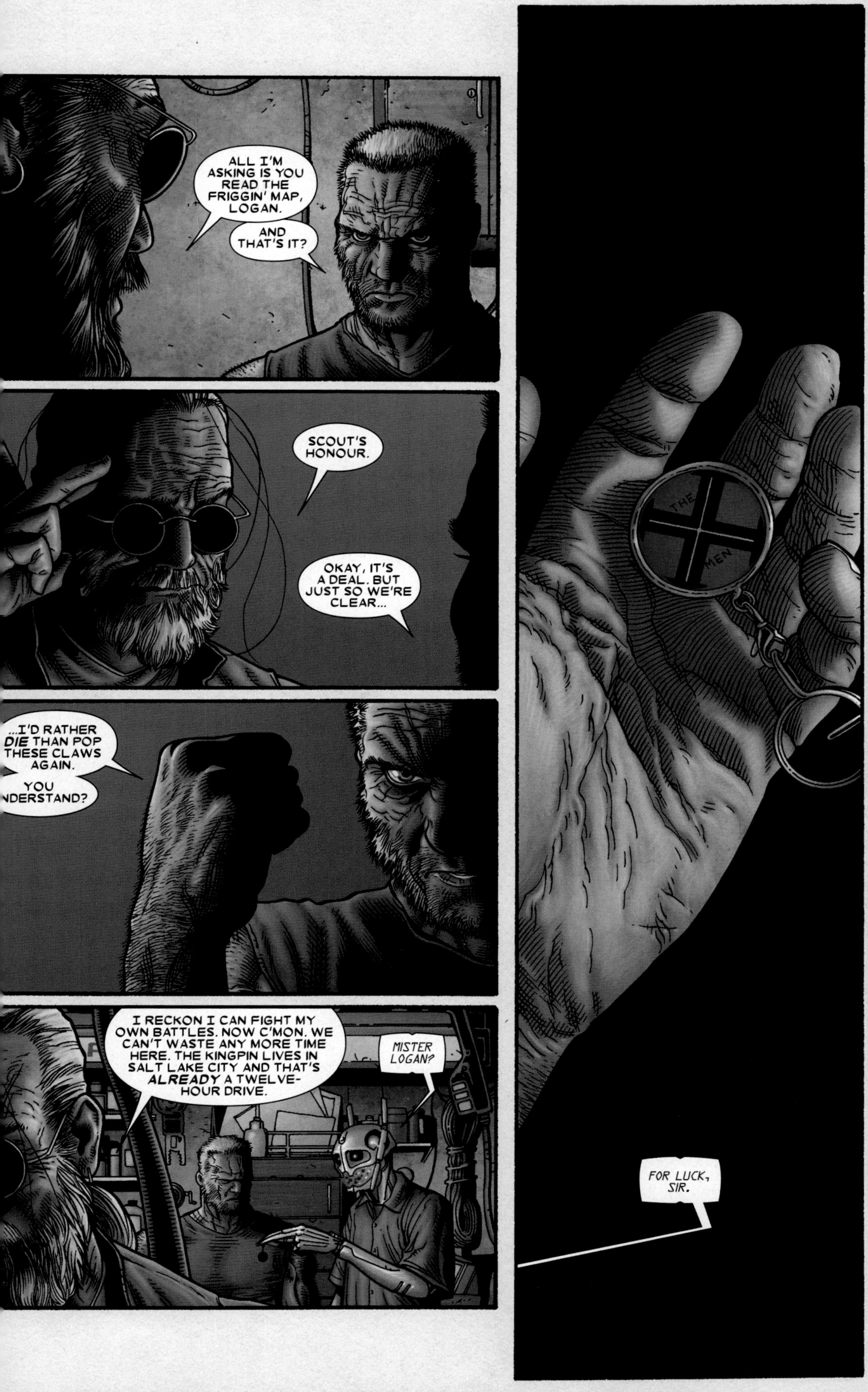
ALL I'M ASKING IS YOU READ THE FRIGGIN' MAP, LOGAN.
AND THAT'S IT?
SCOUT'S HONOUR.
OKAY, IT'S A DEAL. BUT JUST SO WE'RE CLEAR...
...I'D RATHER DIE THAN POP THESE CLAWS AGAIN.
YOU NDERSTAND?
I RECKON I CAN FIGHT MY OWN BATTLES. NOW C'MON. WE CAN'T WASTE ANY MORE TIME HERE. THE KINGPIN LIVES IN SALT LAKE CITY AND THAT'S ALREADY A TWELVE-HOUR DRIVE.
MISTER LOGAN?
THE MEN
FOR LUCK, SIR.

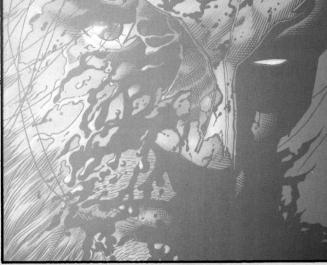

COME ON, DUDE. CHARLIE XAVIER WAS FASTER ON HIS FEET!

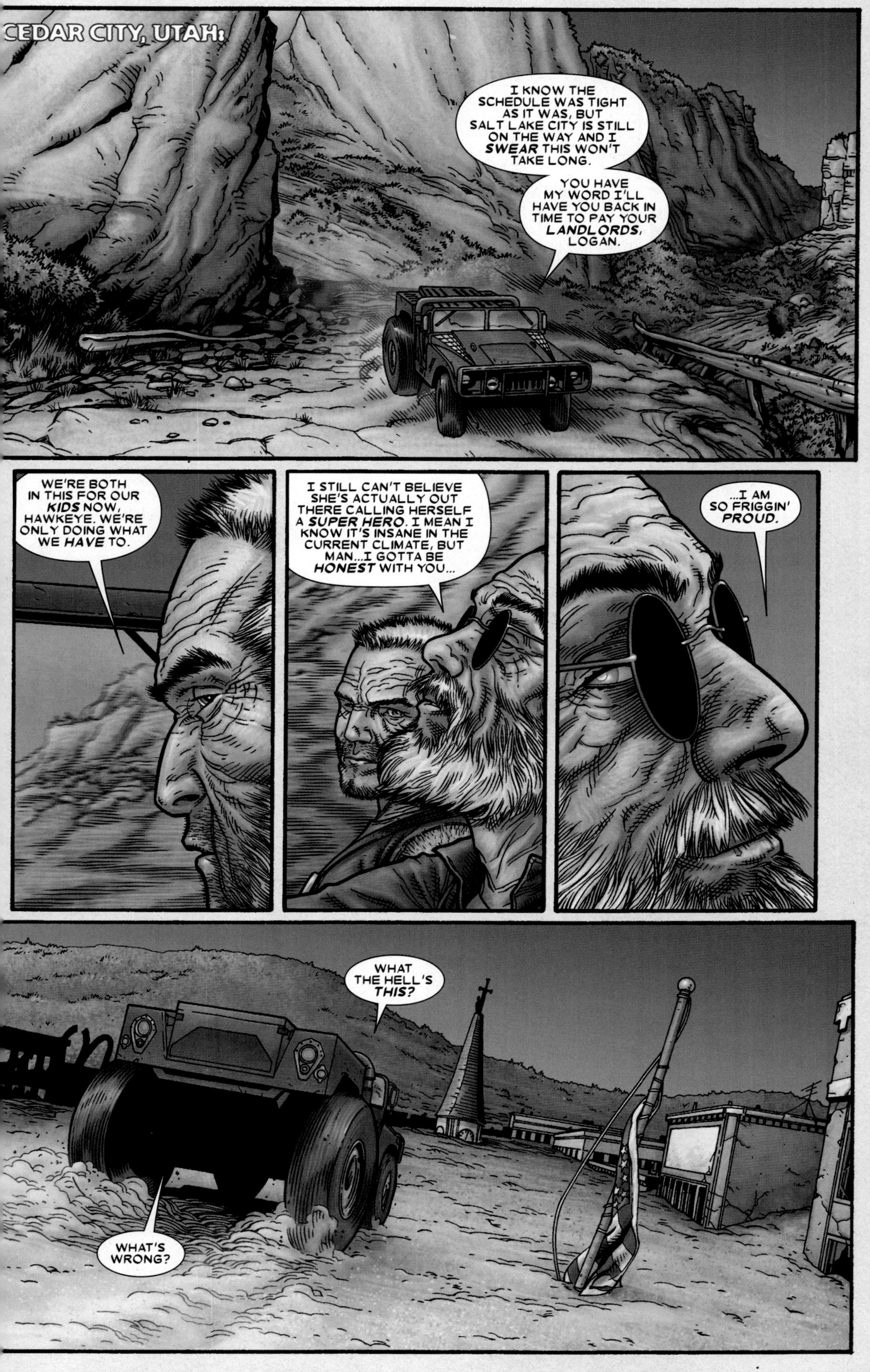
CEDAR CITY, UTAH:
I KNOW THE SCHEDULE WAS TIGHT AS IT WAS, BUT SALT LAKE CITY IS STILL ON THE WAY AND I SWEAR THIS WON'T TAKE LONG.
YOU HAVE MY WORD I'LL HAVE YOU BACK IN TIME TO PAY YOUR LANDLORDS, LOGAN.
WE'RE BOTH IN THIS FOR OUR KIDS NOW, HAWKEYE. WE'RE ONLY DOING WHAT WE HAVE TO.
I STILL CAN'T BELIEVE SHE'S ACTUALLY OUT THERE CALLING HERSELF A SUPER HERO. I MEAN I KNOW IT'S INSANE IN THE CURRENT CLIMATE, BUT MAN...I GOTTA BE HONEST WITH YOU...
...I AM SO FRIGGIN' PROUD.
WHAT THE HELL'S THIS?
WHAT'S WRONG?

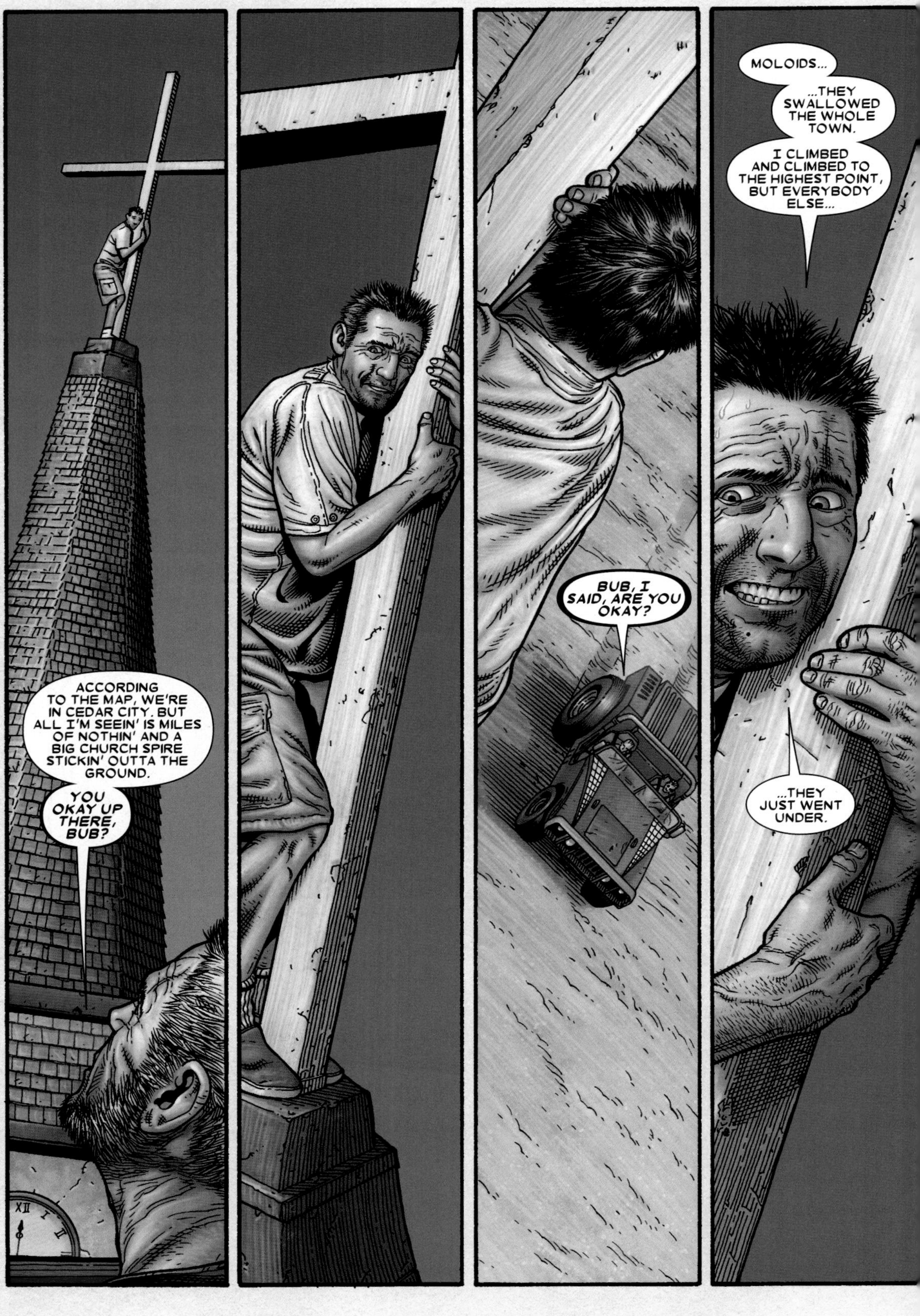
ACCORDING TO THE MAP, WE'RE IN CEDAR CITY. BUT ALL I'M SEEIN' IS MILES OF NOTHIN' AND A BIG CHURCH SPIRE STICKIN' OUTTA THE GROUND.
YOU OKAY UP THERE, BUB?
BUB, I SAID, ARE YOU OKAY?
MOLOIDS...
...THEY SWALLOWED THE WHOLE TOWN.
I CLIMBED AND CLIMBED TO THE HIGHEST POINT, BUT EVERYBODY ELSE...
...THEY JUST WENT UNDER.

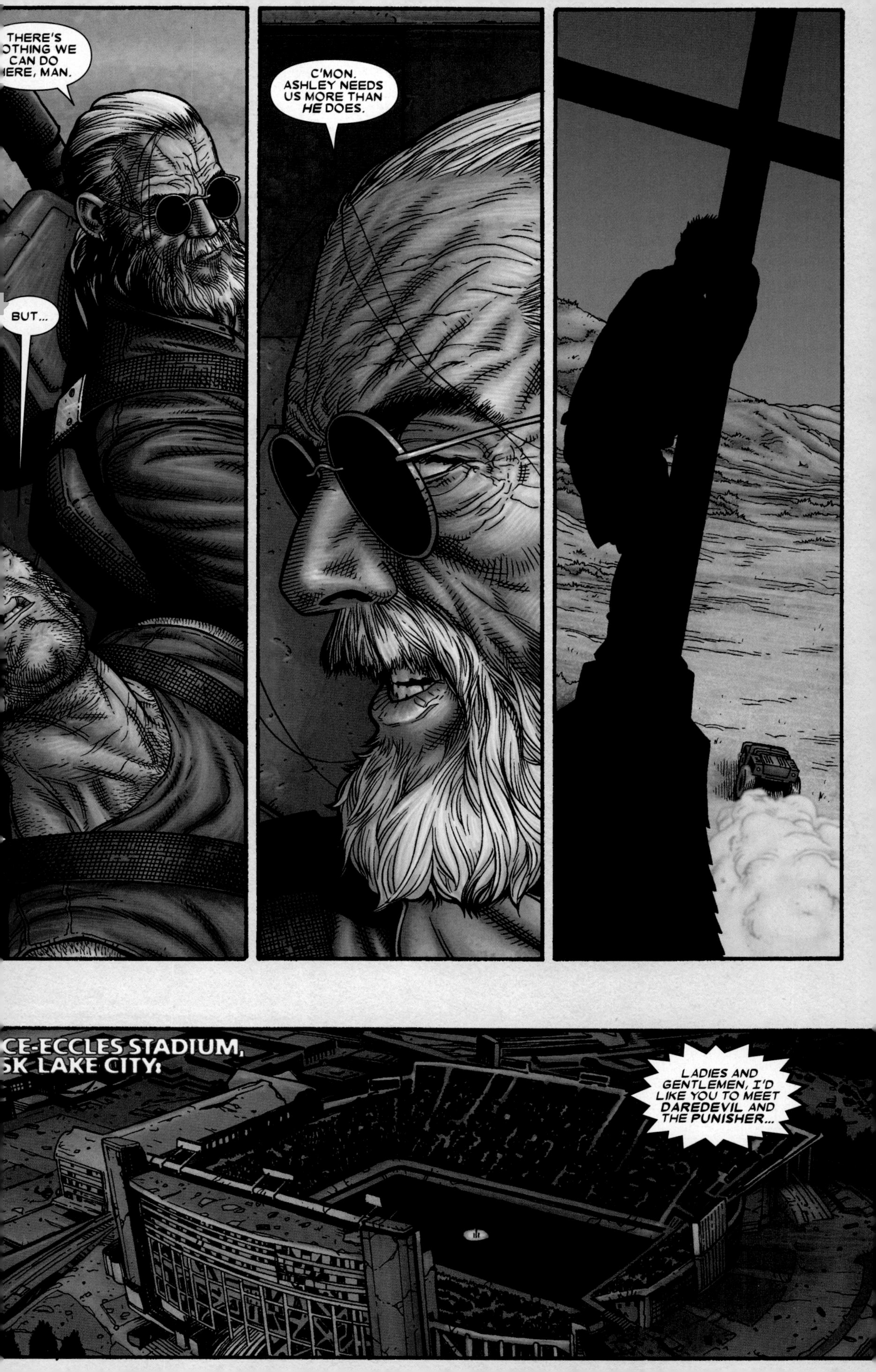
THERE'S
OTHING WE
CAN DO
ERE, MAN.
BUT...
C'MON. ASHLEY NEEDS US MORE THAN *HE* DOES.
CE-ECCLES STADIUM,
SK LAKE CITY:
LADIES AND GENTLEMEN, I'D LIKE YOU TO MEET **DAREDEVIL** AND THE **PUNISHER**...

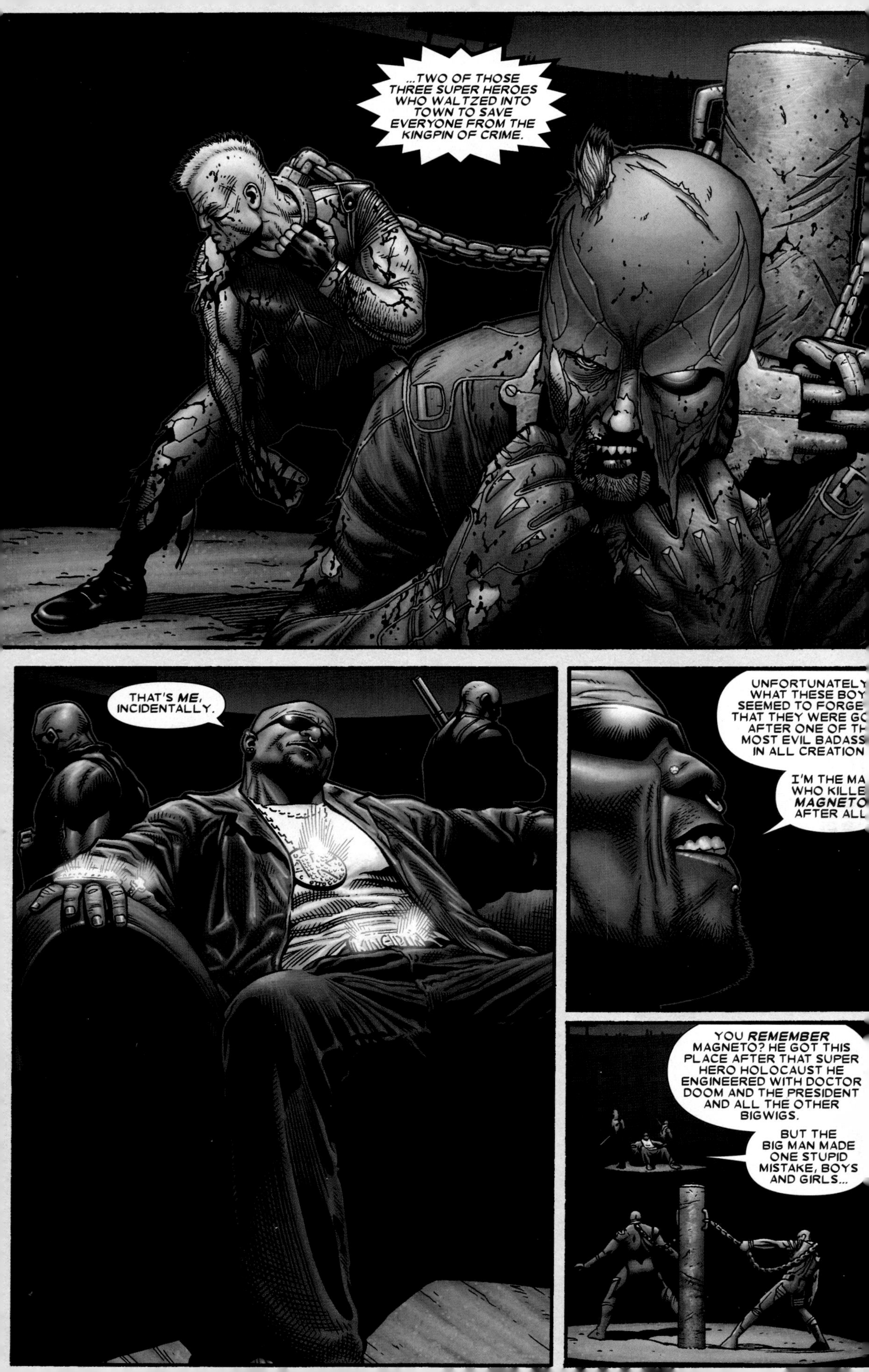
...TWO OF THOSE THREE SUPER HEROES WHO WALTZED INTO TOWN TO SAVE EVERYONE FROM THE KINGPIN OF CRIME.
THAT'S *ME*, INCIDENTALLY.
UNFORTUNATELY WHAT THESE BOY SEEMED TO FORGE THAT THEY WERE GO AFTER ONE OF TH MOST EVIL BADASS IN ALL CREATION
I'M THE MA WHO KILLE *MAGNETO* AFTER ALL
YOU *REMEMBER* MAGNETO? HE GOT THIS PLACE AFTER THAT SUPER HERO HOLOCAUST HE ENGINEERED WITH DOCTOR DOOM AND THE PRESIDENT AND ALL THE OTHER BIGWIGS.
BUT THE BIG MAN MADE ONE STUPID MISTAKE, BOYS AND GIRLS...

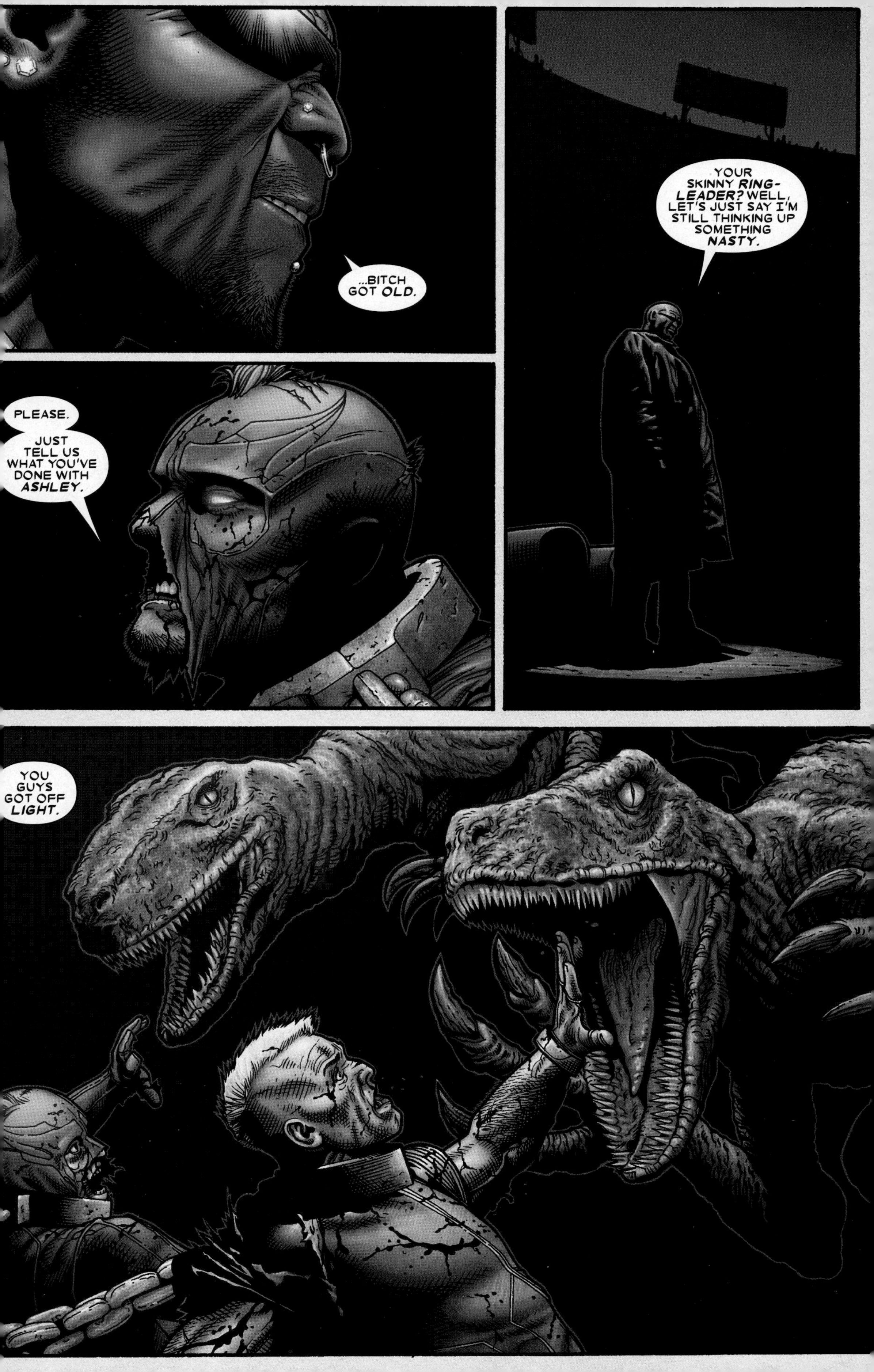
...BITCH GOT OLD.
YOUR SKINNY RING-LEADER? WELL, LET'S JUST SAY I'M STILL THINKING UP SOMETHING NASTY.
PLEASE.
JUST TELL US WHAT YOU'VE DONE WITH ASHLEY.
YOU GUYS GOT OFF LIGHT.

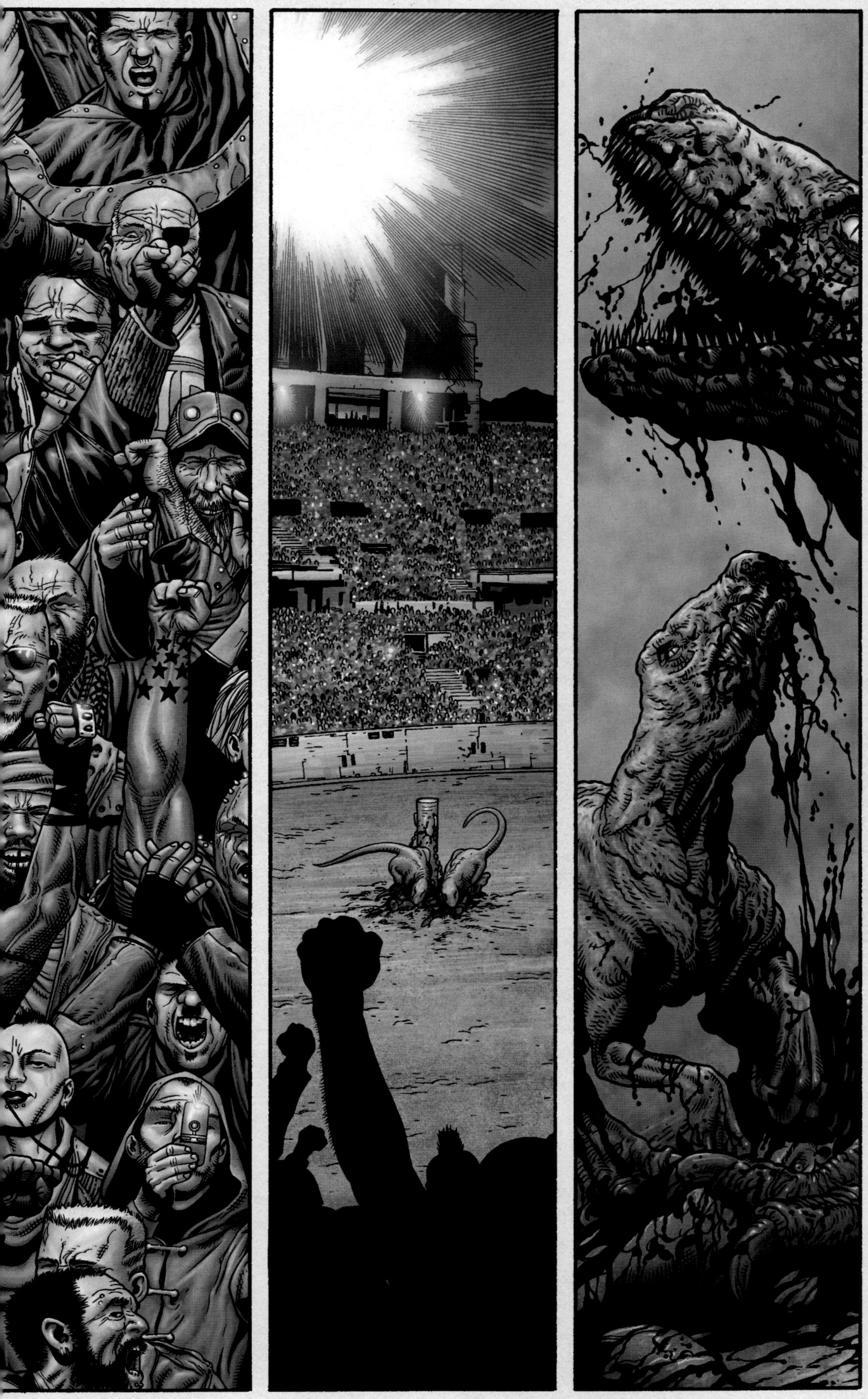

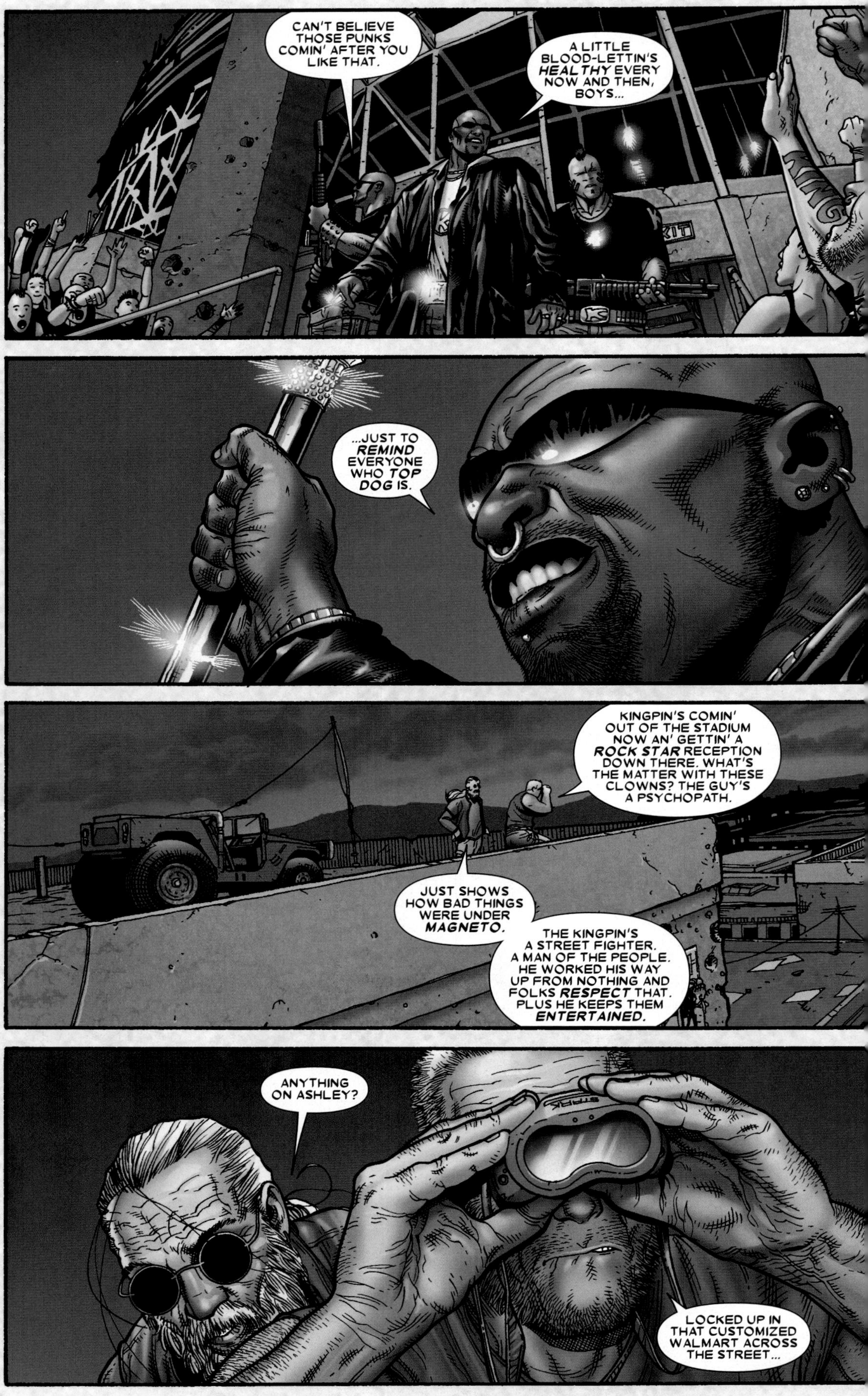
CAN'T BELIEVE THOSE PUNKS COMIN' AFTER YOU LIKE THAT.
A LITTLE BLOOD-LETTIN'S HEALTHY EVERY NOW AND THEN, BOYS...
...JUST TO REMIND EVERYONE WHO TOP DOG IS.
KINGPIN'S COMIN' OUT OF THE STADIUM NOW AN' GETTIN' A ROCK STAR RECEPTION DOWN THERE. WHAT'S THE MATTER WITH THESE CLOWNS? THE GUY'S A PSYCHOPATH.
JUST SHOWS HOW BAD THINGS WERE UNDER MAGNETO.
THE KINGPIN'S A STREET FIGHTER, A MAN OF THE PEOPLE. HE WORKED HIS WAY UP FROM NOTHING AND FOLKS RESPECT THAT. PLUS HE KEEPS THEM ENTERTAINED.
ANYTHING ON ASHLEY?
LOCKED UP IN THAT CUSTOMIZED WALMART ACROSS THE STREET...

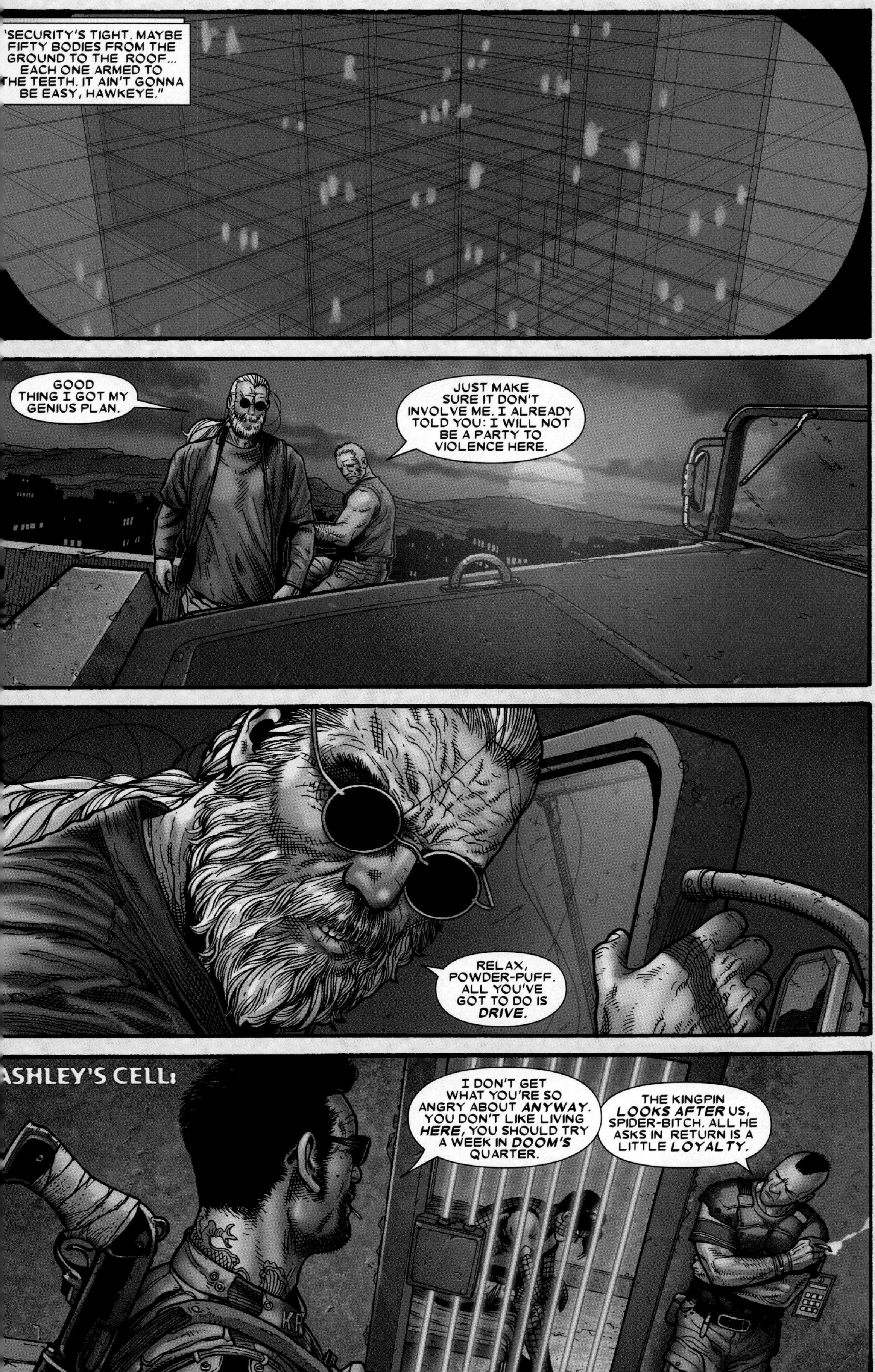
"SECURITY'S TIGHT. MAYBE FIFTY BODIES FROM THE GROUND TO THE ROOF... EACH ONE ARMED TO THE TEETH. IT AIN'T GONNA BE EASY, HAWKEYE."
GOOD THING I GOT MY GENIUS PLAN.
JUST MAKE SURE IT DON'T INVOLVE ME. I ALREADY TOLD YOU: I WILL NOT BE A PARTY TO VIOLENCE HERE.
RELAX, POWDER-PUFF. ALL YOU'VE GOT TO DO IS DRIVE.
ASHLEY'S CELL:
I DON'T GET WHAT YOU'RE SO ANGRY ABOUT ANYWAY. YOU DON'T LIKE LIVING HERE, YOU SHOULD TRY A WEEK IN DOOM'S QUARTER.
THE KINGPIN LOOKS AFTER US, SPIDER-BITCH. ALL HE ASKS IN RETURN IS A LITTLE LOYALTY.

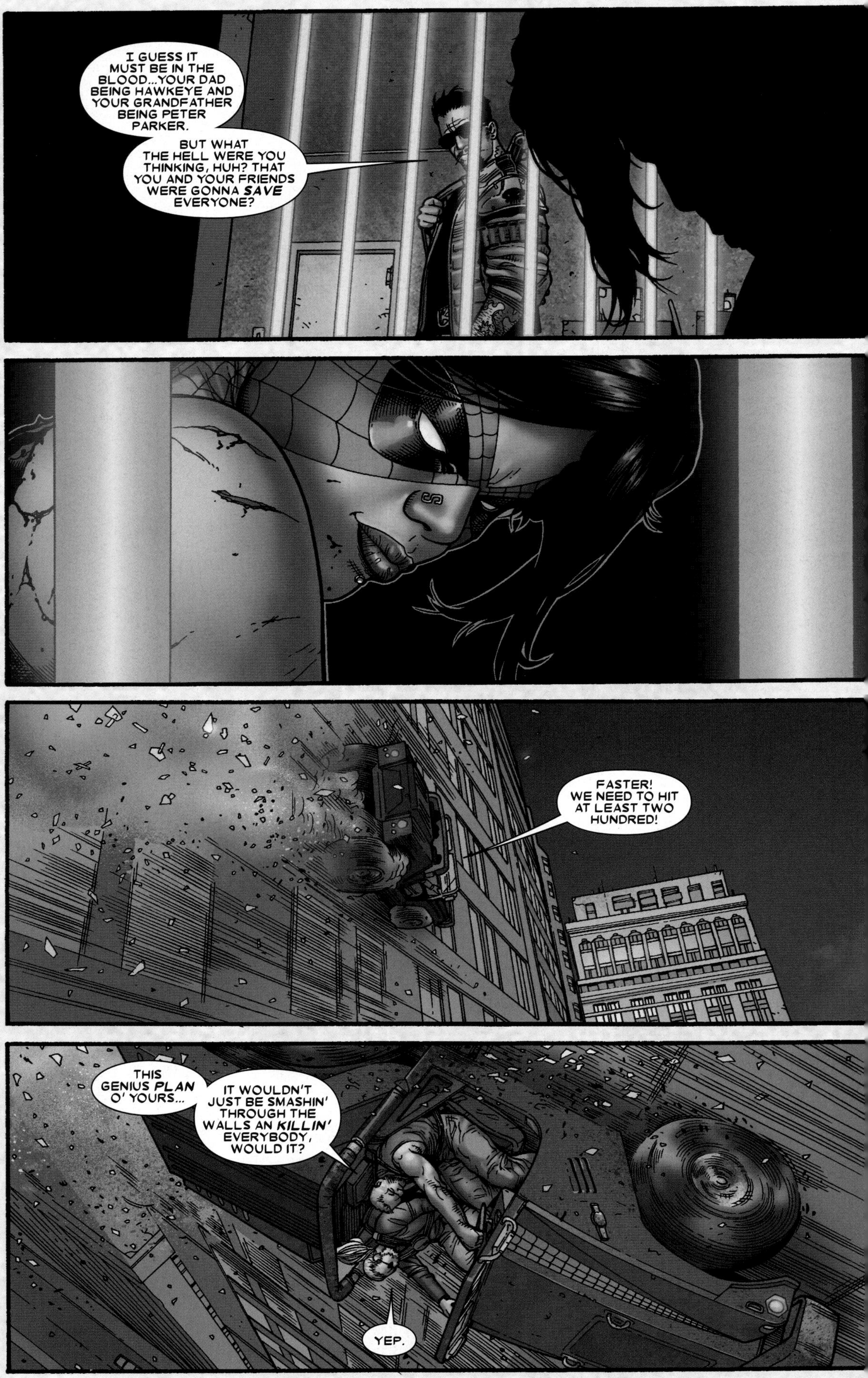
I GUESS IT MUST BE IN THE BLOOD...YOUR DAD BEING HAWKEYE AND YOUR GRANDFATHER BEING PETER PARKER.
BUT WHAT THE HELL WERE YOU THINKING, HUH? THAT YOU AND YOUR FRIENDS WERE GONNA *SAVE* EVERYONE?
FASTER! WE NEED TO HIT AT LEAST TWO HUNDRED!
THIS GENIUS *PLAN* O' YOURS...
IT WOULDN'T JUST BE SMASHIN' THROUGH THE WALLS AN *KILLIN'* EVERYBODY, WOULD IT?
YEP.

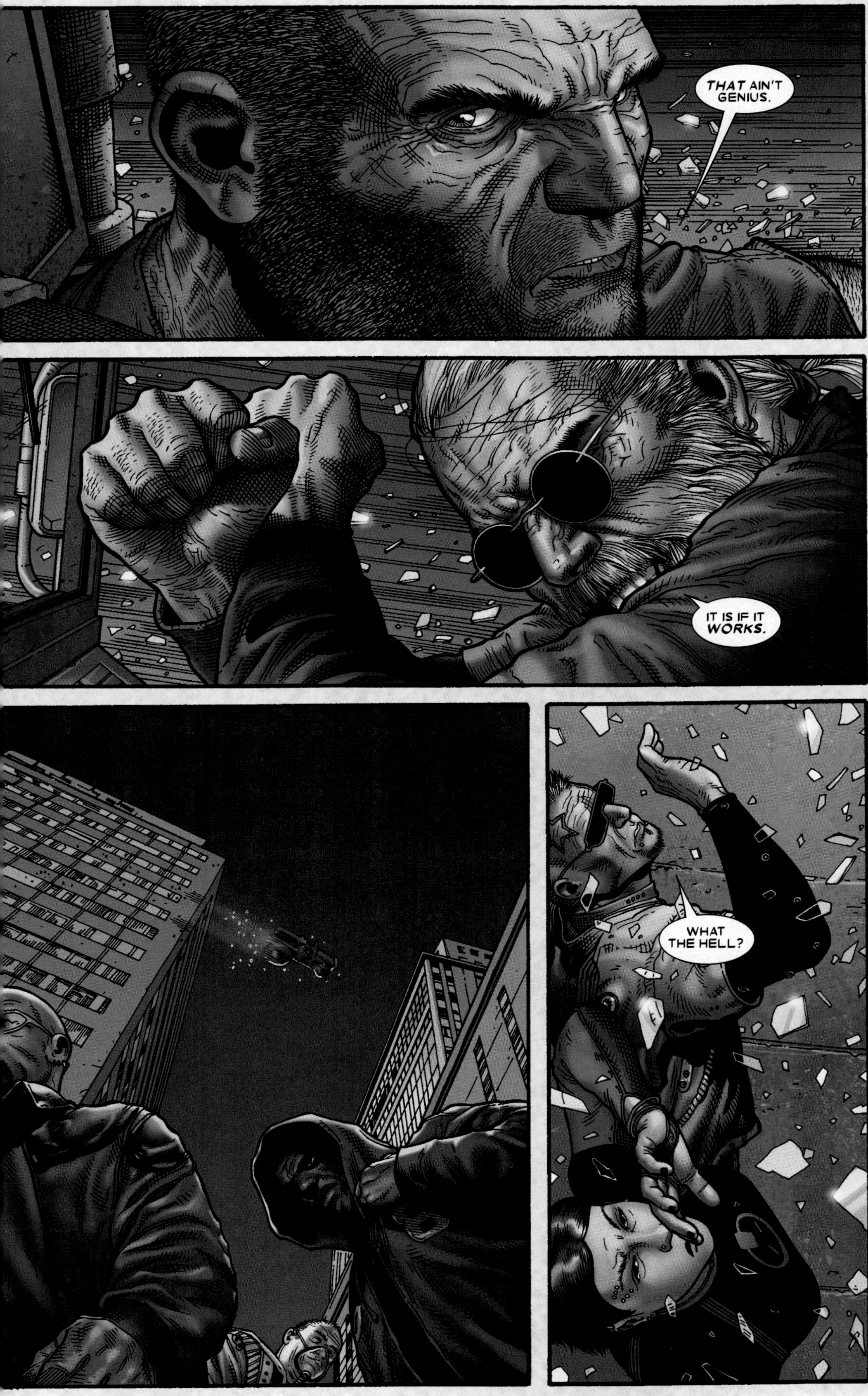
THAT AIN'T GENIUS.
IT IS IF IT WORKS.
WHAT THE HELL?

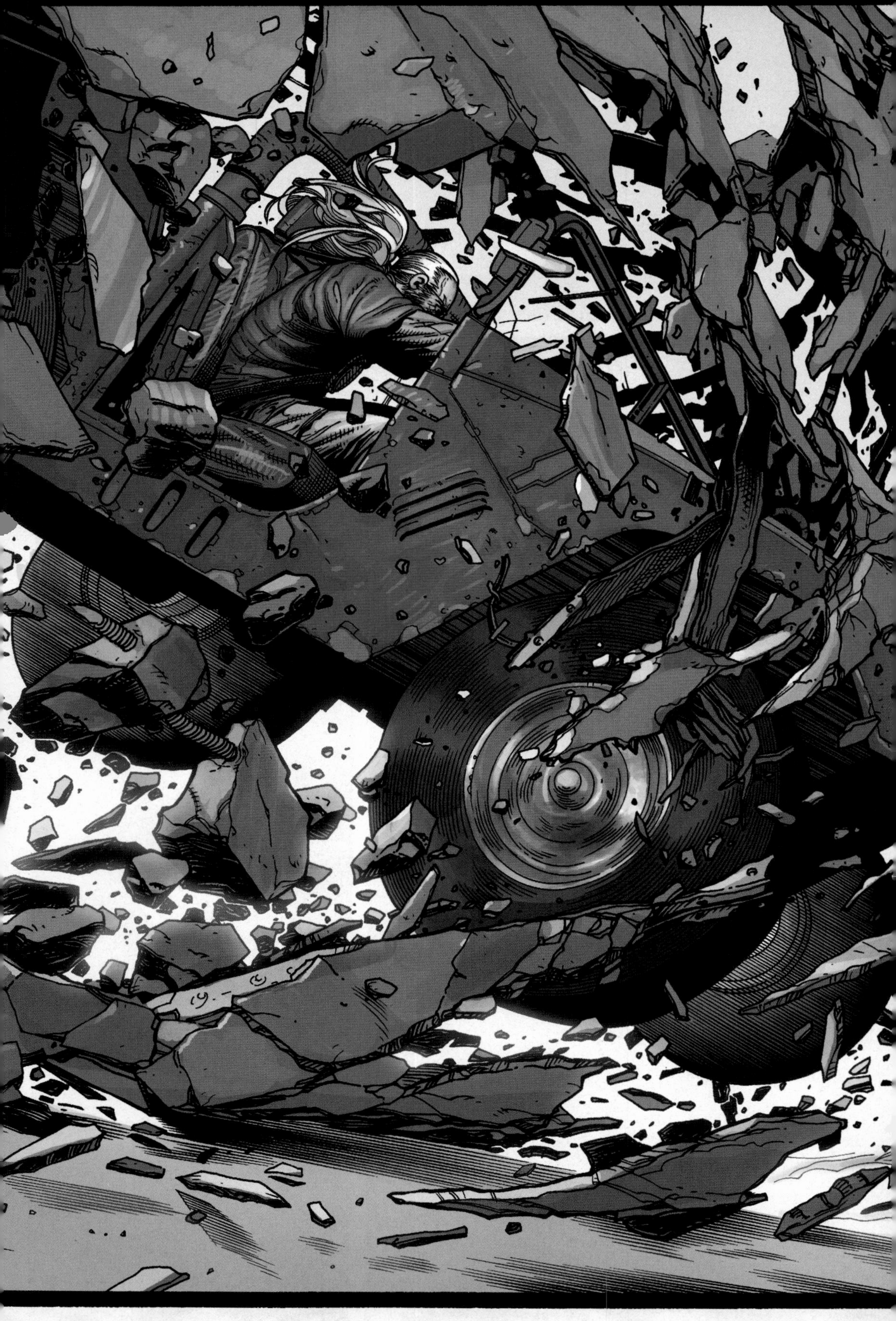

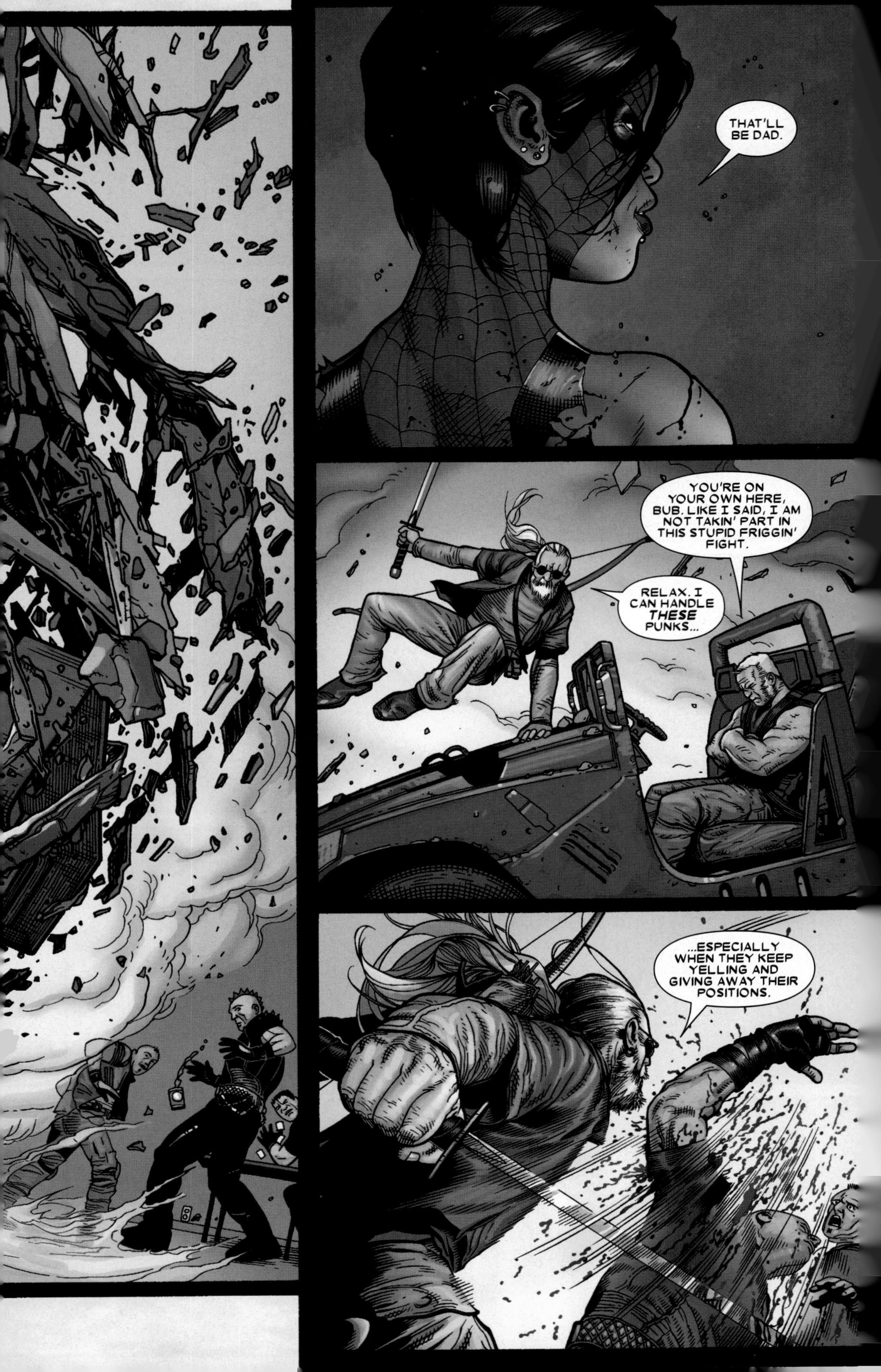
THAT'LL BE DAD.
YOU'RE ON YOUR OWN HERE, BUB. LIKE I SAID, I AM NOT TAKIN' PART IN THIS STUPID FRIGGIN' FIGHT.
RELAX. I CAN HANDLE *THESE* PUNKS...
...ESPECIALLY WHEN THEY KEEP YELLING AND GIVING AWAY THEIR POSITIONS.

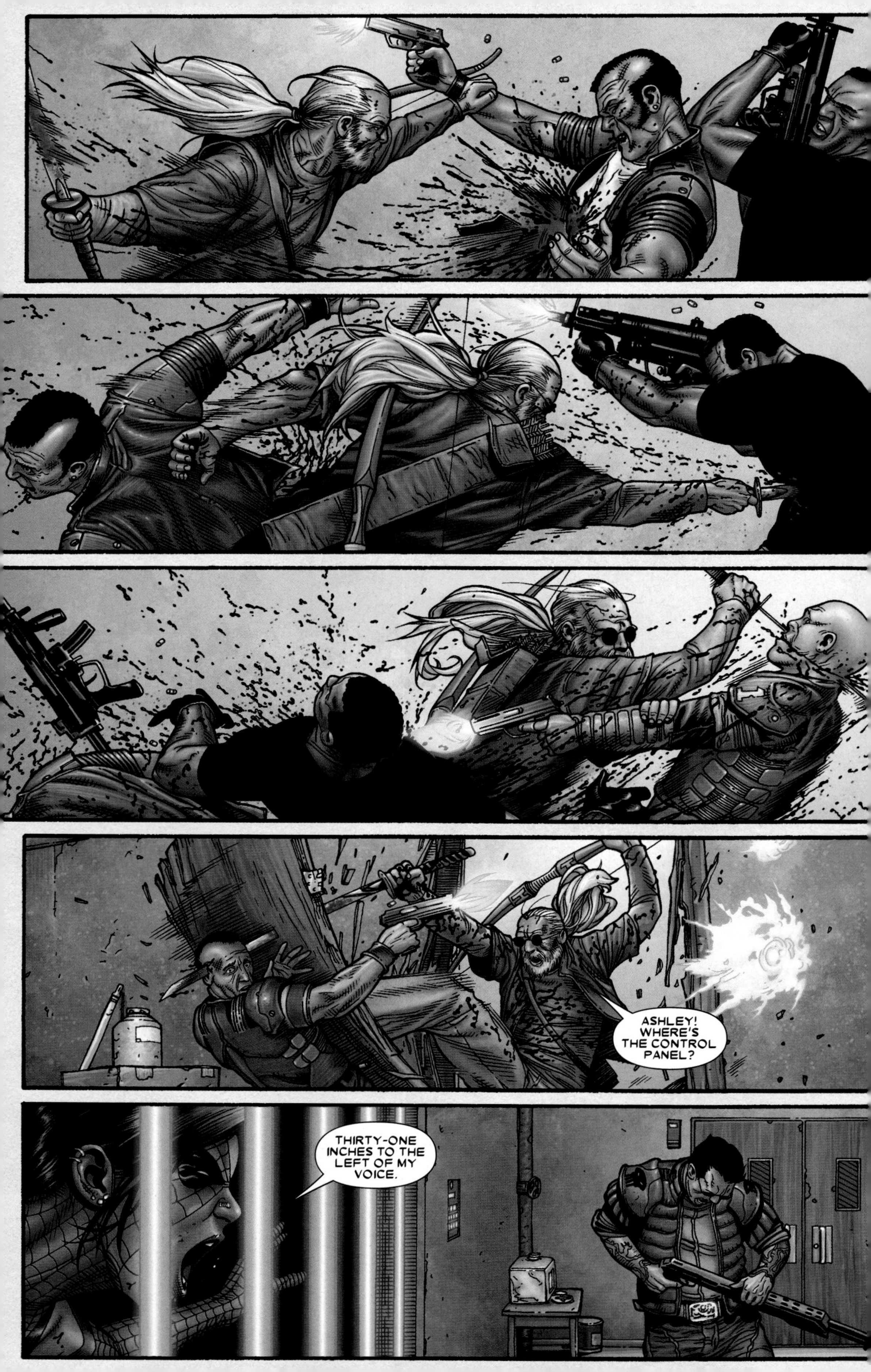

ASHLEY! WHERE'S THE CONTROL PANEL?
THIRTY-ONE INCHES TO THE LEFT OF MY VOICE.

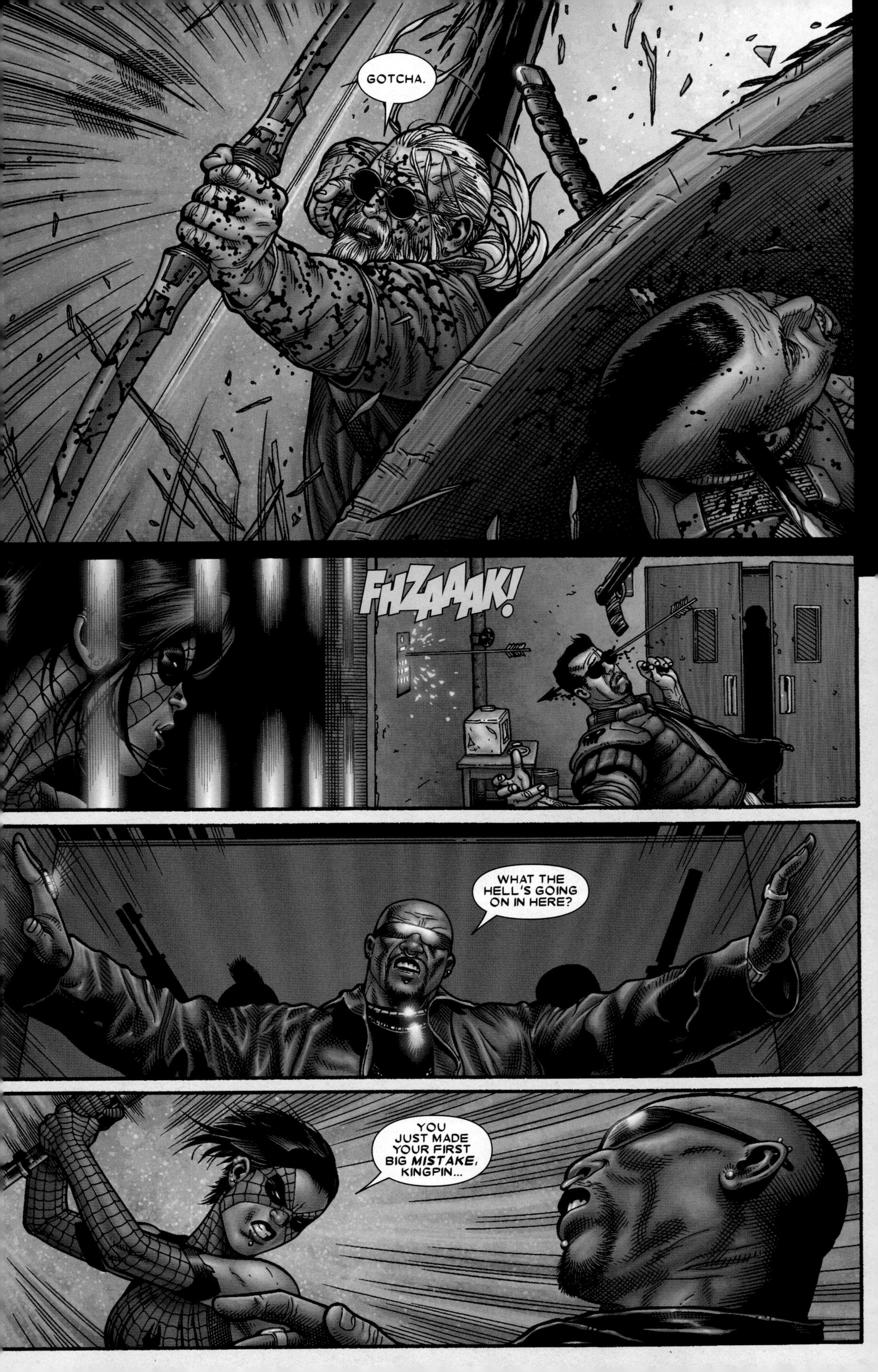
GOTCHA.
FHZAAAK!
WHAT THE HELL'S GOING ON IN HERE?
YOU JUST MADE YOUR FIRST BIG *MISTAKE,* KINGPIN...

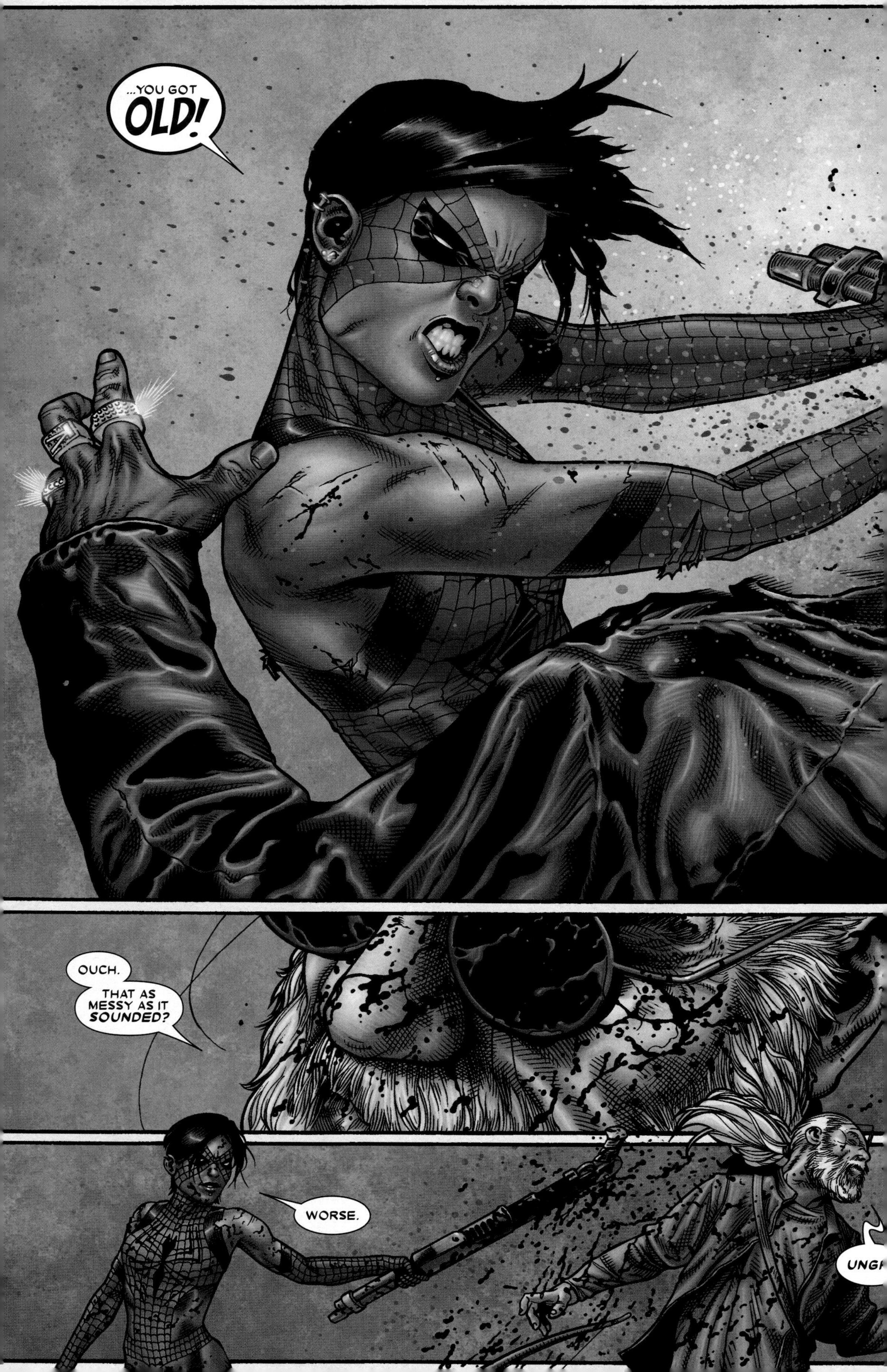
...YOU GOT OLD!
OUCH.
THAT AS MESSY AS IT SOUNDED?
WORSE.

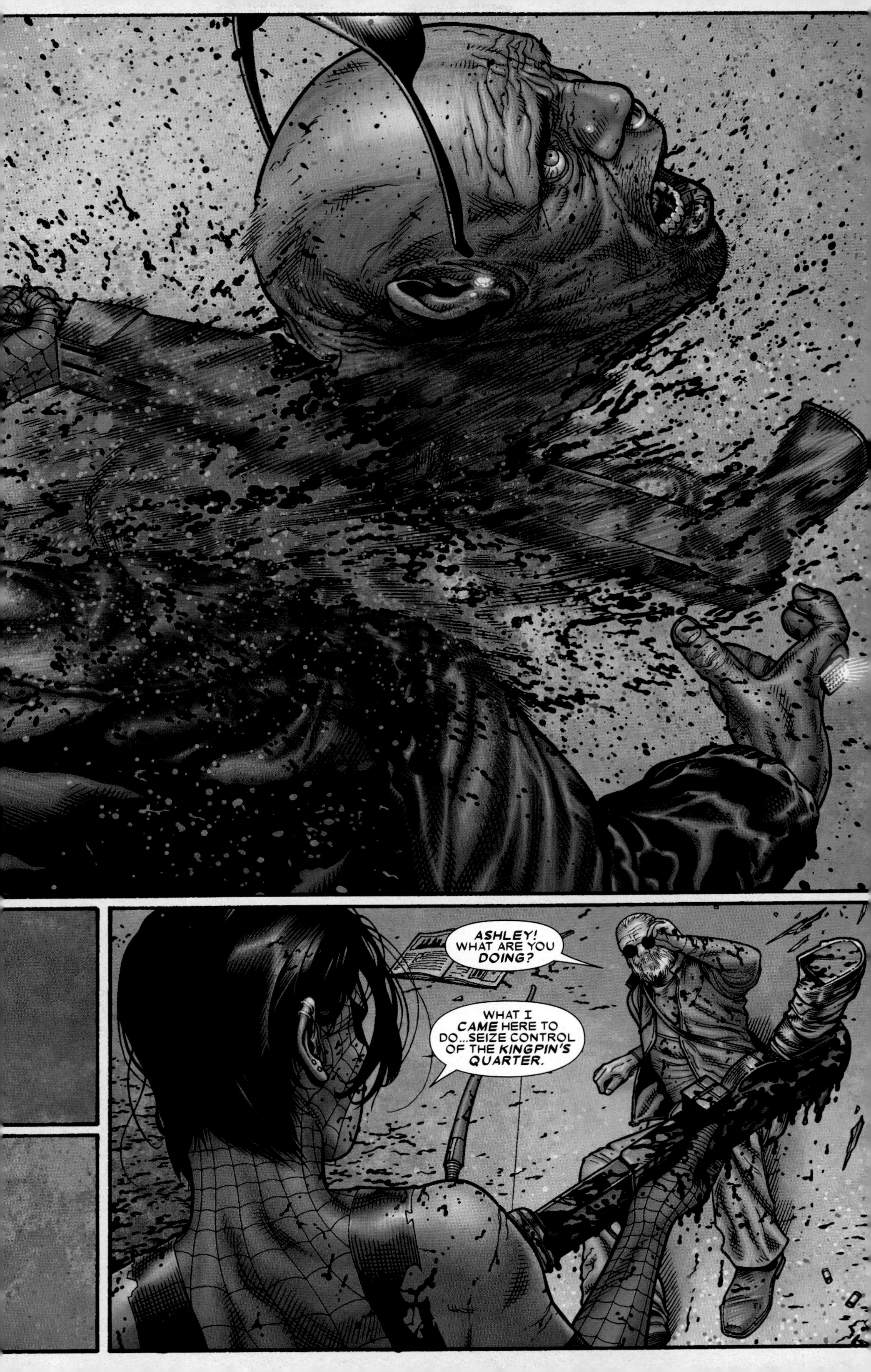
ASHLEY! WHAT ARE YOU DOING?
WHAT I CAME HERE TO DO...SEIZE CONTROL OF THE KINGPIN'S QUARTER.

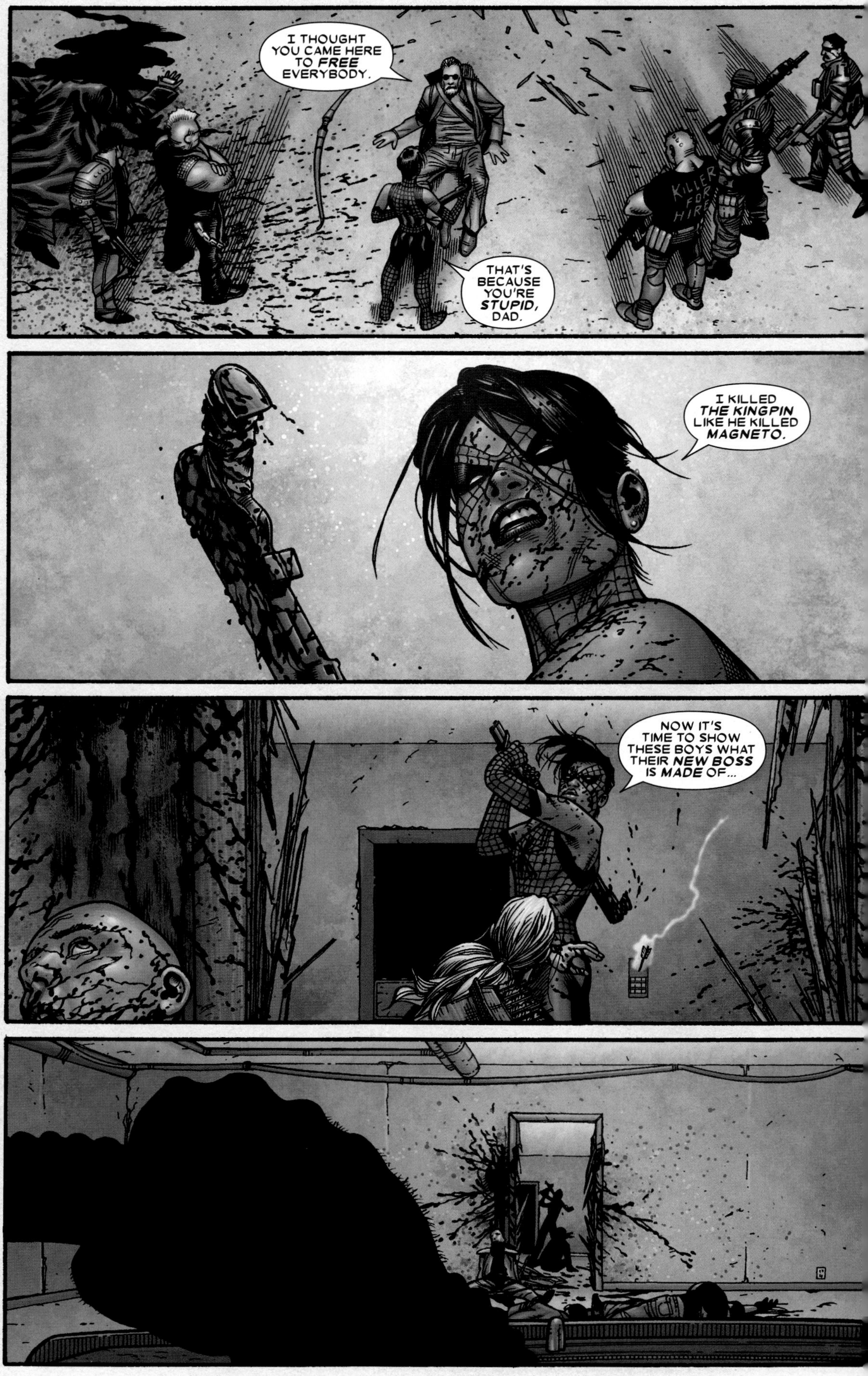
I THOUGHT YOU CAME HERE TO FREE EVERYBODY.
THAT'S BECAUSE YOU'RE STUPID, DAD.
KILLER FOR HIRE
I KILLED THE KINGPIN LIKE HE KILLED MAGNETO.
NOW IT'S TIME TO SHOW THESE BOYS WHAT THEIR NEW BOSS IS MADE OF...

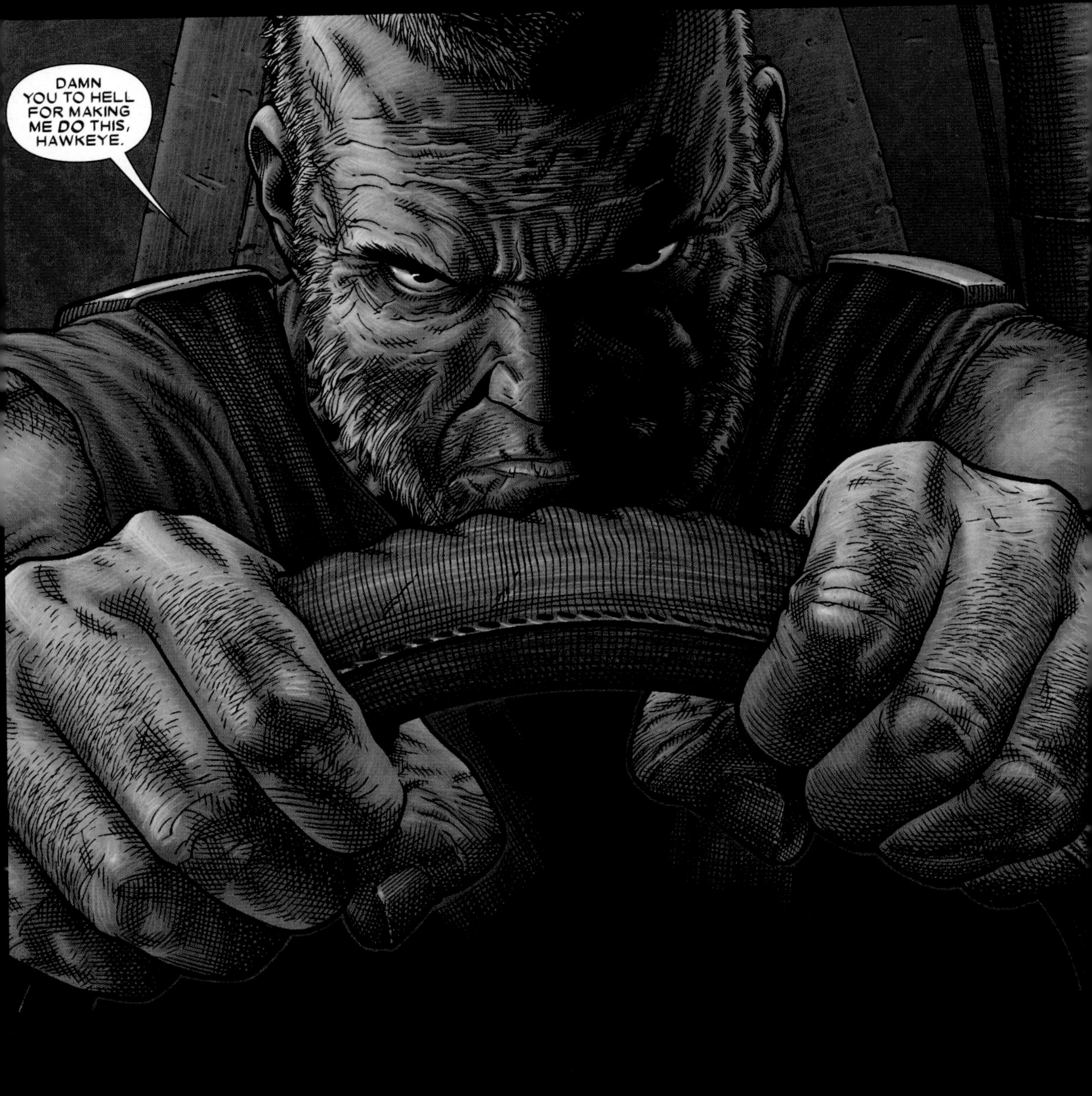
DAMN YOU TO HELL FOR MAKING ME DO THIS, HAWKEYE.

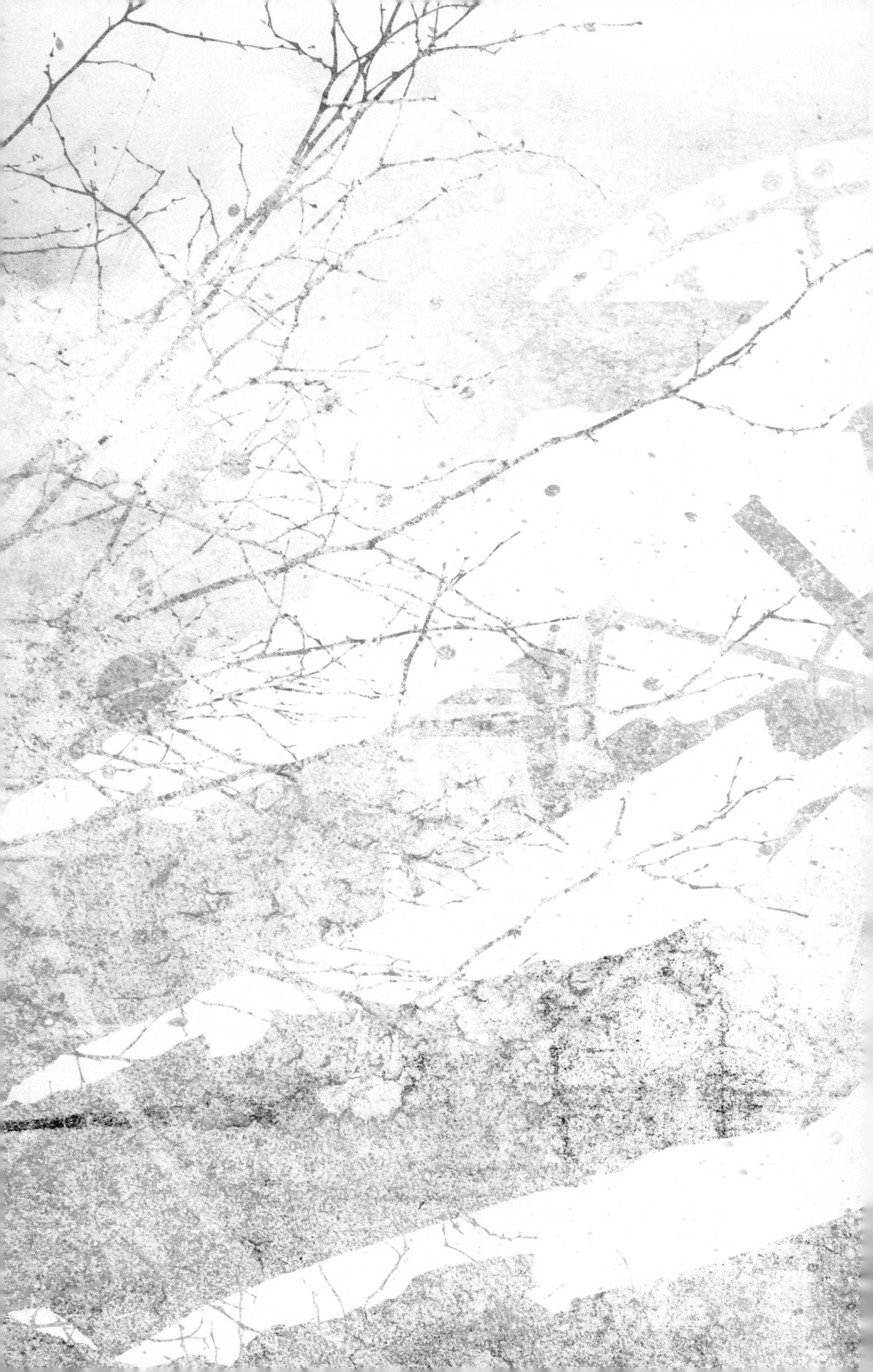

CHAPTER FOUR

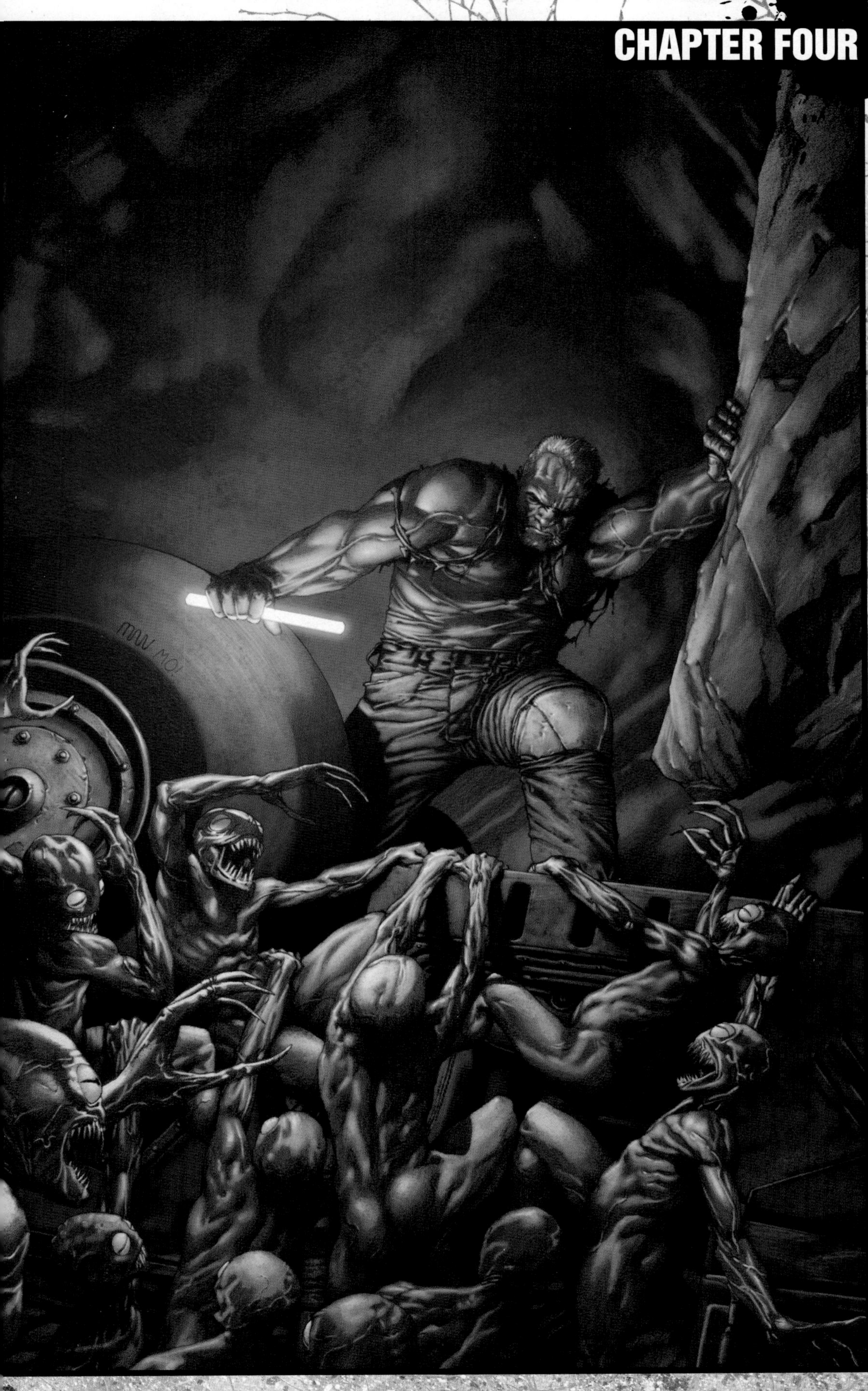

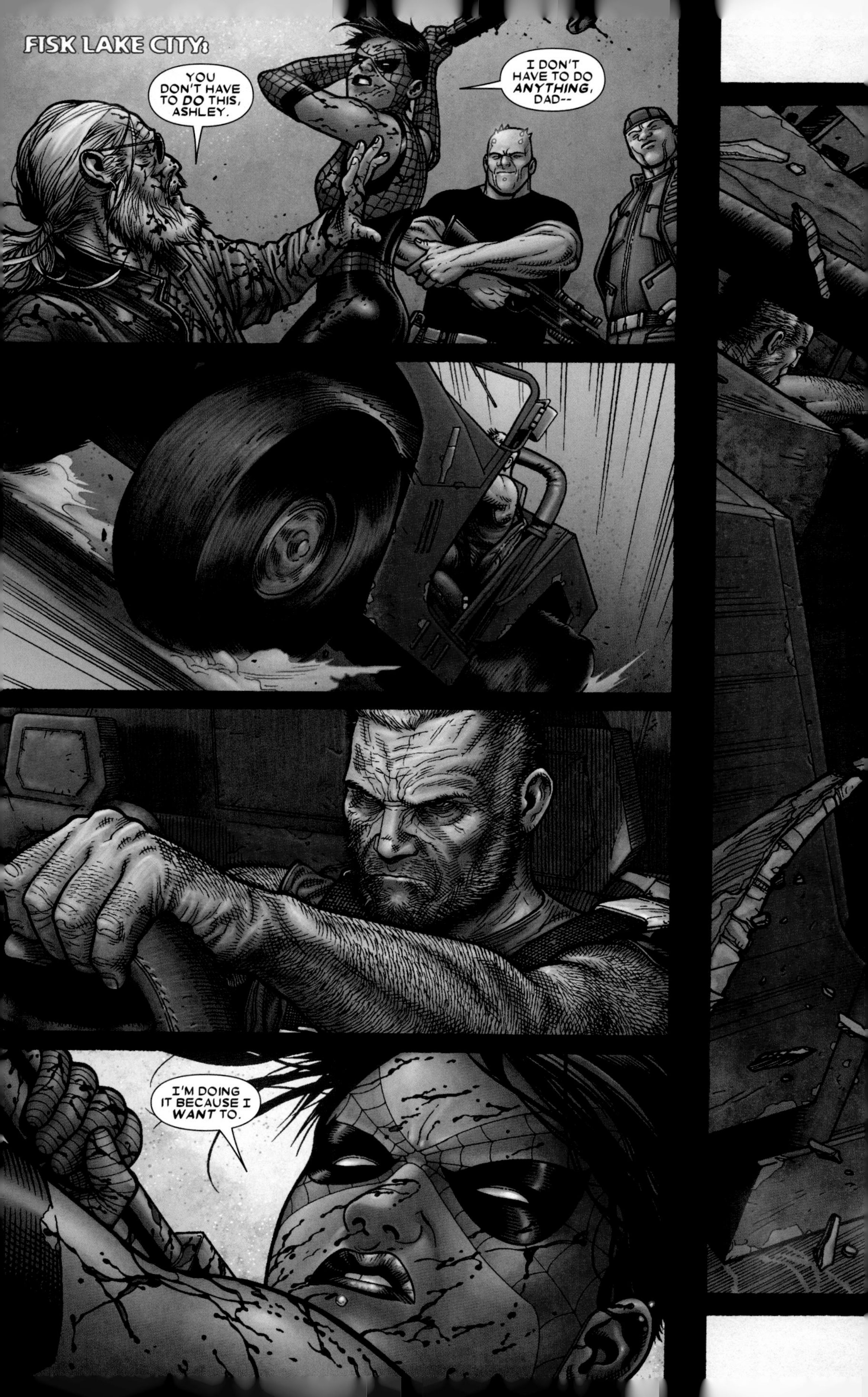
FISK LAKE CITY:
YOU DON'T HAVE TO DO THIS, ASHLEY.
I DON'T HAVE TO DO ANYTHING, DAD--
I'M DOING IT BECAUSE I WANT TO.

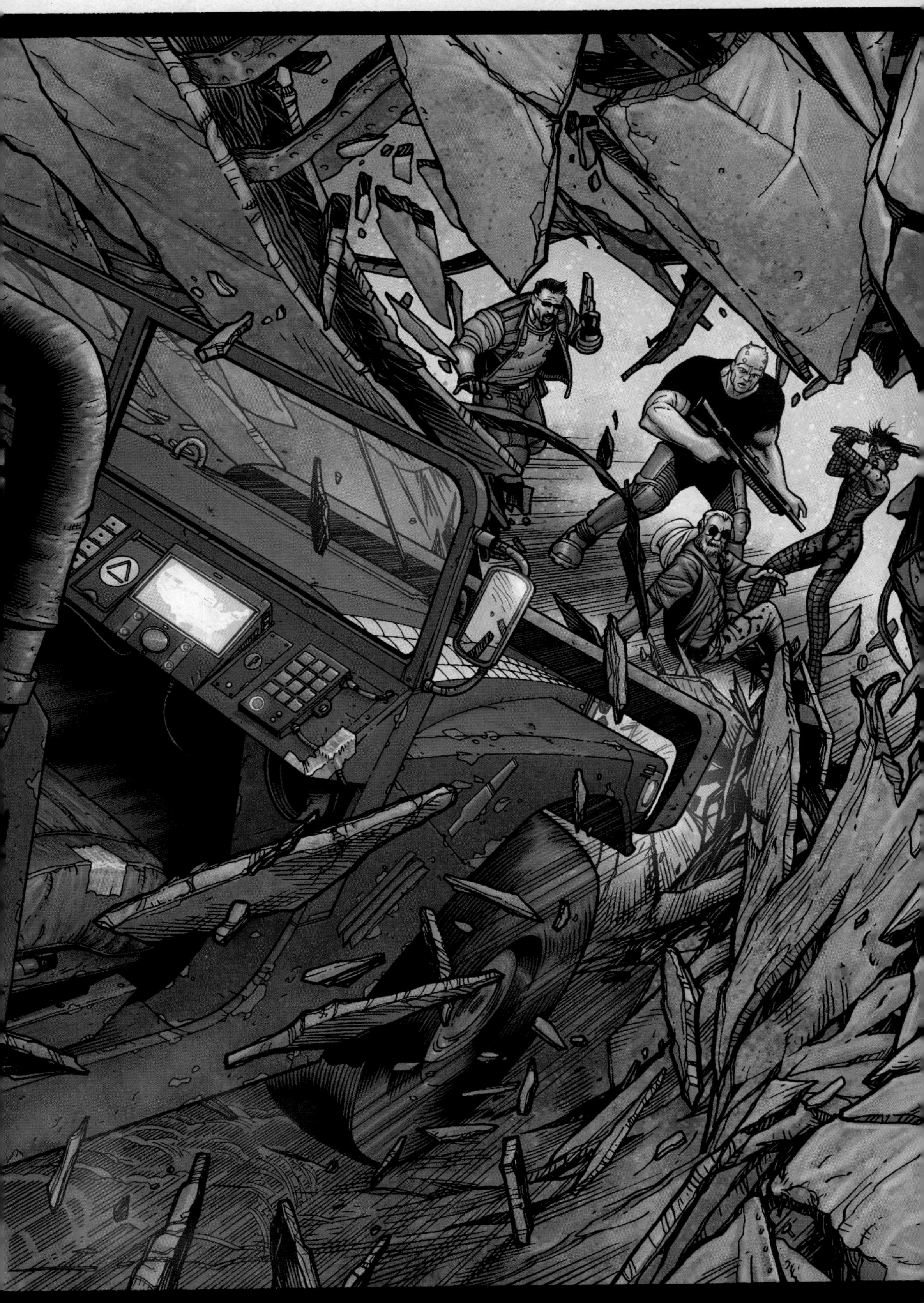

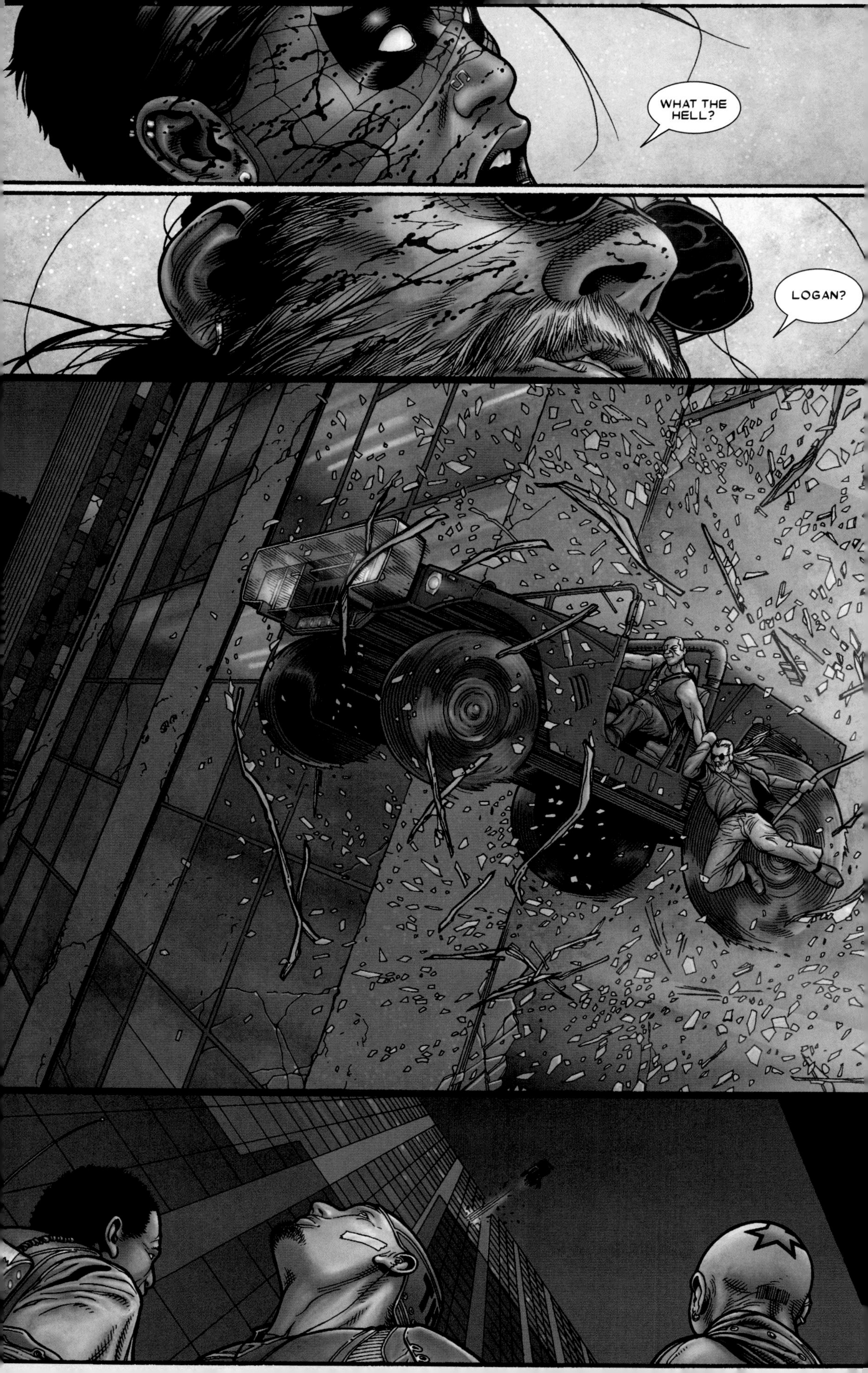
WHAT THE HELL?
LOGAN?

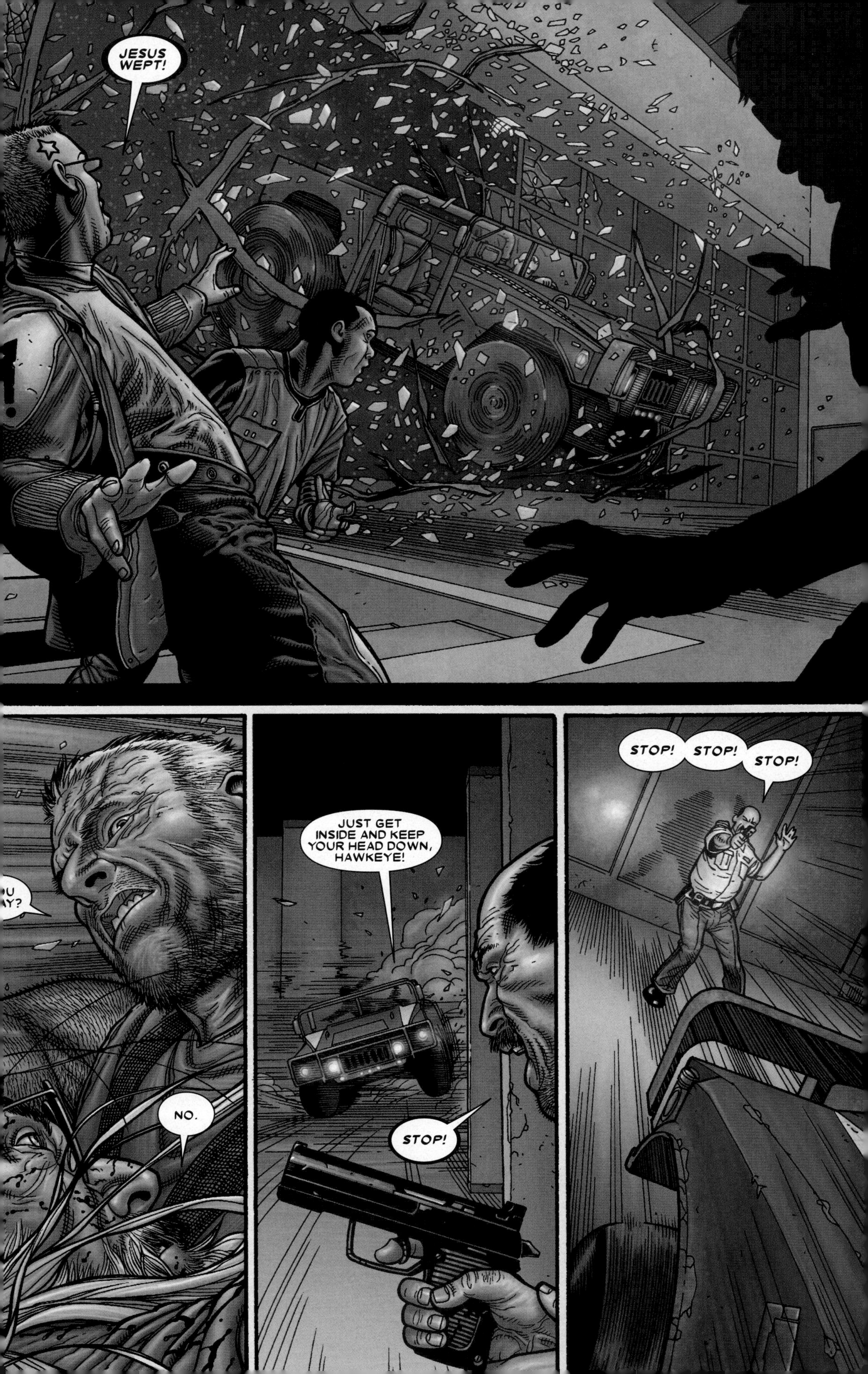
JESUS WEPT!
NO.
JUST GET INSIDE AND KEEP YOUR HEAD DOWN, HAWKEYE!
STOP!
STOP!
STOP!
STOP!

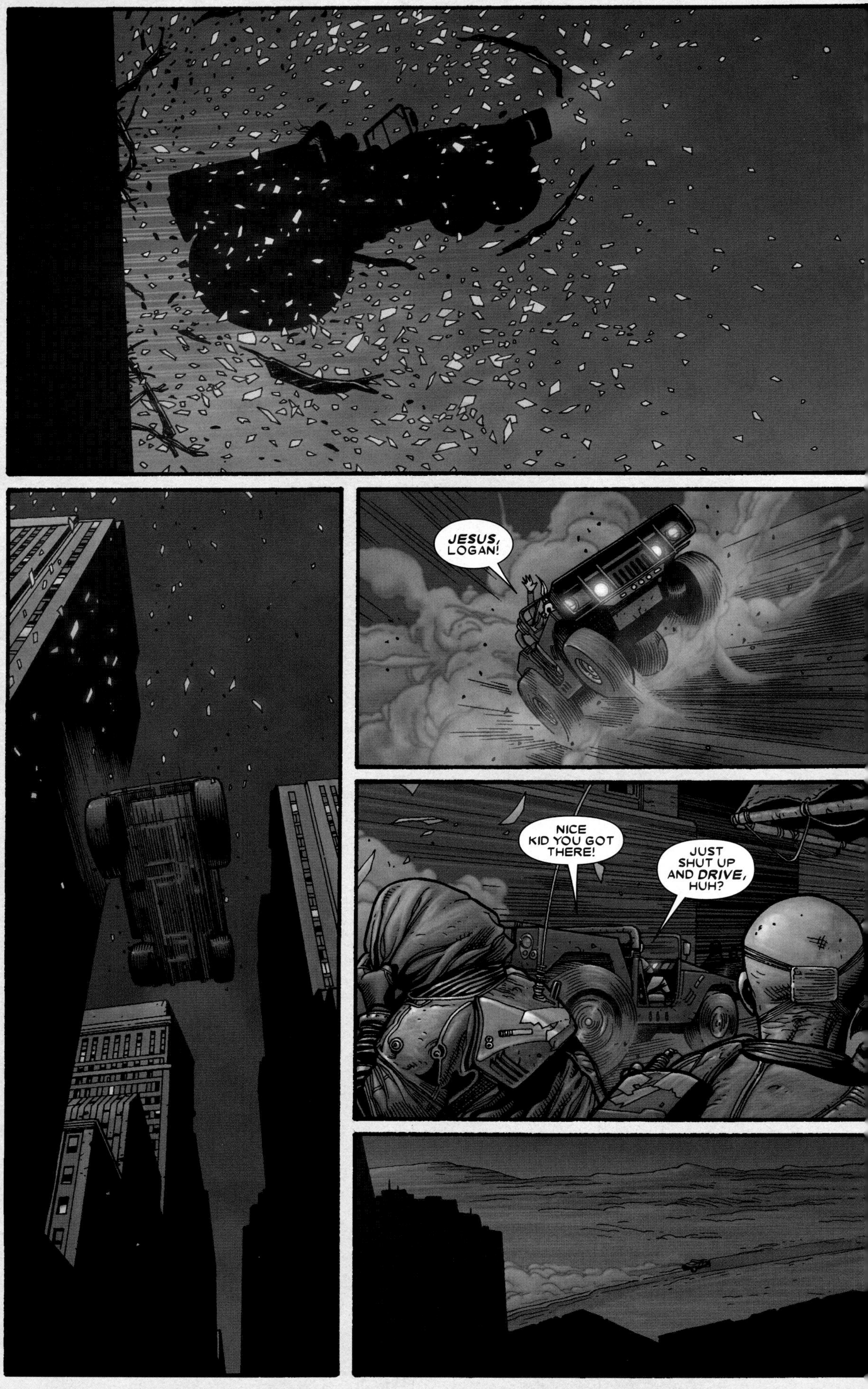
JESUS, LOGAN!
NICE KID YOU GOT THERE!
JUST SHUT UP AND DRIVE, HUH?

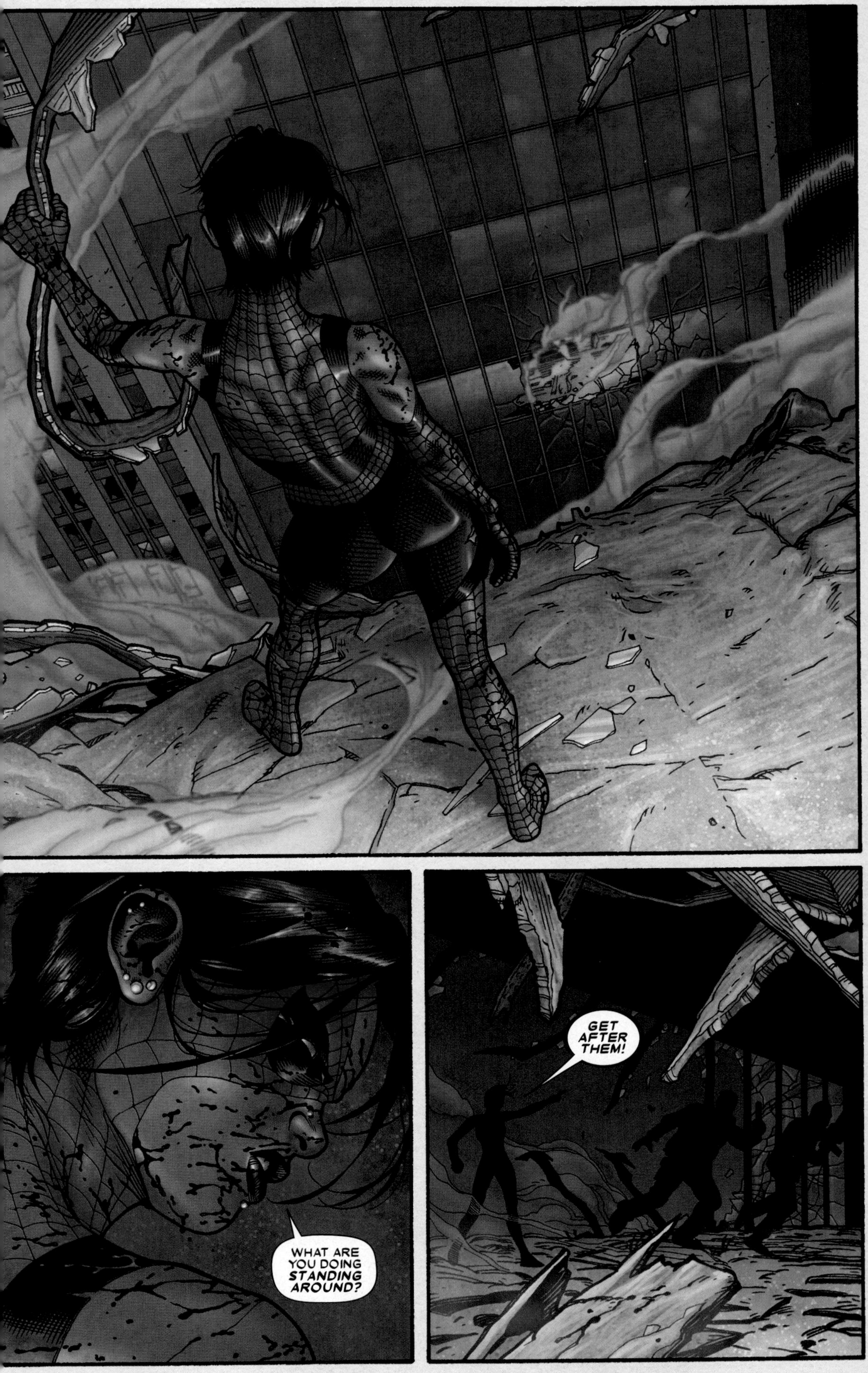
WHAT ARE YOU DOING STANDING AROUND?
GET AFTER THEM!

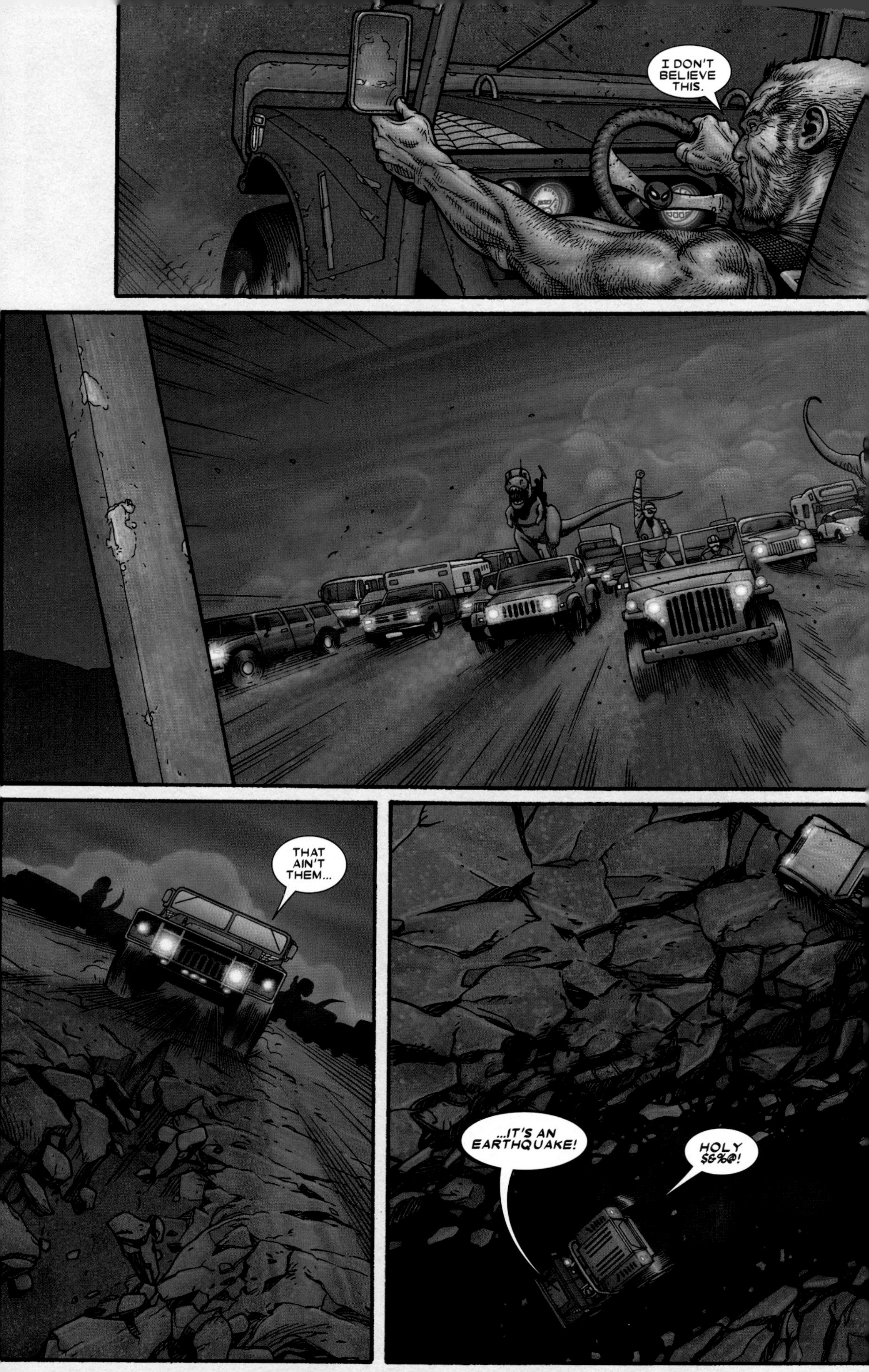
I DON'T BELIEVE THIS.
THAT AIN'T THEM...
...IT'S AN EARTHQUAKE!
HOLY $&%@!

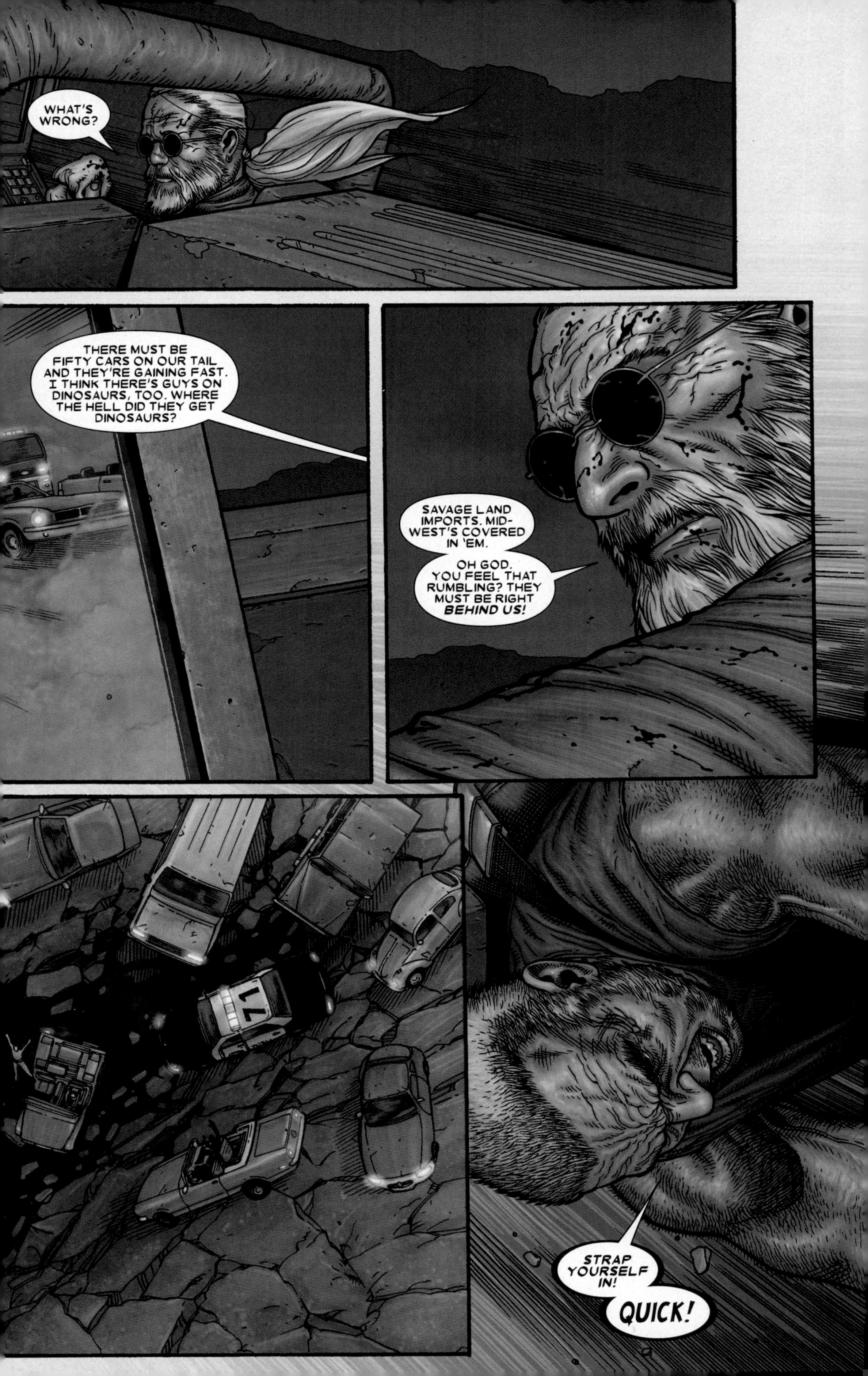
WHAT'S WRONG?
THERE MUST BE FIFTY CARS ON OUR TAIL AND THEY'RE GAINING FAST. I THINK THERE'S GUYS ON DINOSAURS, TOO. WHERE THE HELL DID THEY GET DINOSAURS?
SAVAGE LAND IMPORTS. MID-WEST'S COVERED IN 'EM.
OH GOD. YOU FEEL THAT RUMBLING? THEY MUST BE RIGHT BEHIND US!
STRAP YOURSELF IN!
QUICK!

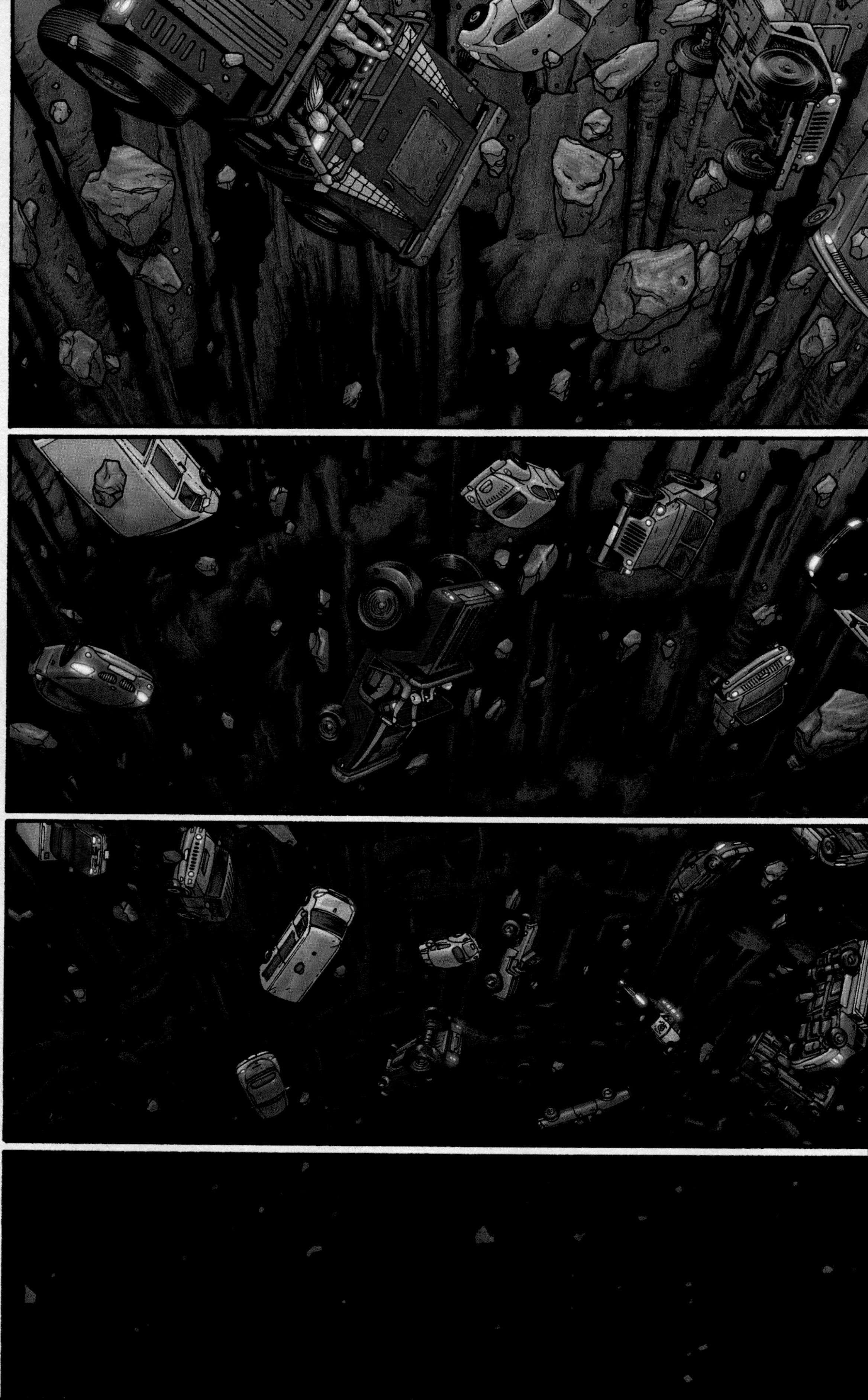

TWO HOURS PASS:

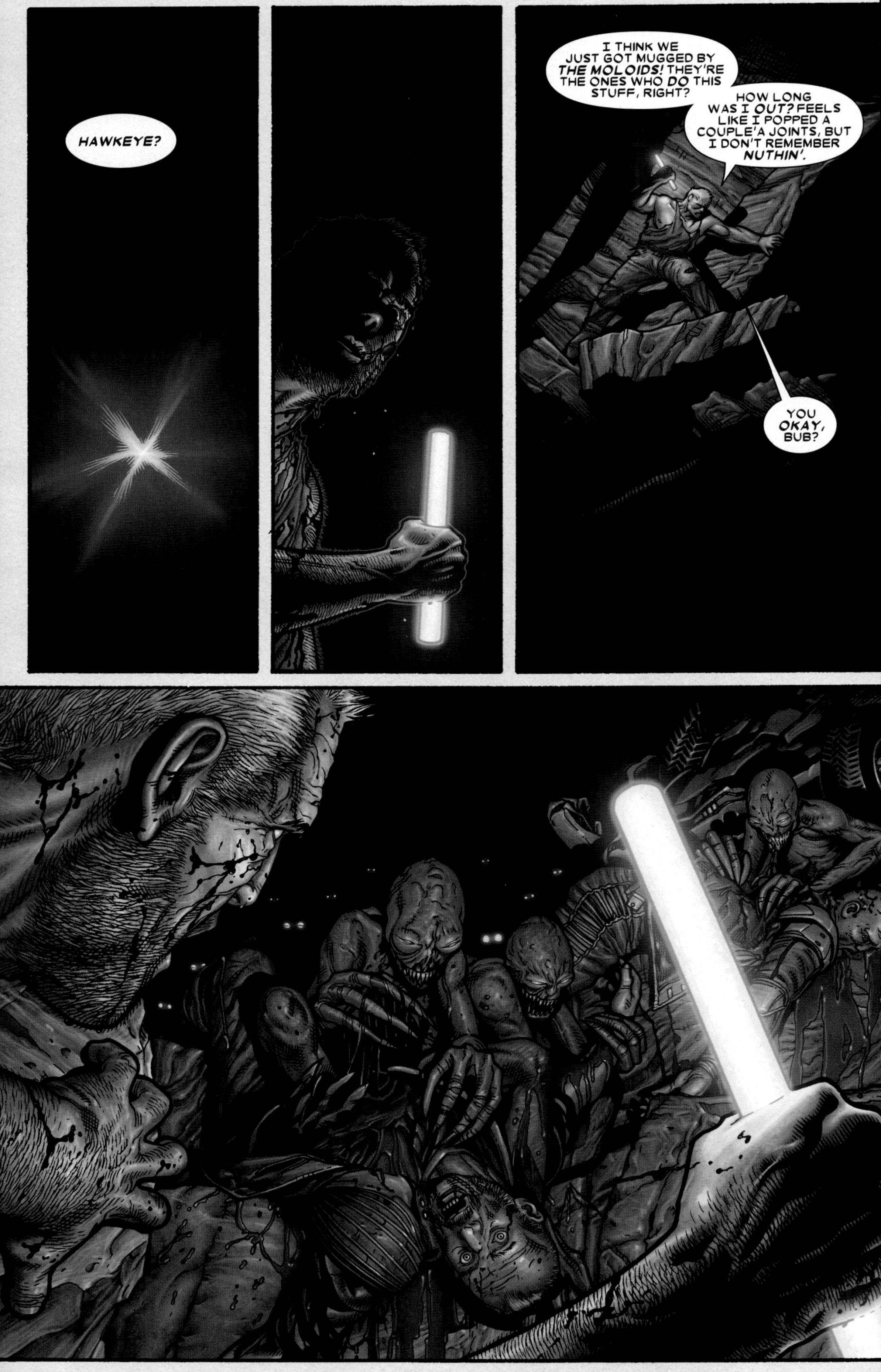
HAWKEYE?
I THINK WE JUST GOT MUGGED BY THE MOLOIDS! THEY'RE THE ONES WHO DO THIS STUFF, RIGHT?
HOW LONG WAS I OUT? FEELS LIKE I POPPED A COUPLE'A JOINTS, BUT I DON'T REMEMBER NUTHIN'.
YOU OKAY, BUB?

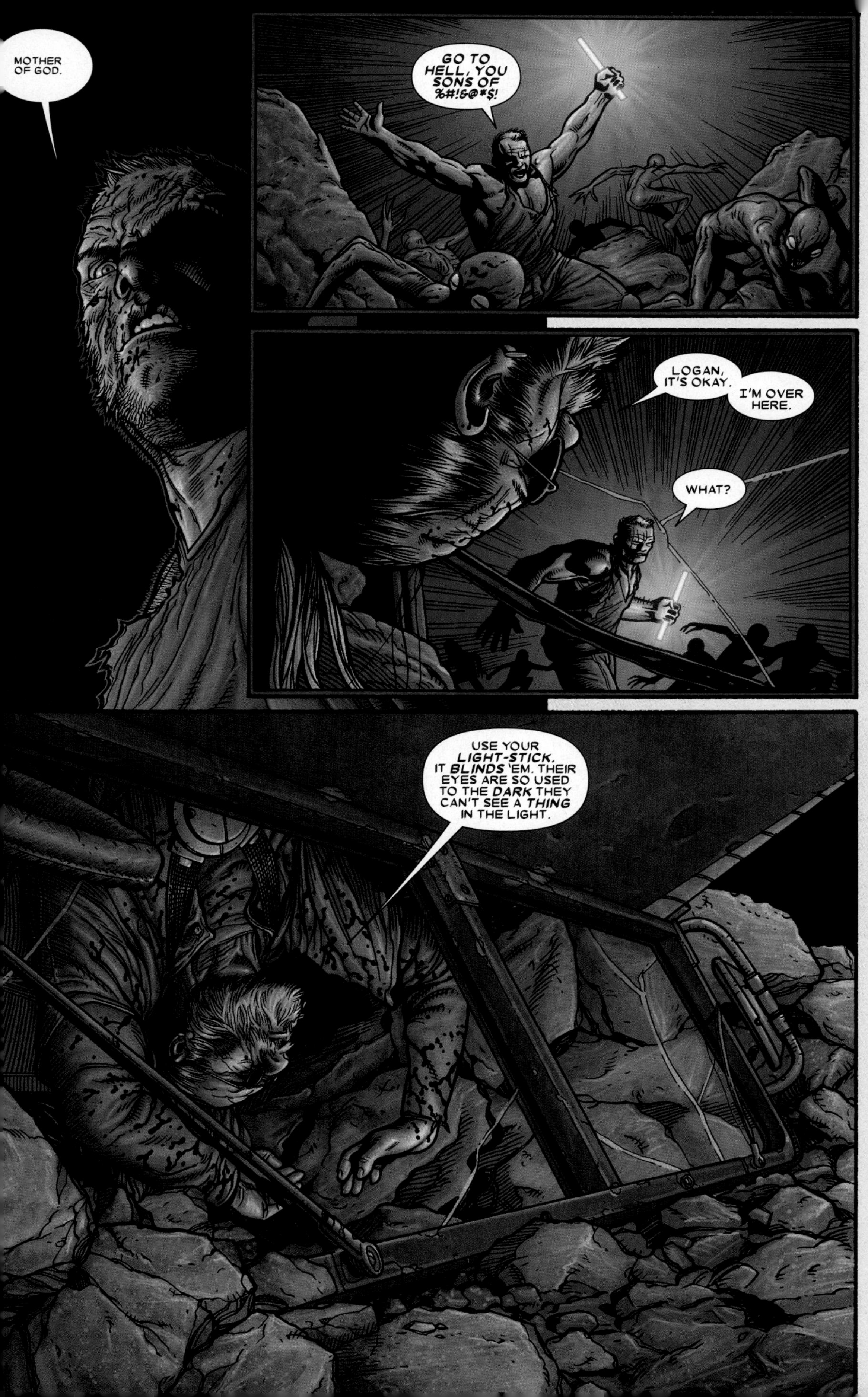
MOTHER OF GOD.
GO TO HELL, YOU SONS OF %#!&@*$!
LOGAN, IT'S OKAY.
I'M OVER HERE.
WHAT?
USE YOUR LIGHT-STICK. IT BLINDS 'EM. THEIR EYES ARE SO USED TO THE DARK THEY CAN'T SEE A THING IN THE LIGHT.

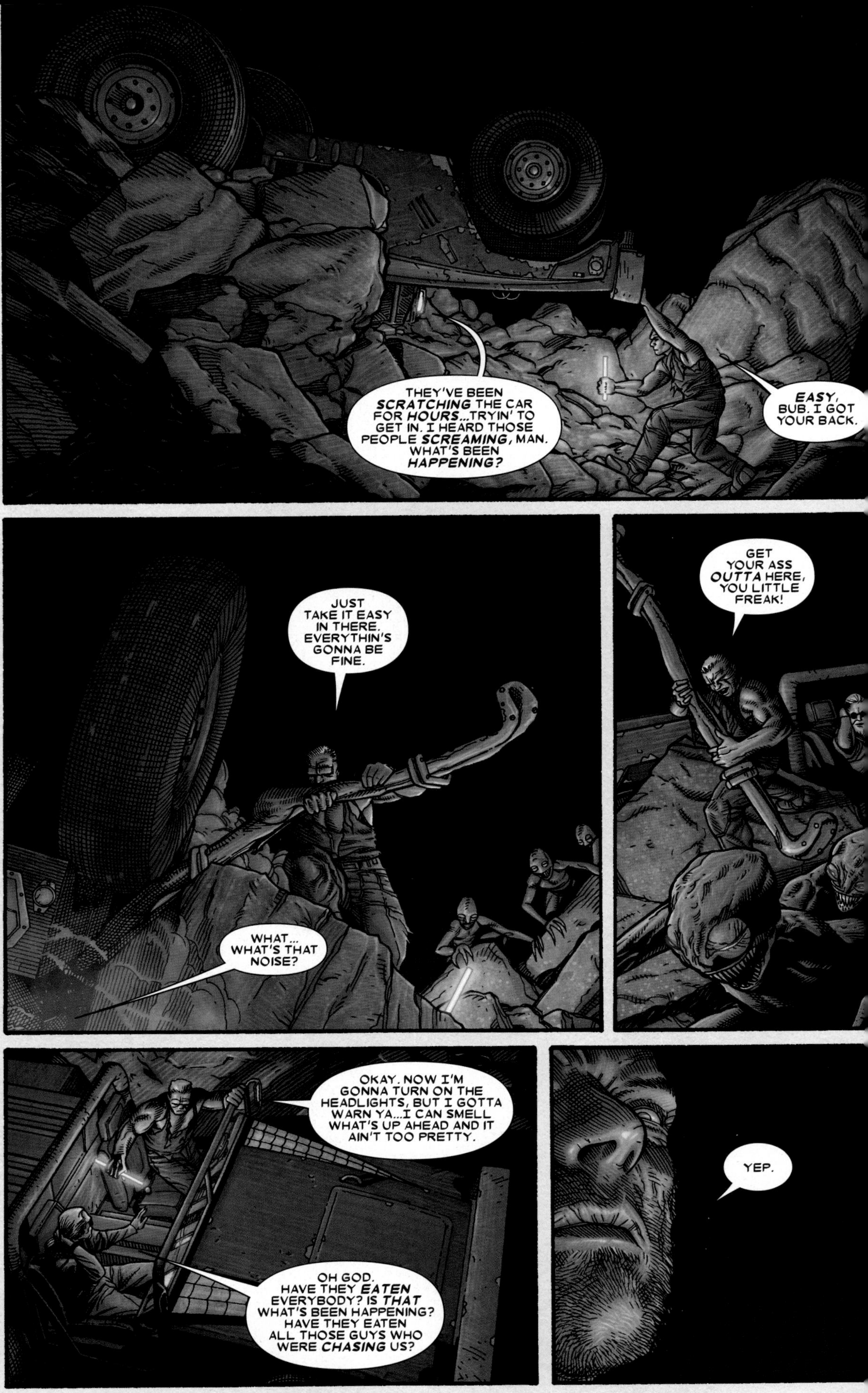
THEY'VE BEEN SCRATCHING THE CAR FOR HOURS...TRYIN' TO GET IN. I HEARD THOSE PEOPLE SCREAMING, MAN. WHAT'S BEEN HAPPENING?
EASY, BUB. I GOT YOUR BACK.
JUST TAKE IT EASY IN THERE. EVERYTHIN'S GONNA BE FINE.
WHAT... WHAT'S THAT NOISE?
GET YOUR ASS OUTTA HERE, YOU LITTLE FREAK!
OKAY. NOW I'M GONNA TURN ON THE HEADLIGHTS, BUT I GOTTA WARN YA...I CAN SMELL WHAT'S UP AHEAD AND IT AIN'T TOO PRETTY.
OH GOD. HAVE THEY EATEN EVERYBODY? IS THAT WHAT'S BEEN HAPPENING? HAVE THEY EATEN ALL THOSE GUYS WHO WERE CHASING US?
YEP.

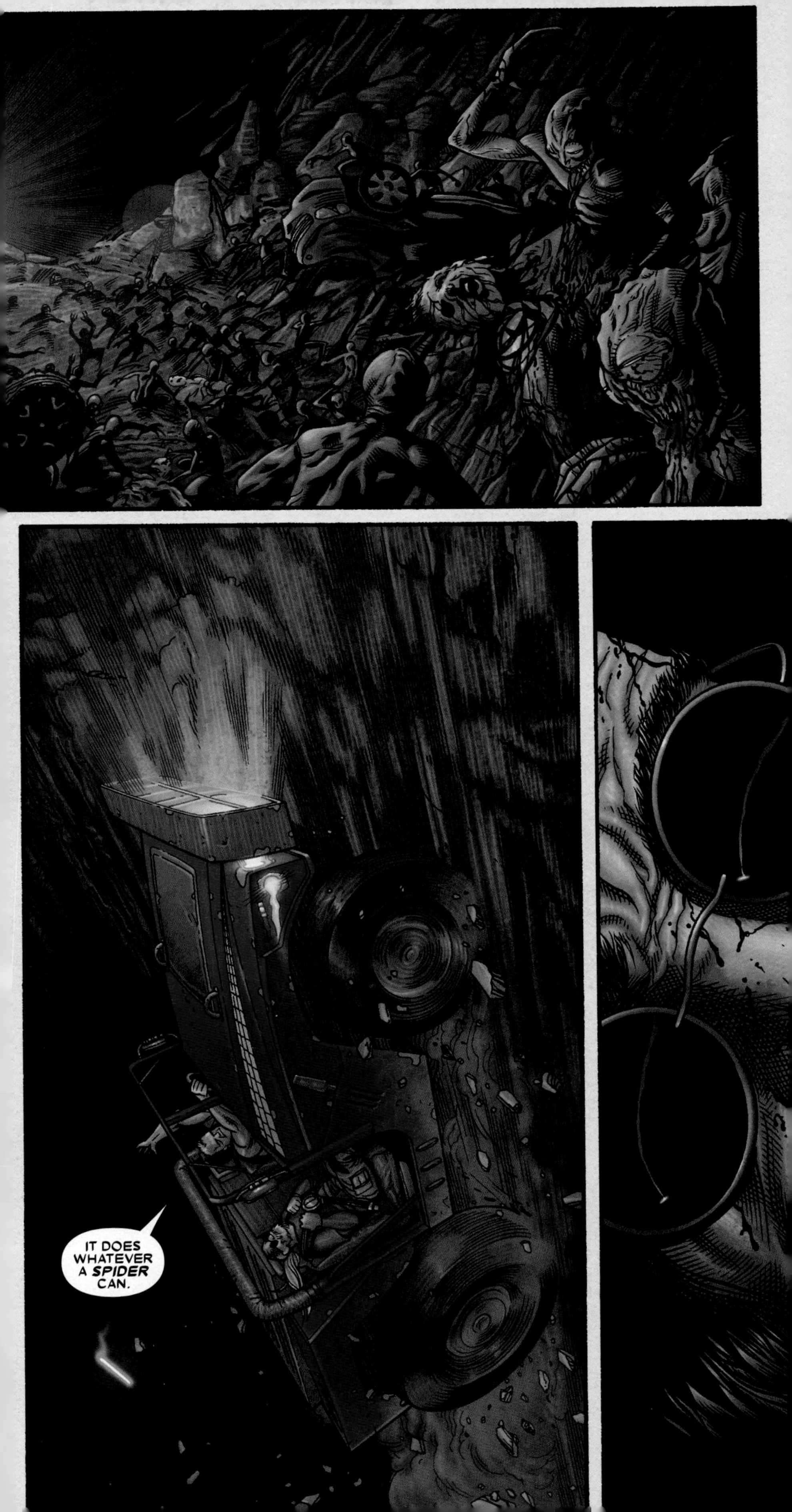
IT DOES WHATEVER A SPIDER CAN.

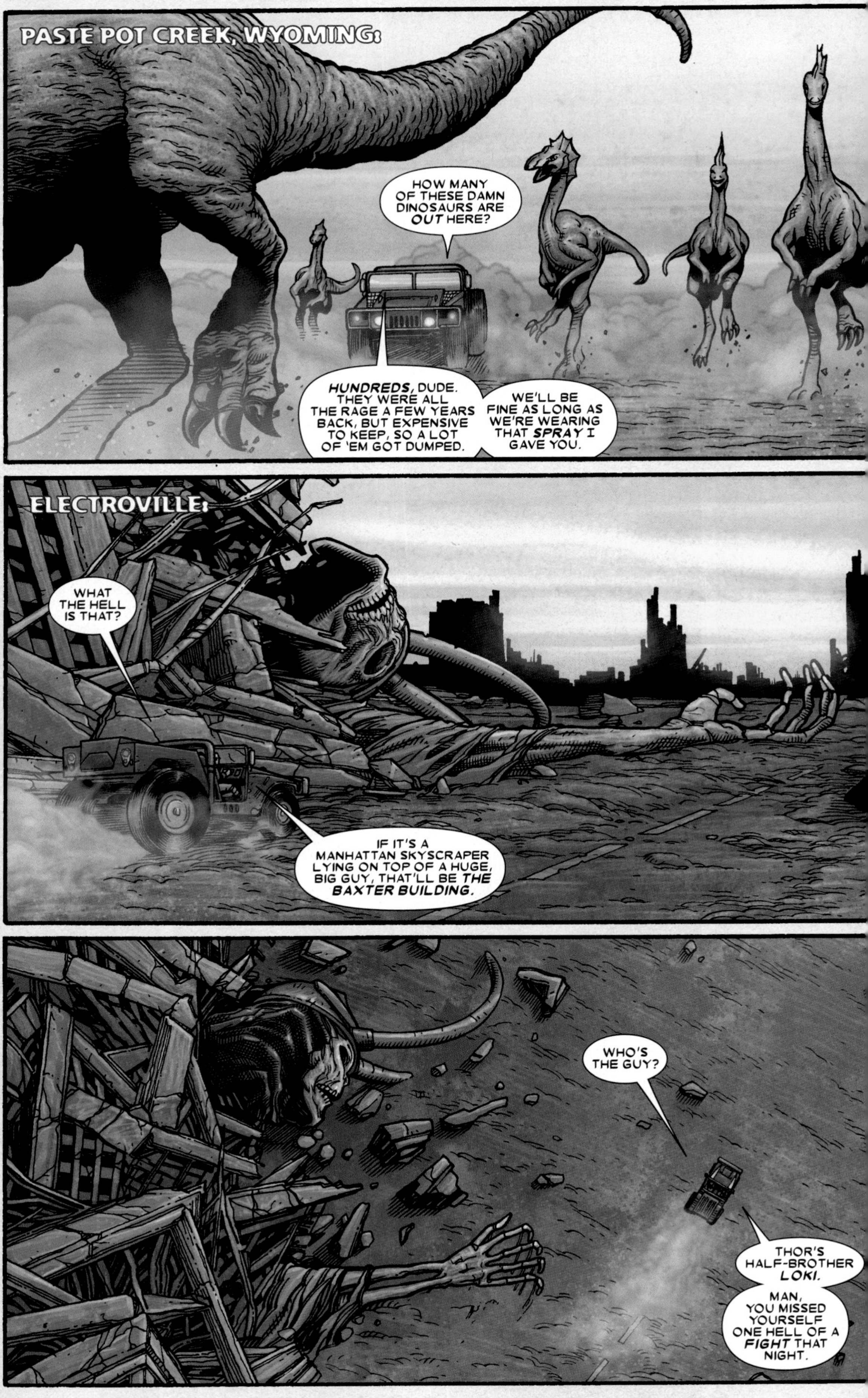
PASTE POT CREEK, WYOMING:
HOW MANY OF THESE DAMN DINOSAURS ARE OUT HERE?
HUNDREDS, DUDE. THEY WERE ALL THE RAGE A FEW YEARS BACK, BUT EXPENSIVE TO KEEP, SO A LOT OF 'EM GOT DUMPED.
WE'LL BE FINE AS LONG AS WE'RE WEARING THAT SPRAY I GAVE YOU.
ELECTROVILLE:
WHAT THE HELL IS THAT?
IF IT'S A MANHATTAN SKYSCRAPER LYING ON TOP OF A HUGE, BIG GUY, THAT'LL BE THE BAXTER BUILDING.
WHO'S THE GUY?
THOR'S HALF-BROTHER LOKI.
MAN, YOU MISSED YOURSELF ONE HELL OF A FIGHT THAT NIGHT.

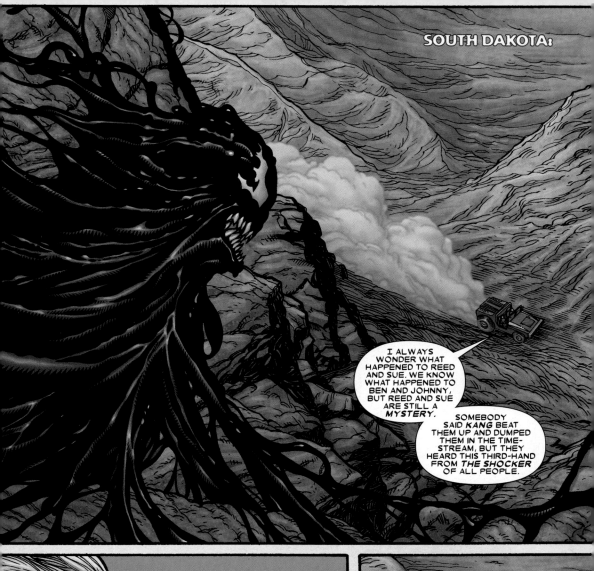

I ALWAYS WONDER WHAT HAPPENED TO REED AND SUE. WE KNOW WHAT HAPPENED TO BEN AND JOHNNY, BUT REED AND SUE ARE STILL A *MYSTERY*.

SOMEBODY SAID *KANG* BEAT THEM UP AND DUMPED THEM IN THE TIME-STREAM, BUT THEY HEARD THIS THIRD-HAND FROM *THE SHOCKER* OF ALL PEOPLE.

MAYBE THEY'LL COME BACK AND *SAVE THE WORLD*.

Y'KNOW, LIKE THE *OLD* DAYS.

YEAH, RIGHT.

A LITTLE LATE FOR *THAT*, DON'T YOU THINK?

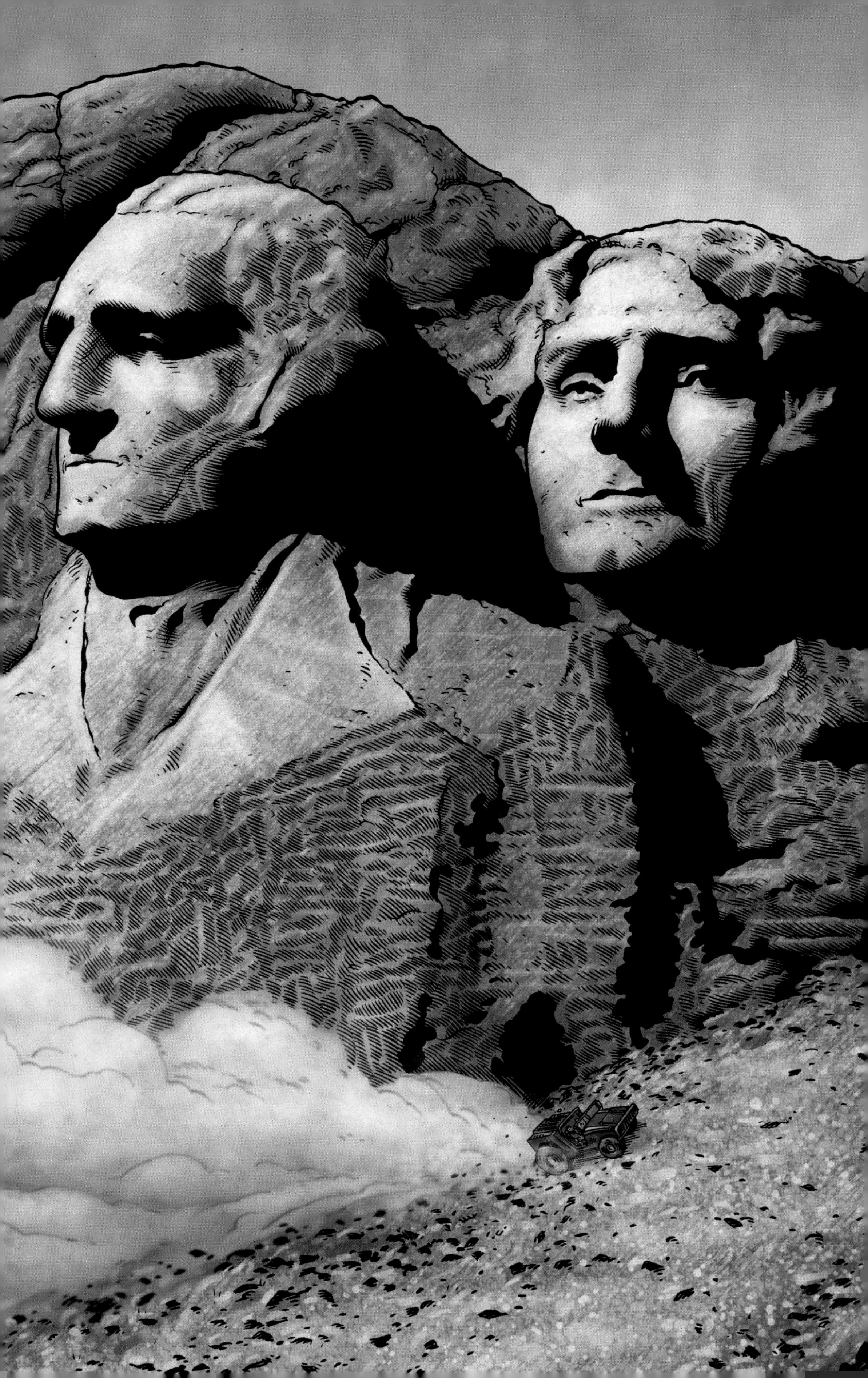

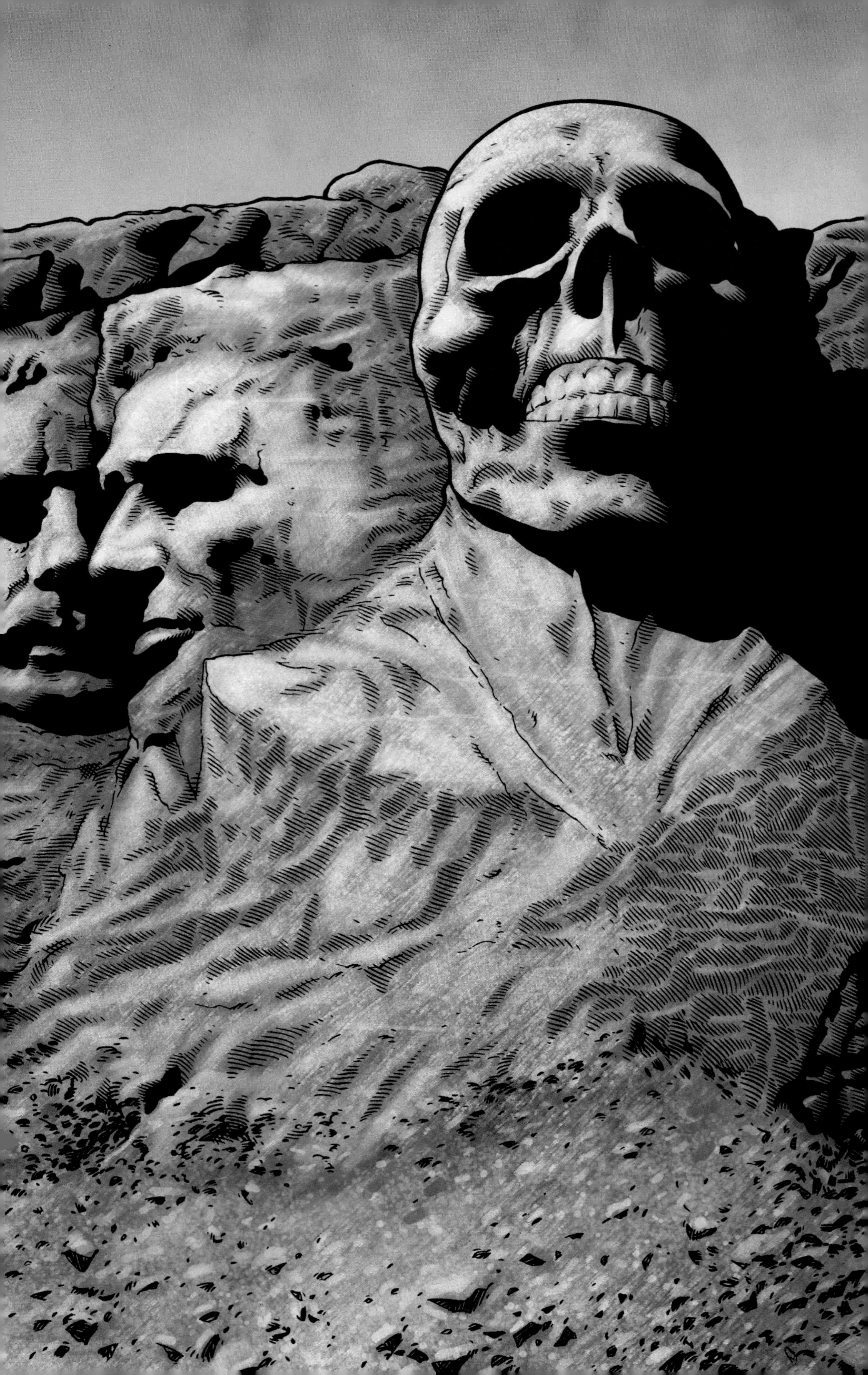

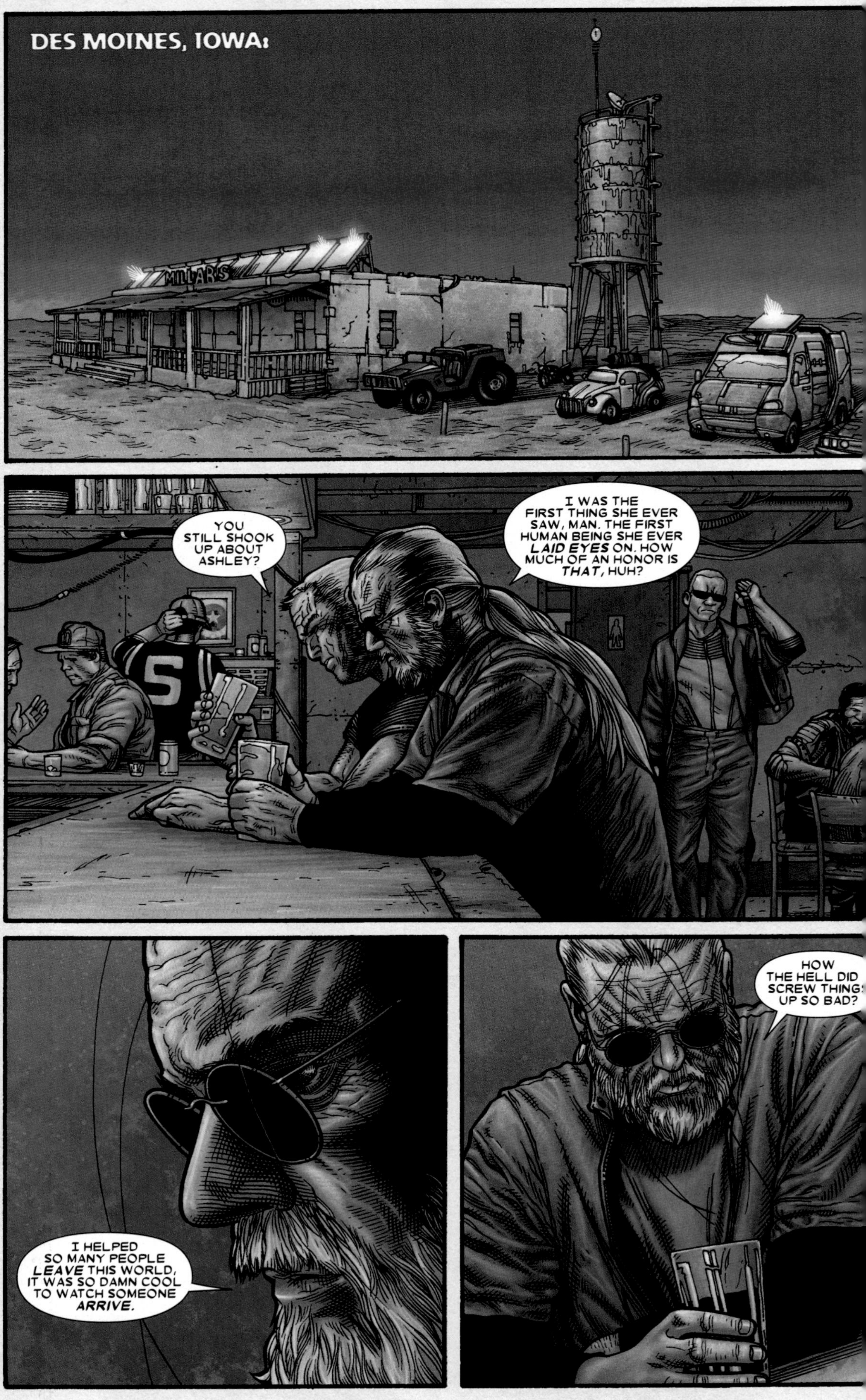
DES MOINES, IOWA:
MILLAR'S
YOU STILL SHOOK UP ABOUT ASHLEY?
I WAS THE FIRST THING SHE EVER SAW, MAN. THE FIRST HUMAN BEING SHE EVER LAID EYES ON. HOW MUCH OF AN HONOR IS THAT, HUH?
I HELPED SO MANY PEOPLE LEAVE THIS WORLD, IT WAS SO DAMN COOL TO WATCH SOMEONE ARRIVE.
HOW THE HELL DID SCREW THING UP SO BAD?

AT LEAST *YOU* SEEM A LITTLE MORE LIKE YOUR OLD SELF.

THAT'S WHAT I'M AFRAID OF.

WHAT DO YOU MEAN?

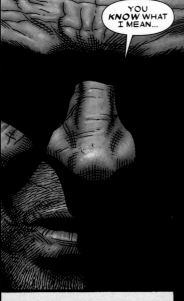

YOU *KNOW* WHAT I MEAN...

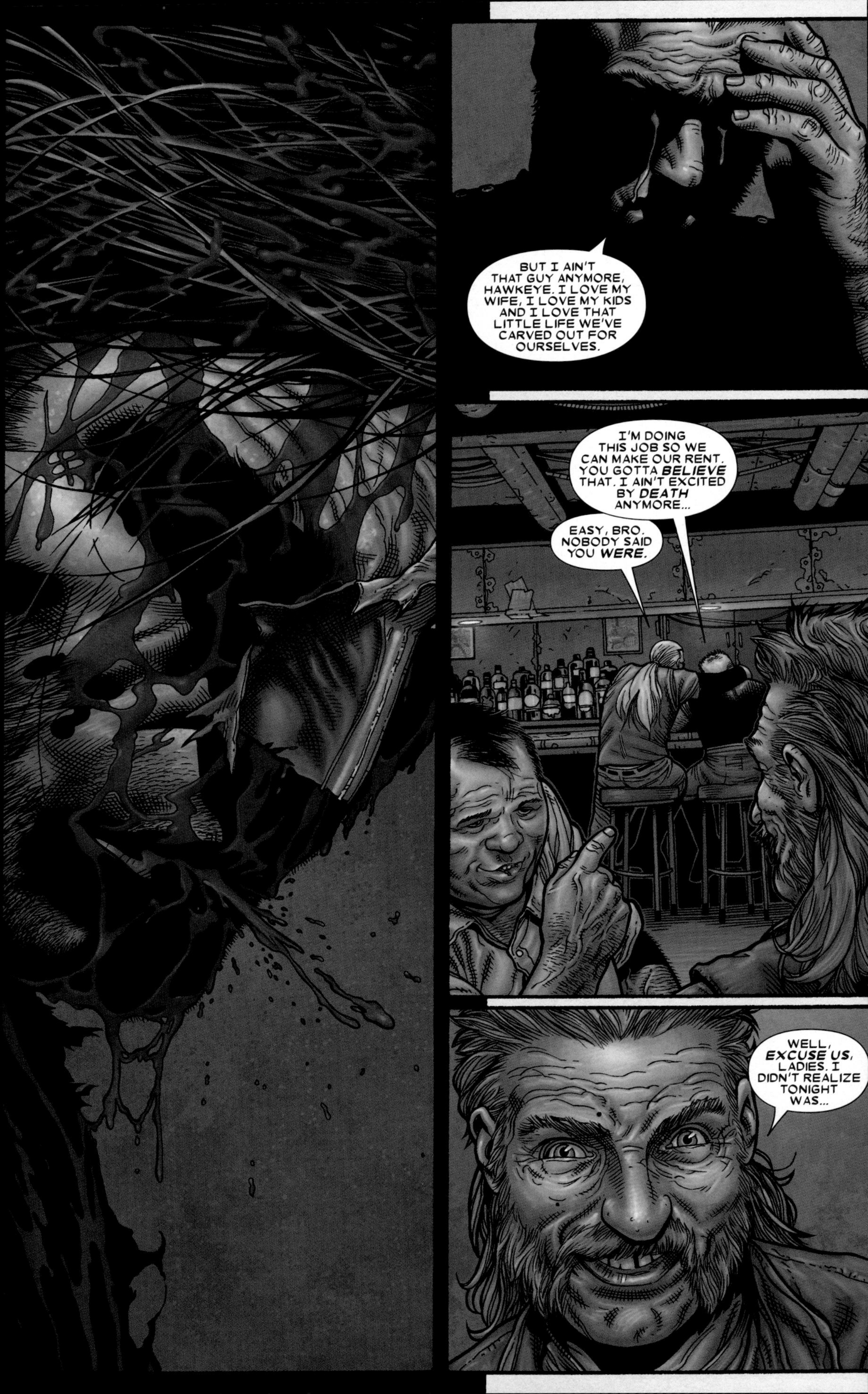
BUT I AIN'T THAT GUY ANYMORE, HAWKEYE. I LOVE MY WIFE, I LOVE MY KIDS AND I LOVE THAT LITTLE LIFE WE'VE CARVED OUT FOR OURSELVES.
I'M DOING THIS JOB SO WE CAN MAKE OUR RENT. YOU GOTTA *BELIEVE* THAT. I AIN'T EXCITED BY *DEATH* ANYMORE...
EASY, BRO. NOBODY SAID YOU *WERE.*
WELL, *EXCUSE US,* LADIES. I DIDN'T REALIZE TONIGHT WAS...

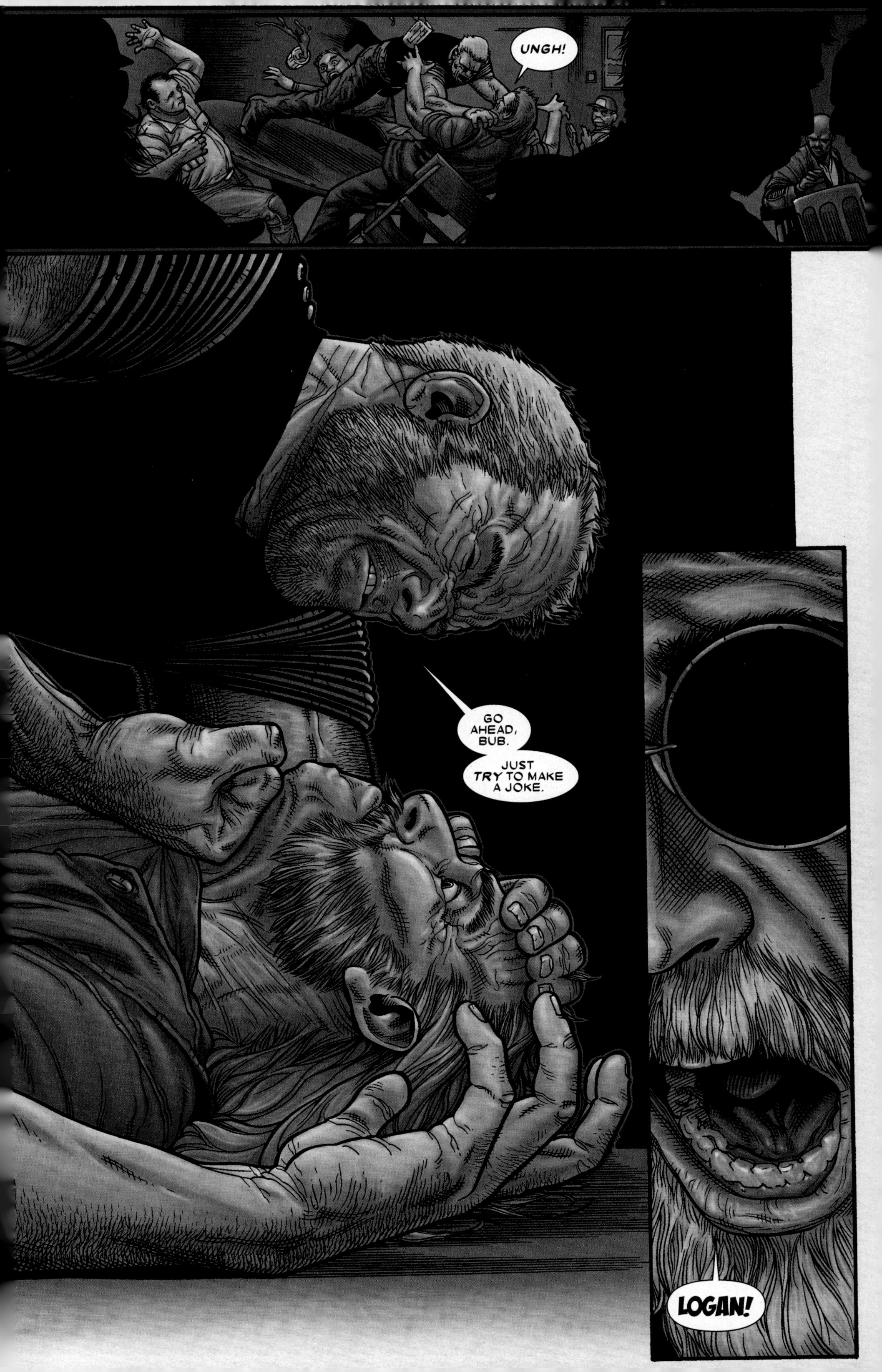
UNGH!
GO AHEAD, BUB.
JUST TRY TO MAKE A JOKE.
LOGAN!

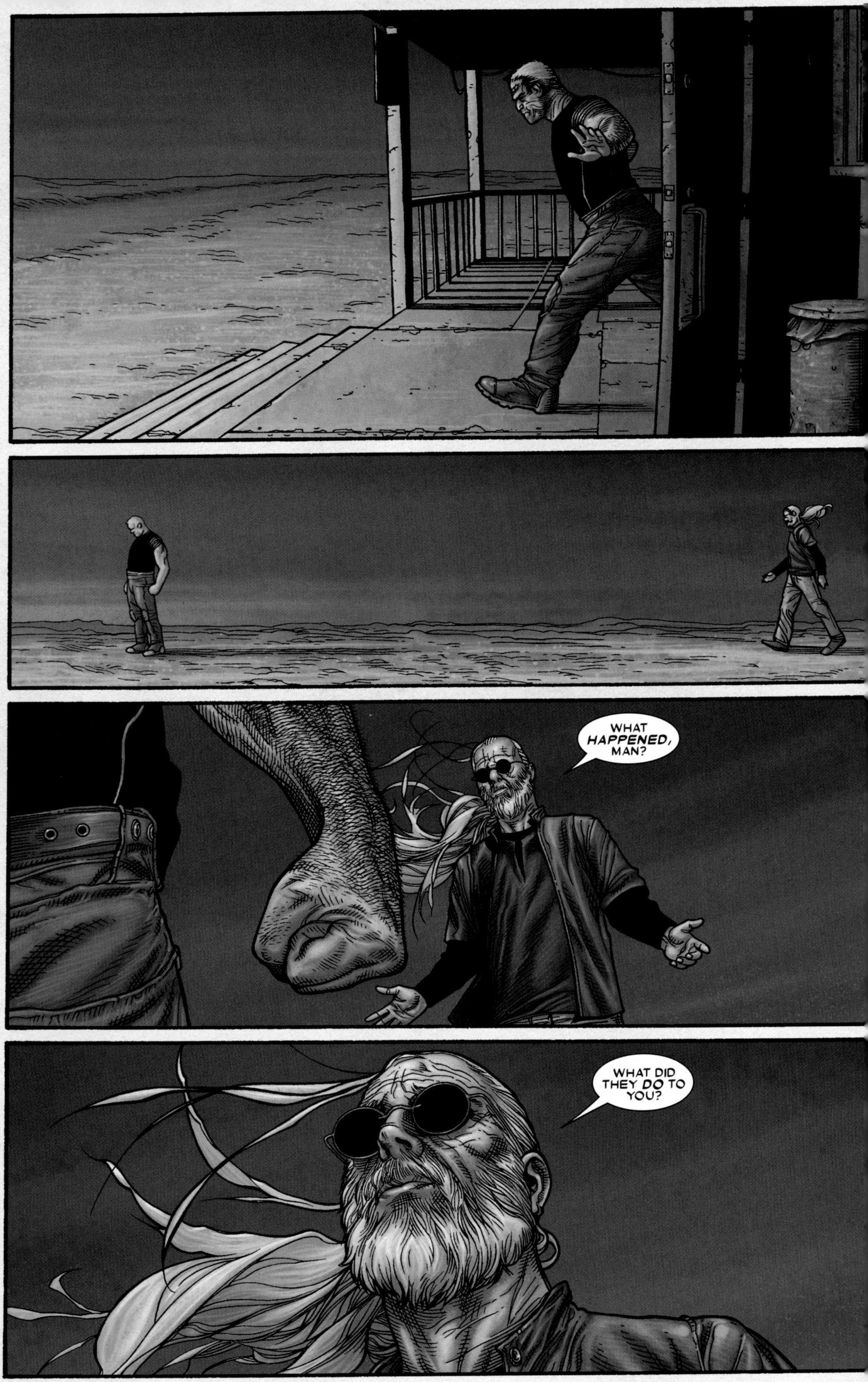
WHAT HAPPENED, MAN?
WHAT DID THEY DO TO YOU?

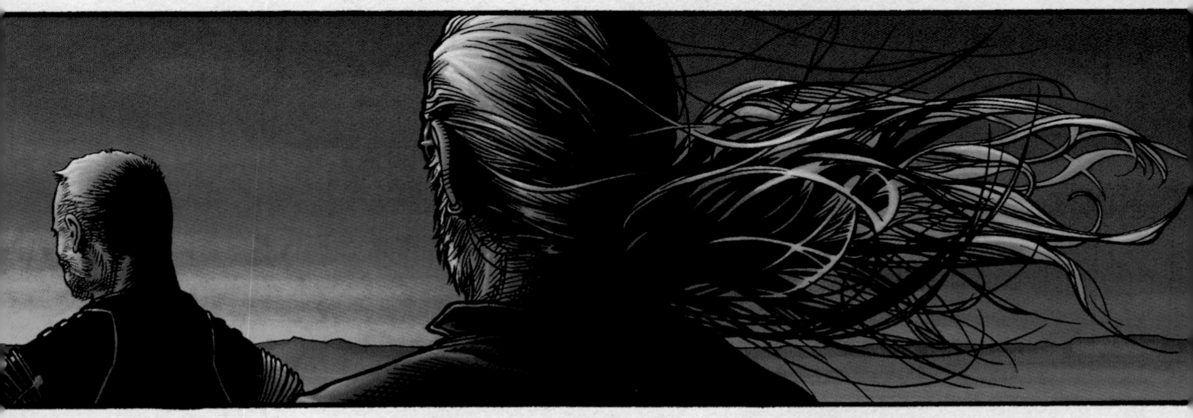

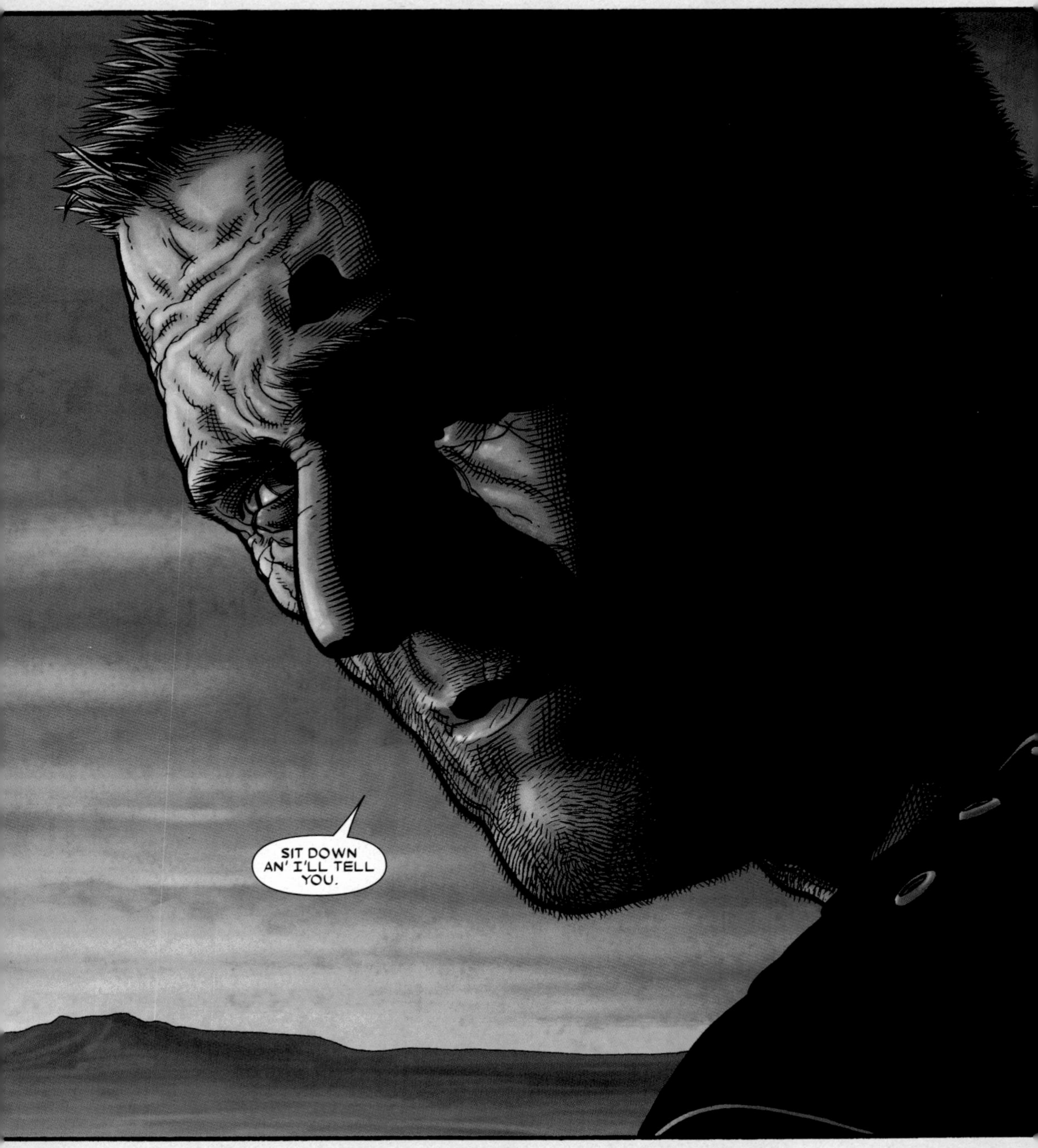
SIT DOWN AN' I'LL TELL YOU.

CHAPTER FIVE

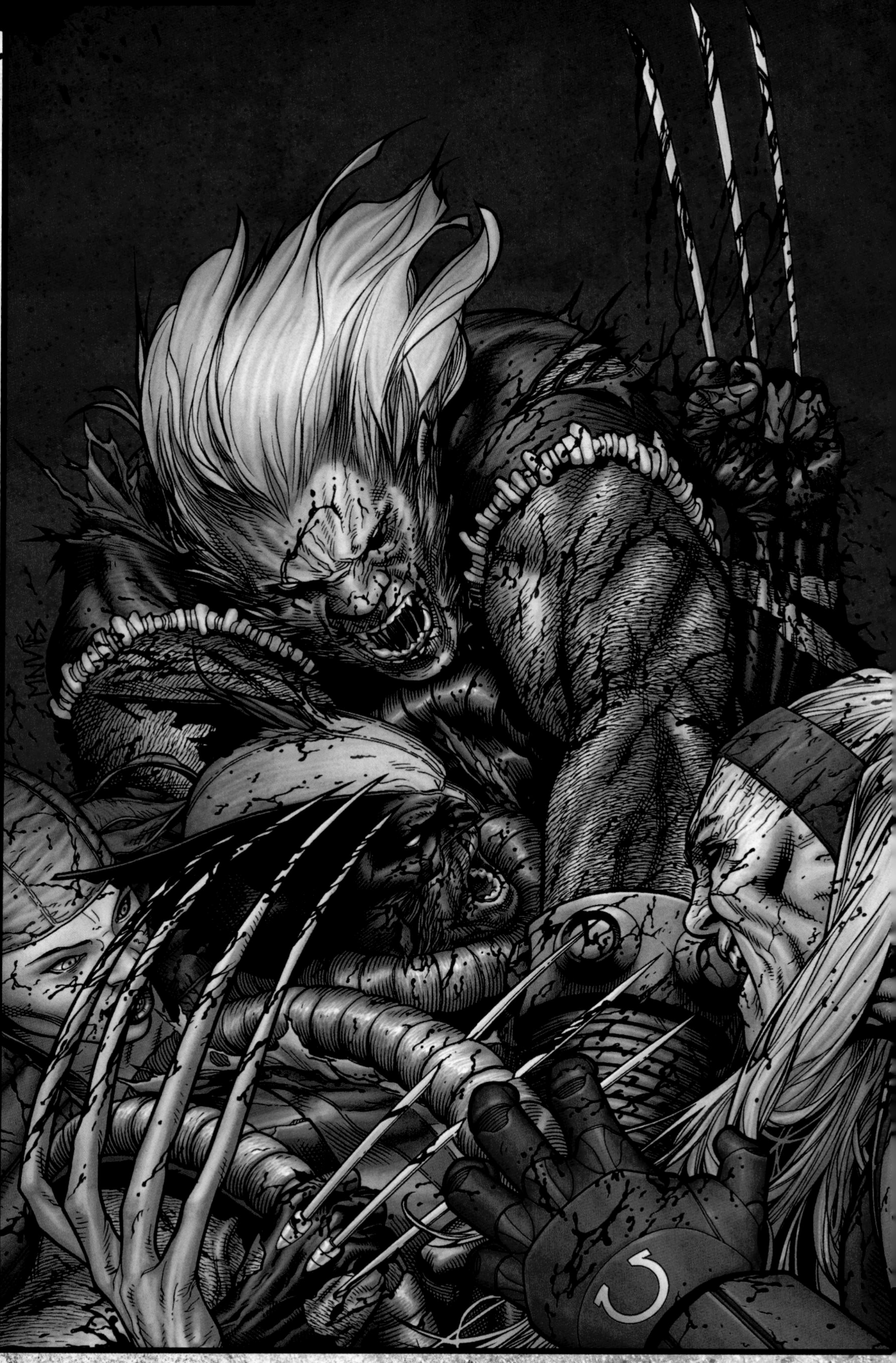

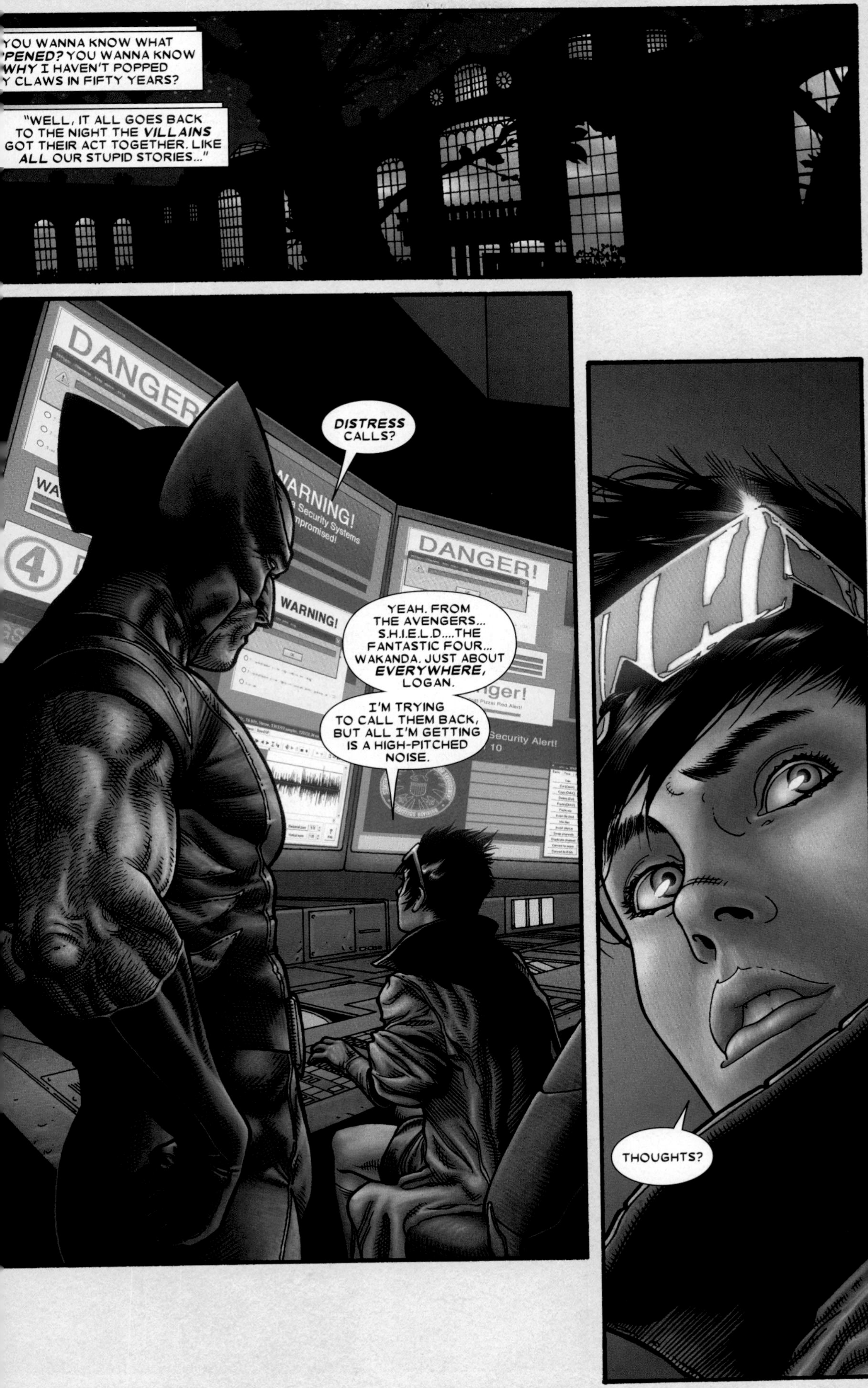
YOU WANNA KNOW WHAT 'PENED? YOU WANNA KNOW WHY I HAVEN'T POPPED Y CLAWS IN FIFTY YEARS?
"WELL, IT ALL GOES BACK TO THE NIGHT THE VILLAINS GOT THEIR ACT TOGETHER. LIKE ALL OUR STUPID STORIES..."
DISTRESS CALLS?
YEAH. FROM THE AVENGERS... S.H.I.E.L.D....THE FANTASTIC FOUR... WAKANDA. JUST ABOUT EVERYWHERE, LOGAN.
I'M TRYING TO CALL THEM BACK, BUT ALL I'M GETTING IS A HIGH-PITCHED NOISE.
THOUGHTS?

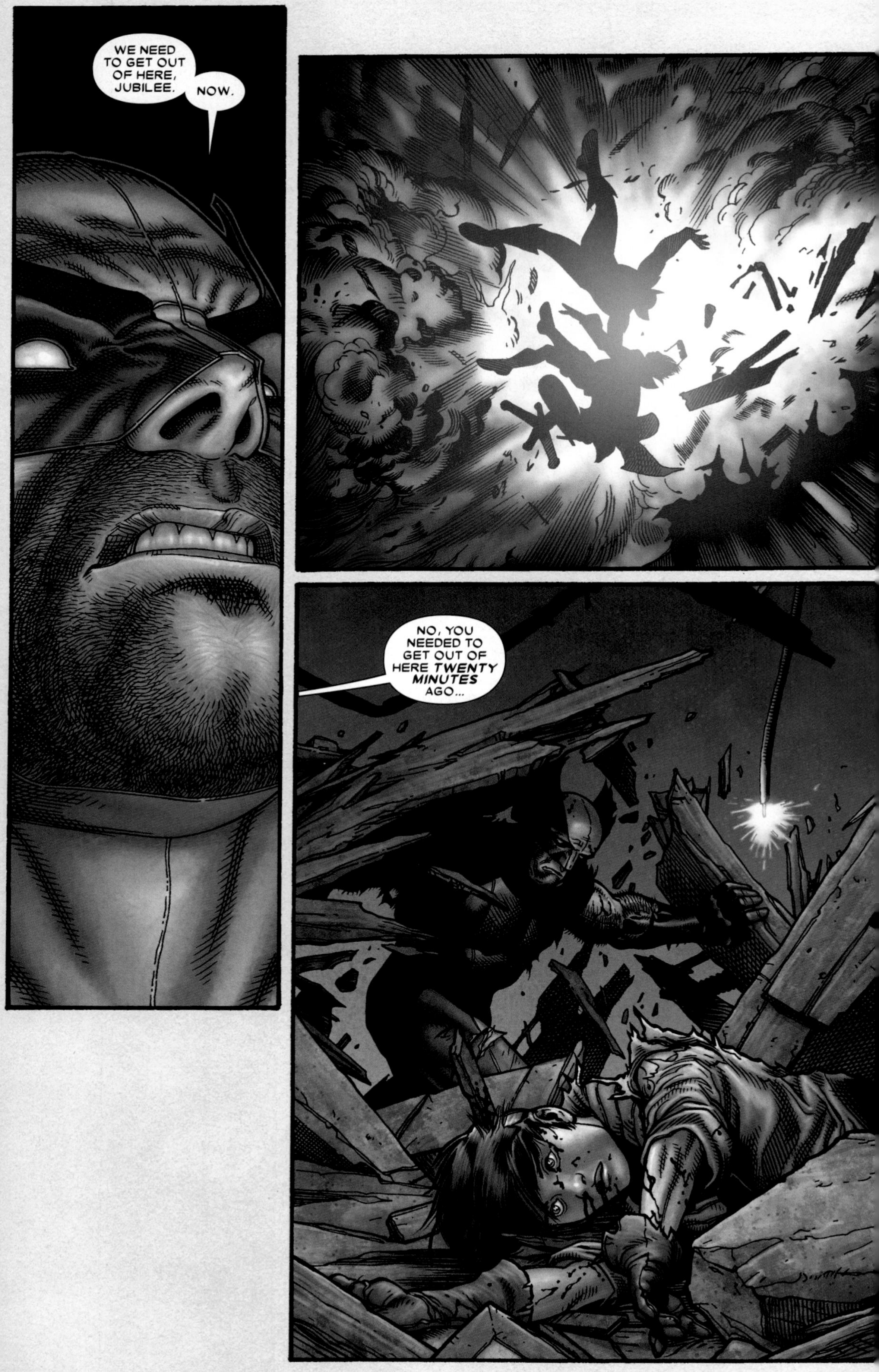
WE NEED TO GET OUT OF HERE, JUBILEE.
NOW.
NO, YOU NEEDED TO GET OUT OF HERE *TWENTY MINUTES* AGO...

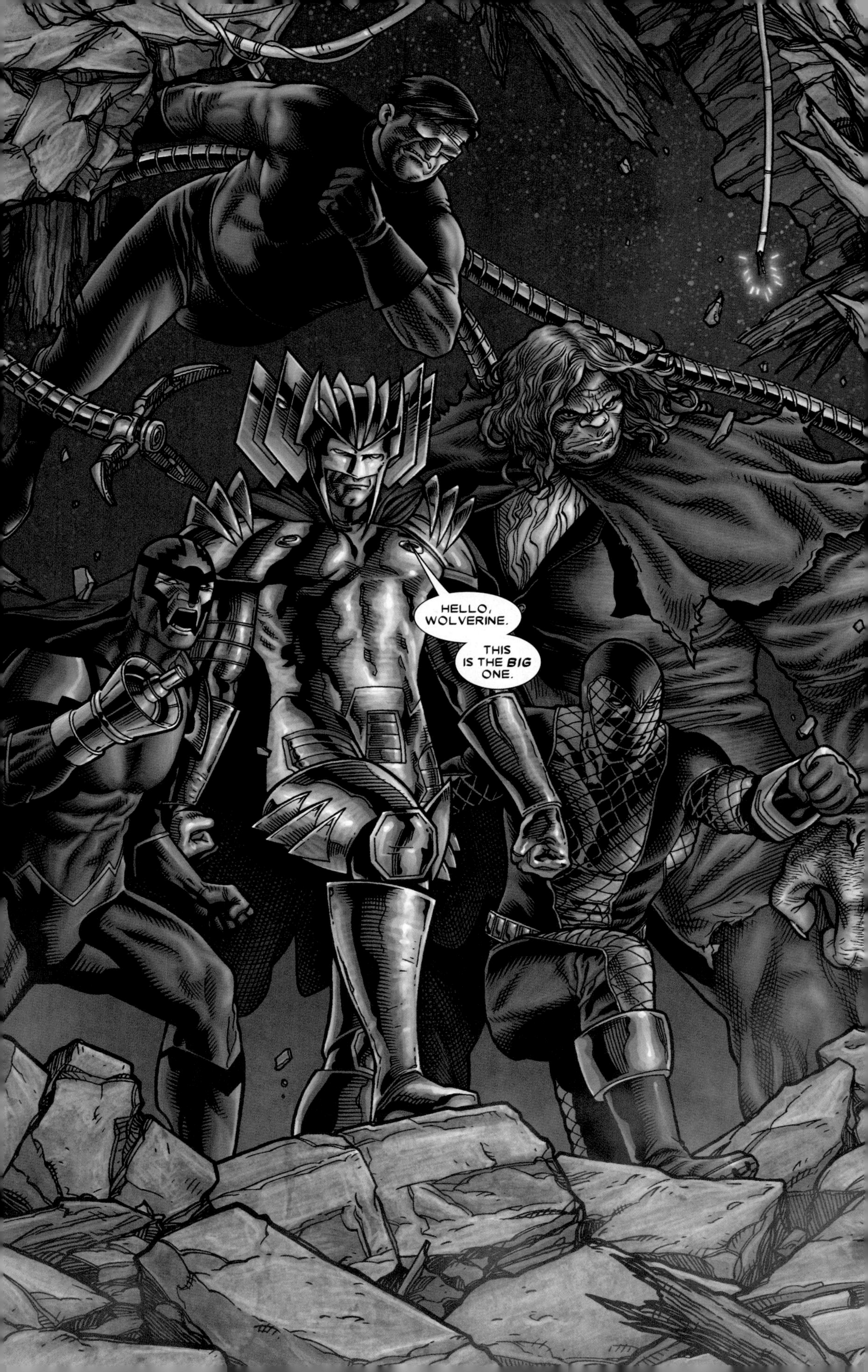
HELLO, WOLVERINE.
THIS IS THE *BIG* ONE.

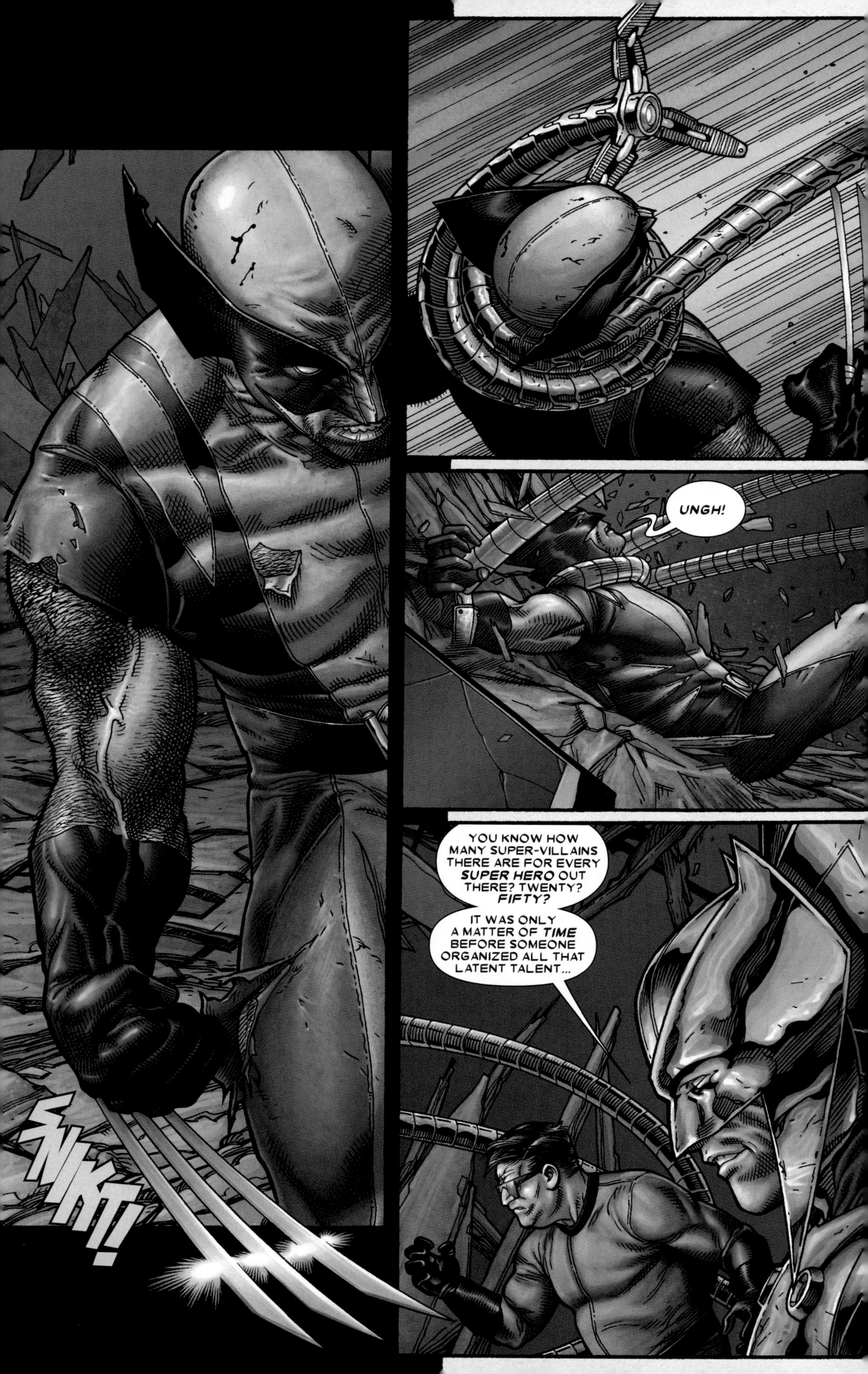
SNIKT!!
UNGH!
YOU KNOW HOW MANY SUPER-VILLAINS THERE ARE FOR EVERY SUPER HERO OUT THERE? TWENTY? FIFTY?
IT WAS ONLY A MATTER OF TIME BEFORE SOMEONE ORGANIZED ALL THAT LATENT TALENT...

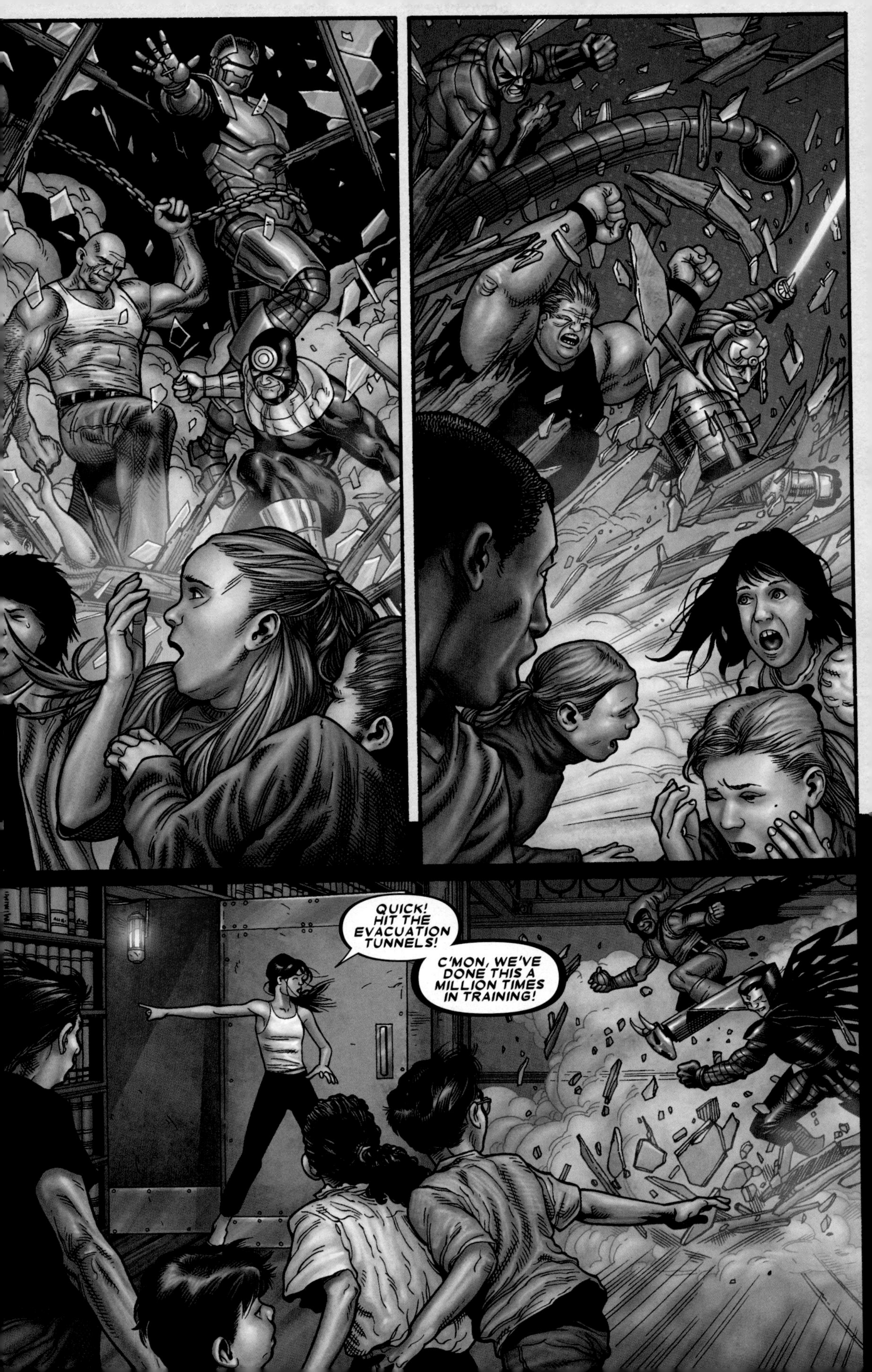
QUICK! HIT THE EVACUATION TUNNELS!
C'MON, WE'VE DONE THIS A MILLION TIMES IN TRAINING!

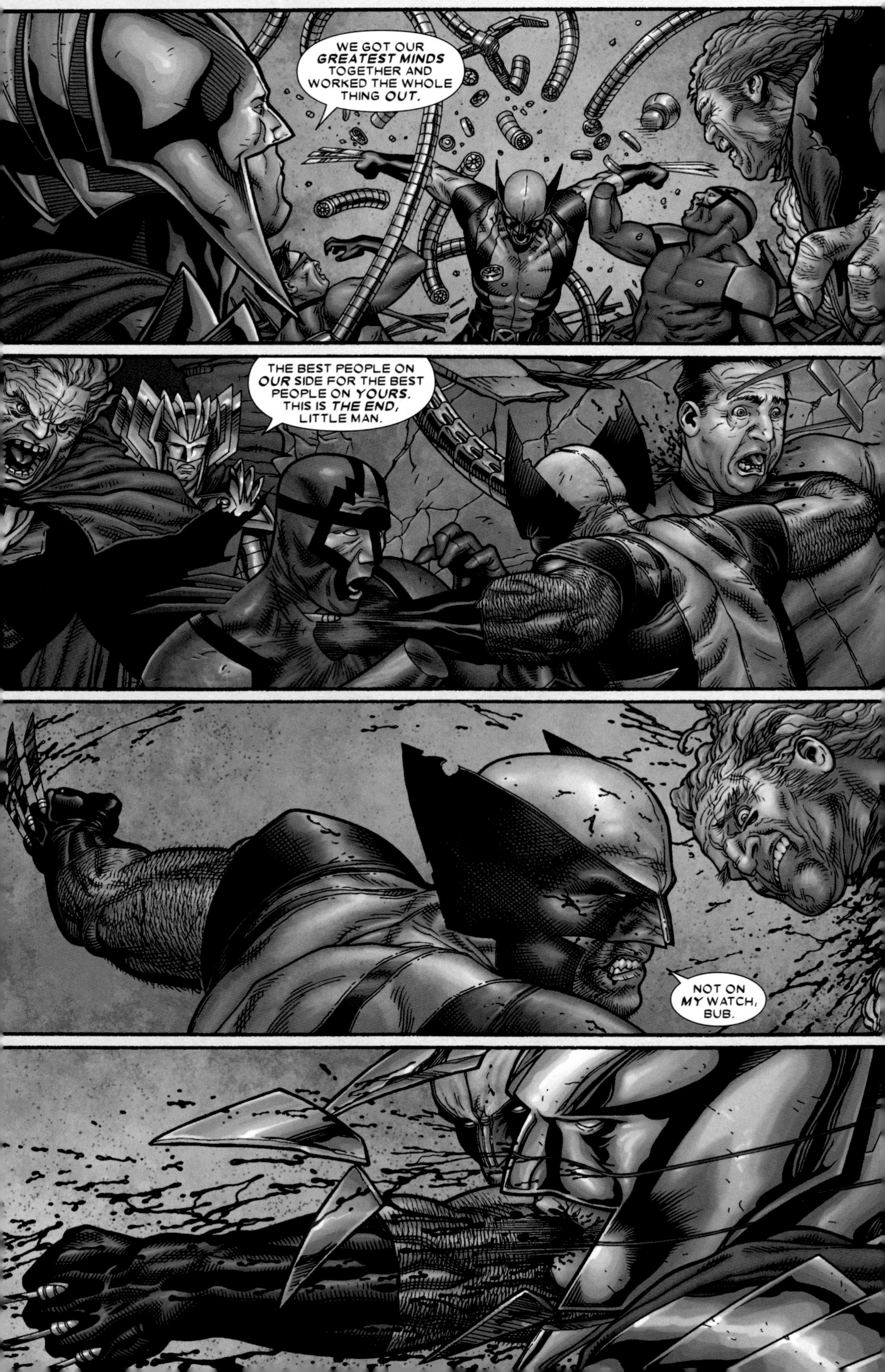
WE GOT OUR GREATEST MINDS TOGETHER AND WORKED THE WHOLE THING OUT.
THE BEST PEOPLE ON OUR SIDE FOR THE BEST PEOPLE ON YOURS. THIS IS THE END, LITTLE MAN.
NOT ON MY WATCH, BUB.

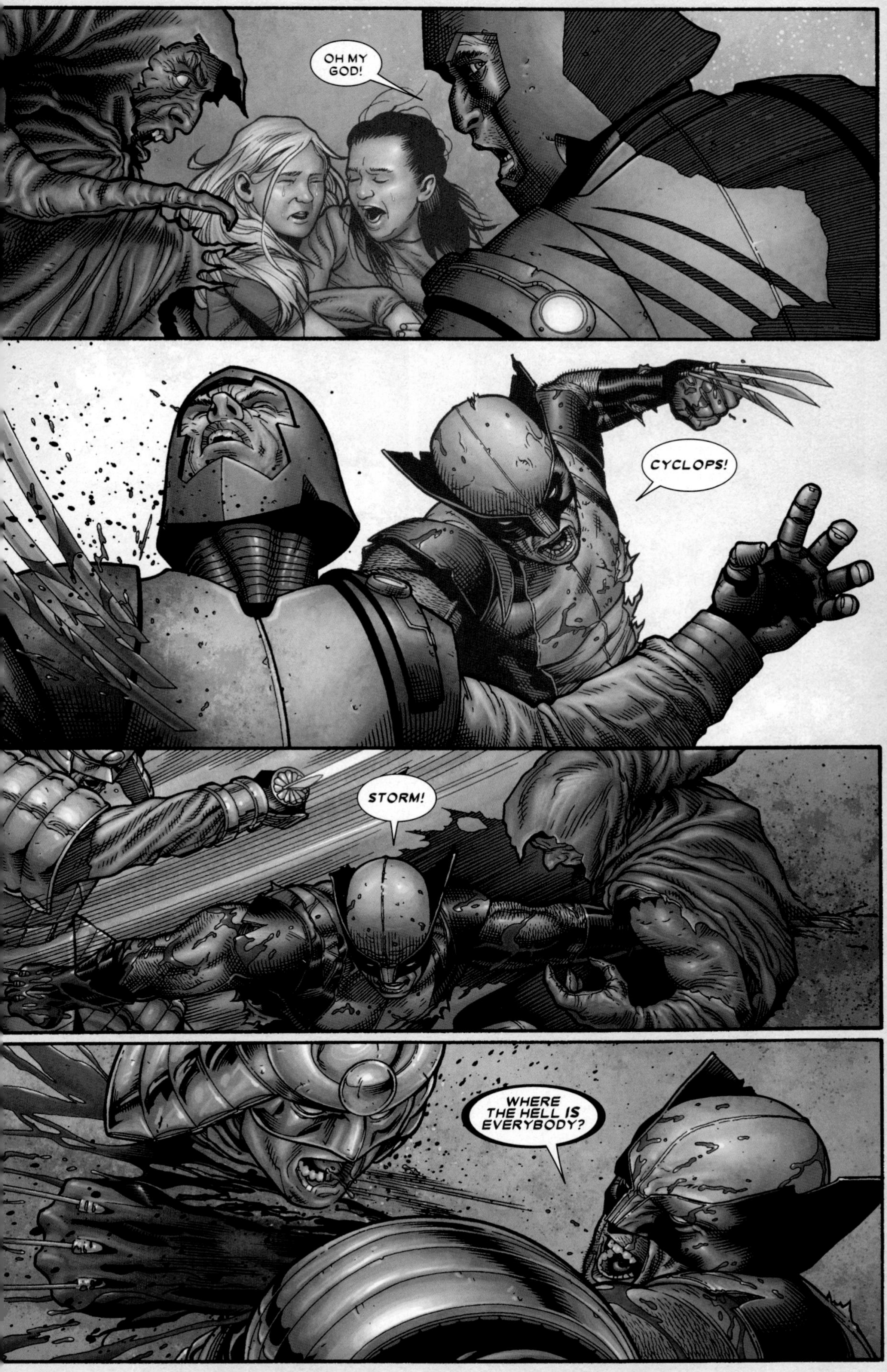
OH MY GOD!
CYCLOPS!
STORM!
WHERE THE HELL IS EVERYBODY?

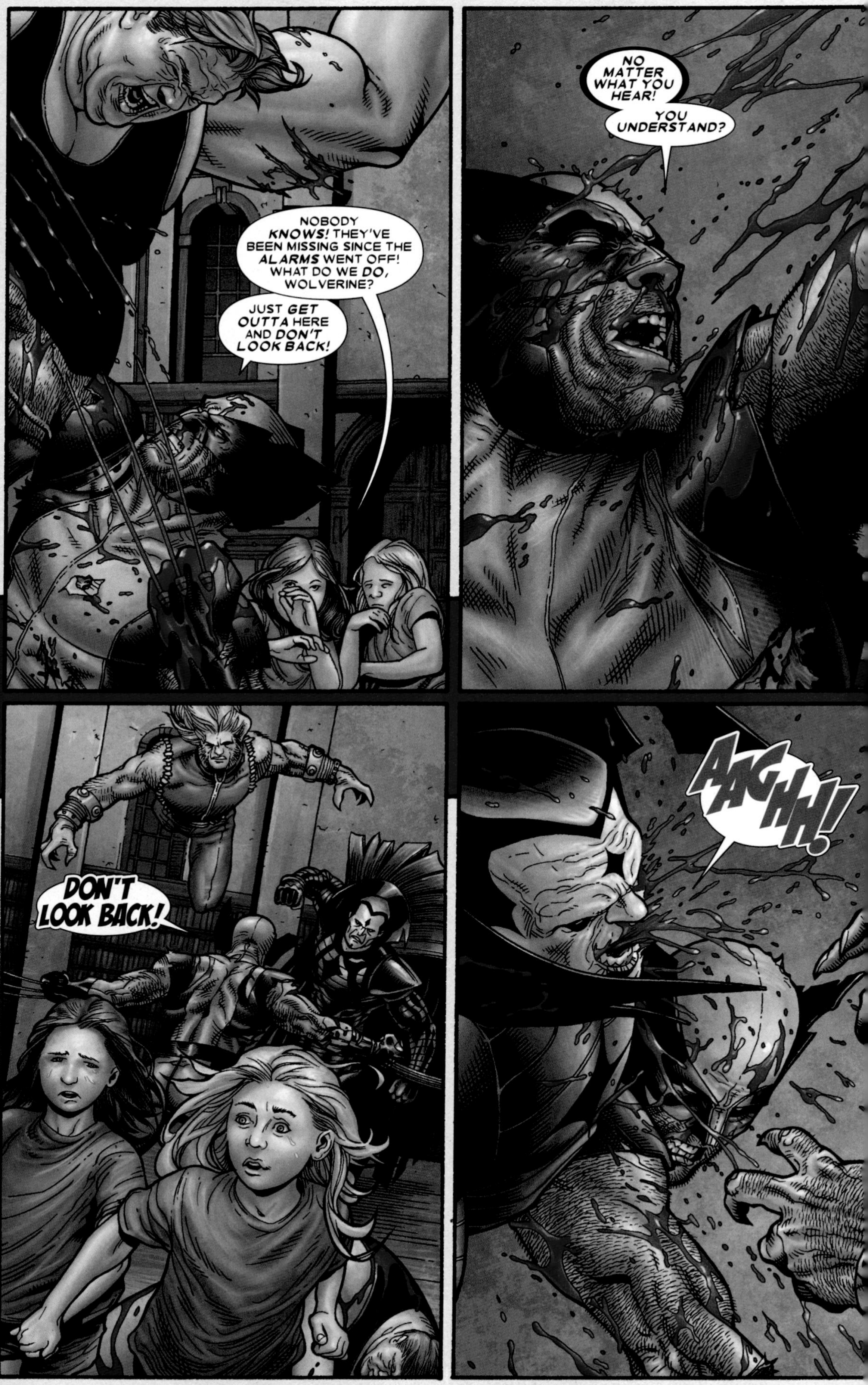
NOBODY KNOWS! THEY'VE BEEN MISSING SINCE THE ALARMS WENT OFF! WHAT DO WE DO, WOLVERINE?
JUST GET OUTTA HERE AND DON'T LOOK BACK!
NO MATTER WHAT YOU HEAR!
YOU UNDERSTAND?
DON'T LOOK BACK!
AAGHH!

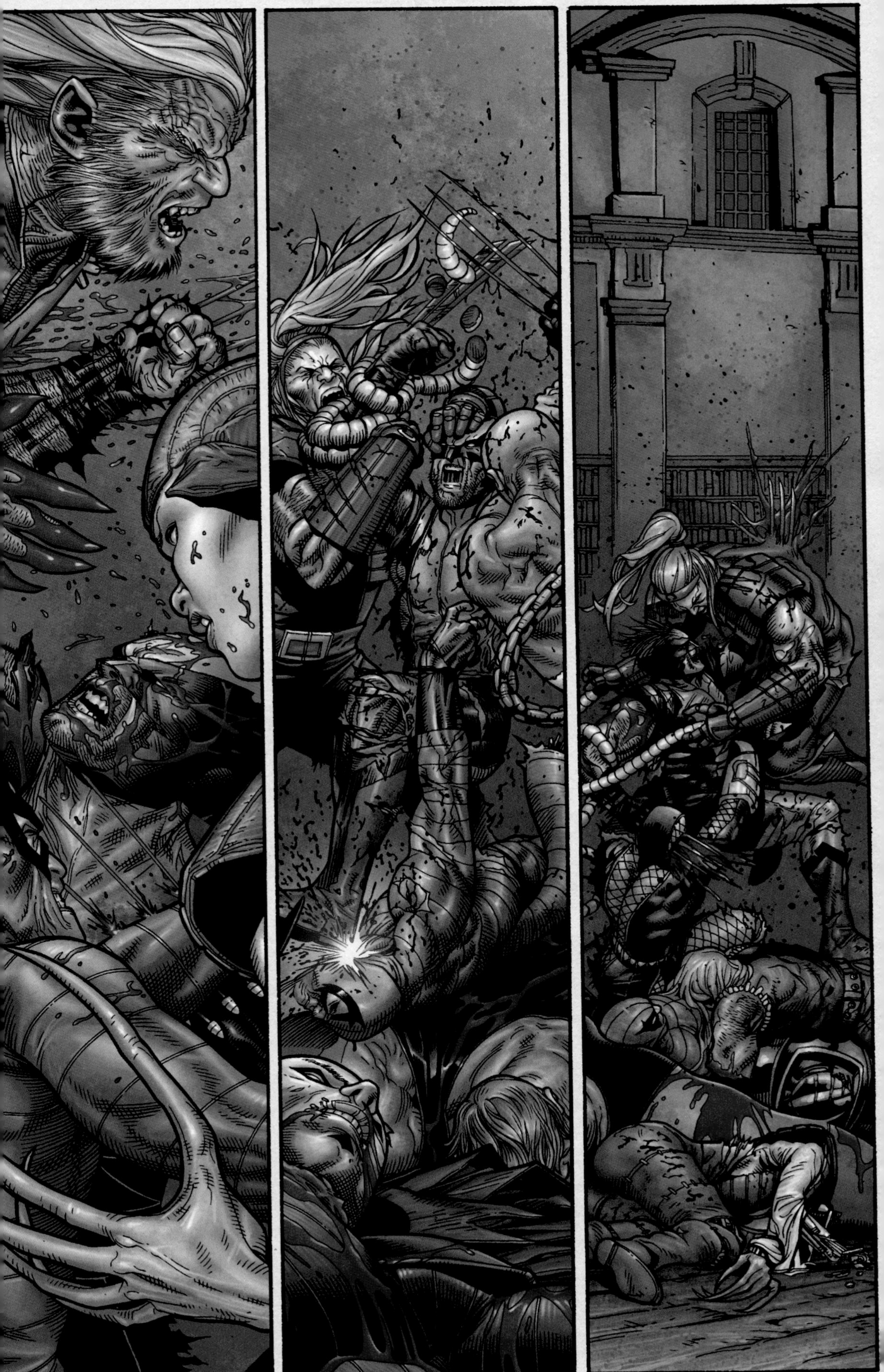

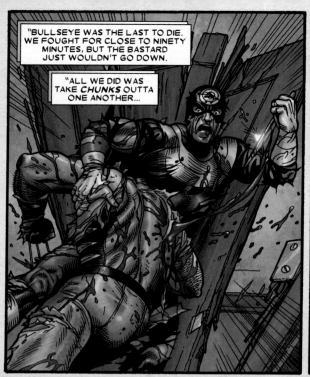

"BULLSEYE WAS THE LAST TO DIE. WE FOUGHT FOR CLOSE TO NINETY MINUTES, BUT THE BASTARD JUST WOULDN'T GO DOWN.

"ALL WE DID WAS TAKE *CHUNKS* OUTTA ONE ANOTHER...

"EVEN WITH HIS KNIVES IN MY BACK, ALL I COULD THINK ABOUT WAS WHAT WAS *GOIN' ON* OUT THERE. WHAT THEY'D DONE TO THE OTHER SUPER HEROES...

"...AND WHAT HE'D DO TO THE KIDS IF I DIDN'T SEIZE MY *CHANCE*."

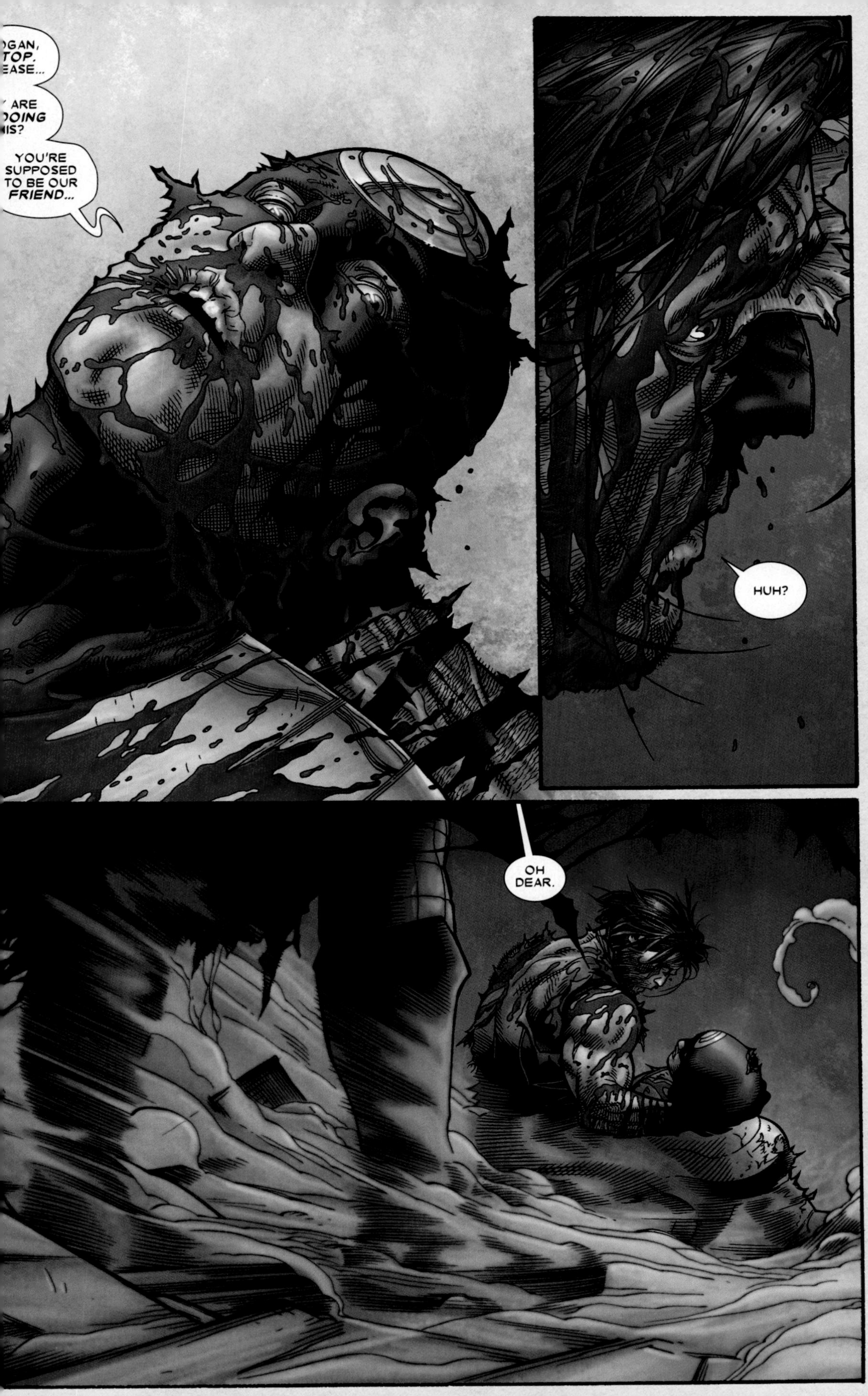

OGAN, TOP. EASE...
ARE DOING IS?
YOU'RE SUPPOSED TO BE OUR FRIEND...
HUH?
OH DEAR.

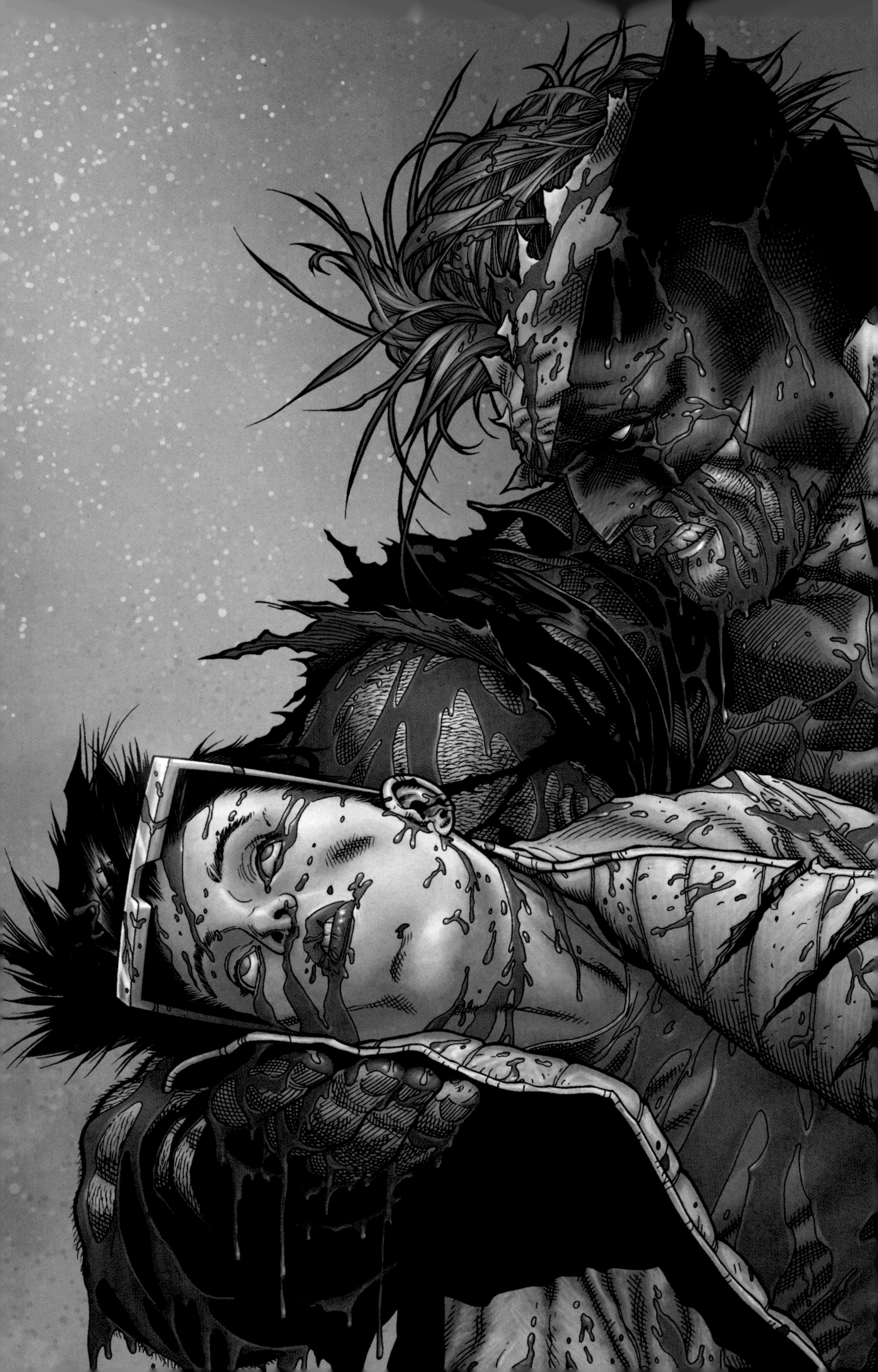

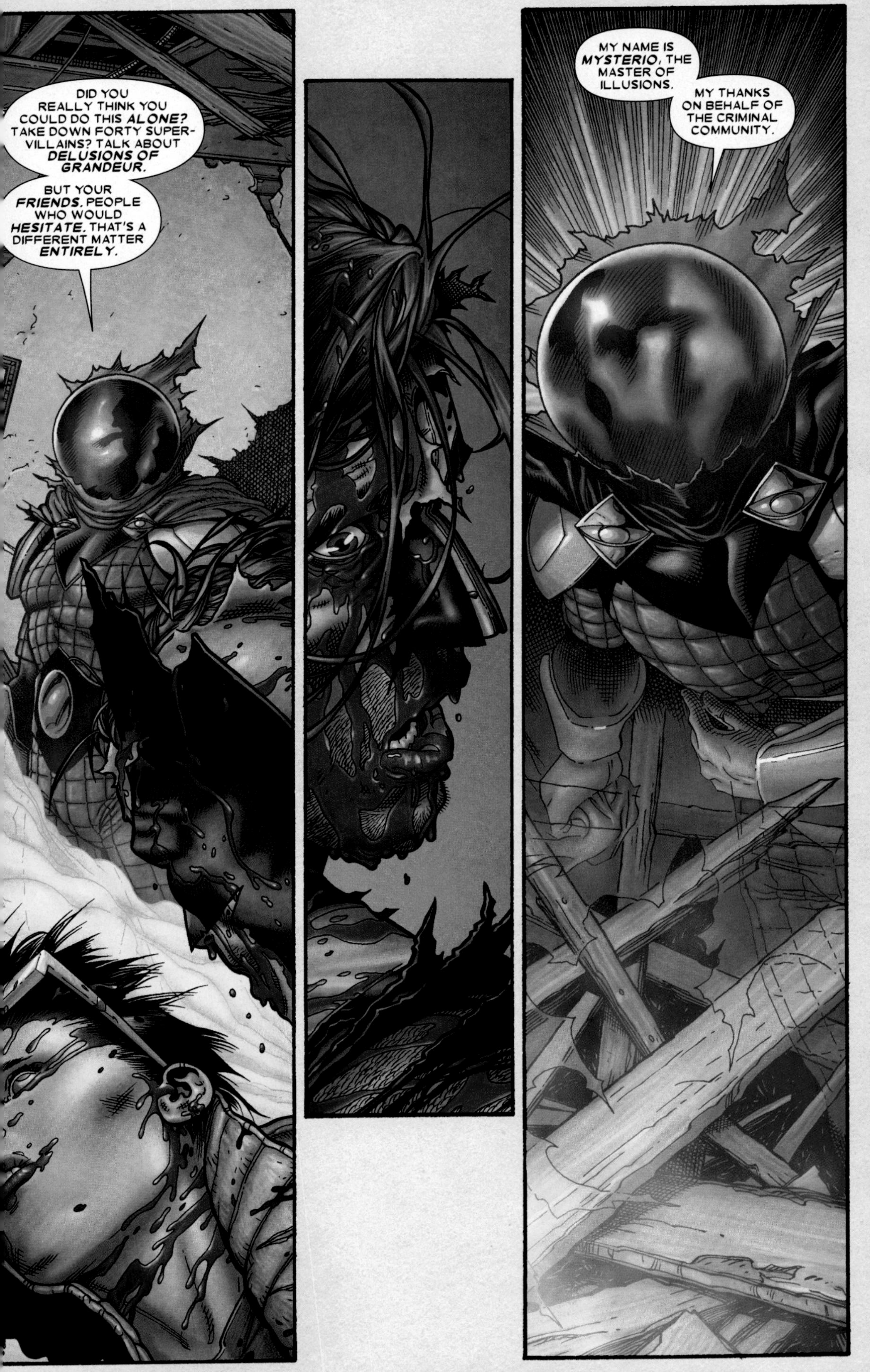
DID YOU REALLY THINK YOU COULD DO THIS ALONE? TAKE DOWN FORTY SUPER-VILLAINS? TALK ABOUT DELUSIONS OF GRANDEUR.
BUT YOUR FRIENDS, PEOPLE WHO WOULD HESITATE. THAT'S A DIFFERENT MATTER ENTIRELY.
MY NAME IS MYSTERIO, THE MASTER OF ILLUSIONS.
MY THANKS ON BEHALF OF THE CRIMINAL COMMUNITY.

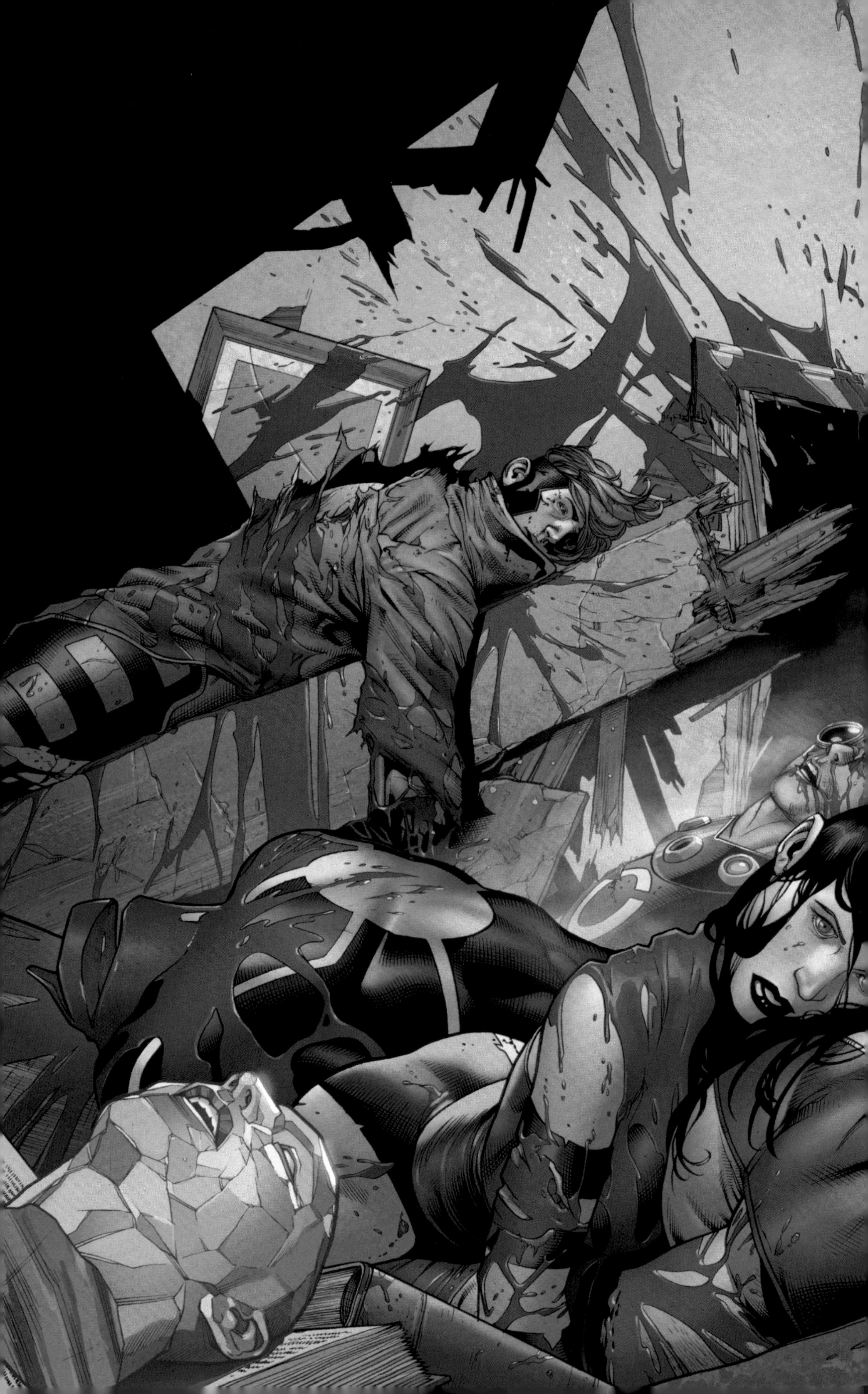

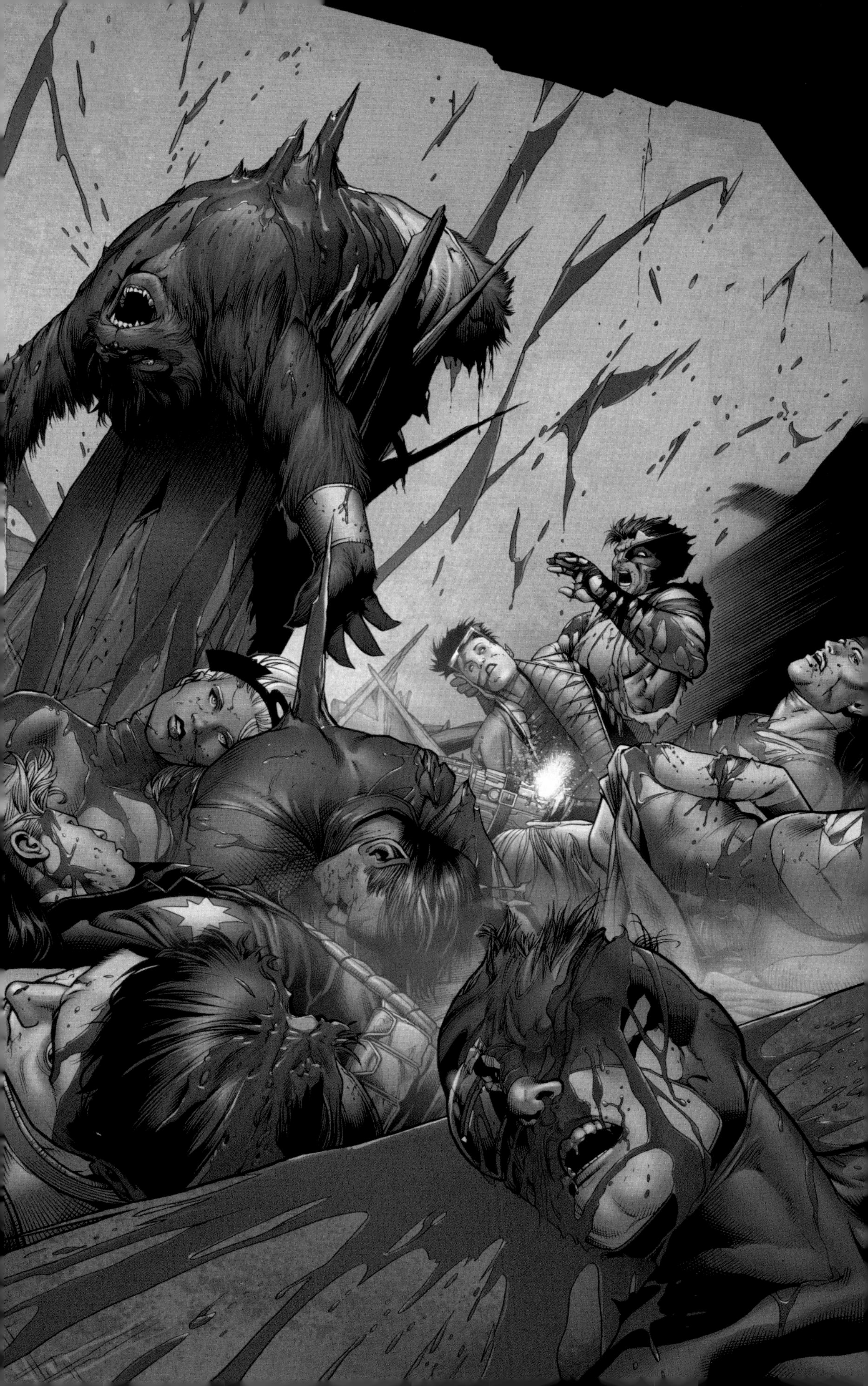

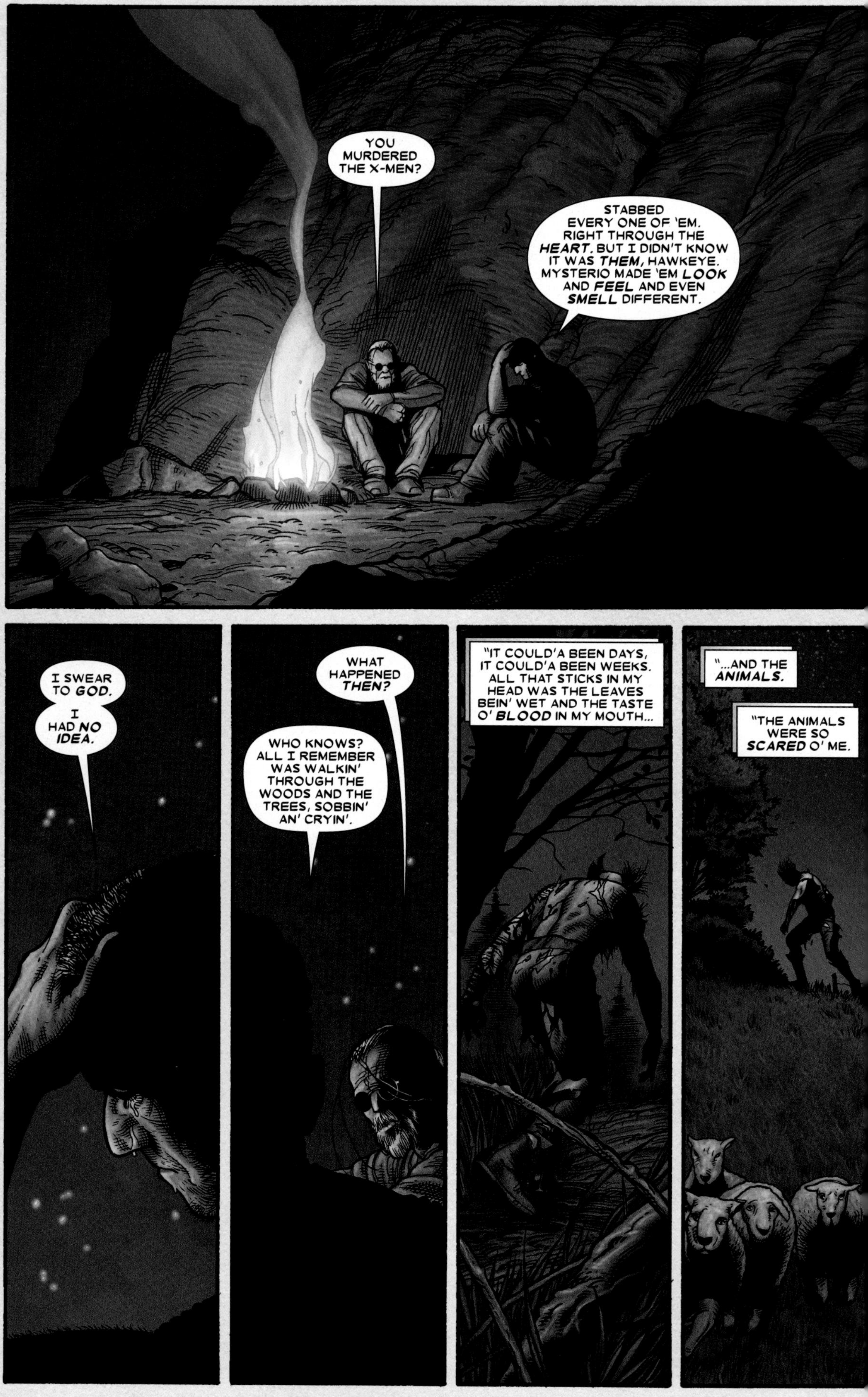
YOU MURDERED THE X-MEN?
STABBED EVERY ONE OF 'EM. RIGHT THROUGH THE HEART. BUT I DIDN'T KNOW IT WAS THEM, HAWKEYE. MYSTERIO MADE 'EM LOOK AND FEEL AND EVEN SMELL DIFFERENT.
I SWEAR TO GOD.
I HAD NO IDEA.
WHAT HAPPENED THEN?
WHO KNOWS? ALL I REMEMBER WAS WALKIN' THROUGH THE WOODS AND THE TREES, SOBBIN' AN' CRYIN'.
"IT COULD'A BEEN DAYS, IT COULD'A BEEN WEEKS. ALL THAT STICKS IN MY HEAD WAS THE LEAVES BEIN' WET AND THE TASTE O' BLOOD IN MY MOUTH...
"...AND THE ANIMALS.
"THE ANIMALS WERE SO SCARED O' ME.

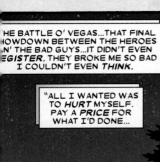

"HE BATTLE O' VEGAS...THAT FINAL HOWDOWN BETWEEN THE HEROES N' THE BAD GUYS...IT DIDN'T EVEN REGISTER. THEY BROKE ME SO BAD I COULDN'T EVEN *THINK*."

"ALL I WANTED WAS TO *HURT* MYSELF. PAY A *PRICE* FOR WHAT I'D DONE..."

"...SO I WAITED ON A *FREIGHT TRAIN*..."

"...AN' *KILLED WOLVERINE DEAD*."

BUT A *TRAIN* COULDN'T KILL YOU. NOT WITH YOUR *HEALING FACTOR.*

NO, BUT IT *HURT*...

...AN' SOMETIMES THAT'S *ENOUGH*.

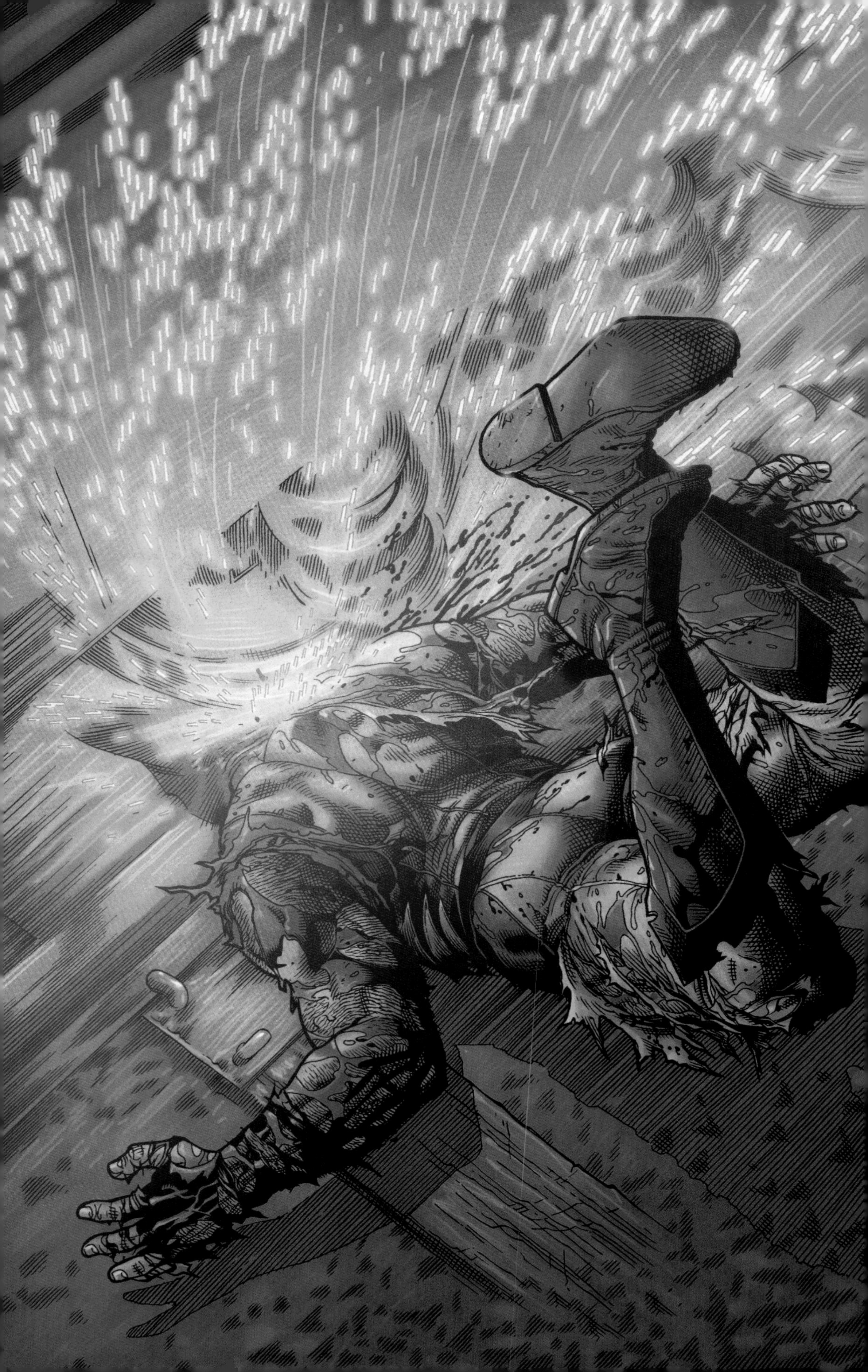

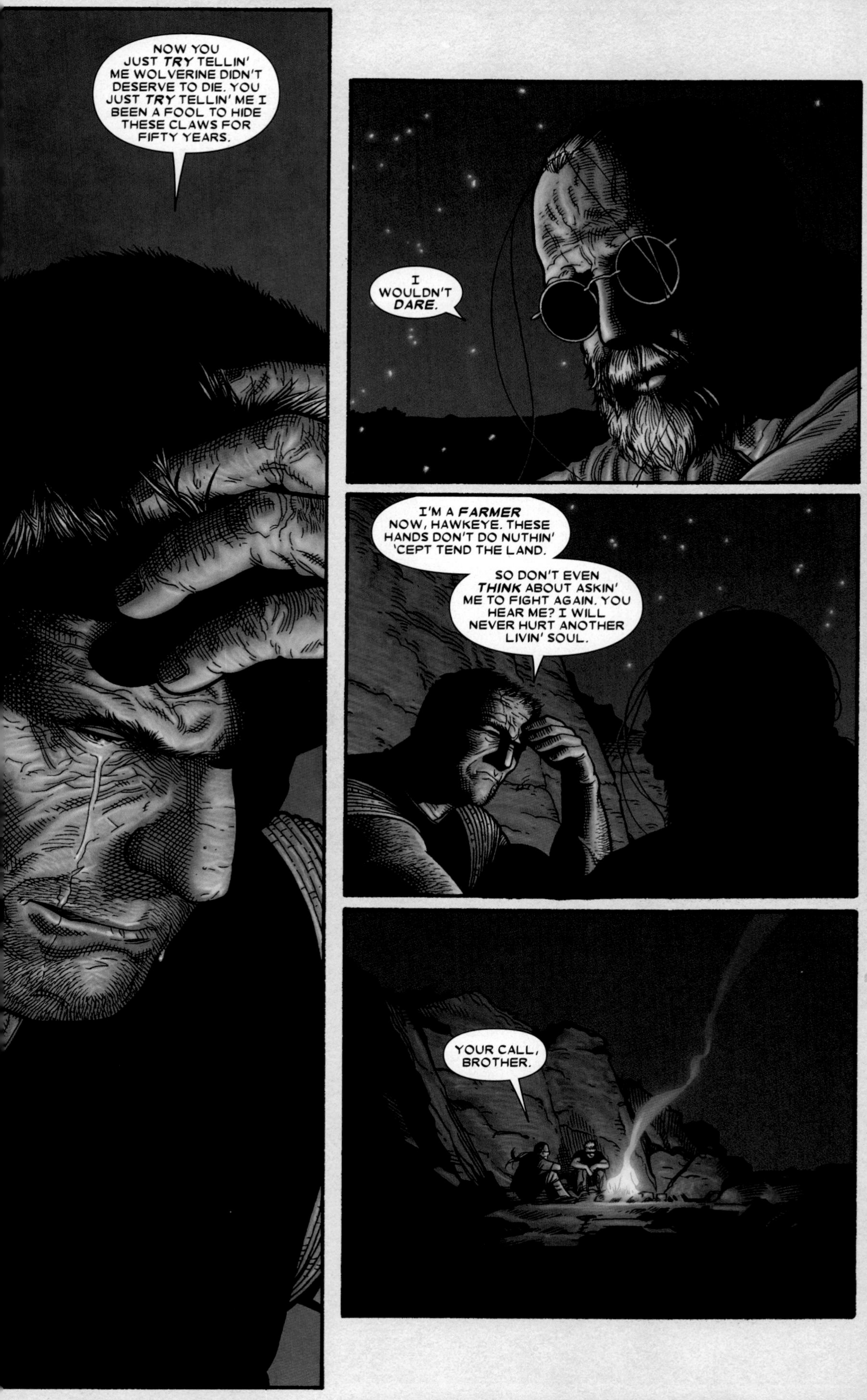
NOW YOU JUST TRY TELLIN' ME WOLVERINE DIDN'T DESERVE TO DIE. YOU JUST TRY TELLIN' ME I BEEN A FOOL TO HIDE THESE CLAWS FOR FIFTY YEARS.
I WOULDN'T DARE.
I'M A FARMER NOW, HAWKEYE. THESE HANDS DON'T DO NUTHIN' 'CEPT TEND THE LAND.
SO DON'T EVEN THINK ABOUT ASKIN' ME TO FIGHT AGAIN. YOU HEAR ME? I WILL NEVER HURT ANOTHER LIVIN' SOUL.
YOUR CALL, BROTHER.

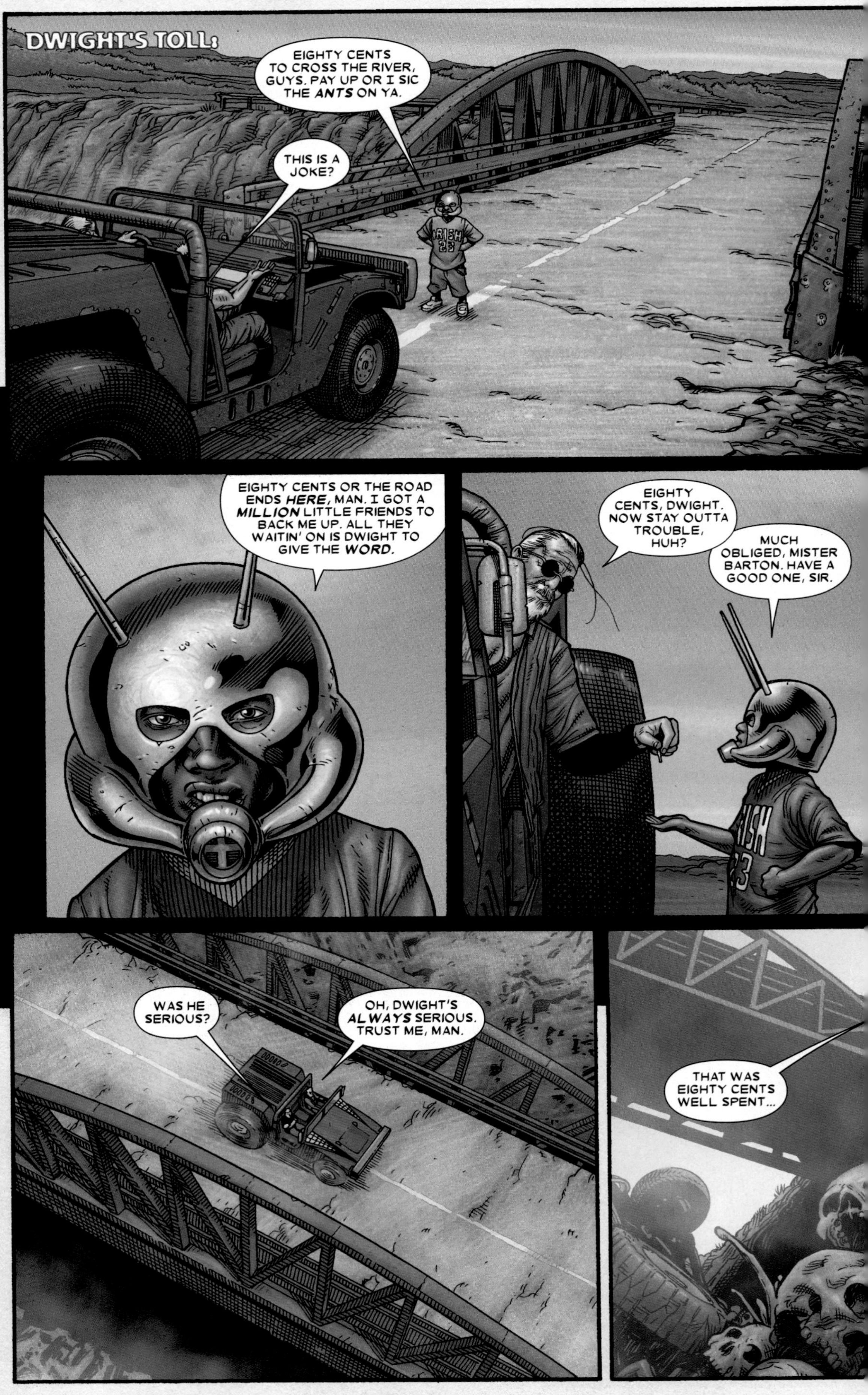
DWIGHT'S TOLL:
EIGHTY CENTS TO CROSS THE RIVER, GUYS. PAY UP OR I SIC THE ANTS ON YA.
THIS IS A JOKE?
EIGHTY CENTS OR THE ROAD ENDS HERE, MAN. I GOT A MILLION LITTLE FRIENDS TO BACK ME UP. ALL THEY WAITIN' ON IS DWIGHT TO GIVE THE WORD.
EIGHTY CENTS, DWIGHT. NOW STAY OUTTA TROUBLE, HUH?
MUCH OBLIGED, MISTER BARTON. HAVE A GOOD ONE, SIR.
WAS HE SERIOUS?
OH, DWIGHT'S ALWAYS SERIOUS. TRUST ME, MAN.
THAT WAS EIGHTY CENTS WELL SPENT...

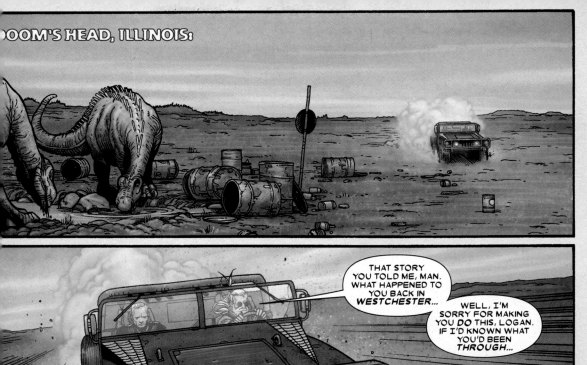

THAT STORY YOU TOLD ME, MAN. WHAT HAPPENED TO YOU BACK IN *WESTCHESTER...*

WELL, I'M SORRY FOR MAKING YOU DO THIS, LOGAN. IF I'D KNOWN WHAT YOU'D BEEN *THROUGH...*

FORGET ABOUT IT, BUB.

THE PAST ONLY HURTS IF WE LET IT *CATCH UP* WITH US.

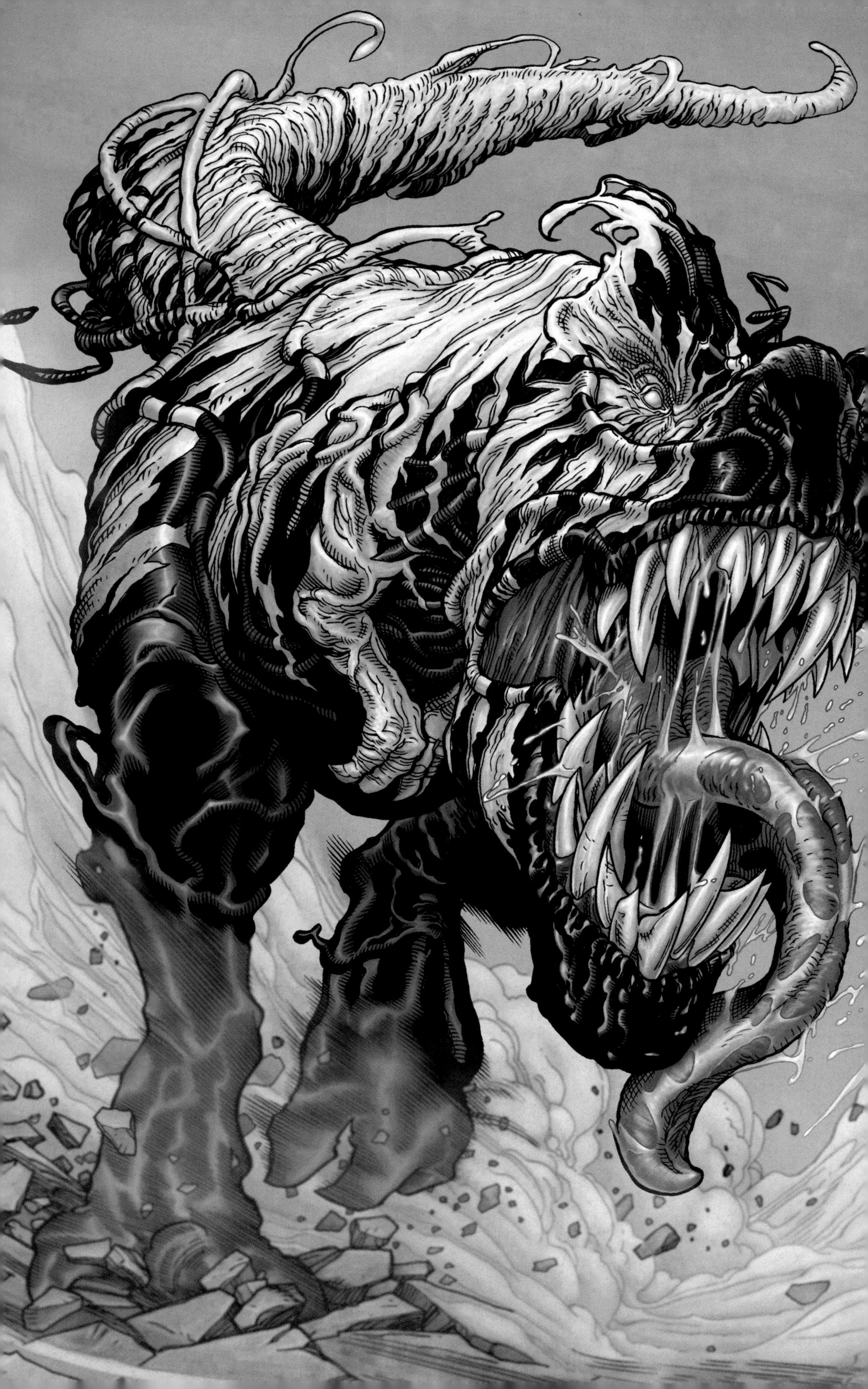

CHAPTER SIX

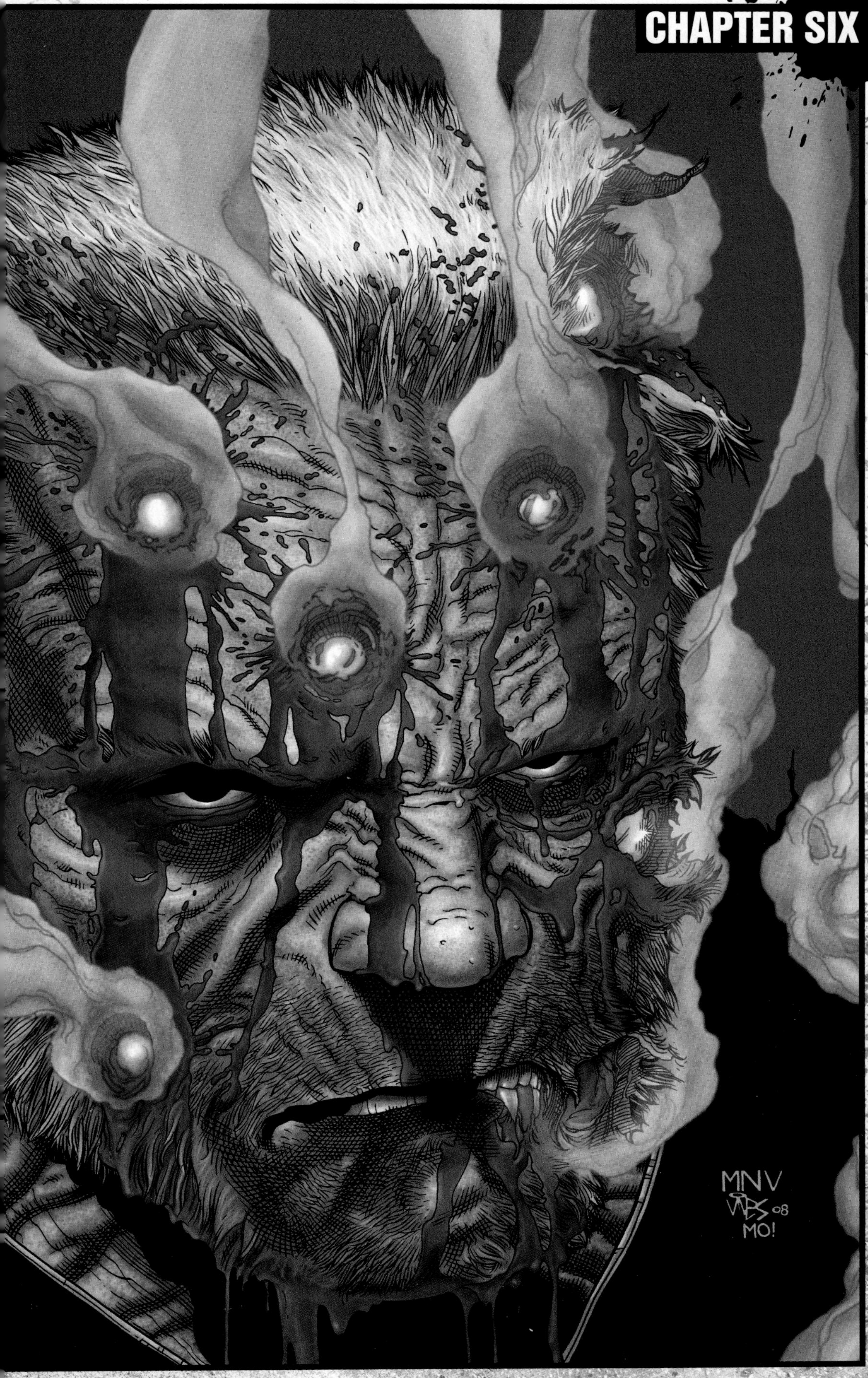

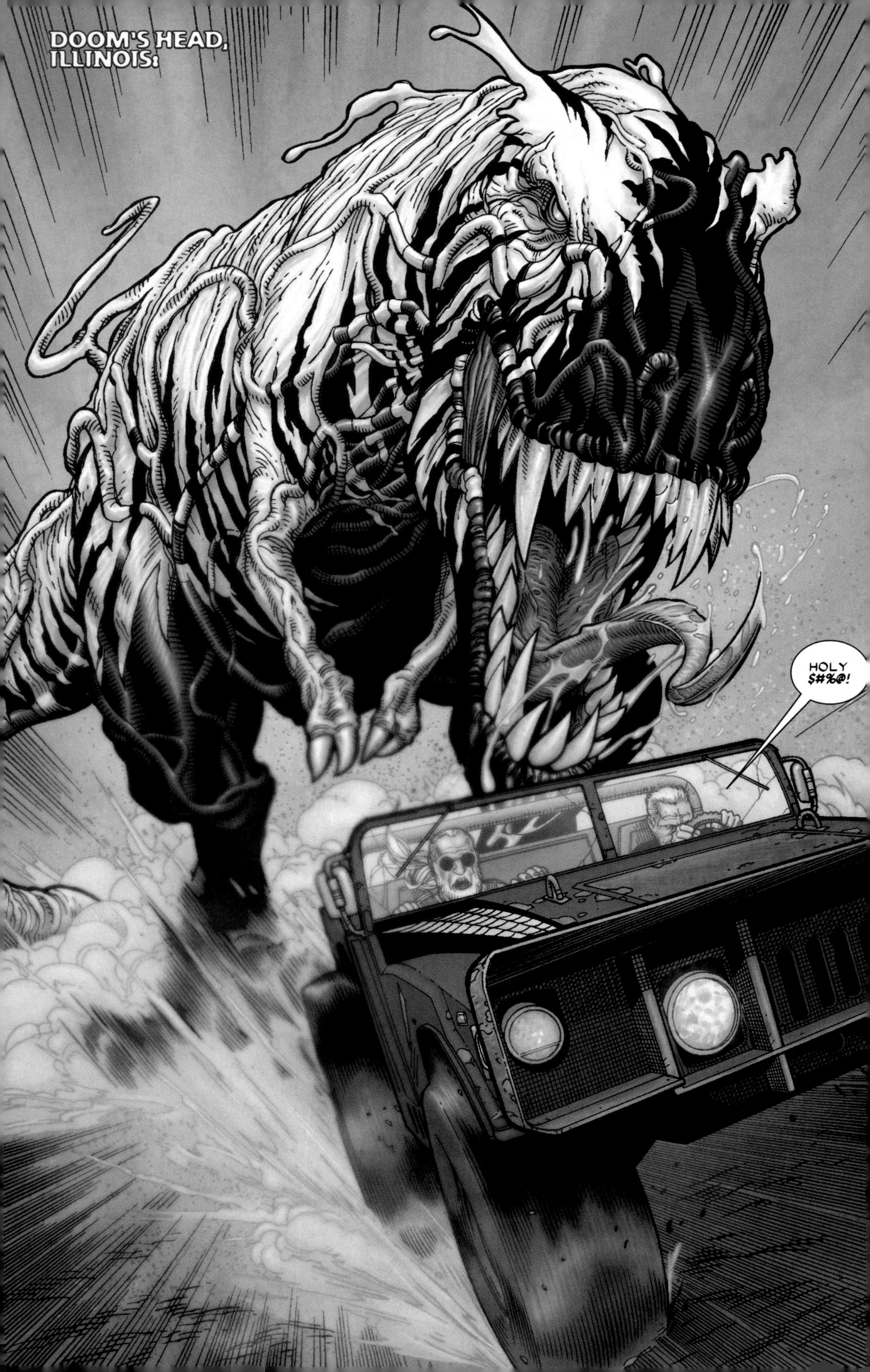
DOOM'S HEAD, ILLINOIS:
HOLY $#%@!

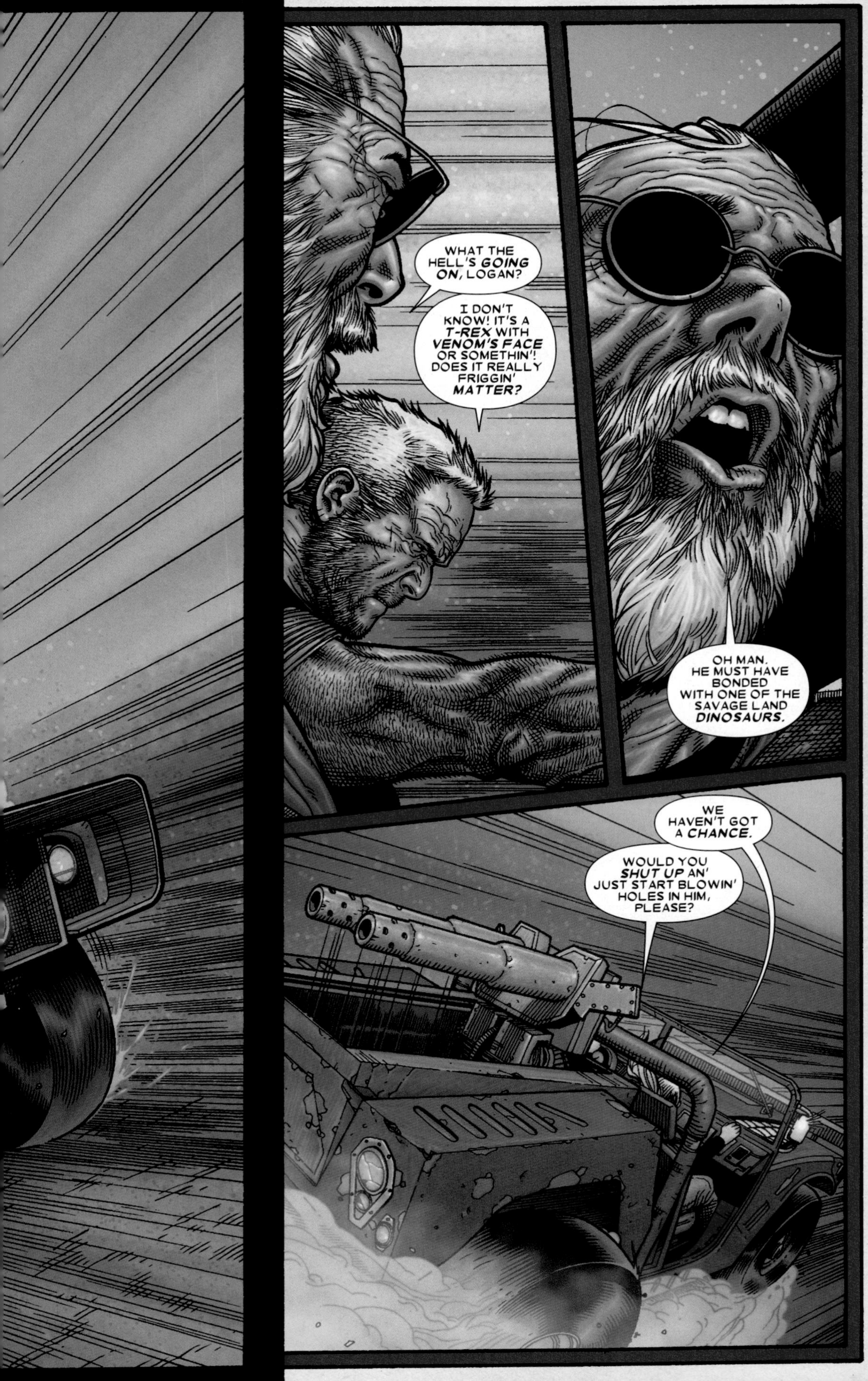
WHAT THE HELL'S GOING ON, LOGAN?
I DON'T KNOW! IT'S A T-REX WITH VENOM'S FACE OR SOMETHIN'! DOES IT REALLY FRIGGIN' MATTER?
OH MAN. HE MUST HAVE BONDED WITH ONE OF THE SAVAGE LAND DINOSAURS.
WE HAVEN'T GOT A CHANCE.
WOULD YOU SHUT UP AN' JUST START BLOWIN' HOLES IN HIM, PLEASE?

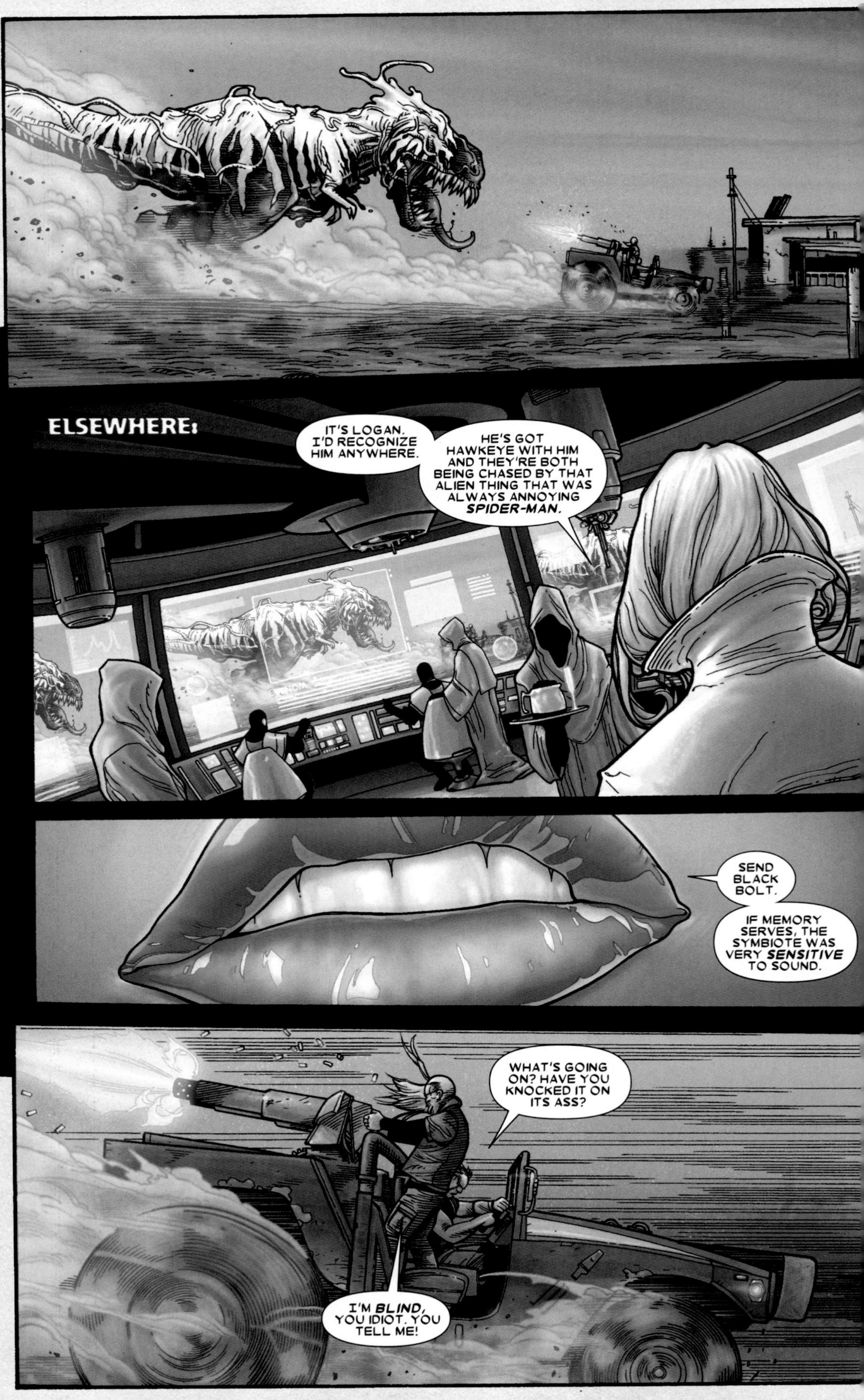
ELSEWHERE:
IT'S LOGAN. I'D RECOGNIZE HIM ANYWHERE.
HE'S GOT HAWKEYE WITH HIM AND THEY'RE BOTH BEING CHASED BY THAT ALIEN THING THAT WAS ALWAYS ANNOYING SPIDER-MAN.
SEND BLACK BOLT.
IF MEMORY SERVES, THE SYMBIOTE WAS VERY SENSITIVE TO SOUND.
WHAT'S GOING ON? HAVE YOU KNOCKED IT ON ITS ASS?
I'M BLIND, YOU IDIOT. YOU TELL ME!

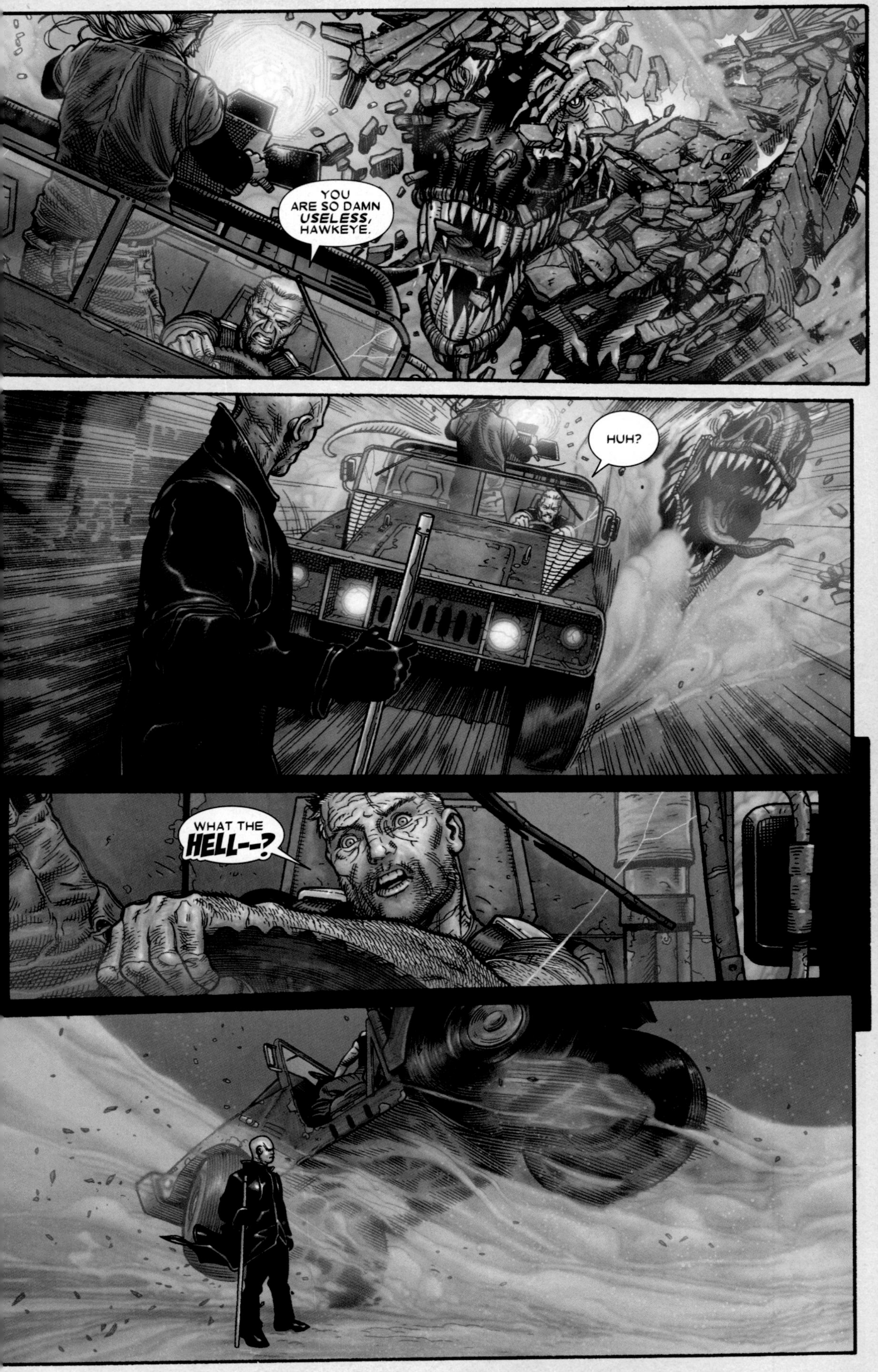
YOU ARE SO DAMN USELESS, HAWKEYE.
HUH?
WHAT THE HELL--?

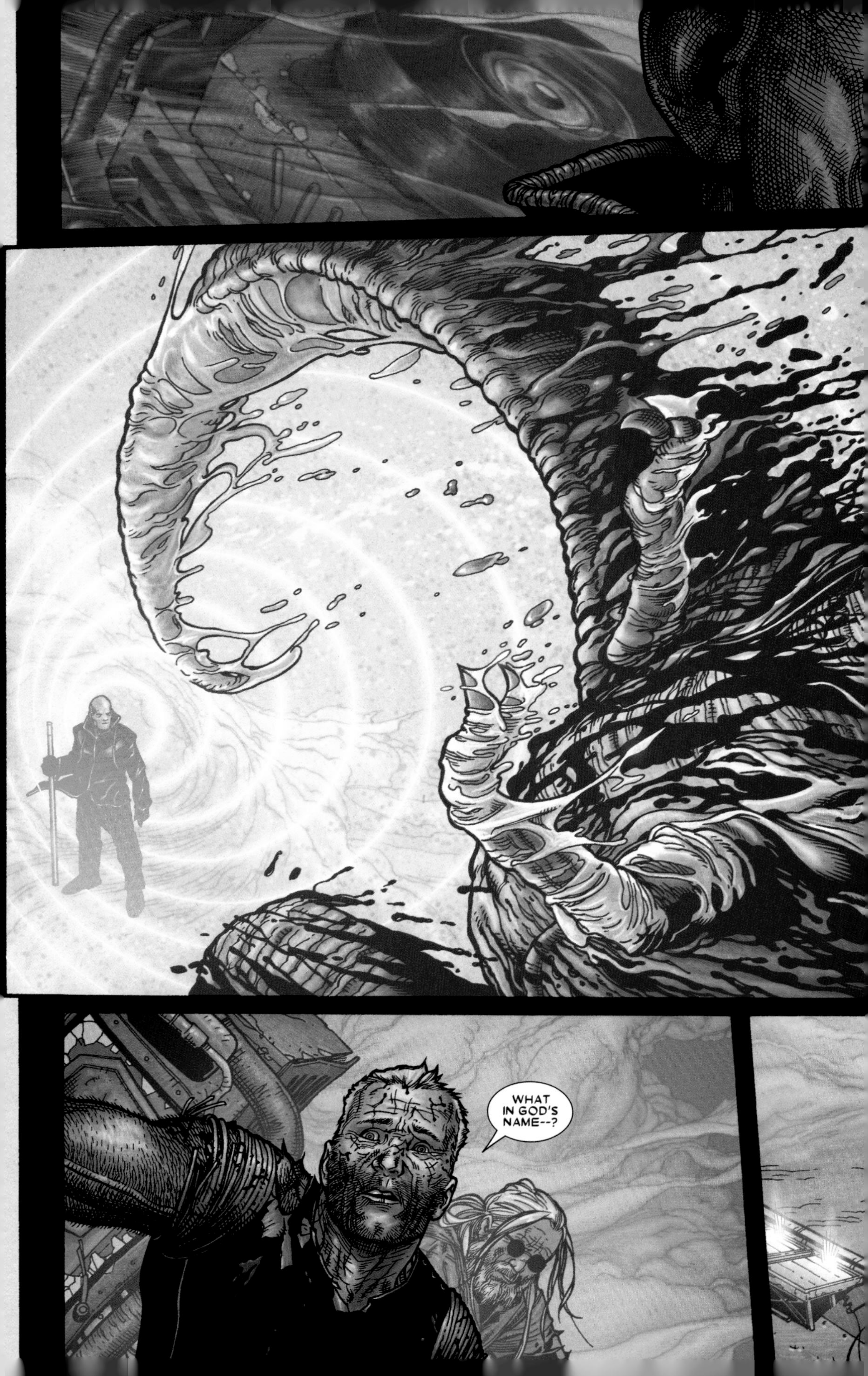
WHAT IN GOD'S NAME--?

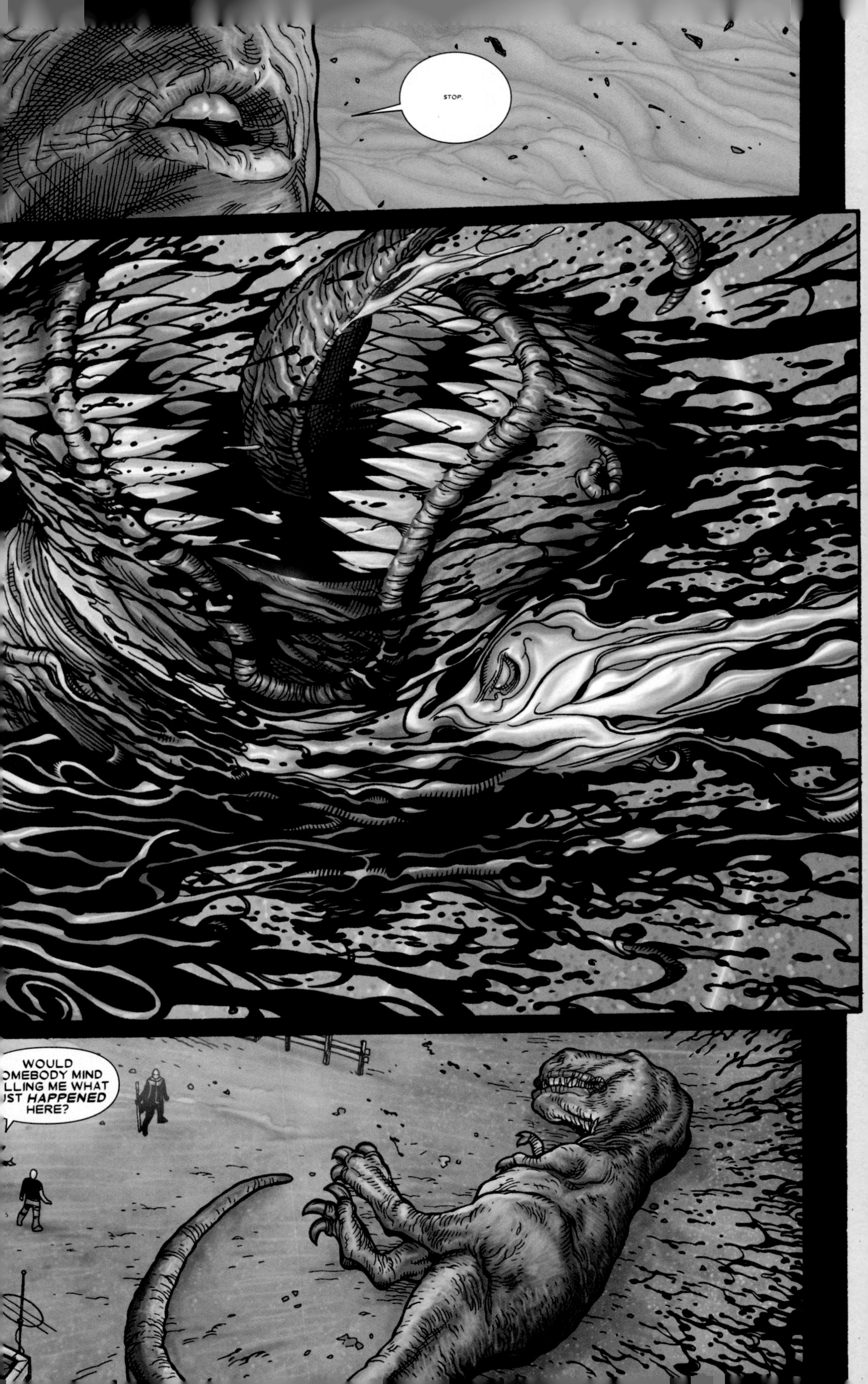
STOP.
WOULD OMEBODY MIND LLING ME WHAT UST *HAPPENED* HERE?

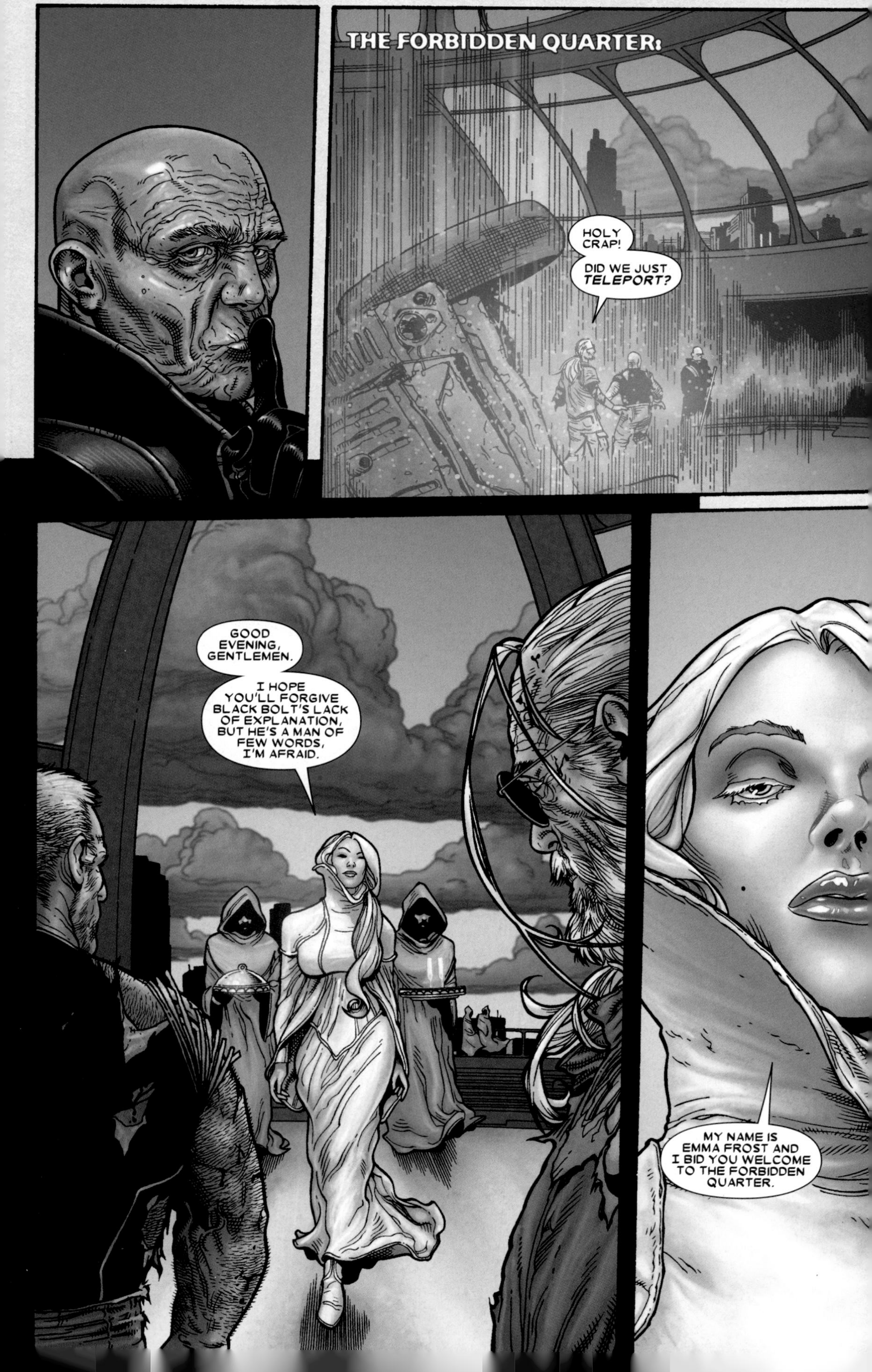
THE FORBIDDEN QUARTER:
HOLY CRAP!
DID WE JUST *TELEPORT?*
GOOD EVENING, GENTLEMEN.
I HOPE YOU'LL FORGIVE BLACK BOLT'S LACK OF EXPLANATION, BUT HE'S A MAN OF FEW WORDS, I'M AFRAID.
MY NAME IS EMMA FROST AND I BID YOU WELCOME TO THE FORBIDDEN QUARTER.

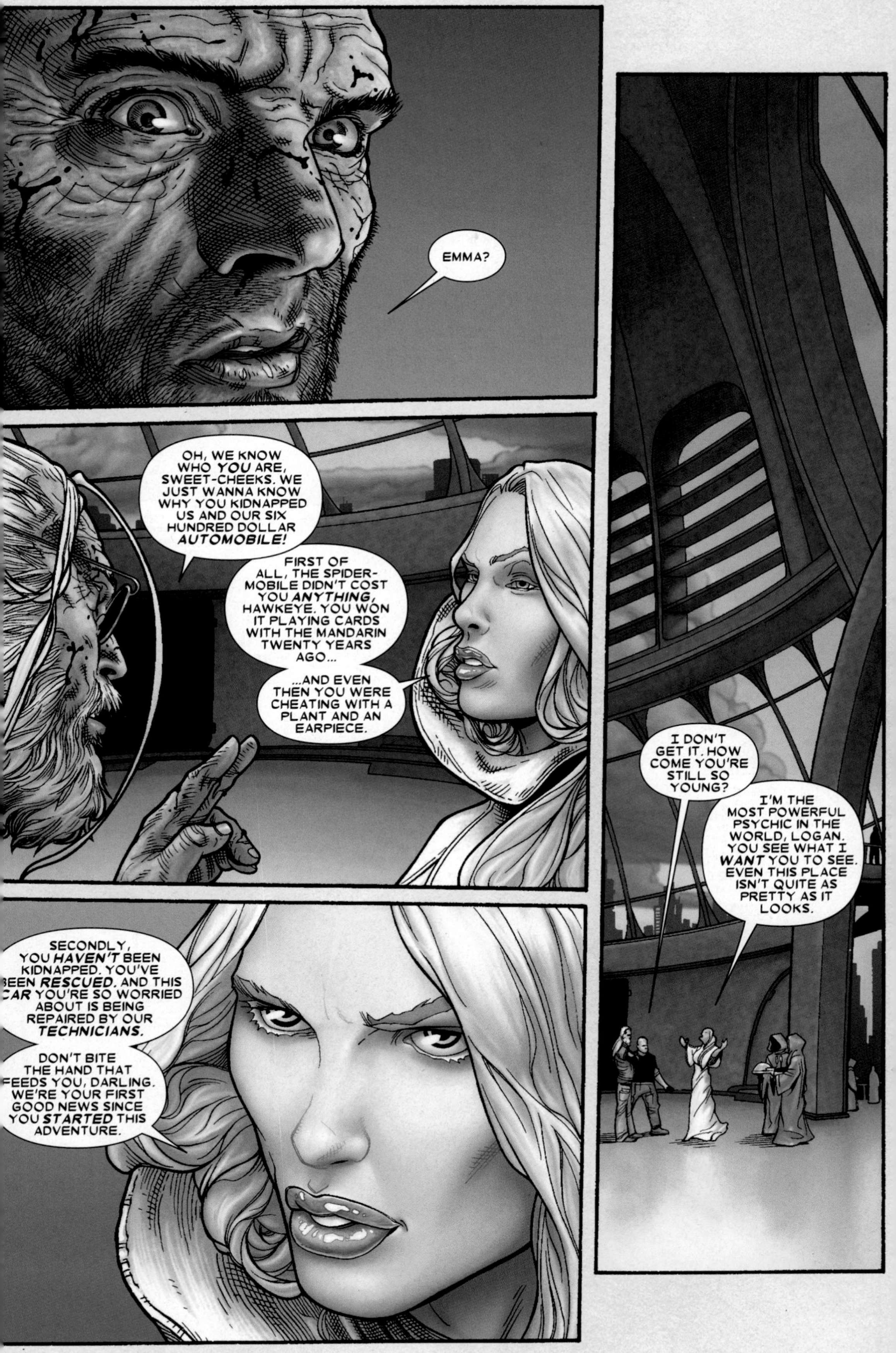
EMMA?
OH, WE KNOW WHO YOU ARE, SWEET-CHEEKS. WE JUST WANNA KNOW WHY YOU KIDNAPPED US AND OUR SIX HUNDRED DOLLAR AUTOMOBILE!
FIRST OF ALL, THE SPIDER-MOBILE DIDN'T COST YOU ANYTHING, HAWKEYE. YOU WON IT PLAYING CARDS WITH THE MANDARIN TWENTY YEARS AGO...
...AND EVEN THEN YOU WERE CHEATING WITH A PLANT AND AN EARPIECE.
SECONDLY, YOU HAVEN'T BEEN KIDNAPPED. YOU'VE BEEN RESCUED. AND THIS CAR YOU'RE SO WORRIED ABOUT IS BEING REPAIRED BY OUR TECHNICIANS.
DON'T BITE THE HAND THAT FEEDS YOU, DARLING. WE'RE YOUR FIRST GOOD NEWS SINCE YOU STARTED THIS ADVENTURE.
I DON'T GET IT. HOW COME YOU'RE STILL SO YOUNG?
I'M THE MOST POWERFUL PSYCHIC IN THE WORLD, LOGAN. YOU SEE WHAT I WANT YOU TO SEE. EVEN THIS PLACE ISN'T QUITE AS PRETTY AS IT LOOKS.

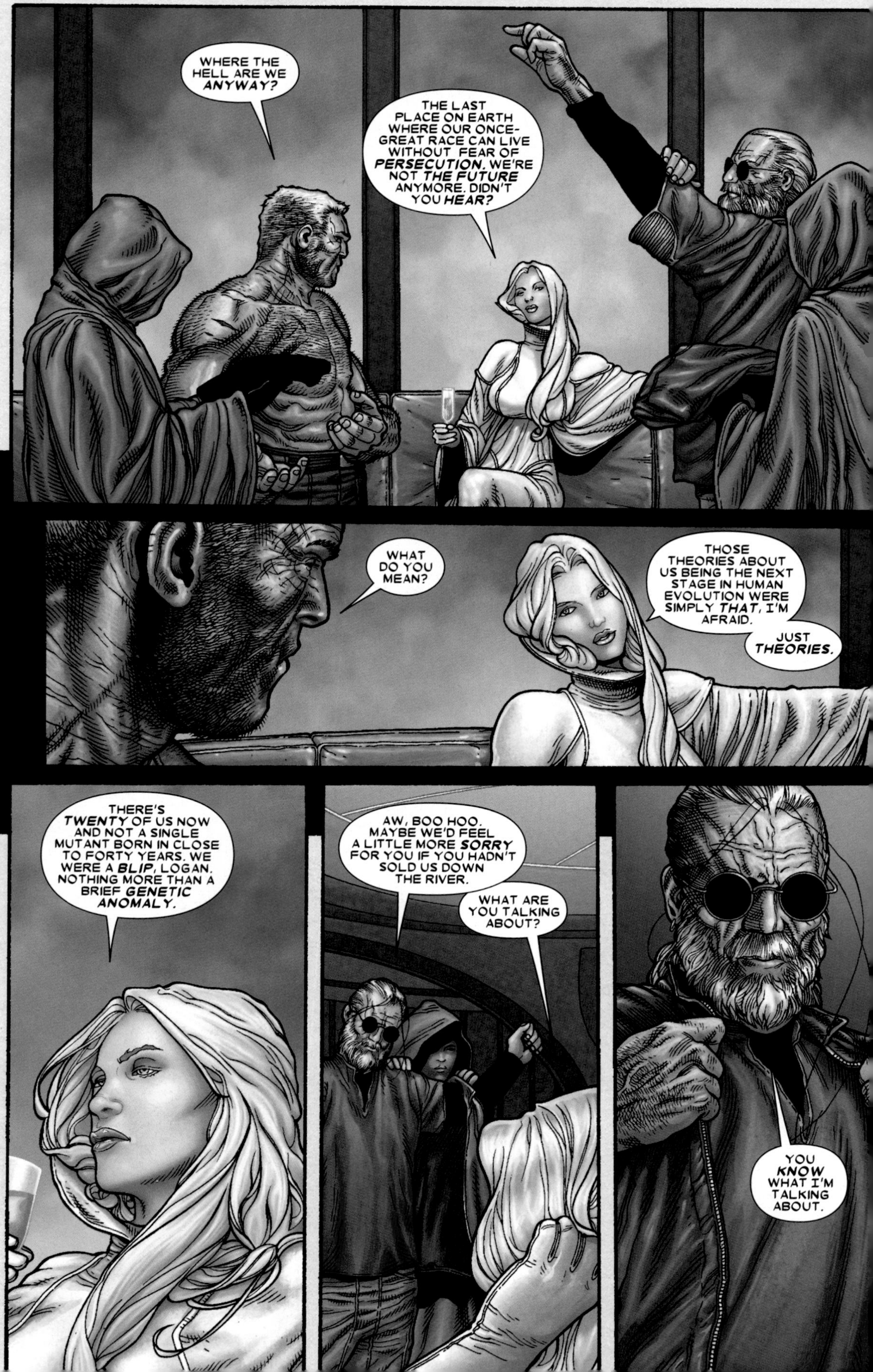
WHERE THE HELL ARE WE *ANYWAY?*
THE LAST PLACE ON EARTH WHERE OUR ONCE-GREAT RACE CAN LIVE WITHOUT FEAR OF *PERSECUTION*. WE'RE NOT *THE FUTURE* ANYMORE. DIDN'T YOU *HEAR?*
WHAT DO YOU MEAN?
THOSE THEORIES ABOUT US BEING THE NEXT STAGE IN HUMAN EVOLUTION WERE SIMPLY *THAT*, I'M AFRAID.
JUST *THEORIES.*
THERE'S *TWENTY* OF US NOW AND NOT A SINGLE MUTANT BORN IN CLOSE TO FORTY YEARS. WE WERE A *BLIP*, LOGAN. NOTHING MORE THAN A BRIEF *GENETIC ANOMALY.*
AW, BOO HOO. MAYBE WE'D FEEL A LITTLE MORE *SORRY* FOR YOU IF YOU HADN'T SOLD US DOWN THE RIVER.
WHAT ARE YOU TALKING ABOUT?
YOU *KNOW* WHAT I'M TALKING ABOUT.

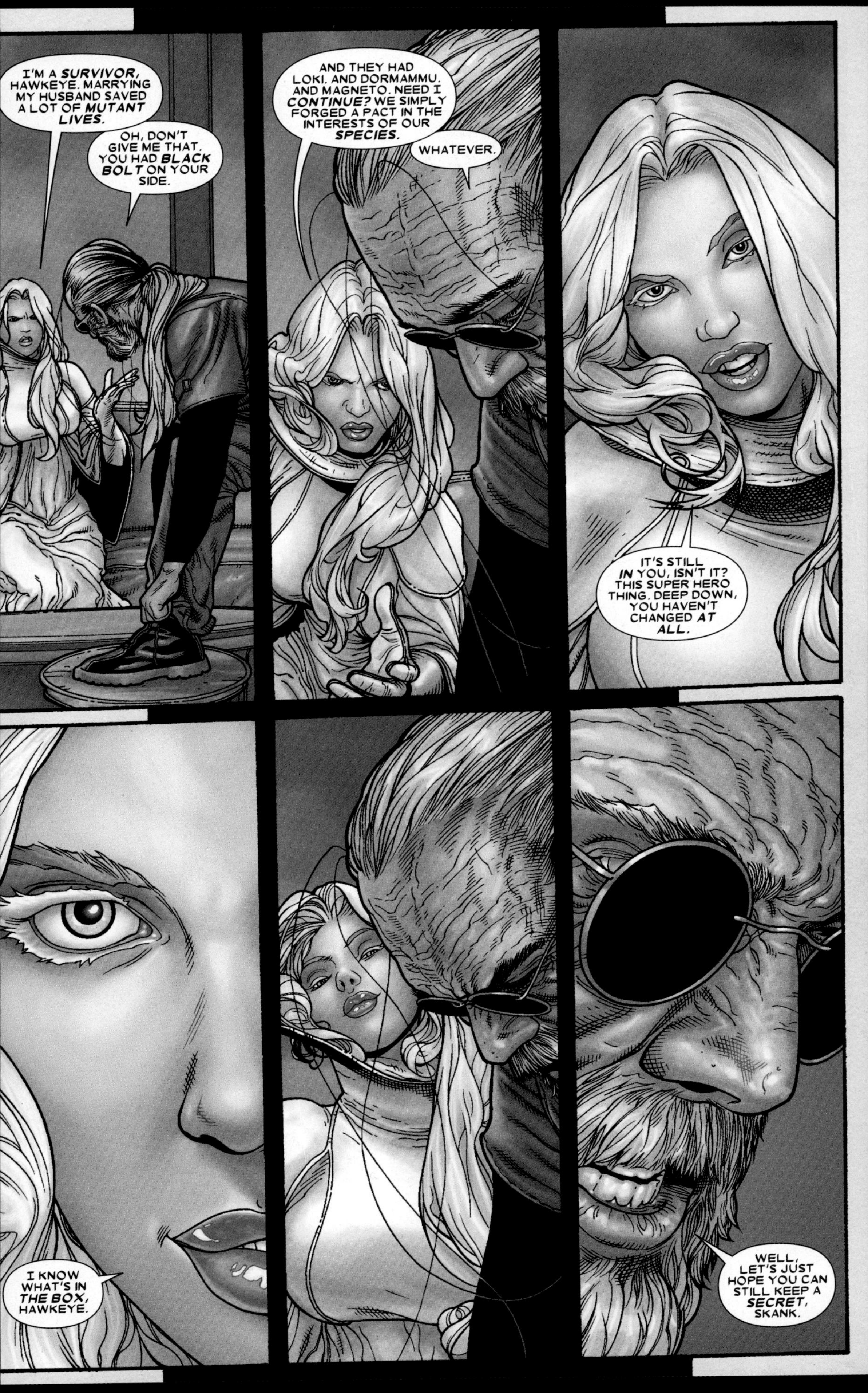
I'M A SURVIVOR, HAWKEYE. MARRYING MY HUSBAND SAVED A LOT OF MUTANT LIVES.
OH, DON'T GIVE ME THAT. YOU HAD BLACK BOLT ON YOUR SIDE.
AND THEY HAD LOKI. AND DORMAMMU. AND MAGNETO. NEED I CONTINUE? WE SIMPLY FORGED A PACT IN THE INTERESTS OF OUR SPECIES.
WHATEVER.
IT'S STILL IN YOU, ISN'T IT? THIS SUPER HERO THING. DEEP DOWN, YOU HAVEN'T CHANGED AT ALL.
I KNOW WHAT'S IN THE BOX, HAWKEYE.
WELL, LET'S JUST HOPE YOU CAN STILL KEEP A SECRET, SKANK.

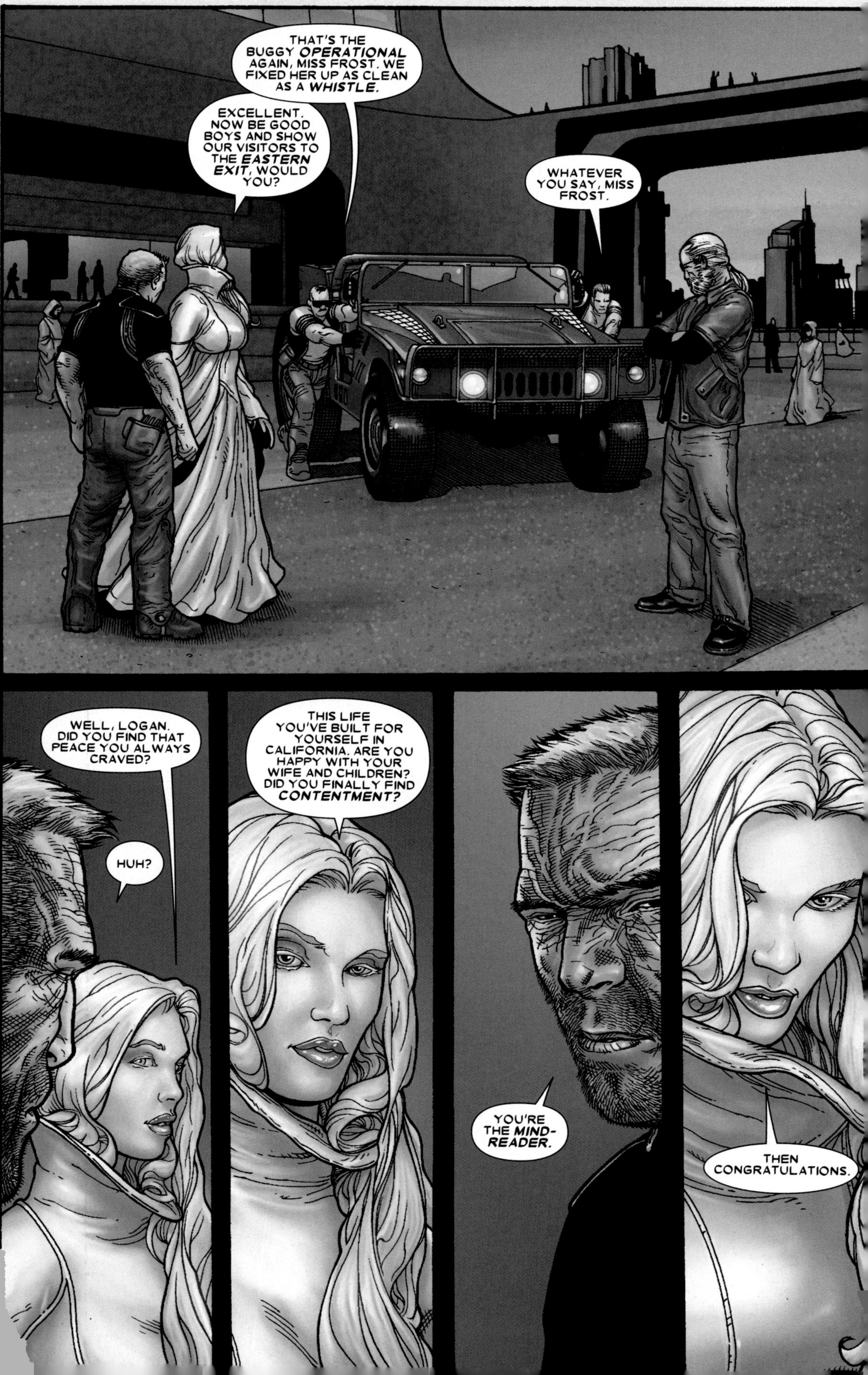
THAT'S THE BUGGY OPERATIONAL AGAIN, MISS FROST. WE FIXED HER UP AS CLEAN AS A WHISTLE.
EXCELLENT. NOW BE GOOD BOYS AND SHOW OUR VISITORS TO THE EASTERN EXIT, WOULD YOU?
WHATEVER YOU SAY, MISS FROST.
WELL, LOGAN. DID YOU FIND THAT PEACE YOU ALWAYS CRAVED?
HUH?
THIS LIFE YOU'VE BUILT FOR YOURSELF IN CALIFORNIA. ARE YOU HAPPY WITH YOUR WIFE AND CHILDREN? DID YOU FINALLY FIND CONTENTMENT?
YOU'RE THE MIND-READER.
THEN CONGRATULATIONS.

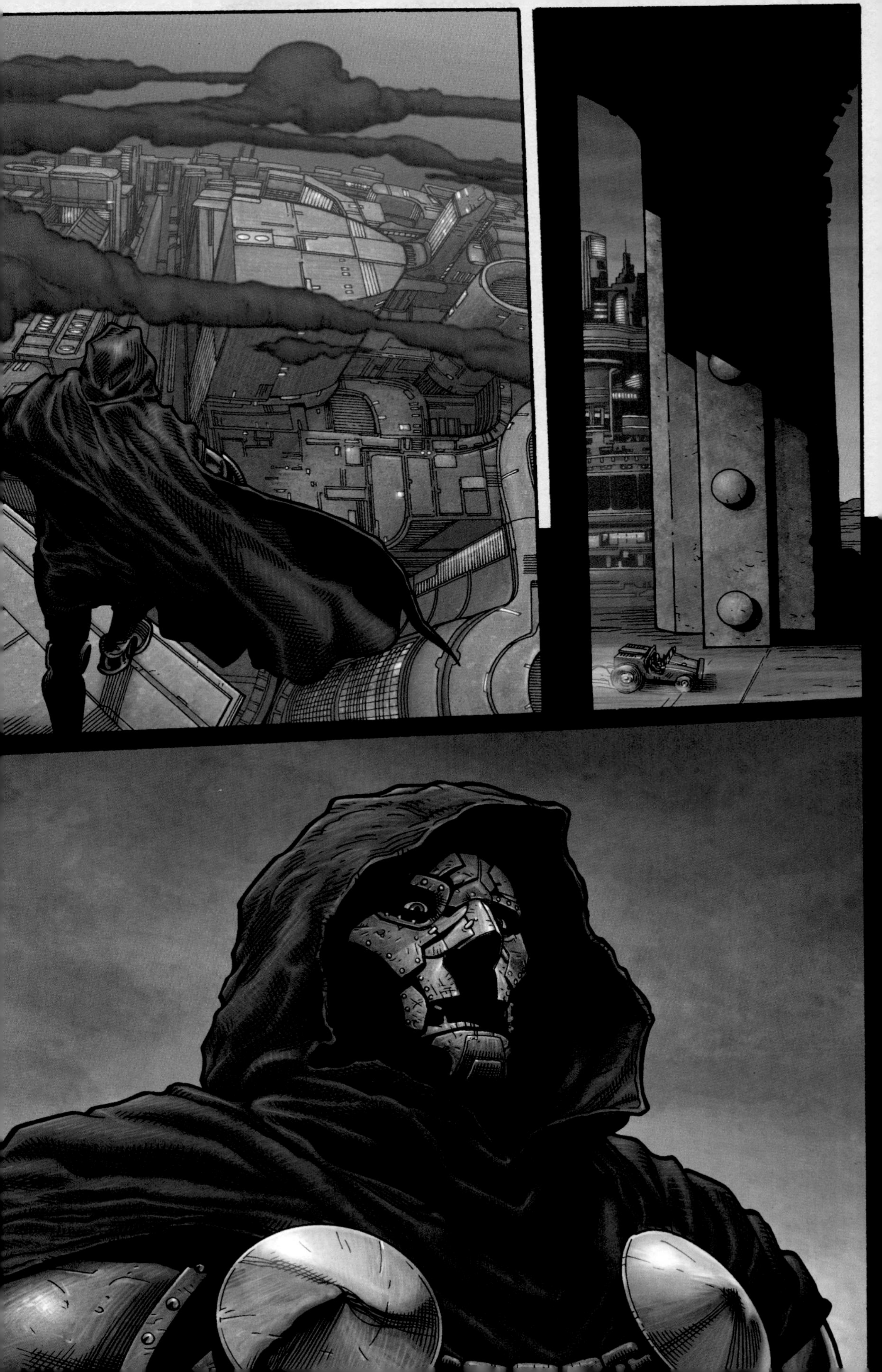

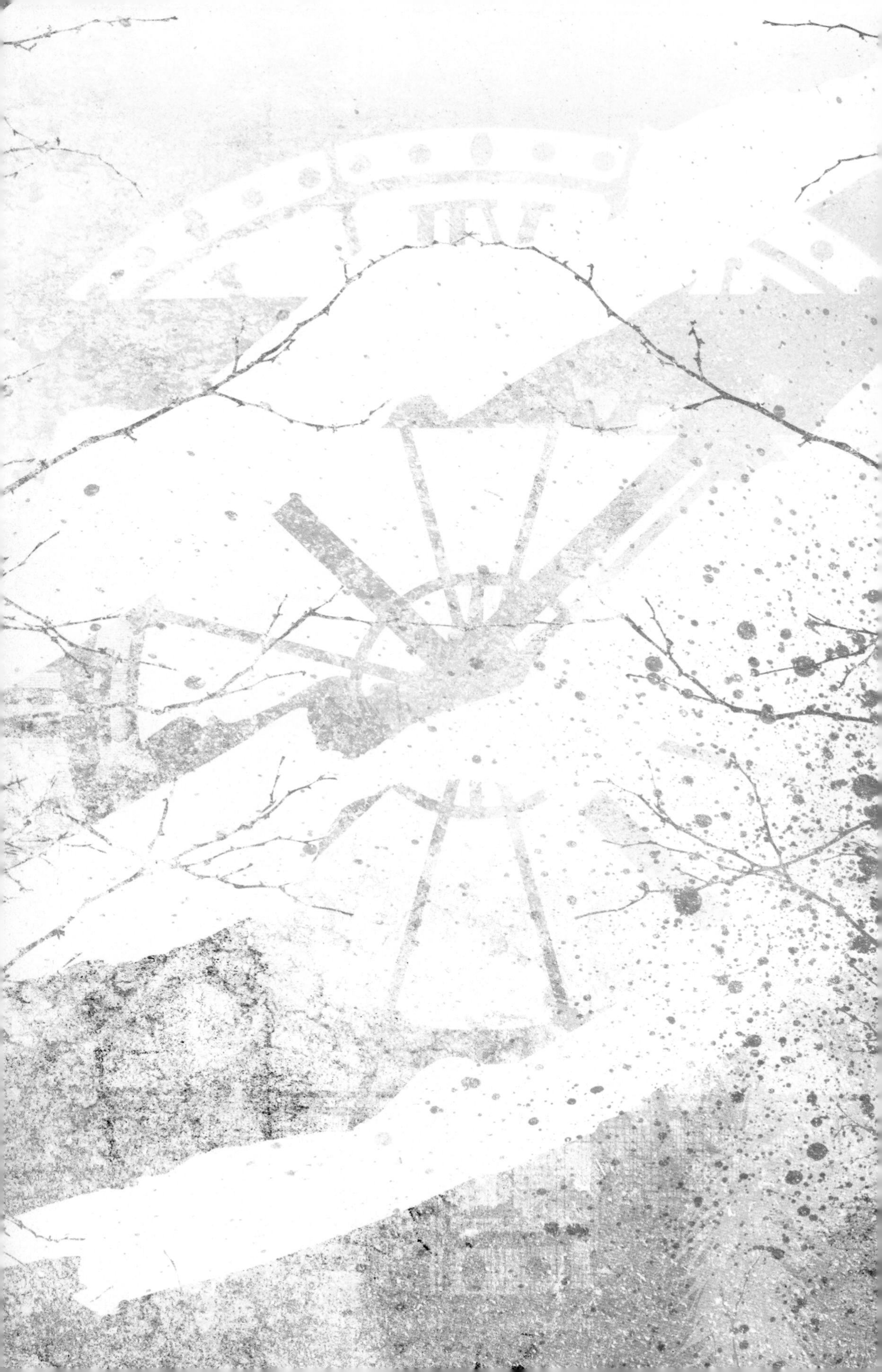

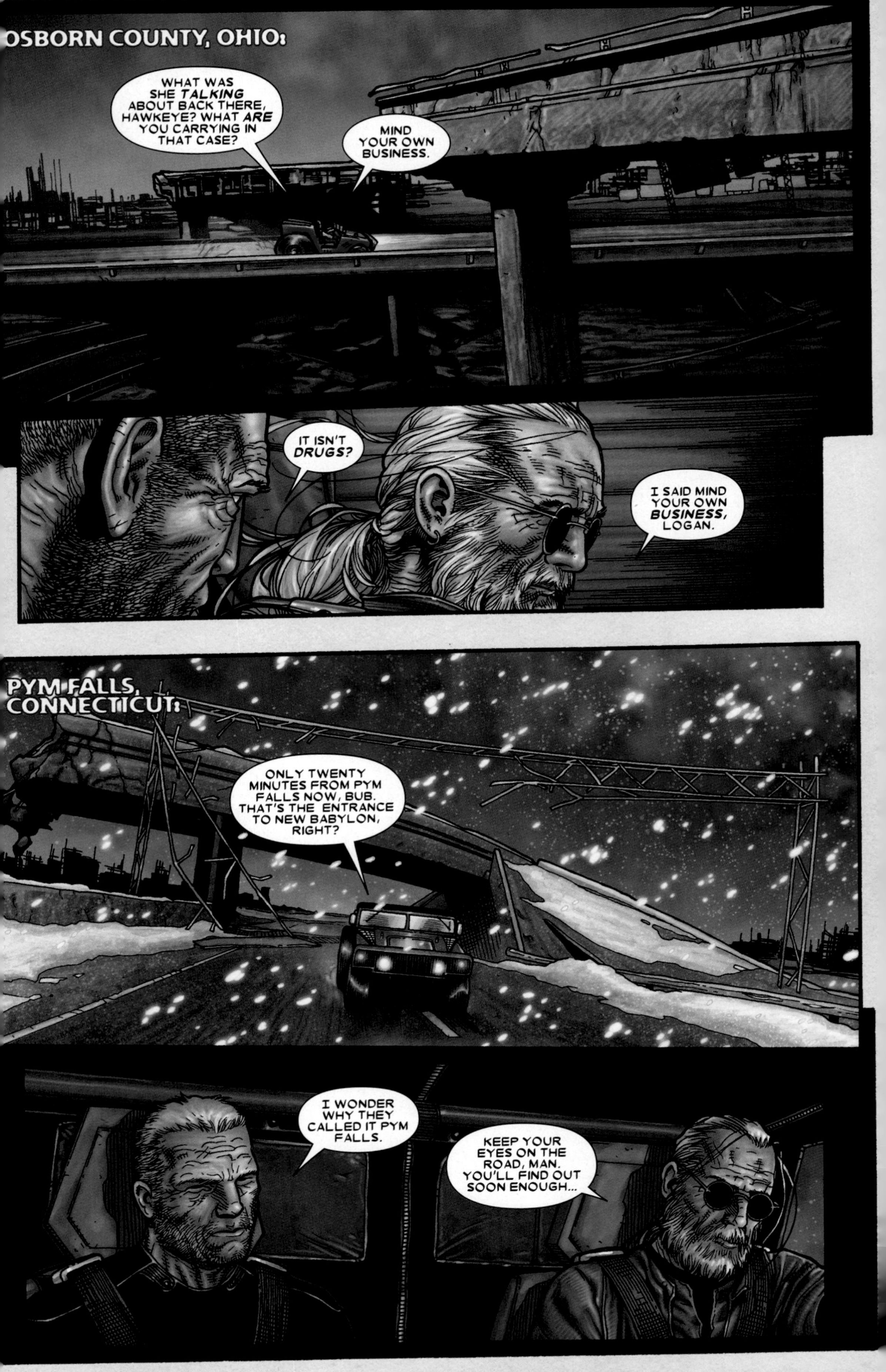
OSBORN COUNTY, OHIO:
WHAT WAS SHE TALKING ABOUT BACK THERE, HAWKEYE? WHAT ARE YOU CARRYING IN THAT CASE?
MIND YOUR OWN BUSINESS.
IT ISN'T DRUGS?
I SAID MIND YOUR OWN BUSINESS, LOGAN.
PYM FALLS, CONNECTICUT:
ONLY TWENTY MINUTES FROM PYM FALLS NOW, BUB. THAT'S THE ENTRANCE TO NEW BABYLON, RIGHT?
I WONDER WHY THEY CALLED IT PYM FALLS.
KEEP YOUR EYES ON THE ROAD, MAN. YOU'LL FIND OUT SOON ENOUGH...

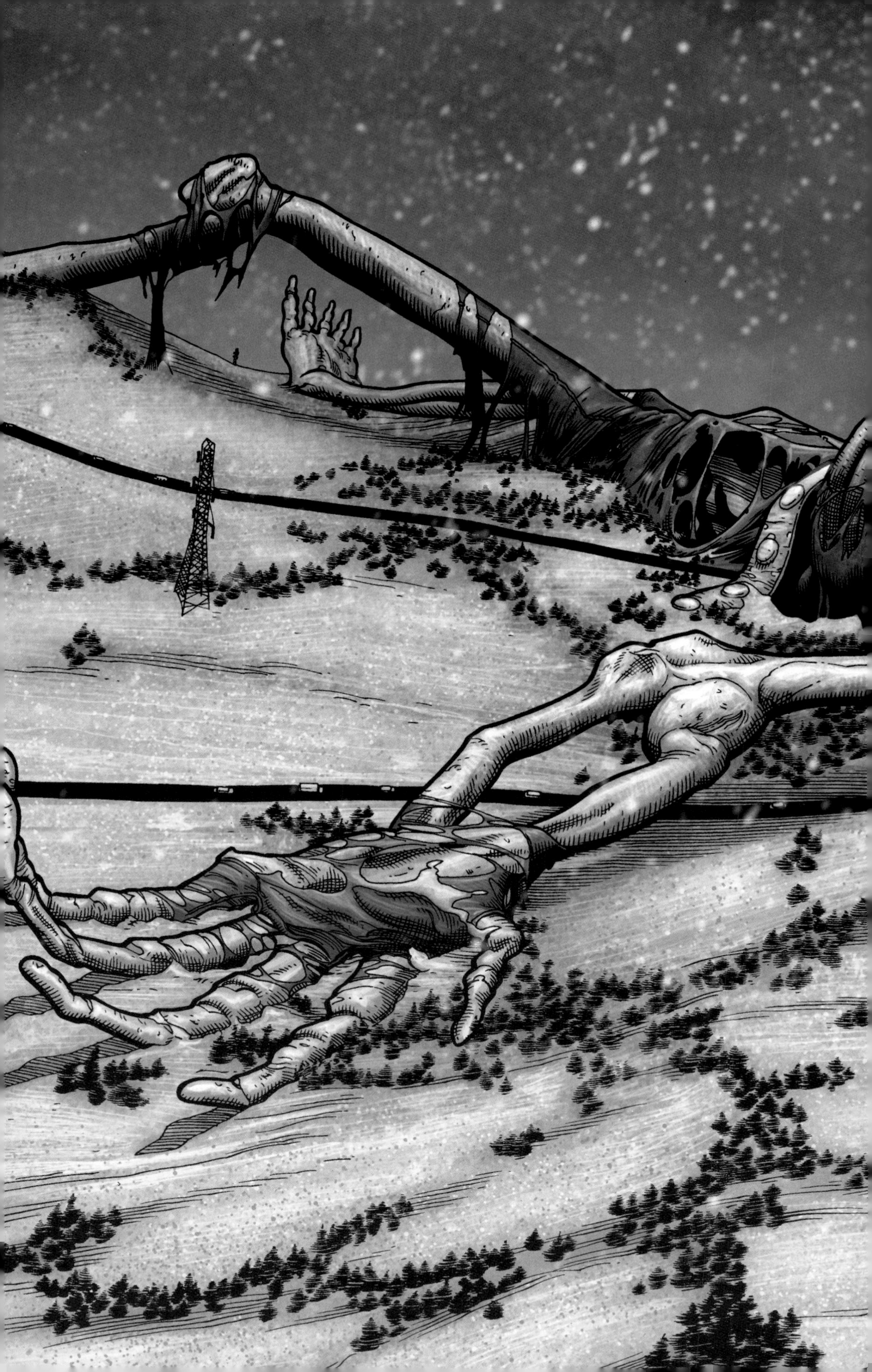

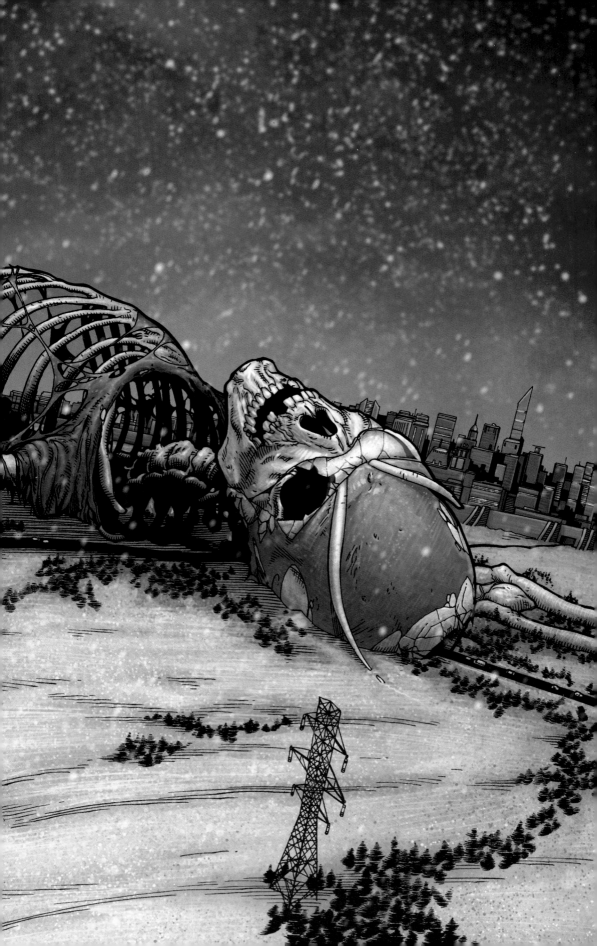

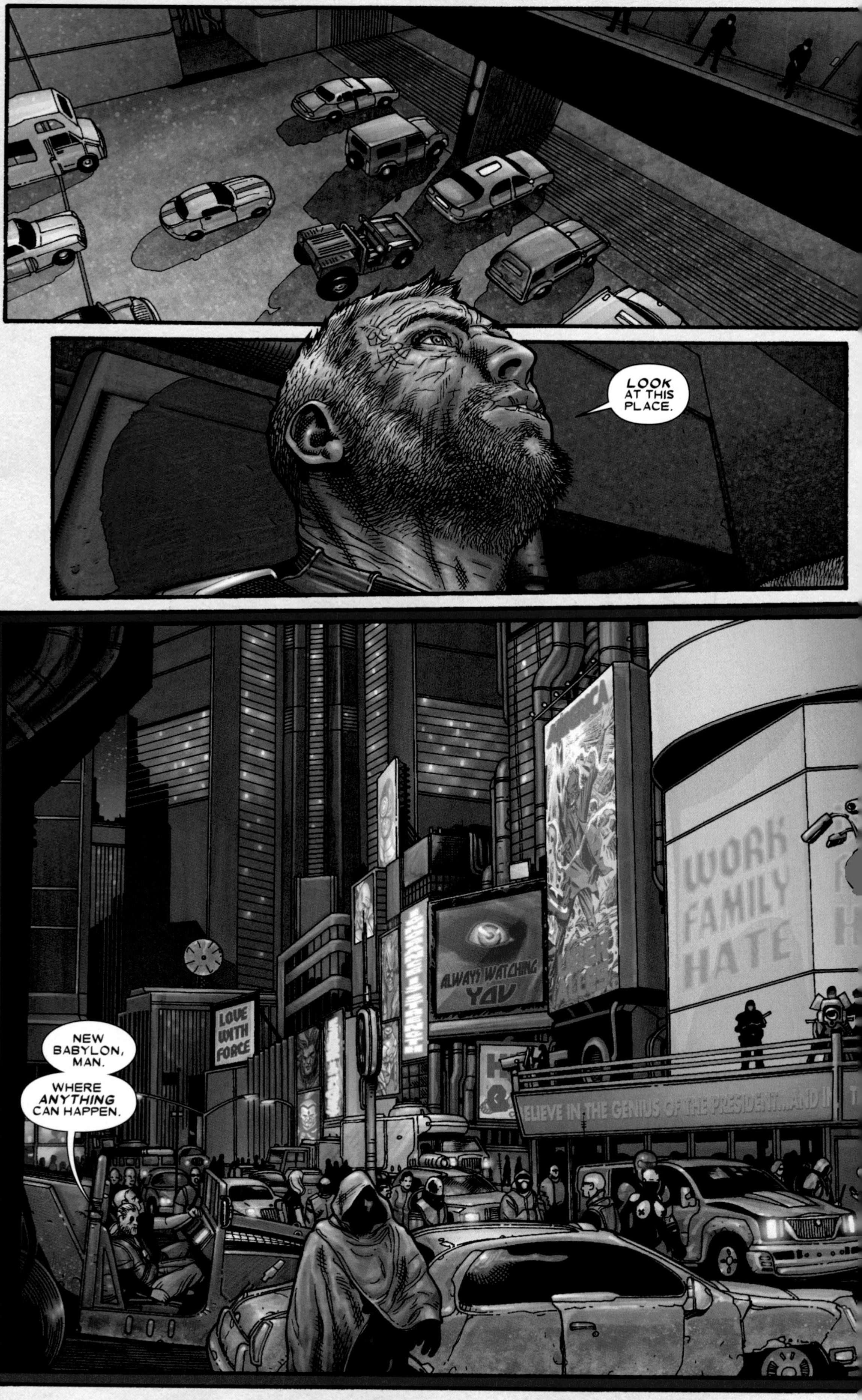
LOOK AT THIS PLACE.
ALWAYS WATCHING YOU
WORK FAMILY HATE
LOVE WITH FORCE
ELIEVE IN THE GENIUS OF THE PRESIDENT...AND I
NEW BABYLON, MAN.
WHERE ANYTHING CAN HAPPEN.

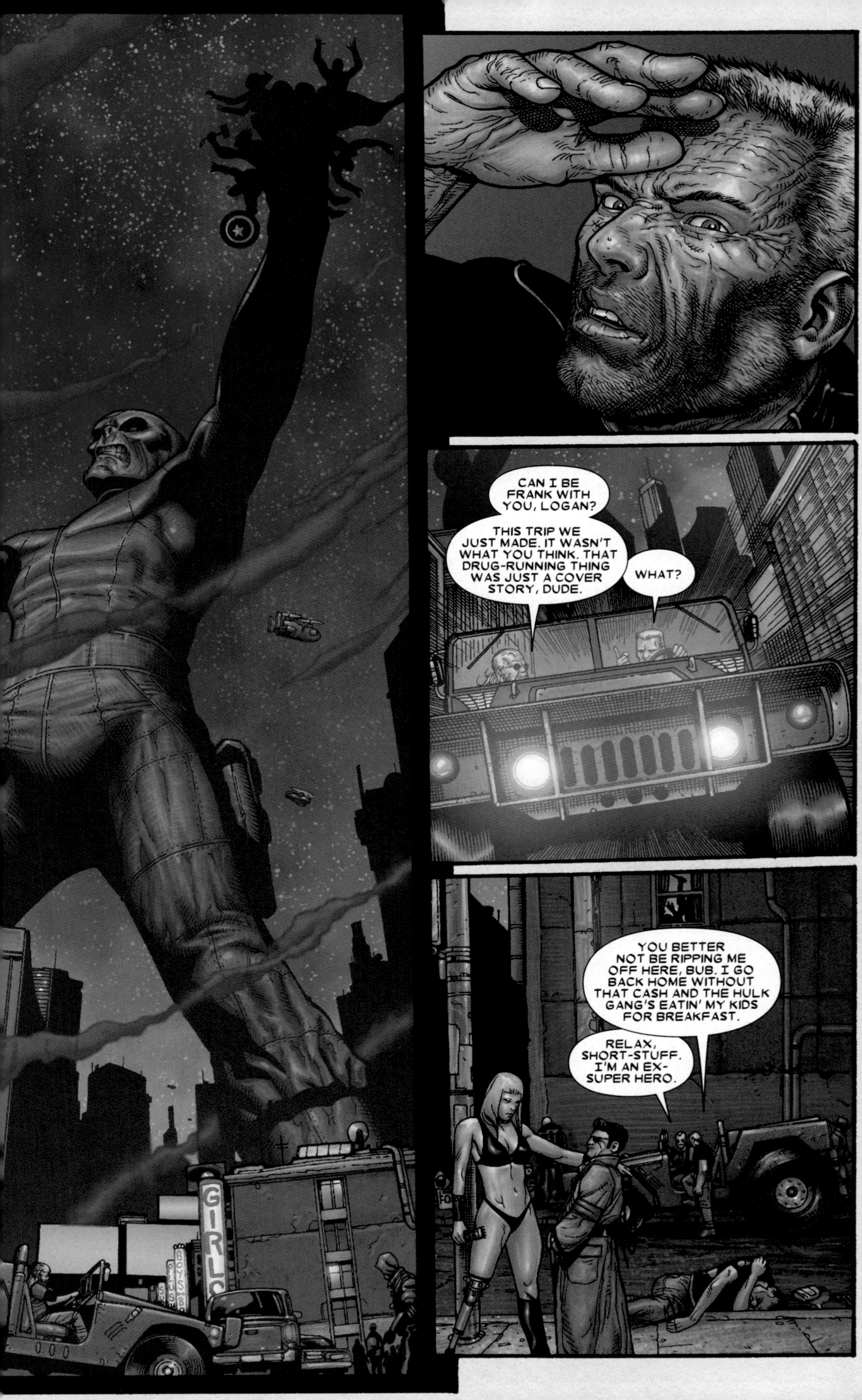
CAN I BE FRANK WITH YOU, LOGAN?
THIS TRIP WE JUST MADE. IT WASN'T WHAT YOU THINK. THAT DRUG-RUNNING THING WAS JUST A COVER STORY, DUDE.
WHAT?
YOU BETTER NOT BE RIPPING ME OFF HERE, BUB. I GO BACK HOME WITHOUT THAT CASH AND THE HULK GANG'S EATIN' MY KIDS FOR BREAKFAST.
RELAX, SHORT-STUFF. I'M AN EX-SUPER HERO.

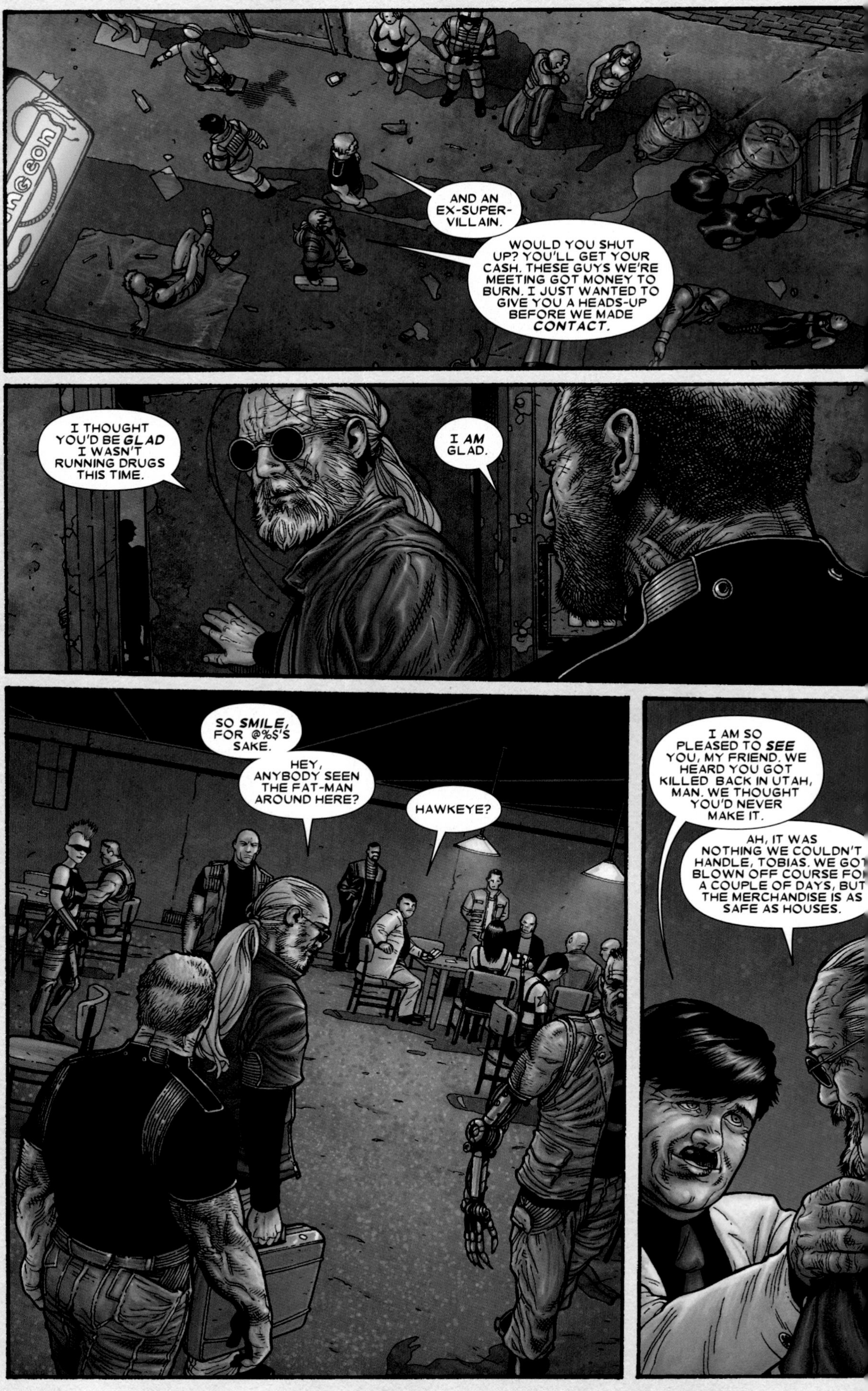
ngeon
AND AN EX-SUPER-VILLAIN.
WOULD YOU SHUT UP? YOU'LL GET YOUR CASH. THESE GUYS WE'RE MEETING GOT MONEY TO BURN. I JUST WANTED TO GIVE YOU A HEADS-UP BEFORE WE MADE CONTACT.
I THOUGHT YOU'D BE GLAD I WASN'T RUNNING DRUGS THIS TIME.
I AM GLAD.
SO SMILE, FOR @%$'S SAKE.
HEY, ANYBODY SEEN THE FAT-MAN AROUND HERE?
HAWKEYE?
I AM SO PLEASED TO SEE YOU, MY FRIEND. WE HEARD YOU GOT KILLED BACK IN UTAH, MAN. WE THOUGHT YOU'D NEVER MAKE IT.
AH, IT WAS NOTHING WE COULDN'T HANDLE, TOBIAS. WE GOT BLOWN OFF COURSE FO A COUPLE OF DAYS, BUT THE MERCHANDISE IS AS SAFE AS HOUSES.

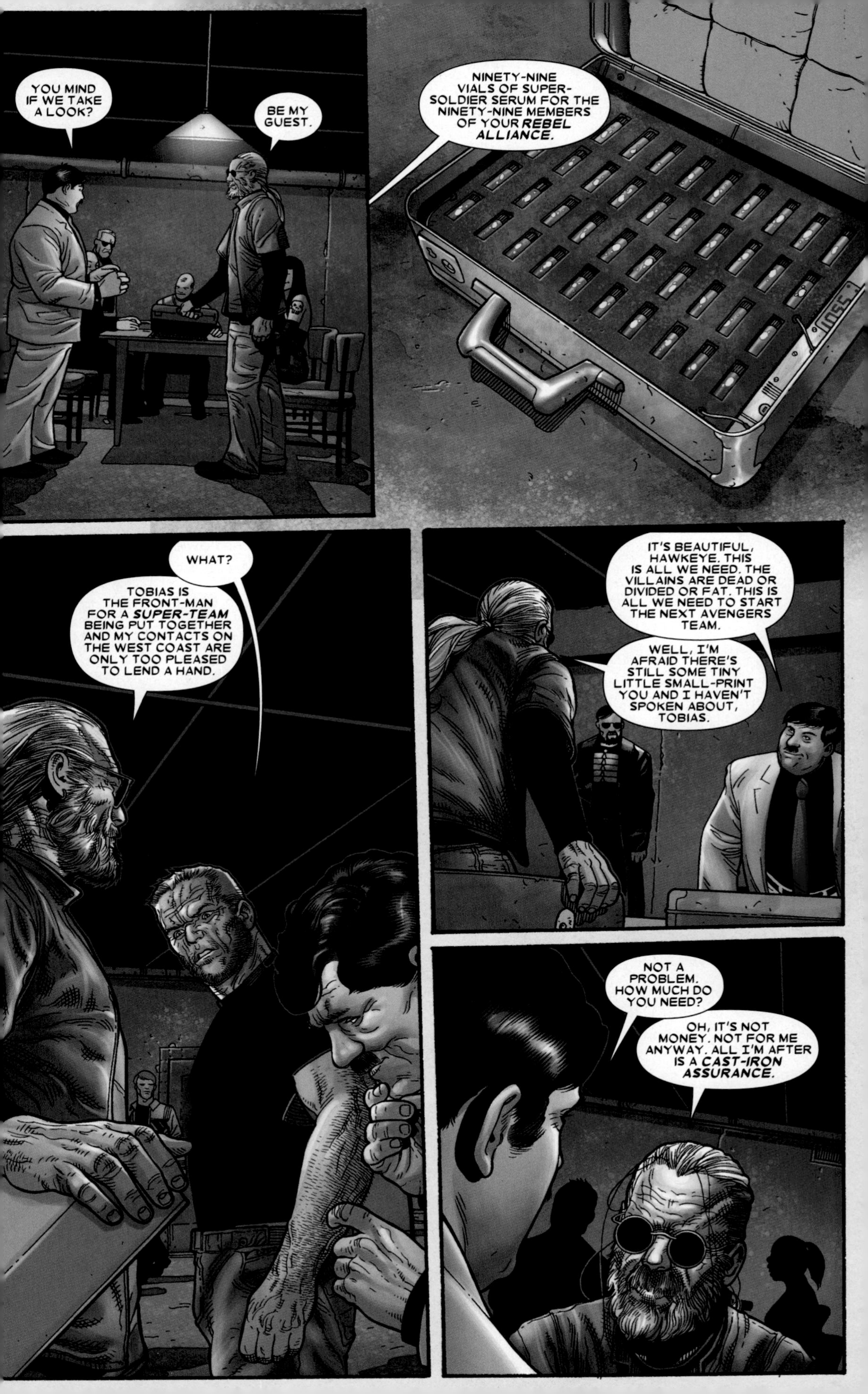
YOU MIND IF WE TAKE A LOOK?
BE MY GUEST.
NINETY-NINE VIALS OF SUPER-SOLDIER SERUM FOR THE NINETY-NINE MEMBERS OF YOUR *REBEL ALLIANCE.*
WHAT?
TOBIAS IS THE FRONT-MAN FOR A *SUPER-TEAM* BEING PUT TOGETHER AND MY CONTACTS ON THE WEST COAST ARE ONLY TOO PLEASED TO LEND A HAND.
IT'S BEAUTIFUL, HAWKEYE. THIS IS ALL WE NEED. THE VILLAINS ARE DEAD OR DIVIDED OR FAT. THIS IS ALL WE NEED TO START THE NEXT AVENGERS TEAM.
WELL, I'M AFRAID THERE'S STILL SOME TINY LITTLE SMALL-PRINT YOU AND I HAVEN'T SPOKEN ABOUT, TOBIAS.
NOT A PROBLEM. HOW MUCH DO YOU NEED?
OH, IT'S NOT MONEY. NOT FOR ME ANYWAY. ALL I'M AFTER IS A *CAST-IRON ASSURANCE.*

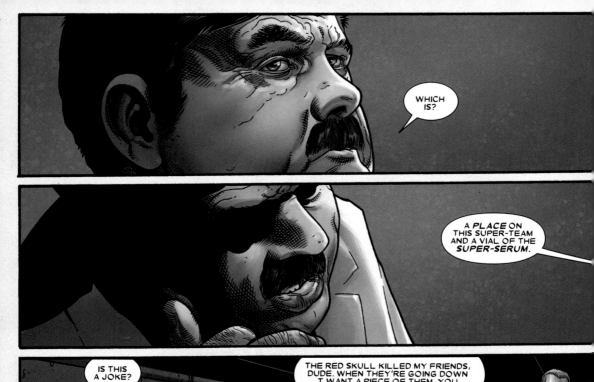

WHICH IS?

A *PLACE* ON THIS SUPER-TEAM AND A VIAL OF THE *SUPER-SERUM.*

IS THIS A JOKE?

THE RED SKULL KILLED MY FRIENDS, DUDE. WHEN THEY'RE GOING DOWN I WANT A PIECE OF THEM. YOU UNDERSTAND? NOW EITHER COUNT ME IN OR THE DEAL IS OFF.

ONCE AN AVENGER, *ALWAYS* AN AVENGER, HUH?

IT'S A DEAL, OLD MAN. YOU'VE GOT YOUR PLACE ON THE TEAM.

AWESOME. YOU HAVE NO IDEA HOW MUCH THIS MEANS TO ME. I FEEL LIKE I FELT WHEN THEY *FIRST* MADE ME AN AVENGER. JUST TO HAVE SOMEONE *BELIEVE* IN ME LIKE THIS...

HAWKEYE?

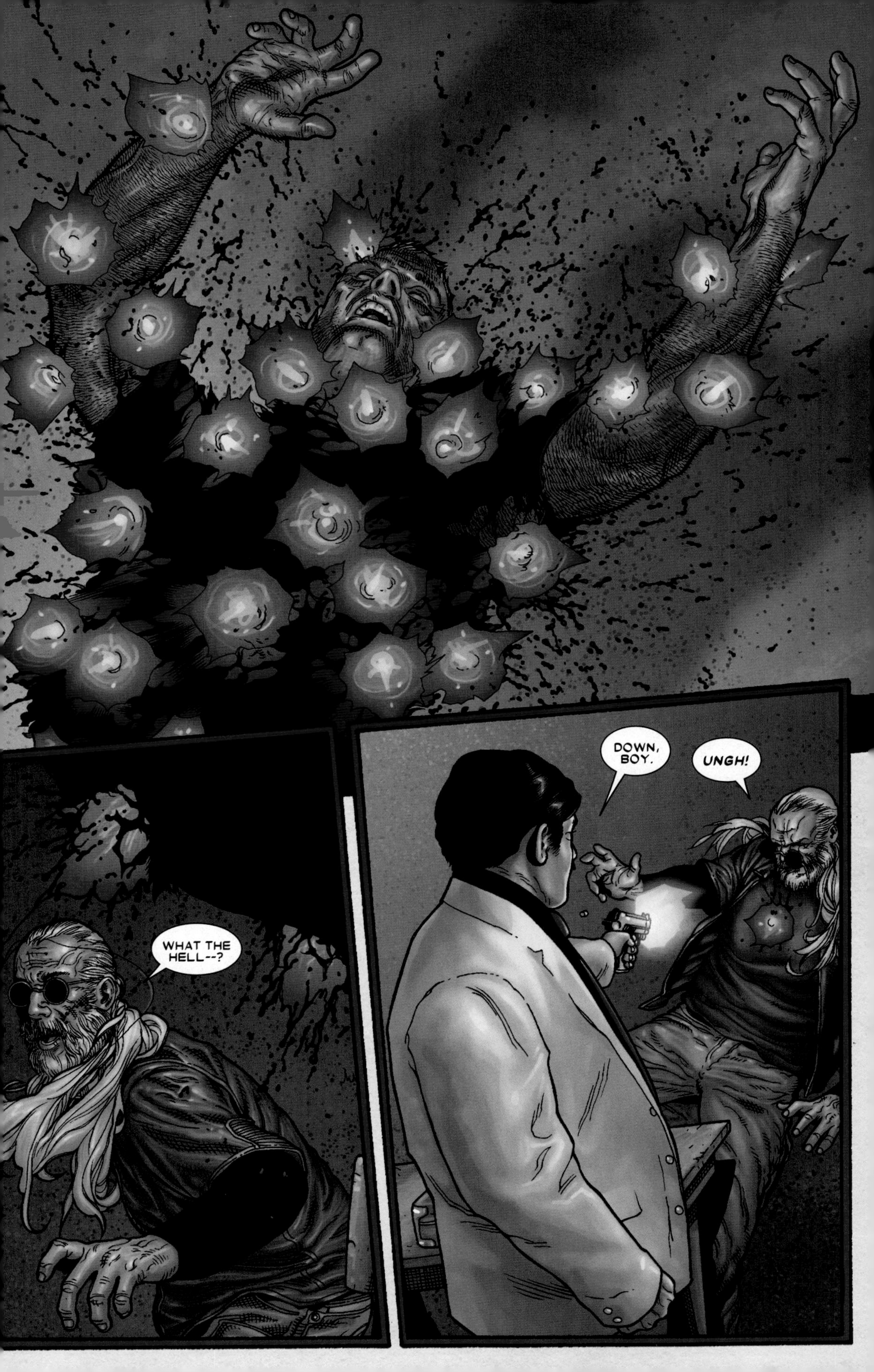
WHAT THE HELL--?
DOWN, BOY.
UNGH!

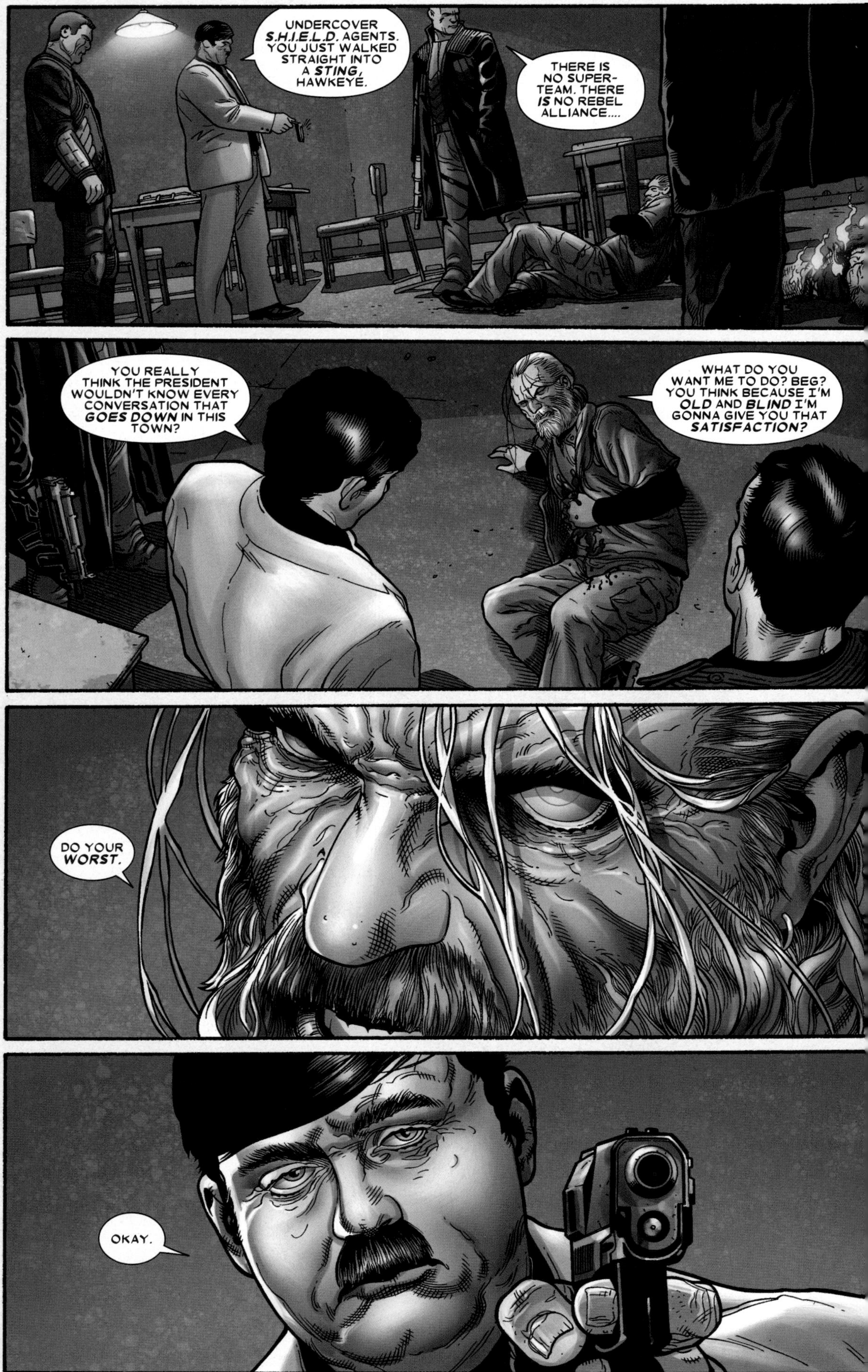
UNDERCOVER S.H.I.E.L.D. AGENTS. YOU JUST WALKED STRAIGHT INTO A STING, HAWKEYE.
THERE IS NO SUPER-TEAM. THERE IS NO REBEL ALLIANCE....
YOU REALLY THINK THE PRESIDENT WOULDN'T KNOW EVERY CONVERSATION THAT GOES DOWN IN THIS TOWN?
WHAT DO YOU WANT ME TO DO? BEG? YOU THINK BECAUSE I'M OLD AND BLIND I'M GONNA GIVE YOU THAT SATISFACTION?
DO YOUR WORST.
OKAY.

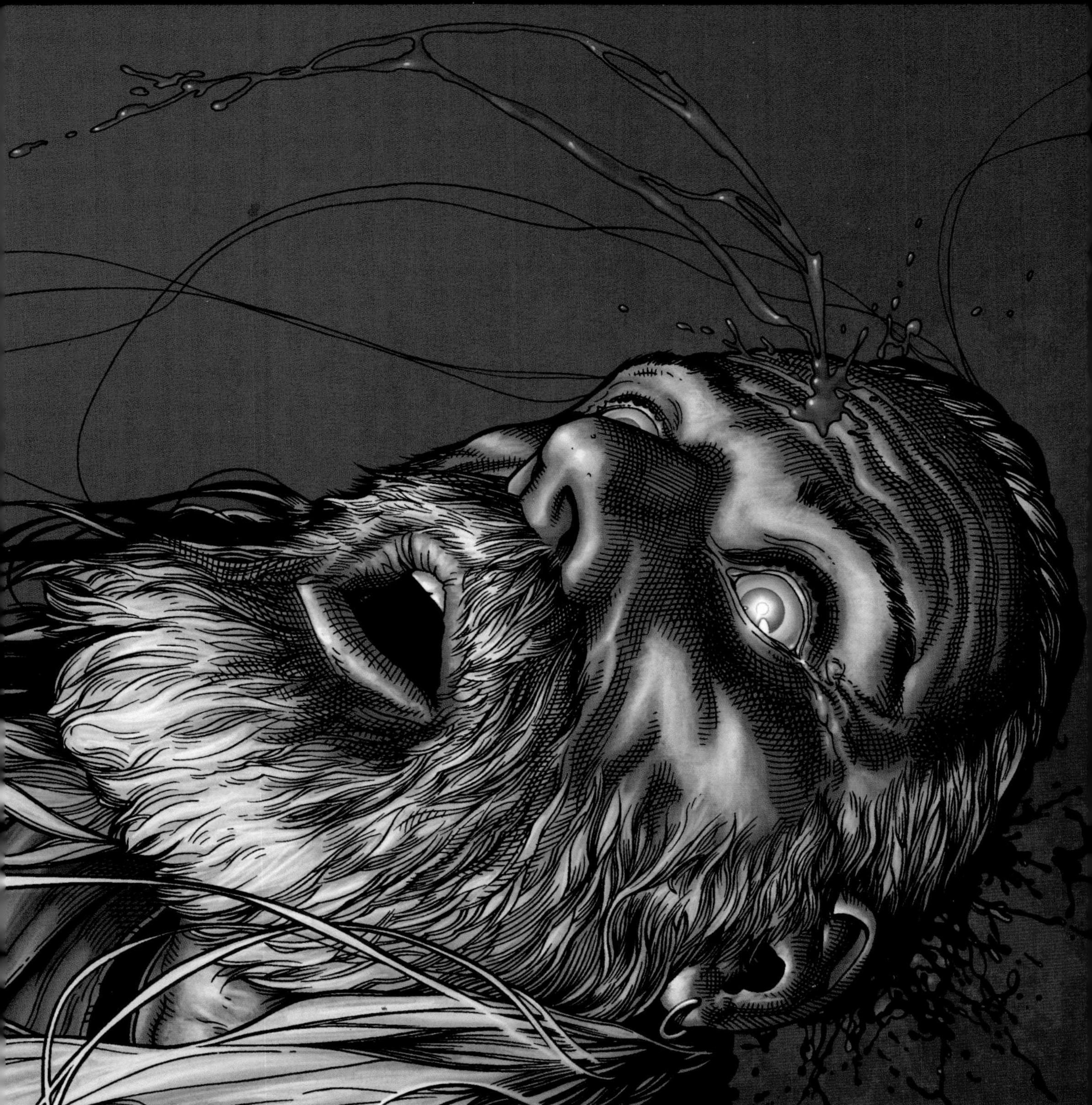

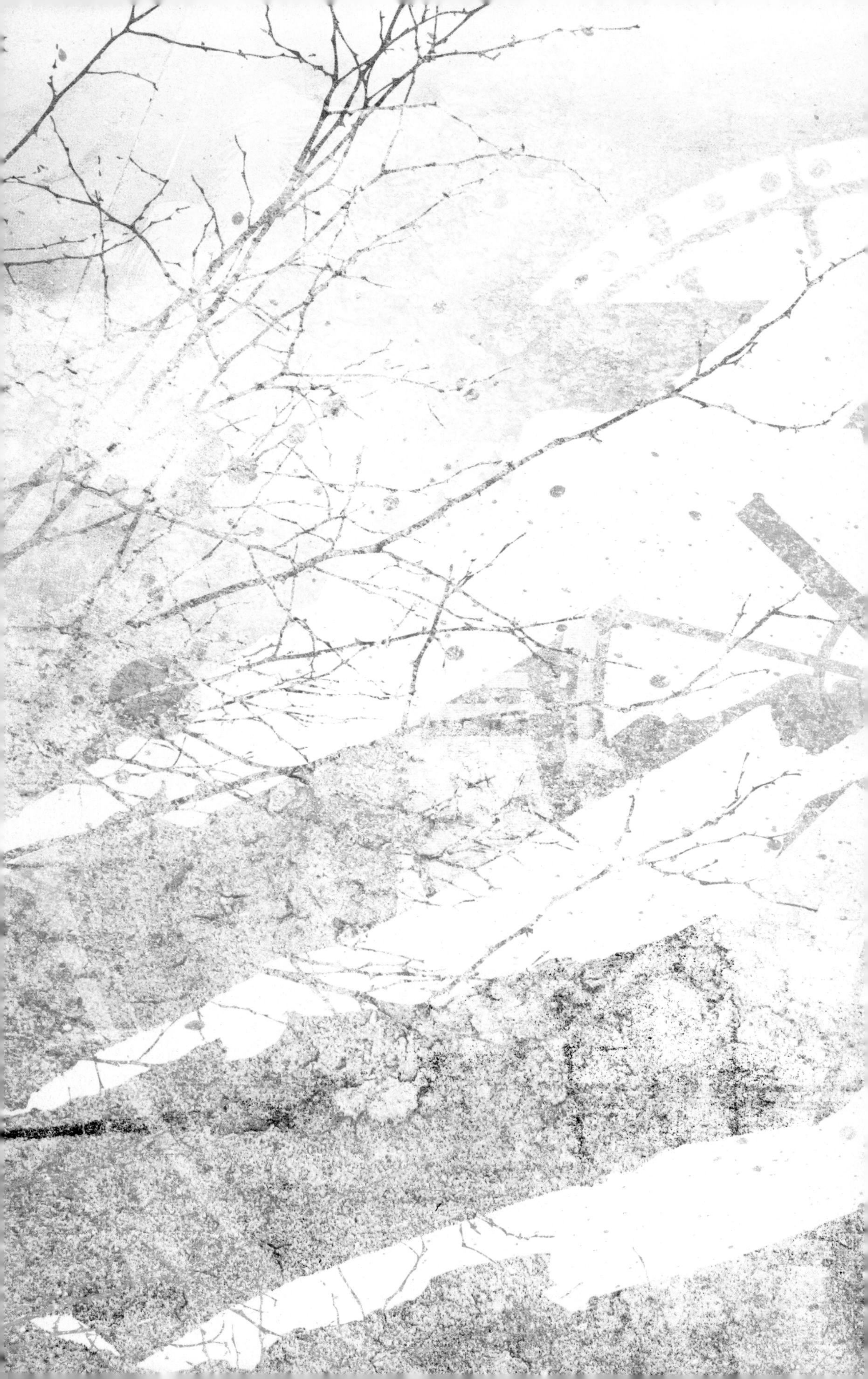

CHAPTER SEVEN

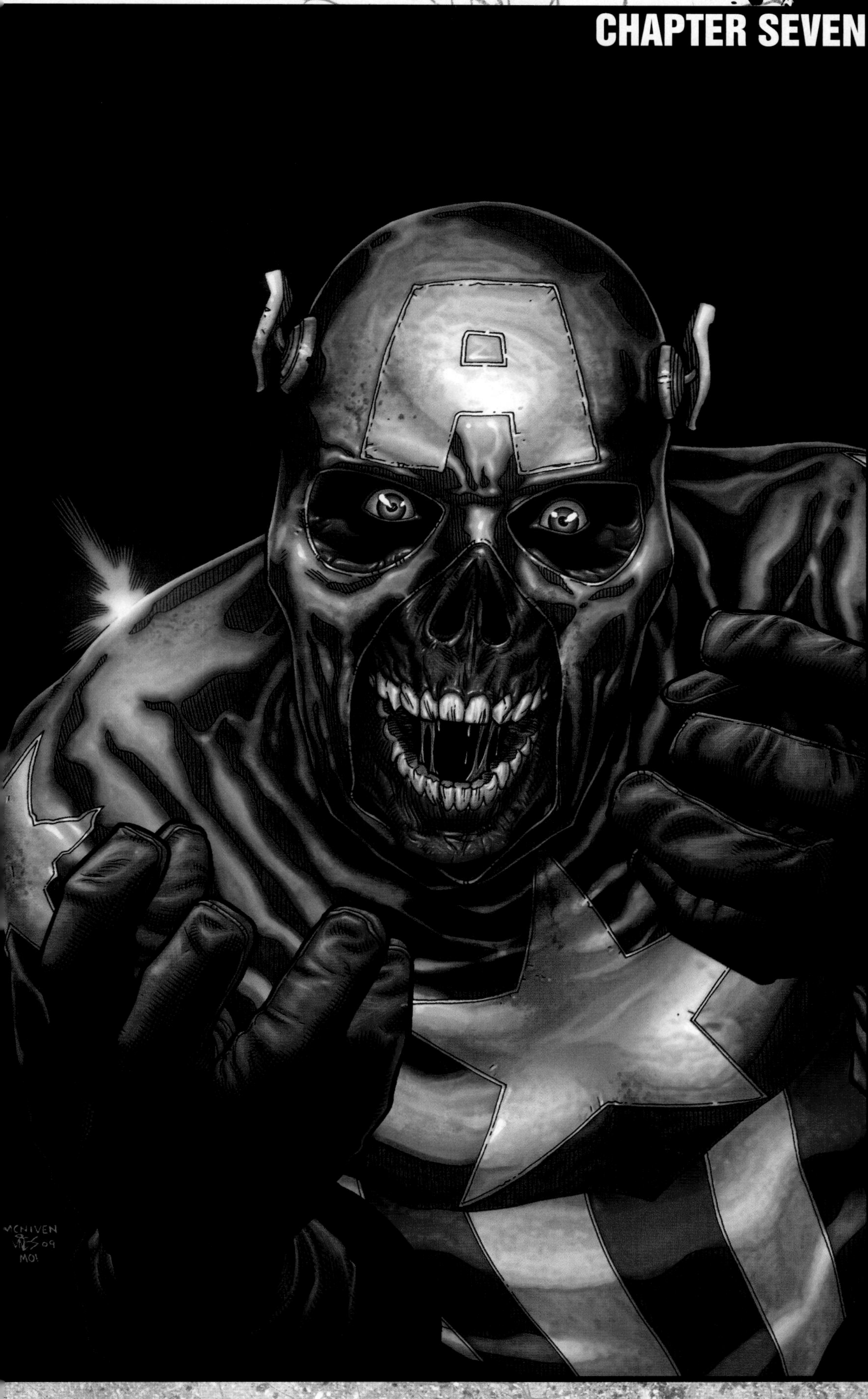

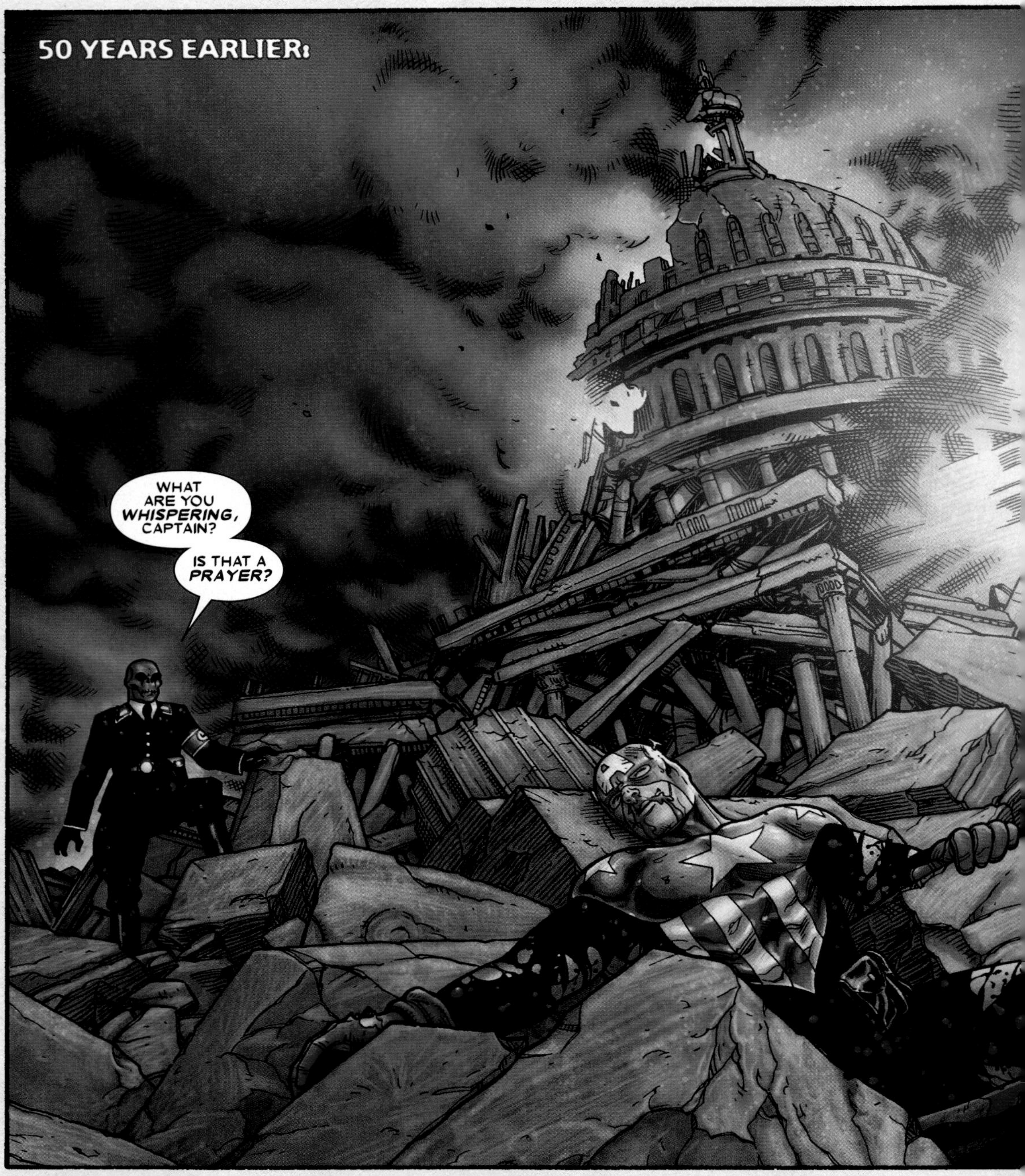
50 YEARS EARLIER:
WHAT ARE YOU WHISPERING, CAPTAIN?
IS THAT A PRAYER?

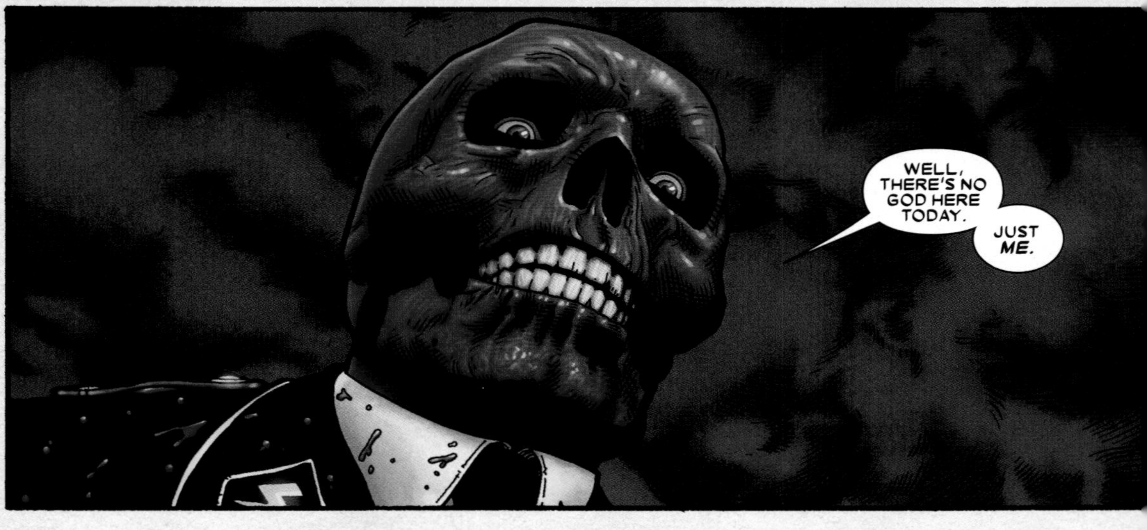
WELL, THERE'S NO GOD HERE TODAY.
JUST ME.

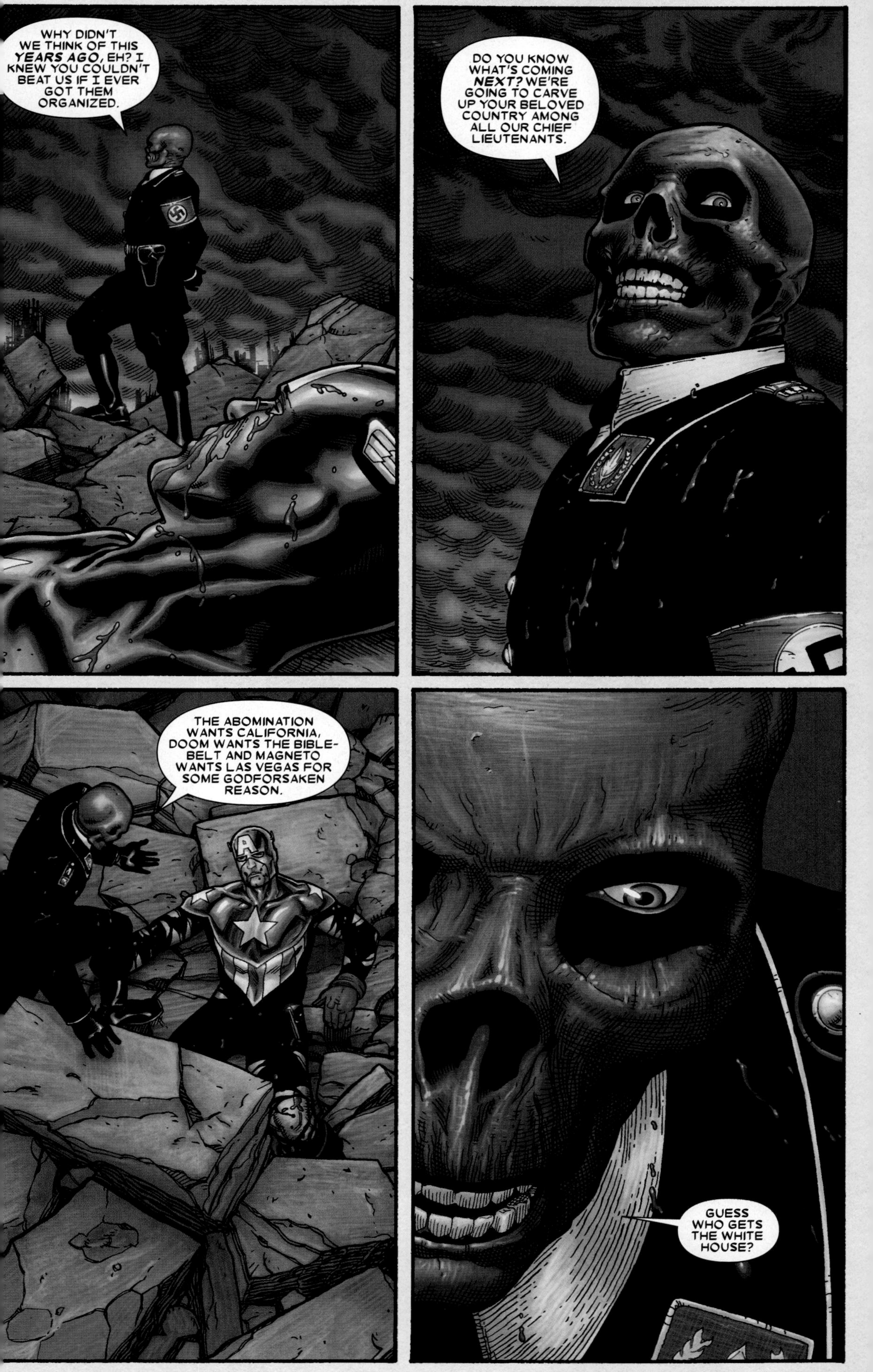
WHY DIDN'T WE THINK OF THIS YEARS AGO, EH? I KNEW YOU COULDN'T BEAT US IF I EVER GOT THEM ORGANIZED.
DO YOU KNOW WHAT'S COMING NEXT? WE'RE GOING TO CARVE UP YOUR BELOVED COUNTRY AMONG ALL OUR CHIEF LIEUTENANTS.
THE ABOMINATION WANTS CALIFORNIA, DOOM WANTS THE BIBLE-BELT AND MAGNETO WANTS LAS VEGAS FOR SOME GODFORSAKEN REASON.
GUESS WHO GETS THE WHITE HOUSE?

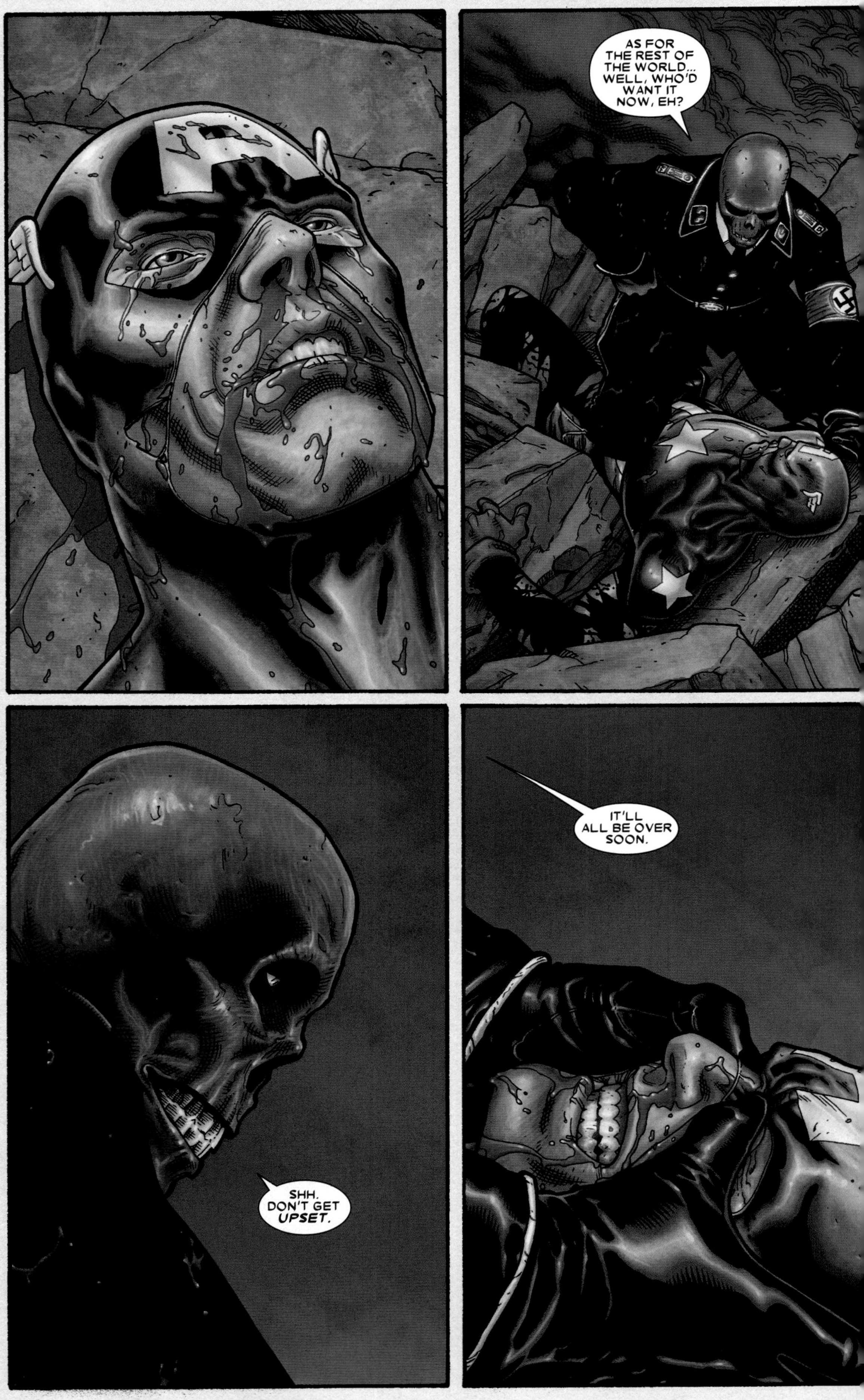
AS FOR THE REST OF THE WORLD... WELL, WHO'D WANT IT NOW, EH?
SHH. DON'T GET *UPSET*.
IT'LL ALL BE OVER SOON.

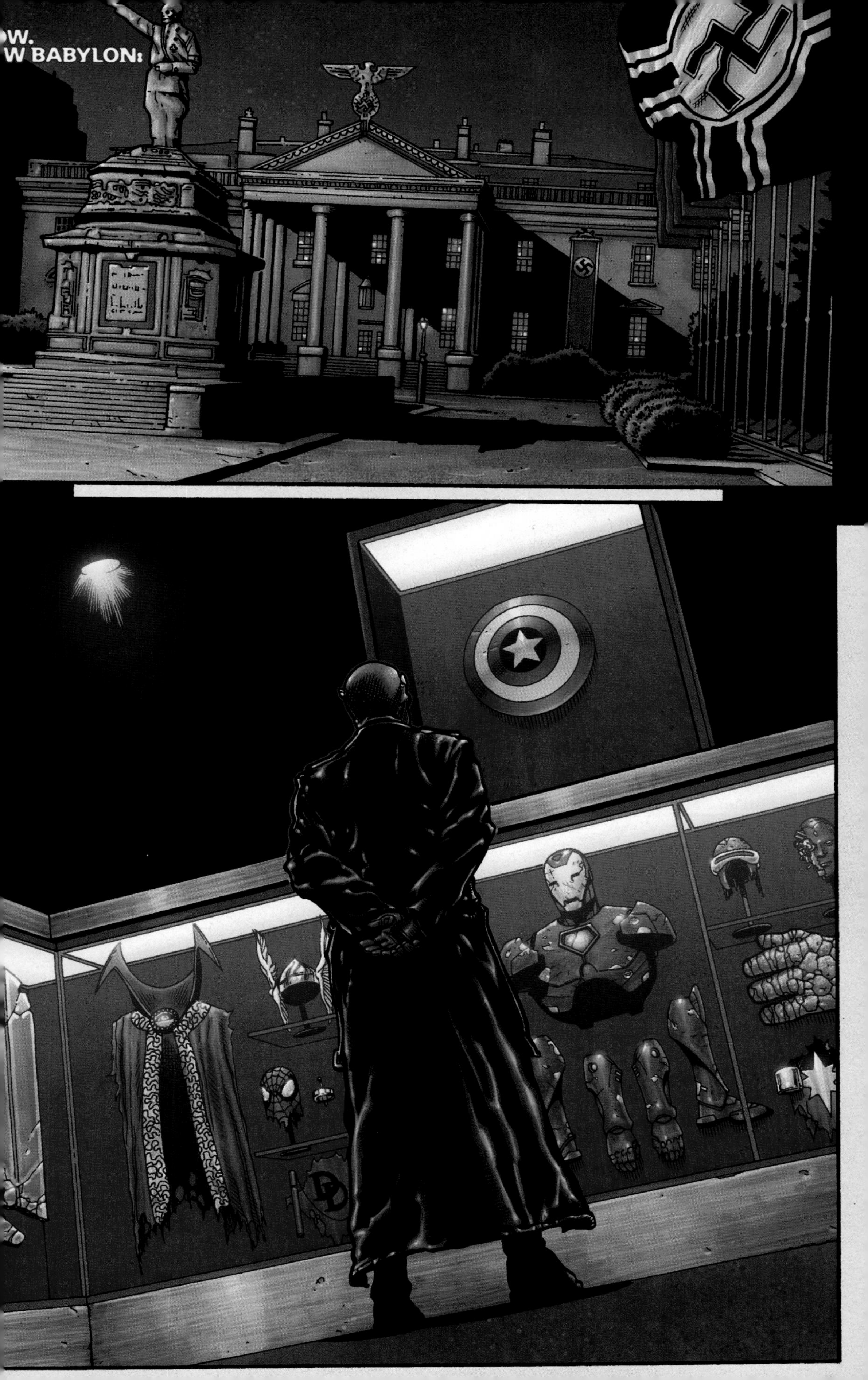
W.
W BABYLON:

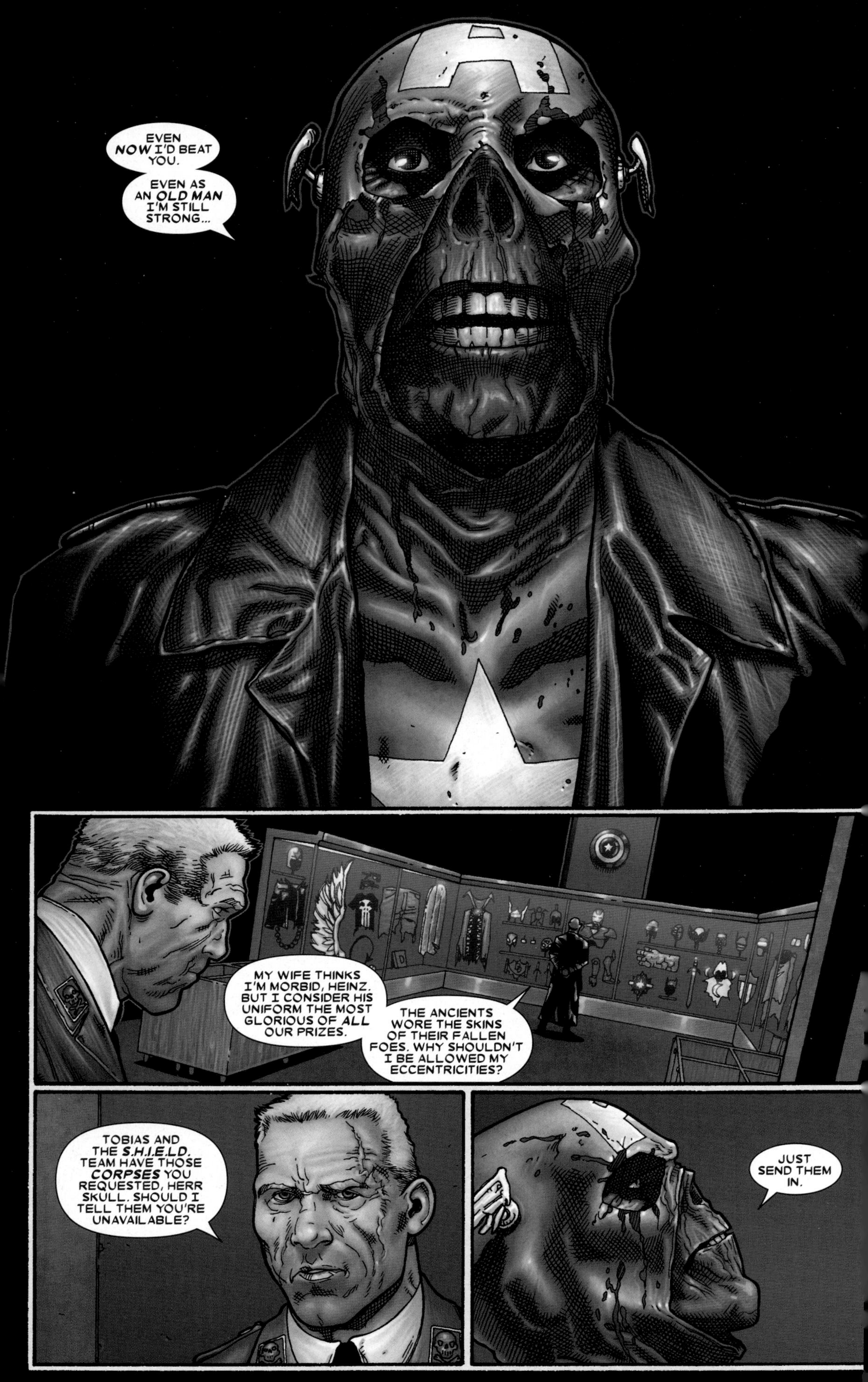
EVEN NOW I'D BEAT YOU.
EVEN AS AN OLD MAN I'M STILL STRONG...
MY WIFE THINKS I'M MORBID, HEINZ. BUT I CONSIDER HIS UNIFORM THE MOST GLORIOUS OF ALL OUR PRIZES.
THE ANCIENTS WORE THE SKINS OF THEIR FALLEN FOES. WHY SHOULDN'T I BE ALLOWED MY ECCENTRICITIES?
TOBIAS AND THE S.H.I.E.L.D. TEAM HAVE THOSE CORPSES YOU REQUESTED, HERR SKULL. SHOULD I TELL THEM YOU'RE UNAVAILABLE?
JUST SEND THEM IN.

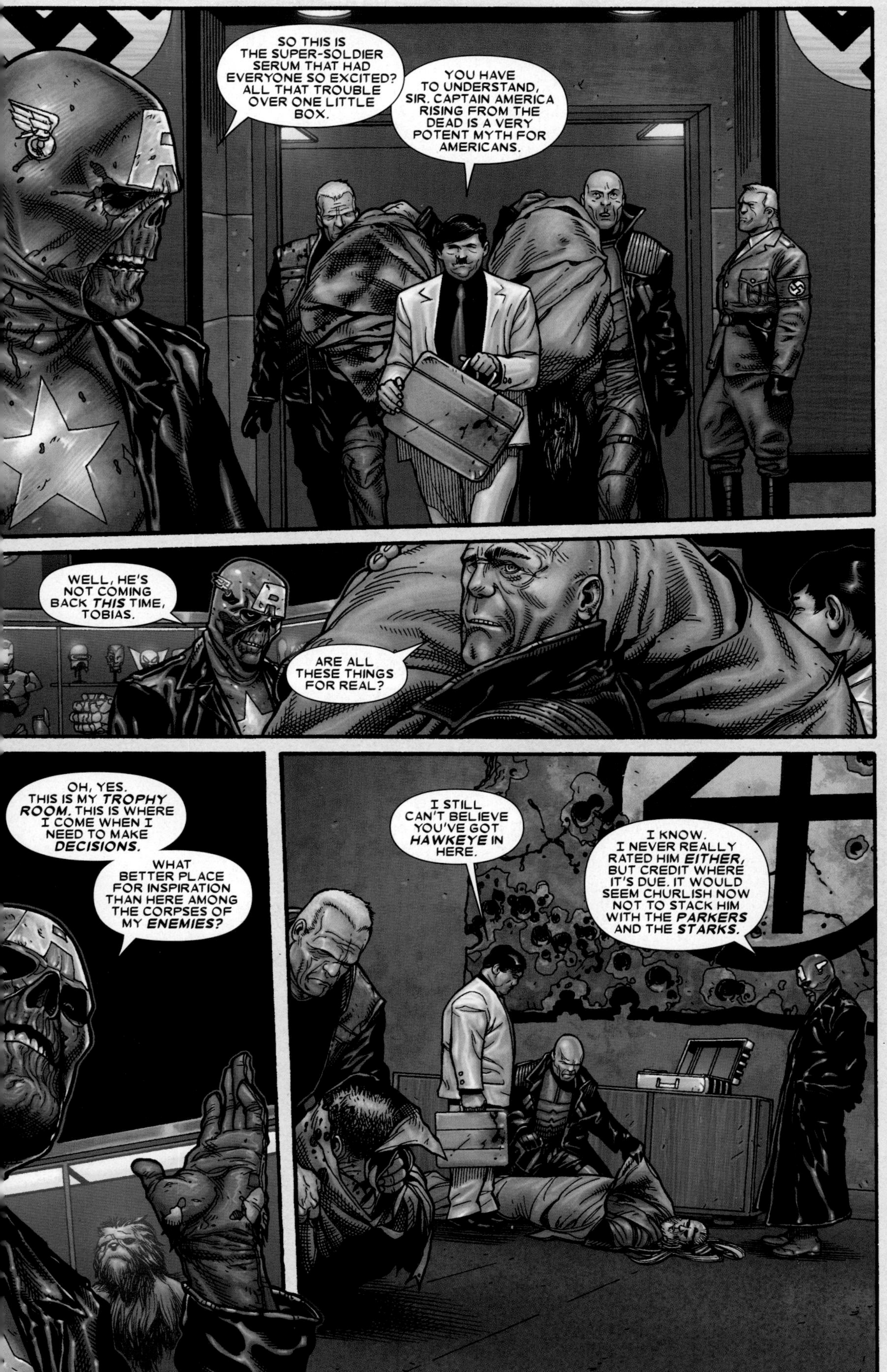
SO THIS IS THE SUPER-SOLDIER SERUM THAT HAD EVERYONE SO EXCITED? ALL THAT TROUBLE OVER ONE LITTLE BOX.
YOU HAVE TO UNDERSTAND, SIR. CAPTAIN AMERICA RISING FROM THE DEAD IS A VERY POTENT MYTH FOR AMERICANS.
WELL, HE'S NOT COMING BACK THIS TIME, TOBIAS.
ARE ALL THESE THINGS FOR REAL?
OH, YES. THIS IS MY TROPHY ROOM. THIS IS WHERE I COME WHEN I NEED TO MAKE DECISIONS.
WHAT BETTER PLACE FOR INSPIRATION THAN HERE AMONG THE CORPSES OF MY ENEMIES?
I STILL CAN'T BELIEVE YOU'VE GOT HAWKEYE IN HERE.
I KNOW. I NEVER REALLY RATED HIM EITHER, BUT CREDIT WHERE IT'S DUE. IT WOULD SEEM CHURLISH NOW NOT TO STACK HIM WITH THE PARKERS AND THE STARKS.

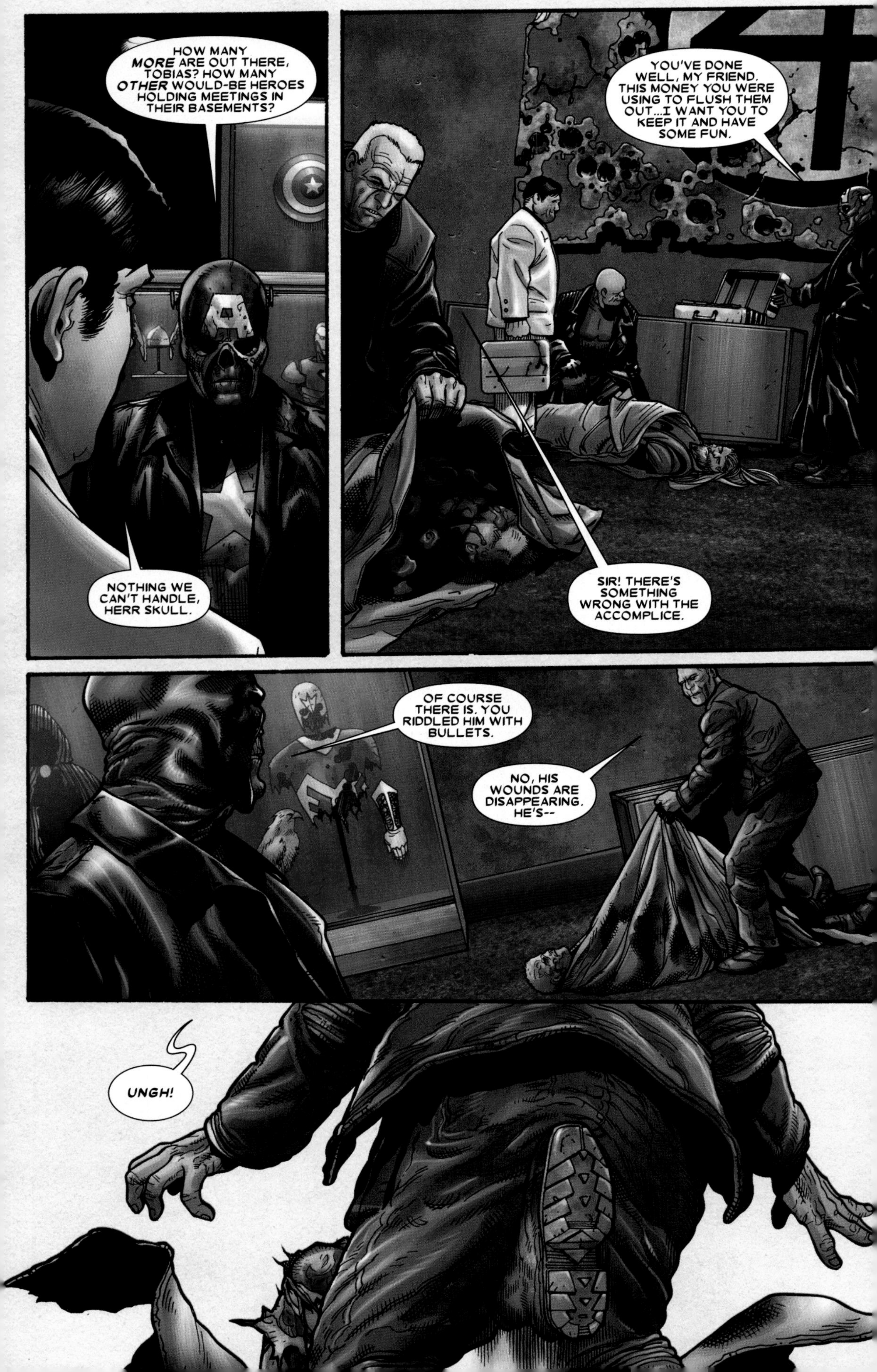
HOW MANY MORE ARE OUT THERE, TOBIAS? HOW MANY OTHER WOULD-BE HEROES HOLDING MEETINGS IN THEIR BASEMENTS?
NOTHING WE CAN'T HANDLE, HERR SKULL.
YOU'VE DONE WELL, MY FRIEND. THIS MONEY YOU WERE USING TO FLUSH THEM OUT...I WANT YOU TO KEEP IT AND HAVE SOME FUN.
SIR! THERE'S SOMETHING WRONG WITH THE ACCOMPLICE.
OF COURSE THERE IS. YOU RIDDLED HIM WITH BULLETS.
NO, HIS WOUNDS ARE DISAPPEARING. HE'S--
UNGH!

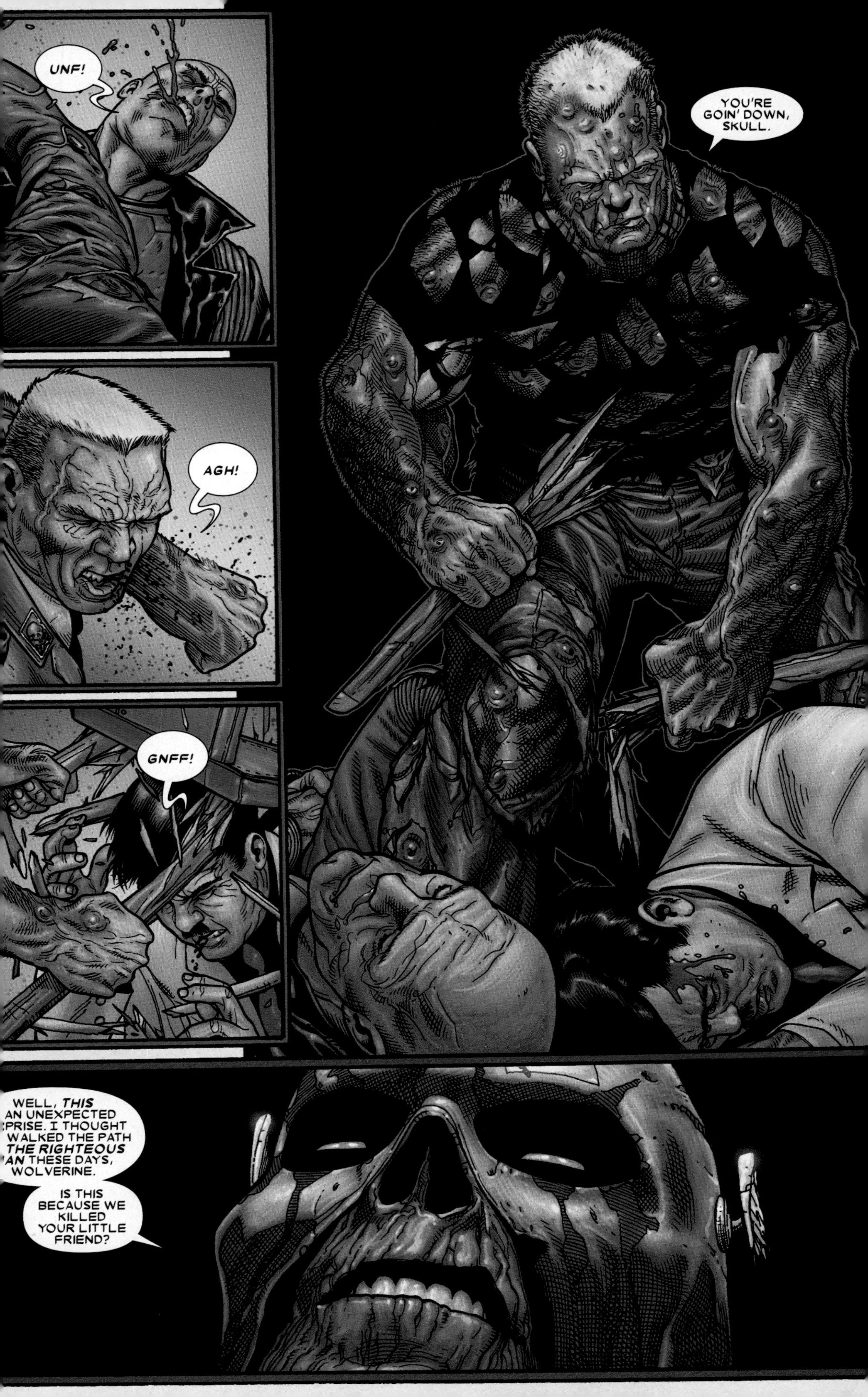
UNF!
YOU'RE GOIN' DOWN, SKULL.
AGH!
GNFF!
WELL, *THIS* AN UNEXPECTED PRISE. I THOUGHT WALKED THE PATH *THE RIGHTEOUS AN* THESE DAYS, WOLVERINE.
IS THIS BECAUSE WE KILLED YOUR LITTLE FRIEND?

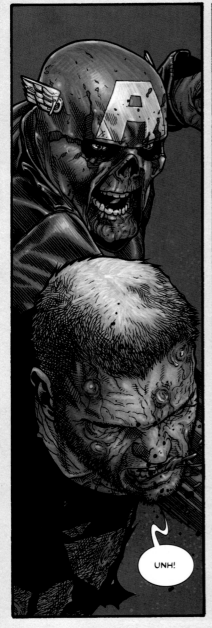

UNH!

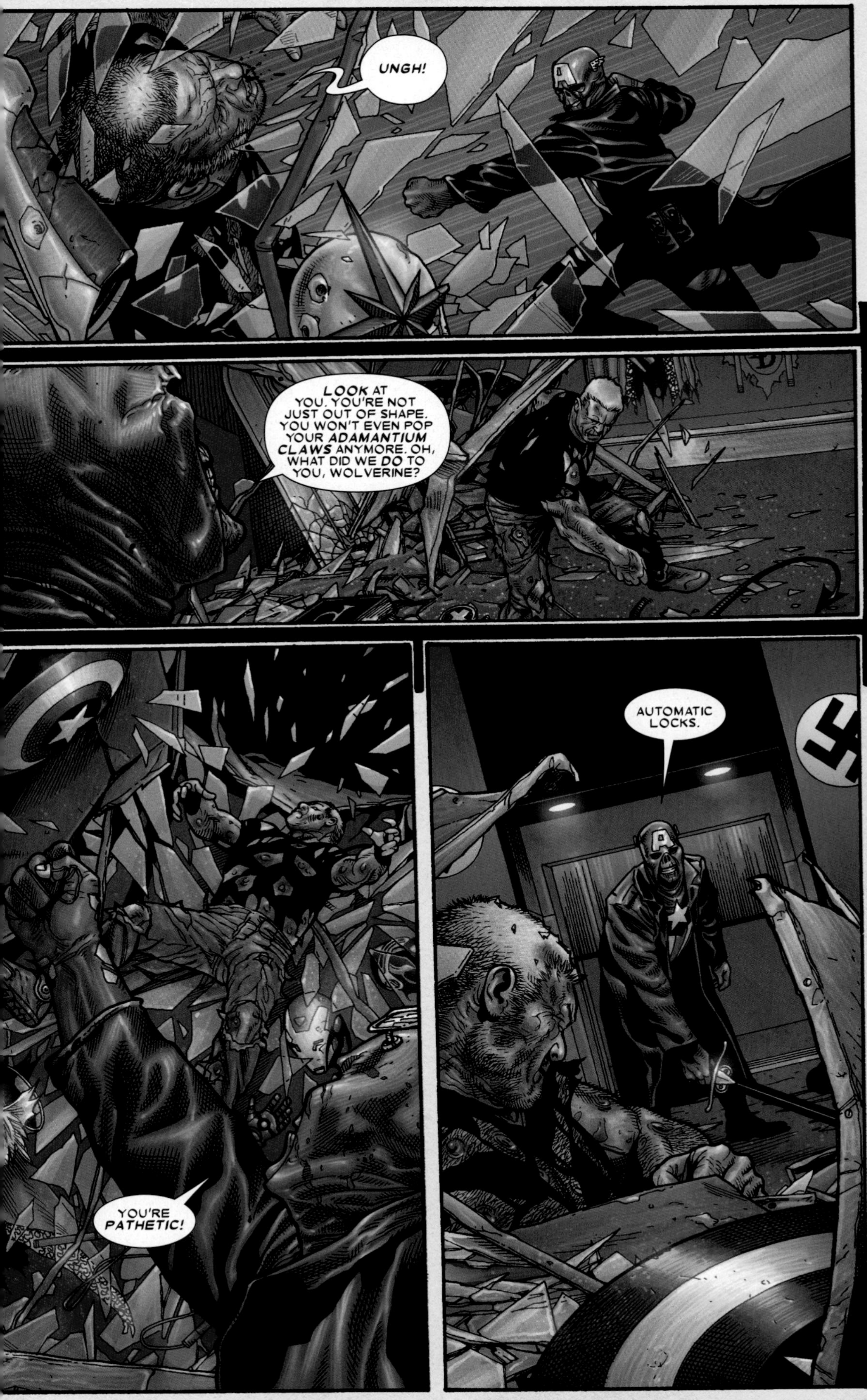
UNGH!
LOOK AT YOU. YOU'RE NOT JUST OUT OF SHAPE. YOU WON'T EVEN POP YOUR ADAMANTIUM CLAWS ANYMORE. OH, WHAT DID WE DO TO YOU, WOLVERINE?
YOU'RE PATHETIC!
AUTOMATIC LOCKS.

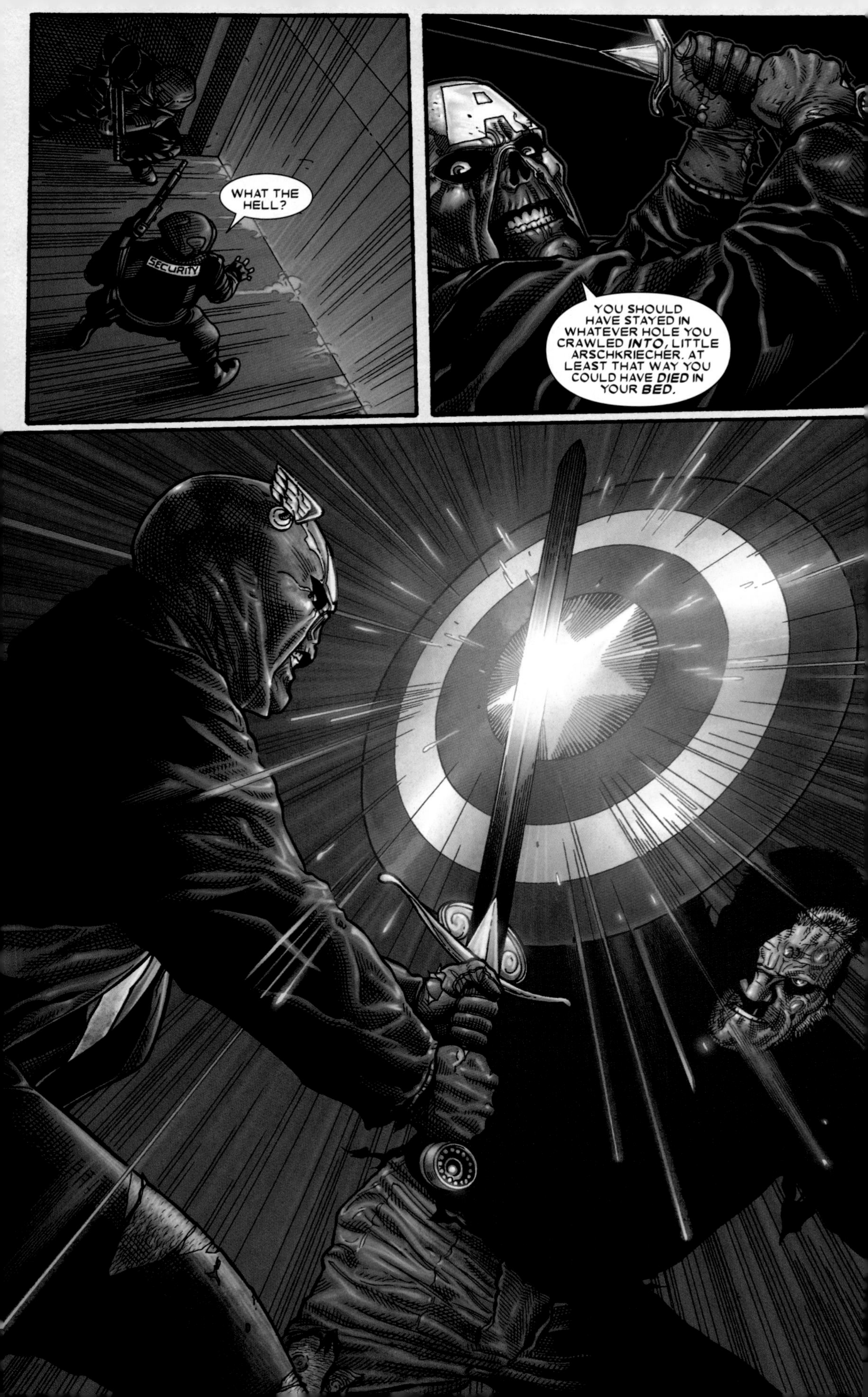
WHAT THE HELL?
SECURITY
YOU SHOULD HAVE STAYED IN WHATEVER HOLE YOU CRAWLED *INTO*, LITTLE ARSCHKRIECHER. AT LEAST THAT WAY YOU COULD HAVE *DIED* IN YOUR *BED*.

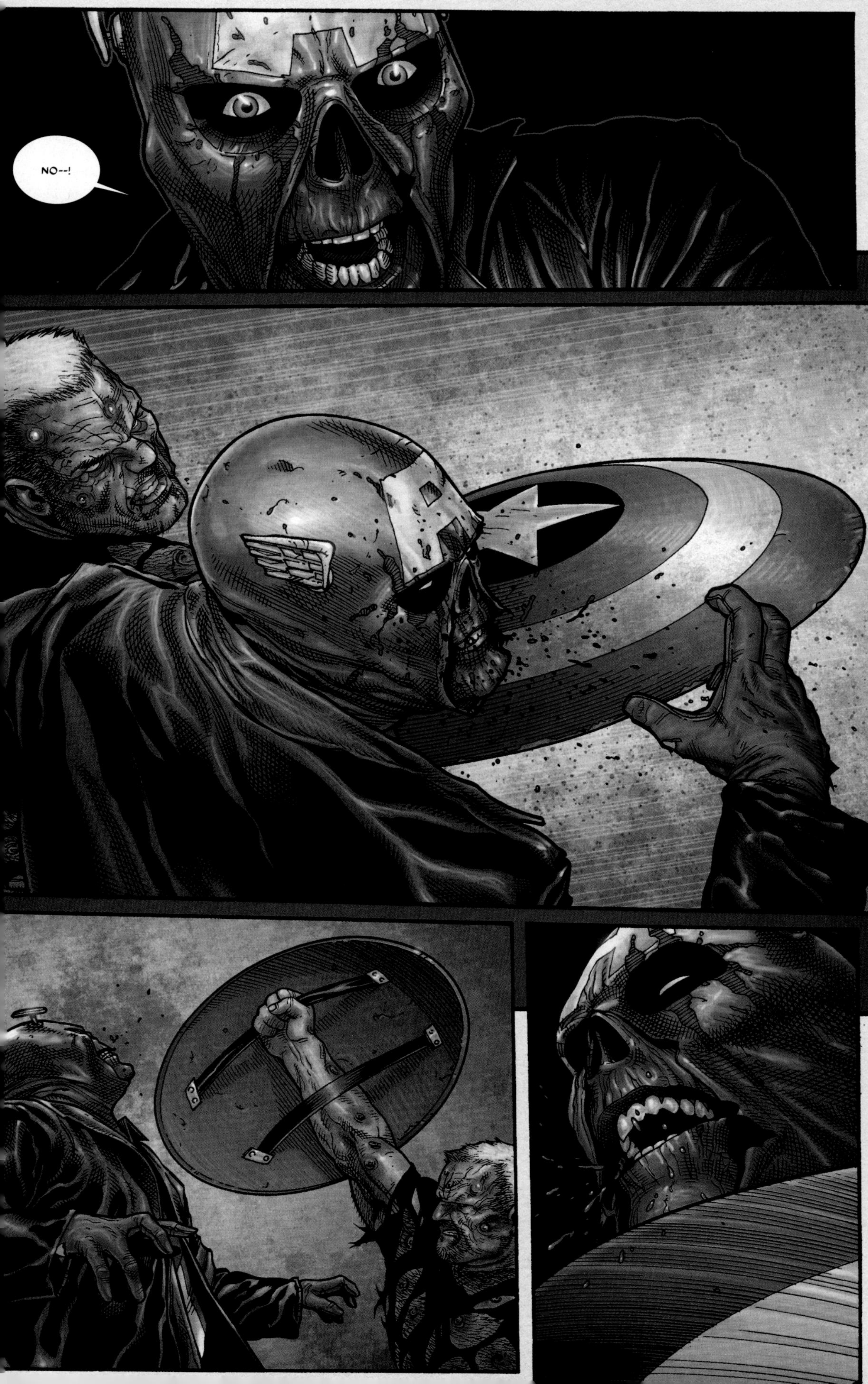
NO--!

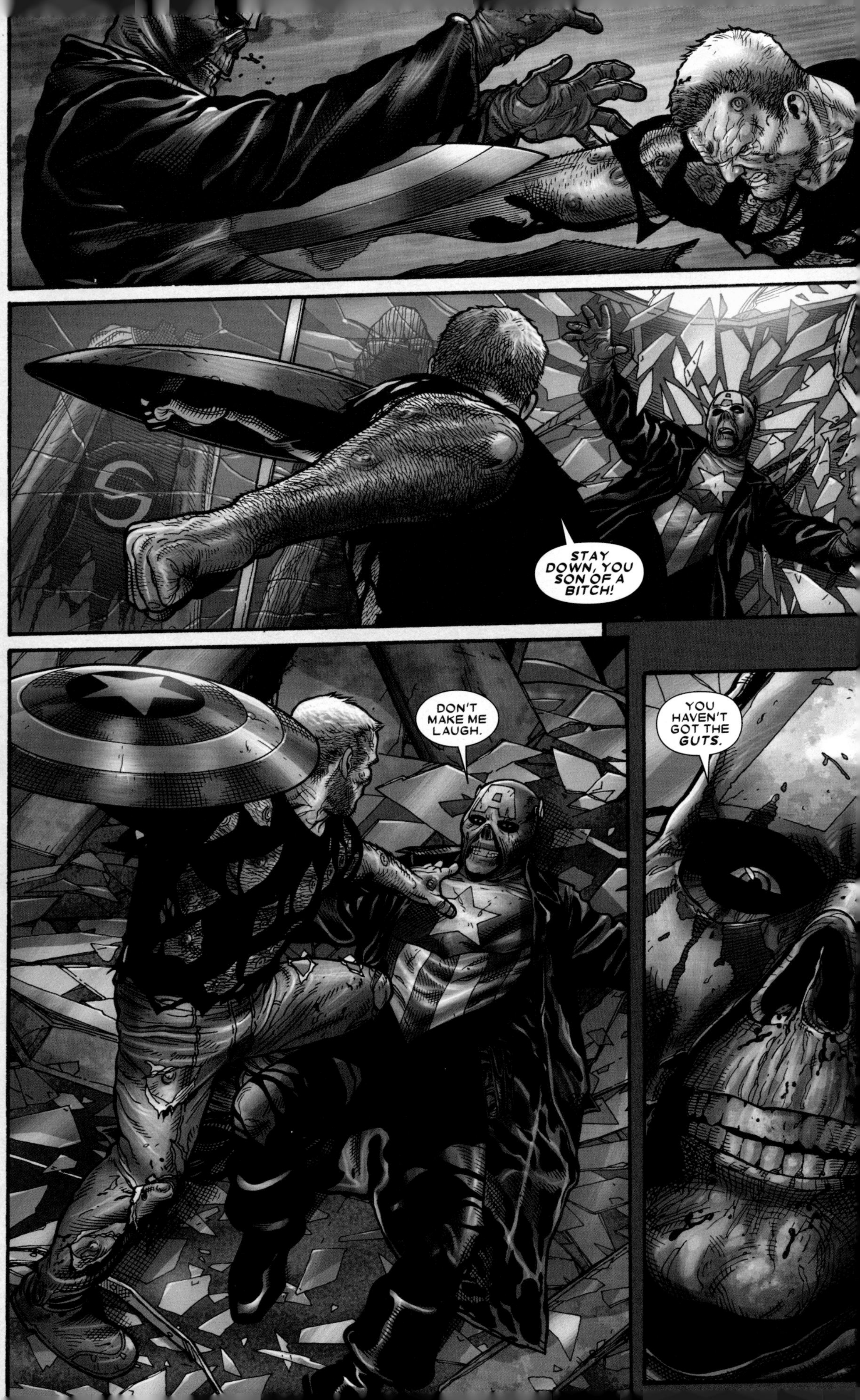
STAY DOWN, YOU SON OF A BITCH!
DON'T MAKE ME LAUGH.
YOU HAVEN'T GOT THE GUTS.

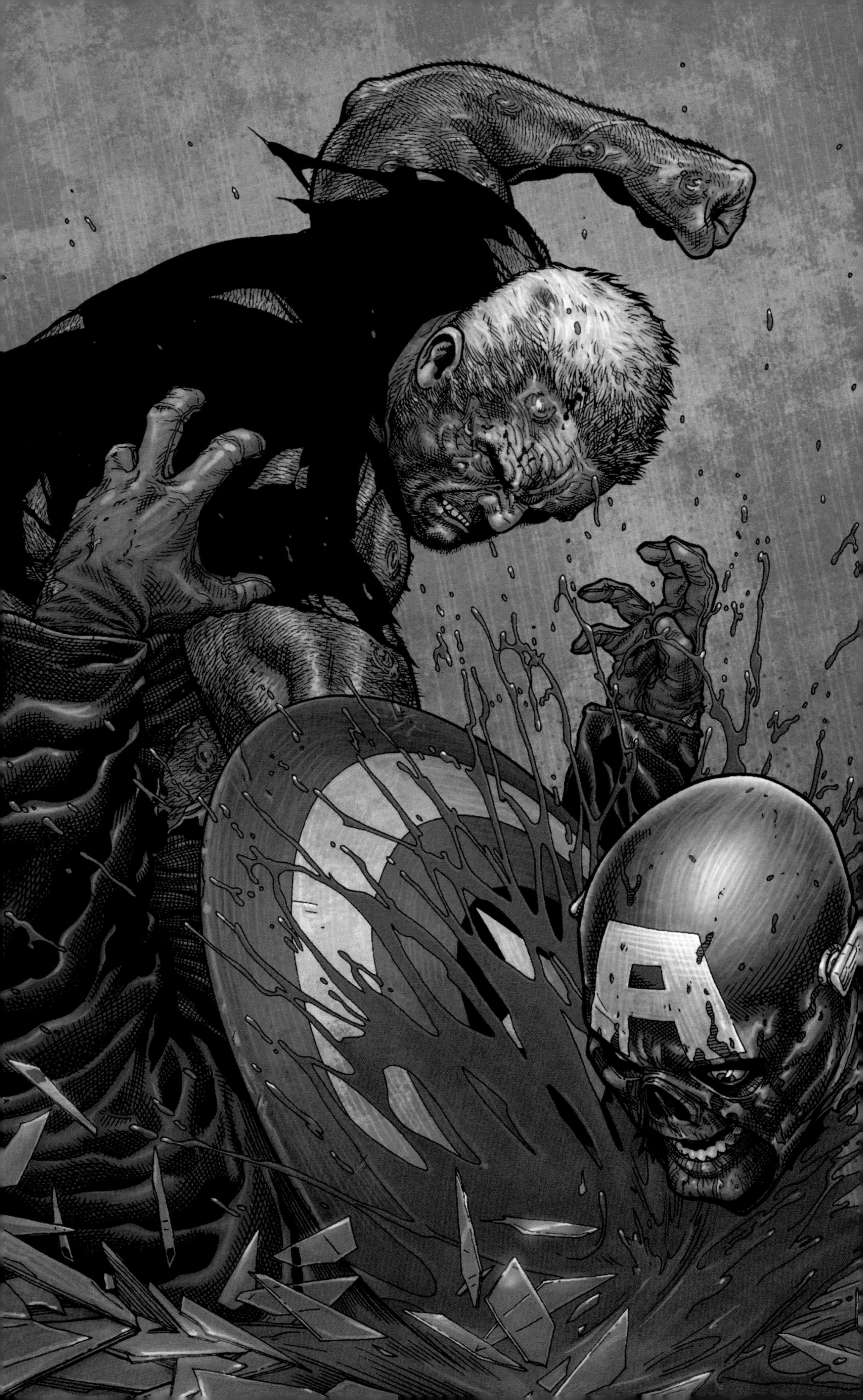

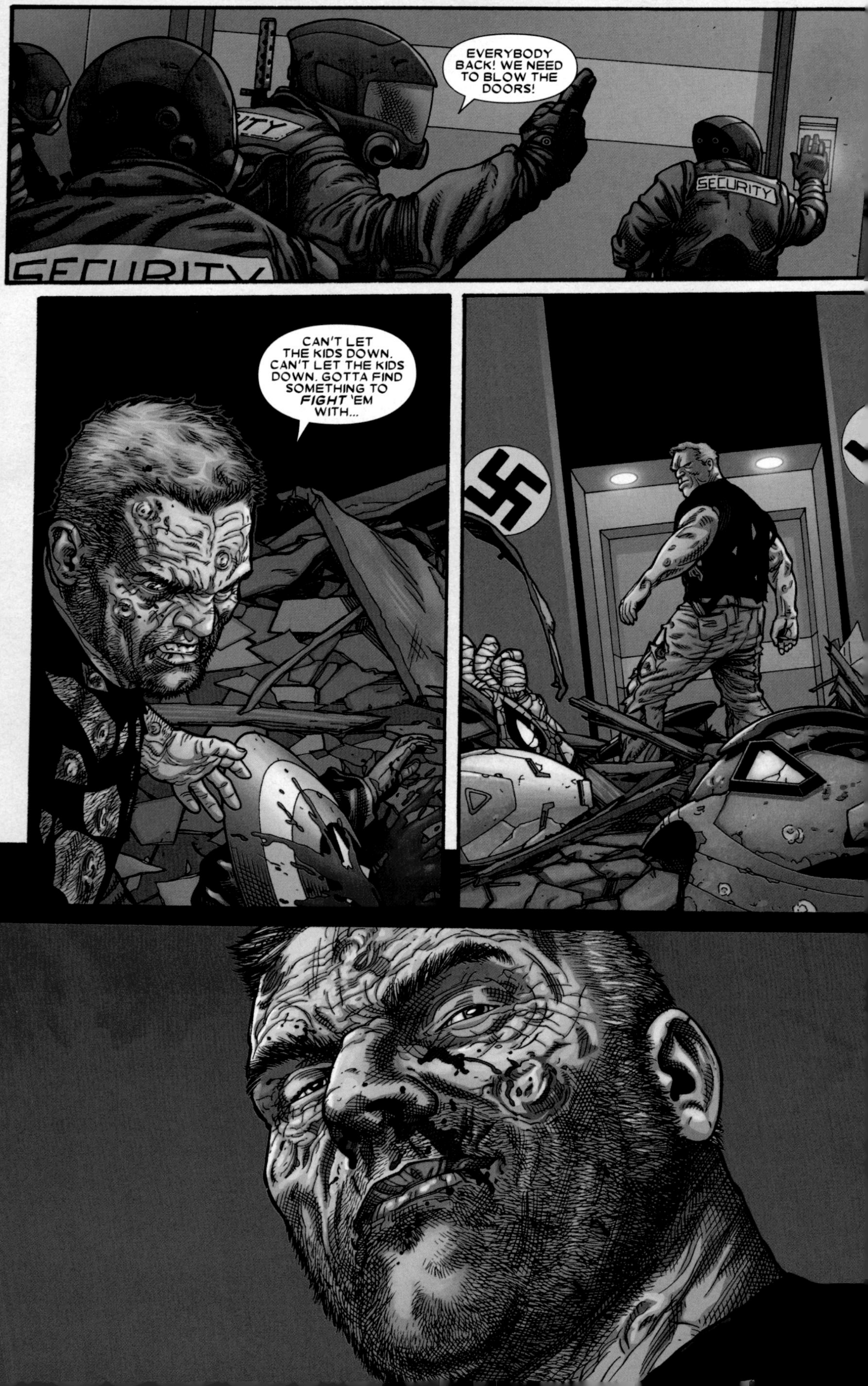
EVERYBODY BACK! WE NEED TO BLOW THE DOORS!
SECURITY
SECURITY
CAN'T LET THE KIDS DOWN. CAN'T LET THE KIDS DOWN. GOTTA FIND SOMETHING TO FIGHT 'EM WITH...

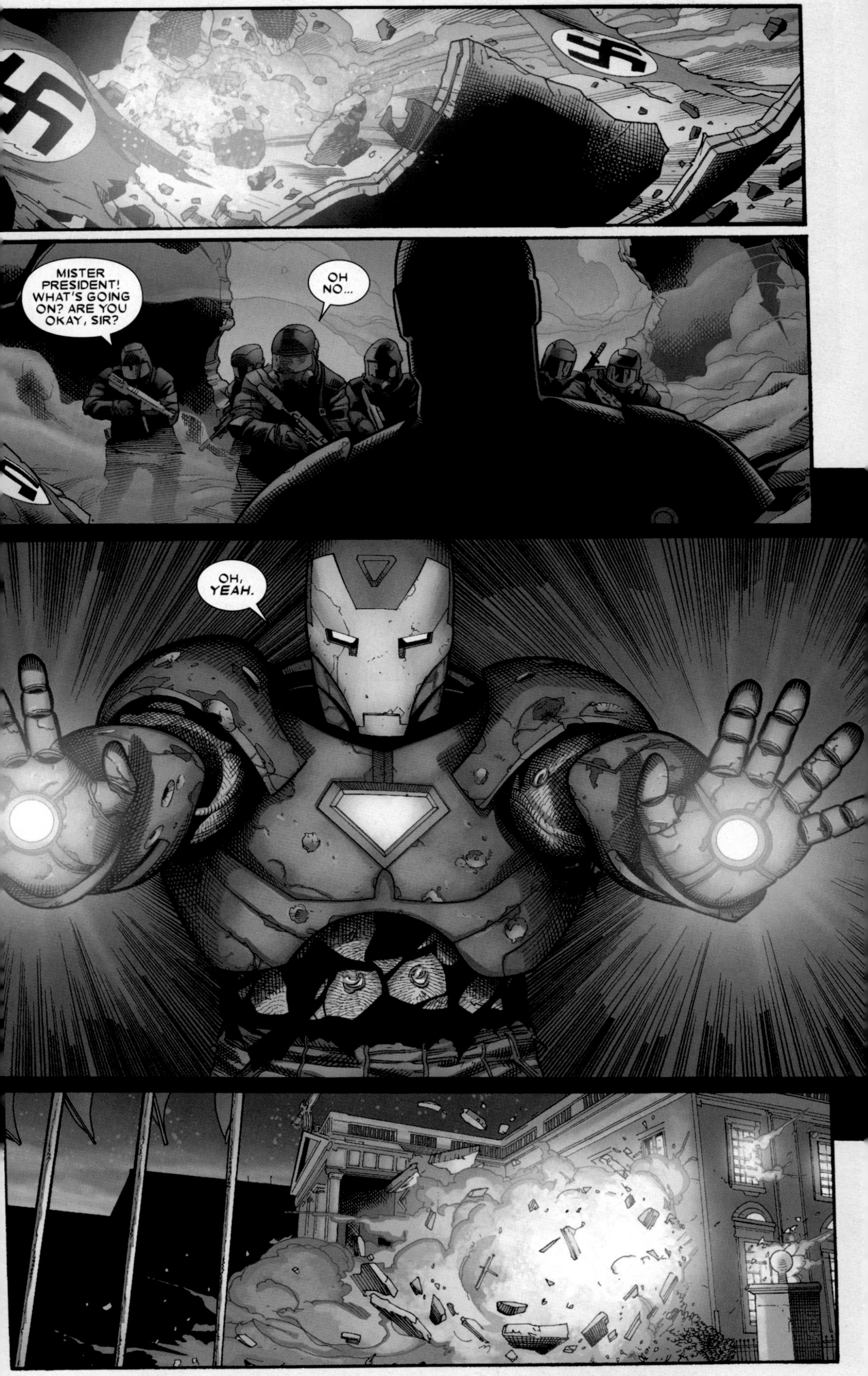
MISTER PRESIDENT! WHAT'S GOING ON? ARE YOU OKAY, SIR?
OH NO...
OH, YEAH.

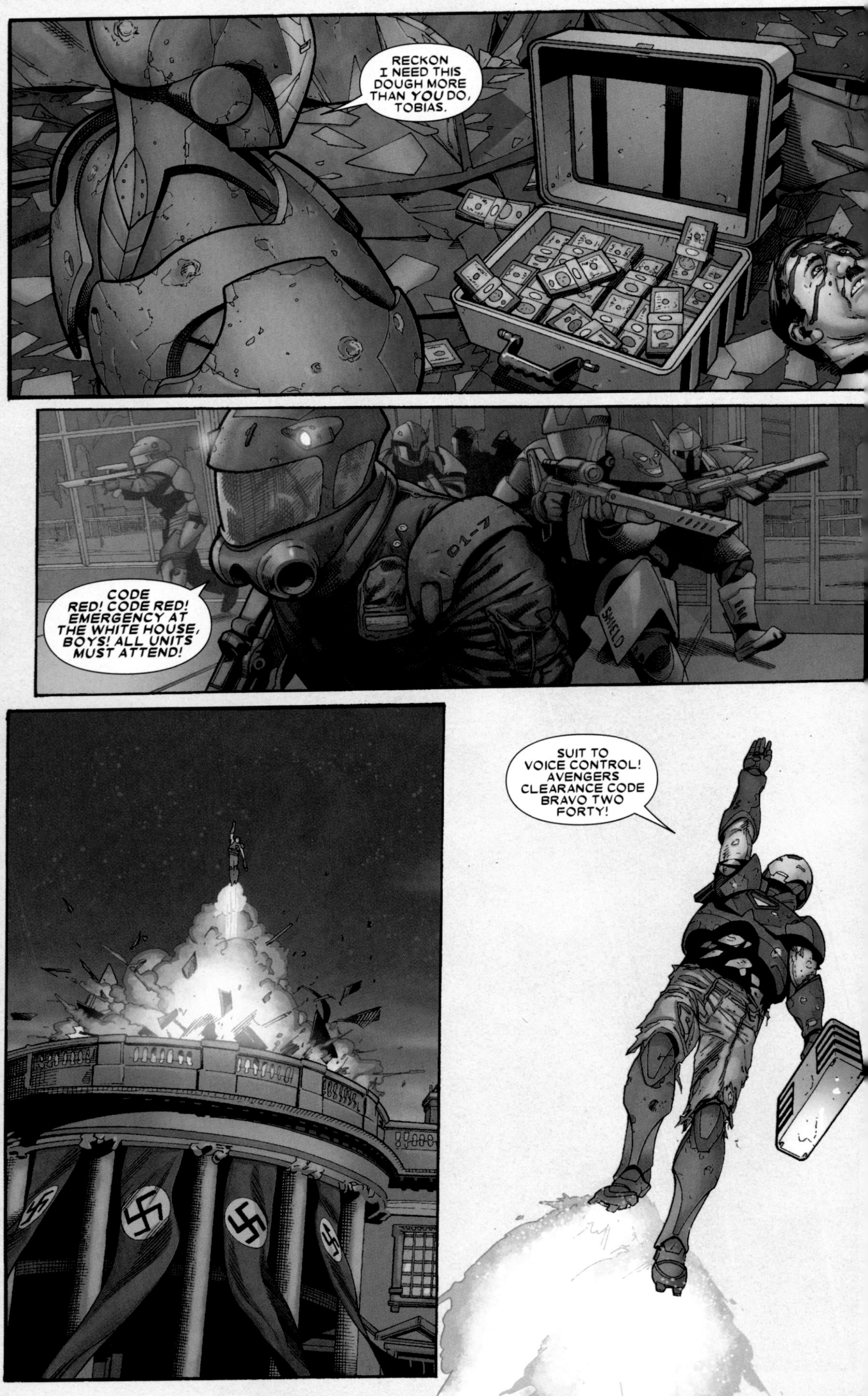
RECKON I NEED THIS DOUGH MORE THAN YOU DO, TOBIAS.
CODE RED! CODE RED! EMERGENCY AT THE WHITE HOUSE, BOYS! ALL UNITS MUST ATTEND!
SUIT TO VOICE CONTROL! AVENGERS CLEARANCE CODE BRAVO TWO FORTY!

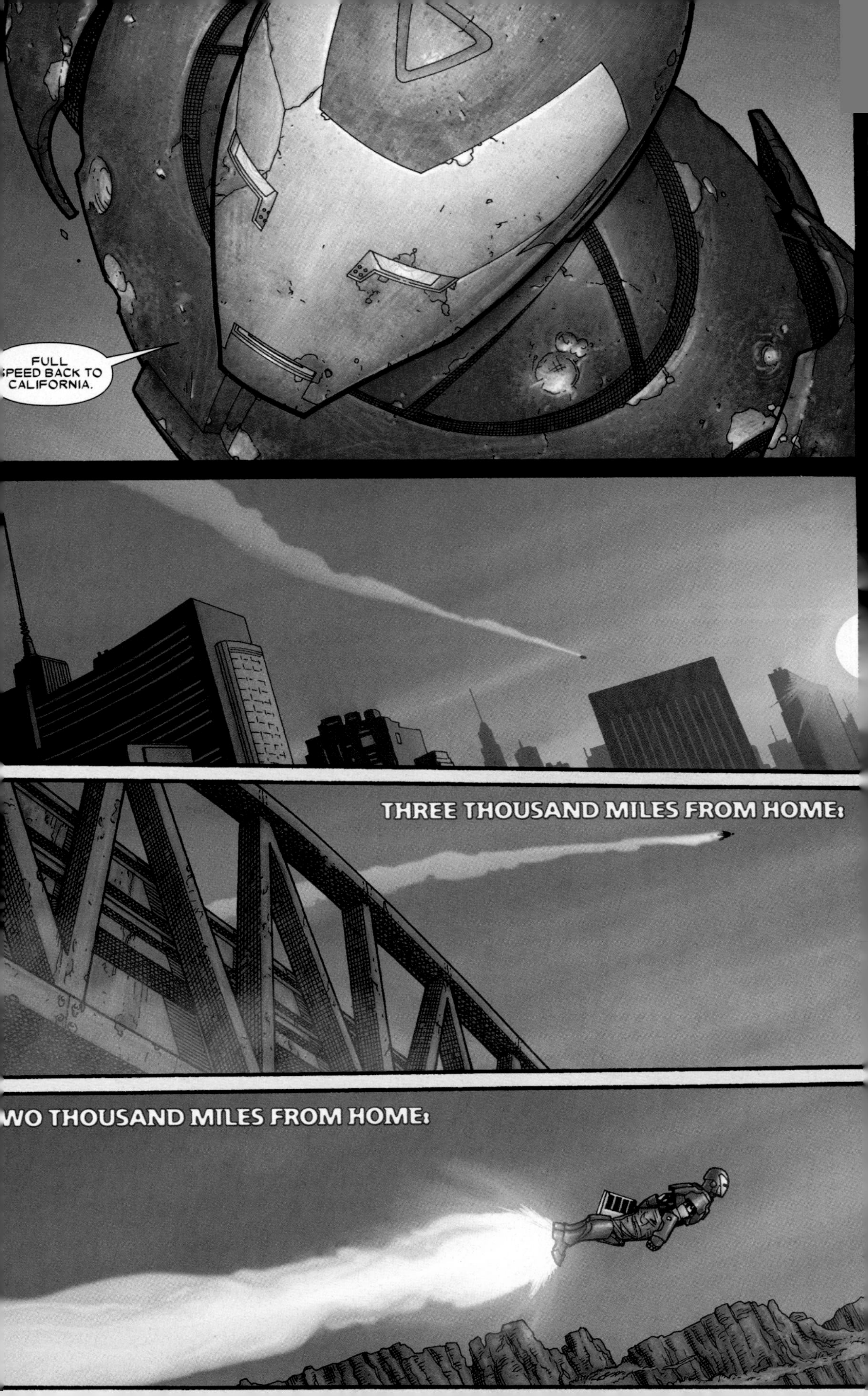
FULL SPEED BACK TO CALIFORNIA.
THREE THOUSAND MILES FROM HOME:
WO THOUSAND MILES FROM HOME:

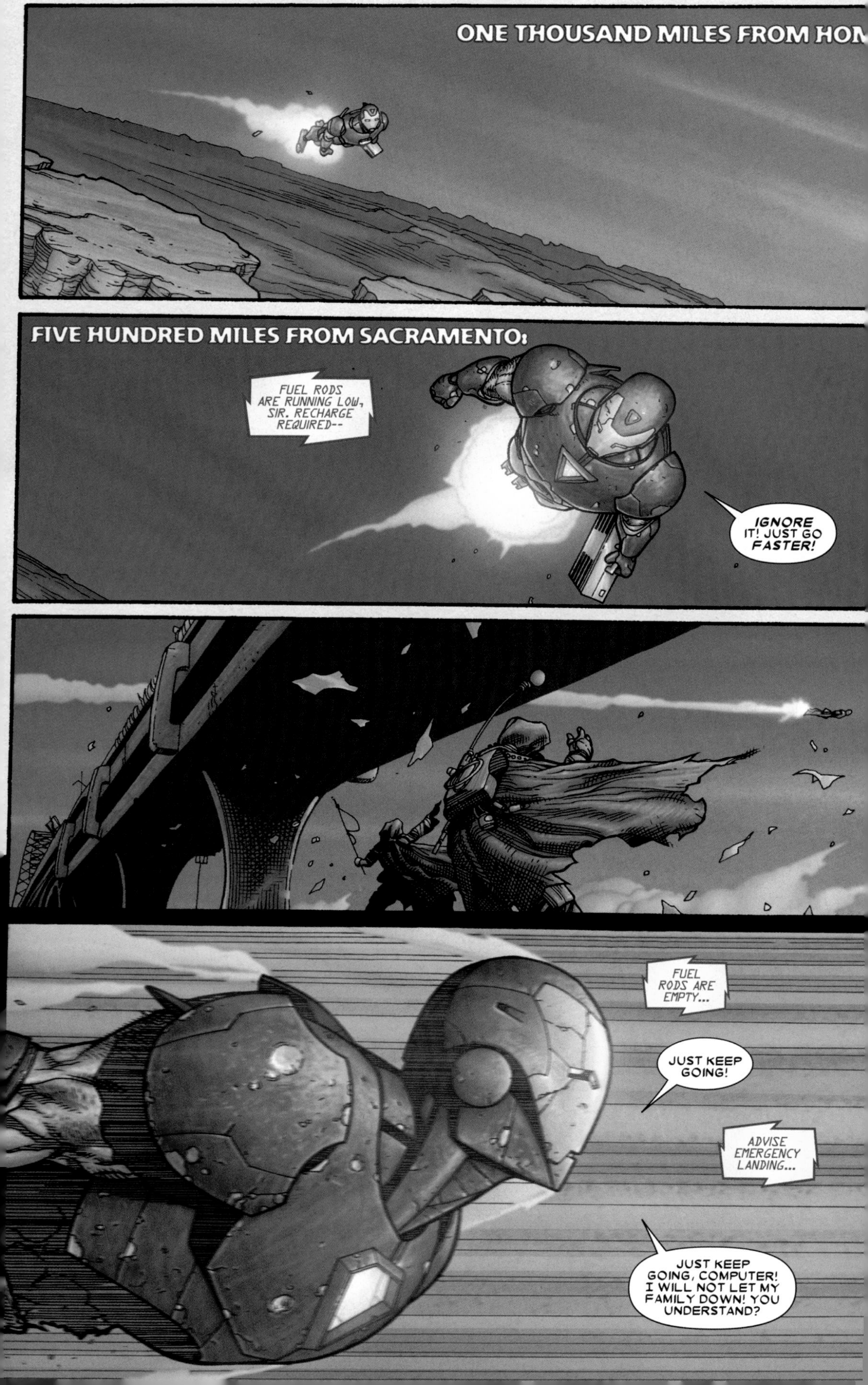
ONE THOUSAND MILES FROM HOM
FIVE HUNDRED MILES FROM SACRAMENTO:
FUEL RODS ARE RUNNING LOW, SIR. RECHARGE REQUIRED--
IGNORE IT! JUST GO FASTER!
FUEL RODS ARE EMPTY...
JUST KEEP GOING!
ADVISE EMERGENCY LANDING...
JUST KEEP GOING, COMPUTER! I WILL NOT LET MY FAMILY DOWN! YOU UNDERSTAND?

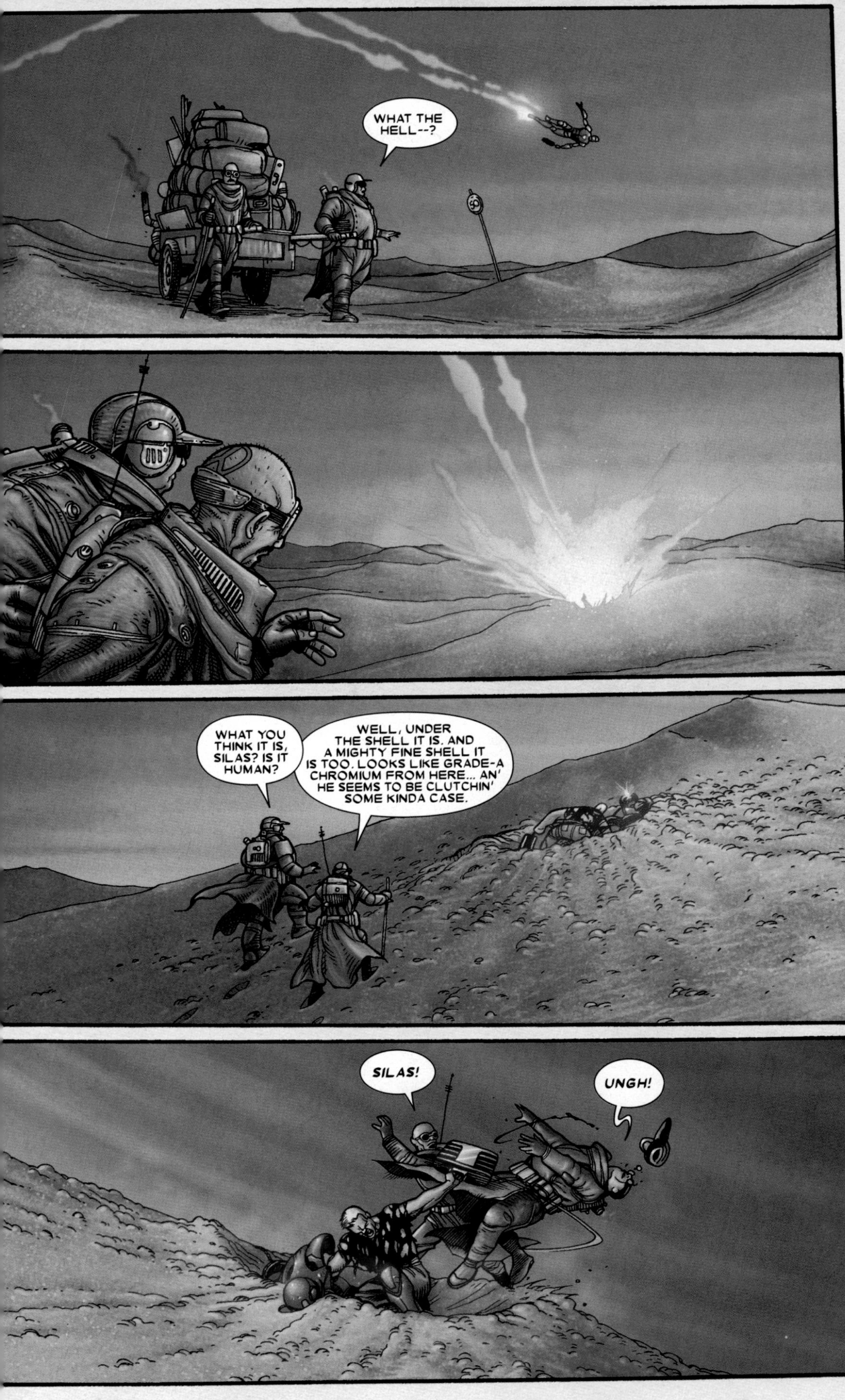
WHAT THE HELL--?
WHAT YOU THINK IT IS, SILAS? IS IT HUMAN?
WELL, UNDER THE SHELL IT IS. AND A MIGHTY FINE SHELL IT IS TOO. LOOKS LIKE GRADE-A CHROMIUM FROM HERE... AN' HE SEEMS TO BE CLUTCHIN' SOME KINDA CASE.
SILAS!
UNGH!

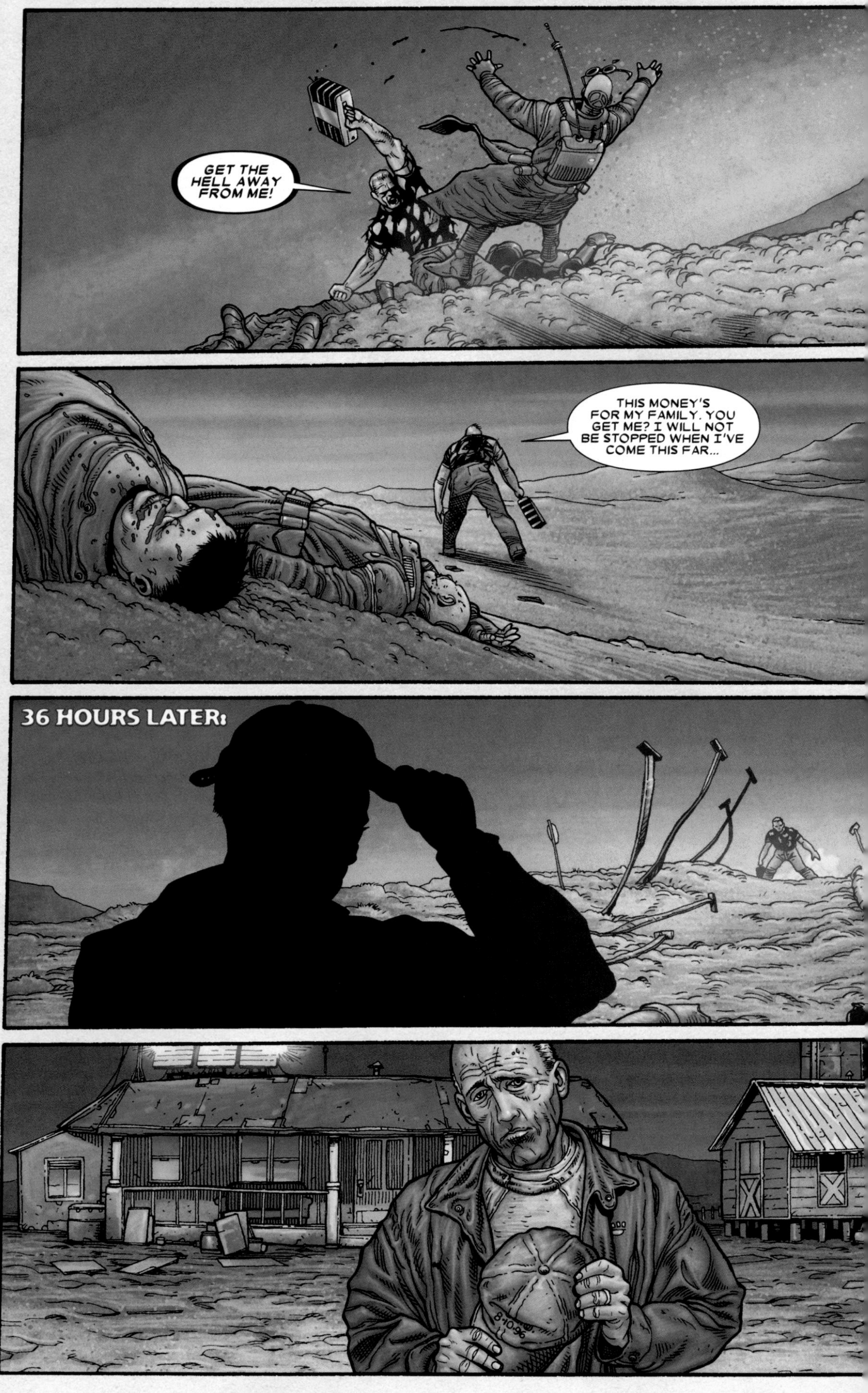
GET THE HELL AWAY FROM ME!
THIS MONEY'S FOR MY FAMILY. YOU GET ME? I WILL NOT BE STOPPED WHEN I'VE COME THIS FAR...
36 HOURS LATER:
8-10-96

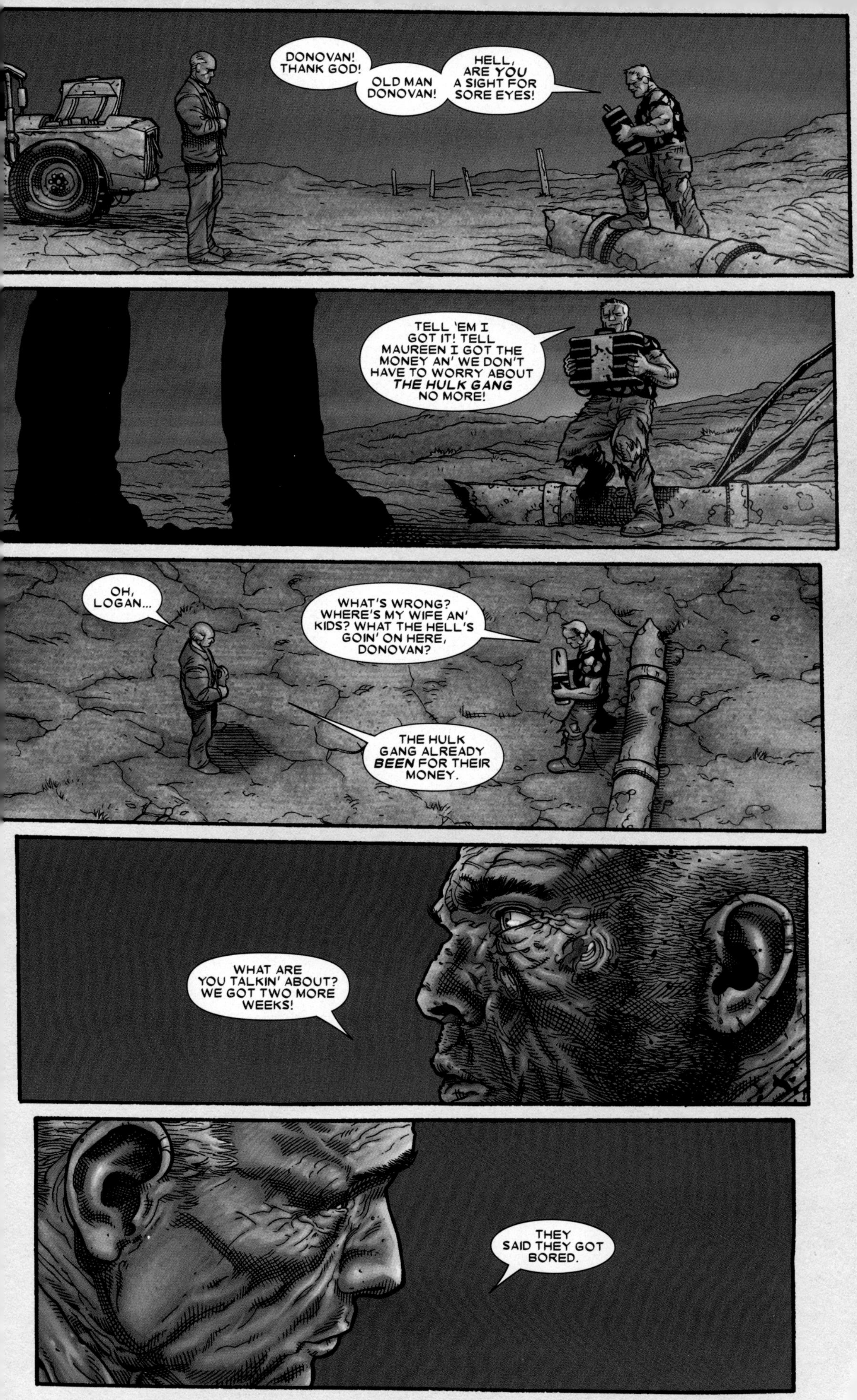
DONOVAN! THANK GOD!
OLD MAN DONOVAN!
HELL, ARE YOU A SIGHT FOR SORE EYES!
TELL 'EM I GOT IT! TELL MAUREEN I GOT THE MONEY AN' WE DON'T HAVE TO WORRY ABOUT THE HULK GANG NO MORE!
OH, LOGAN...
WHAT'S WRONG? WHERE'S MY WIFE AN' KIDS? WHAT THE HELL'S GOIN' ON HERE, DONOVAN?
THE HULK GANG ALREADY BEEN FOR THEIR MONEY.
WHAT ARE YOU TALKIN' ABOUT? WE GOT TWO MORE WEEKS!
THEY SAID THEY GOT BORED.

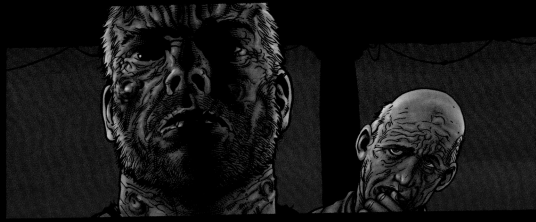

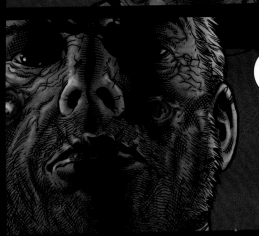

NOW DON'T YOU GO DOIN' SOMETHIN' STUPID. THEY'LL ONLY TAKE IT OUT ON THE REST OF US AN' YOU AIN'T THE MAN YOU *USED* TO BE, LOGAN.

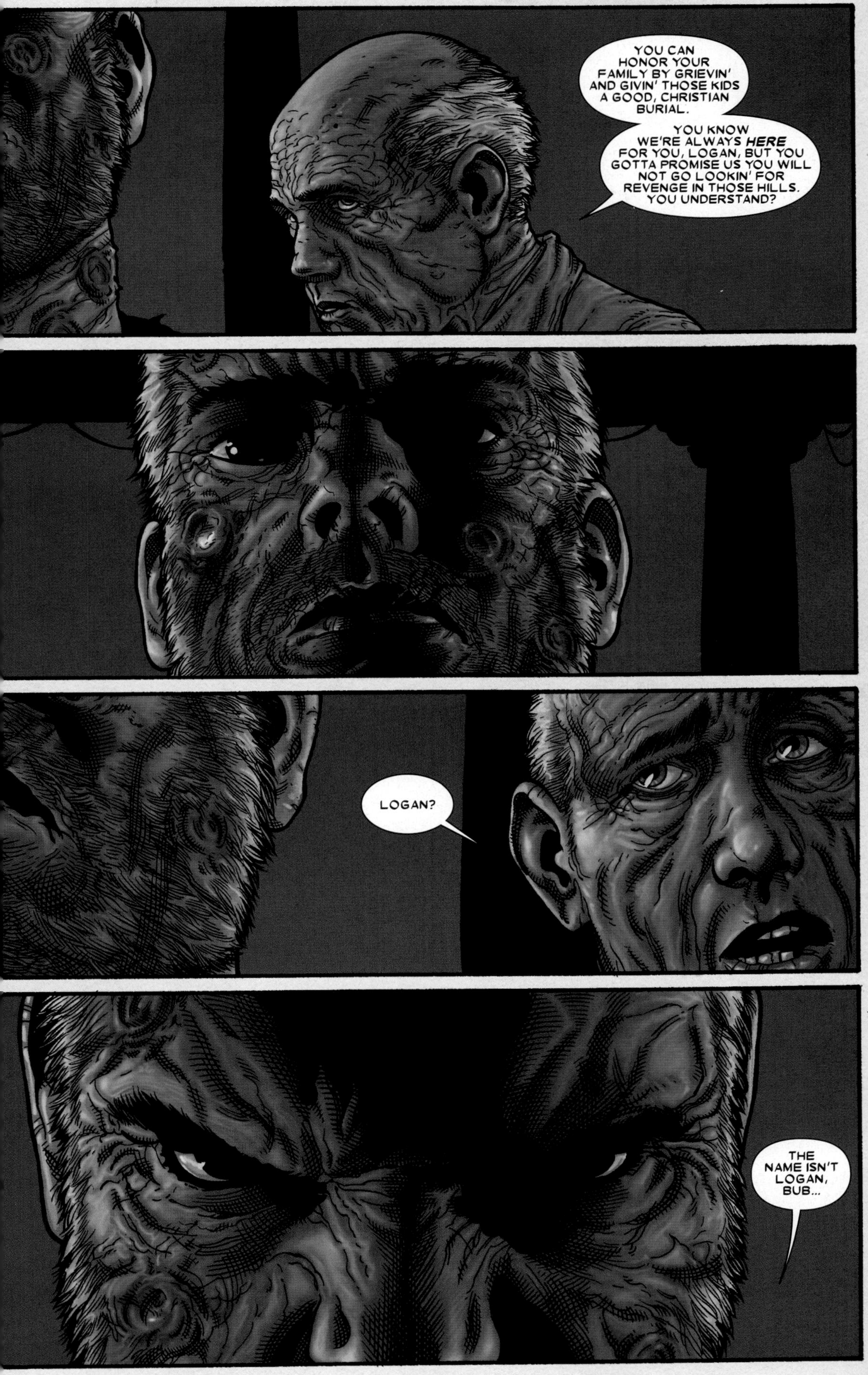
YOU CAN HONOR YOUR FAMILY BY GRIEVIN' AND GIVIN' THOSE KIDS A GOOD, CHRISTIAN BURIAL.
YOU KNOW WE'RE ALWAYS *HERE* FOR YOU, LOGAN, BUT YOU GOTTA PROMISE US YOU WILL NOT GO LOOKIN' FOR REVENGE IN THOSE HILLS. YOU UNDERSTAND?
LOGAN?
THE NAME ISN'T LOGAN, BUB...

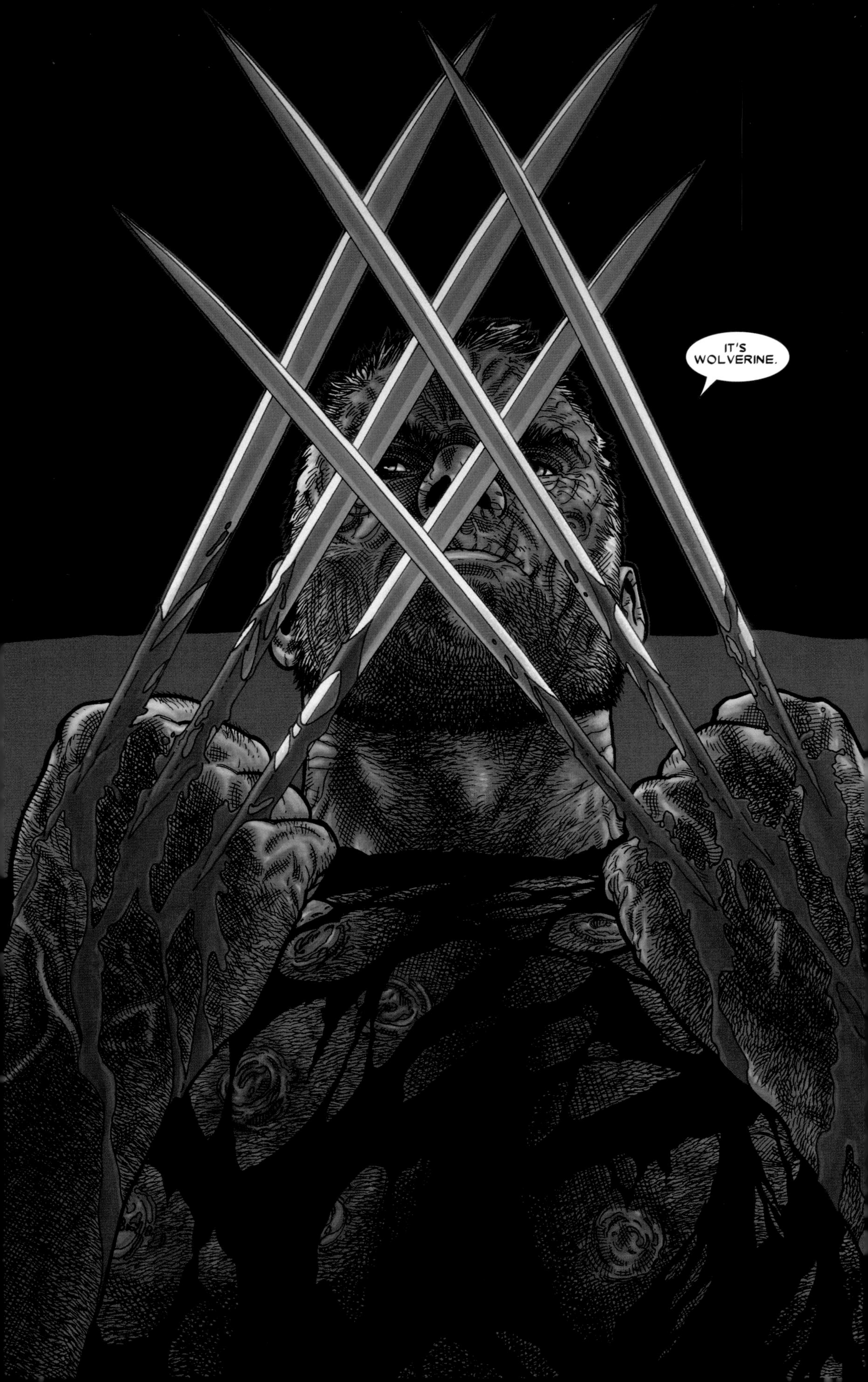
IT'S WOLVERINE.

FINAL CHAPTER

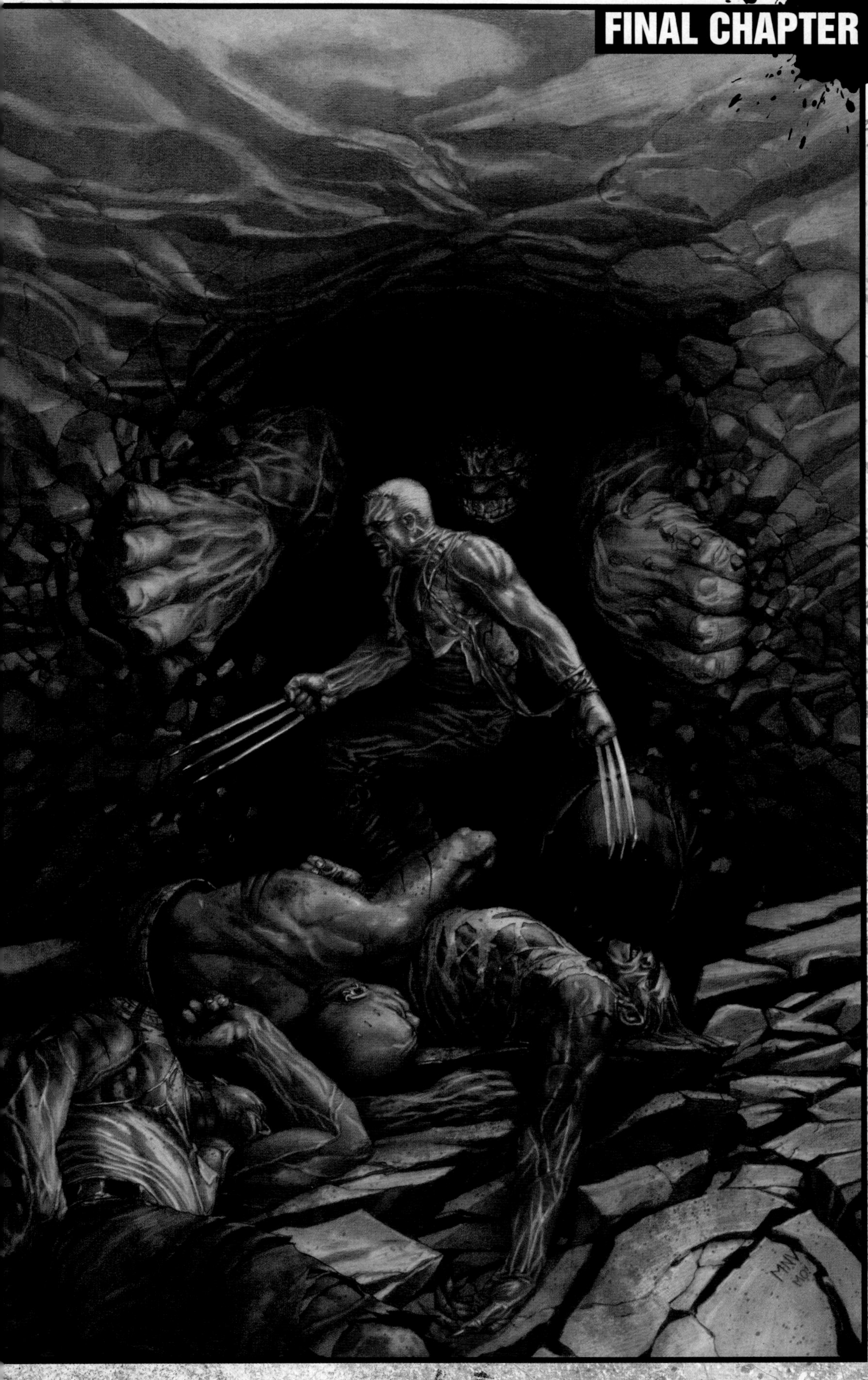

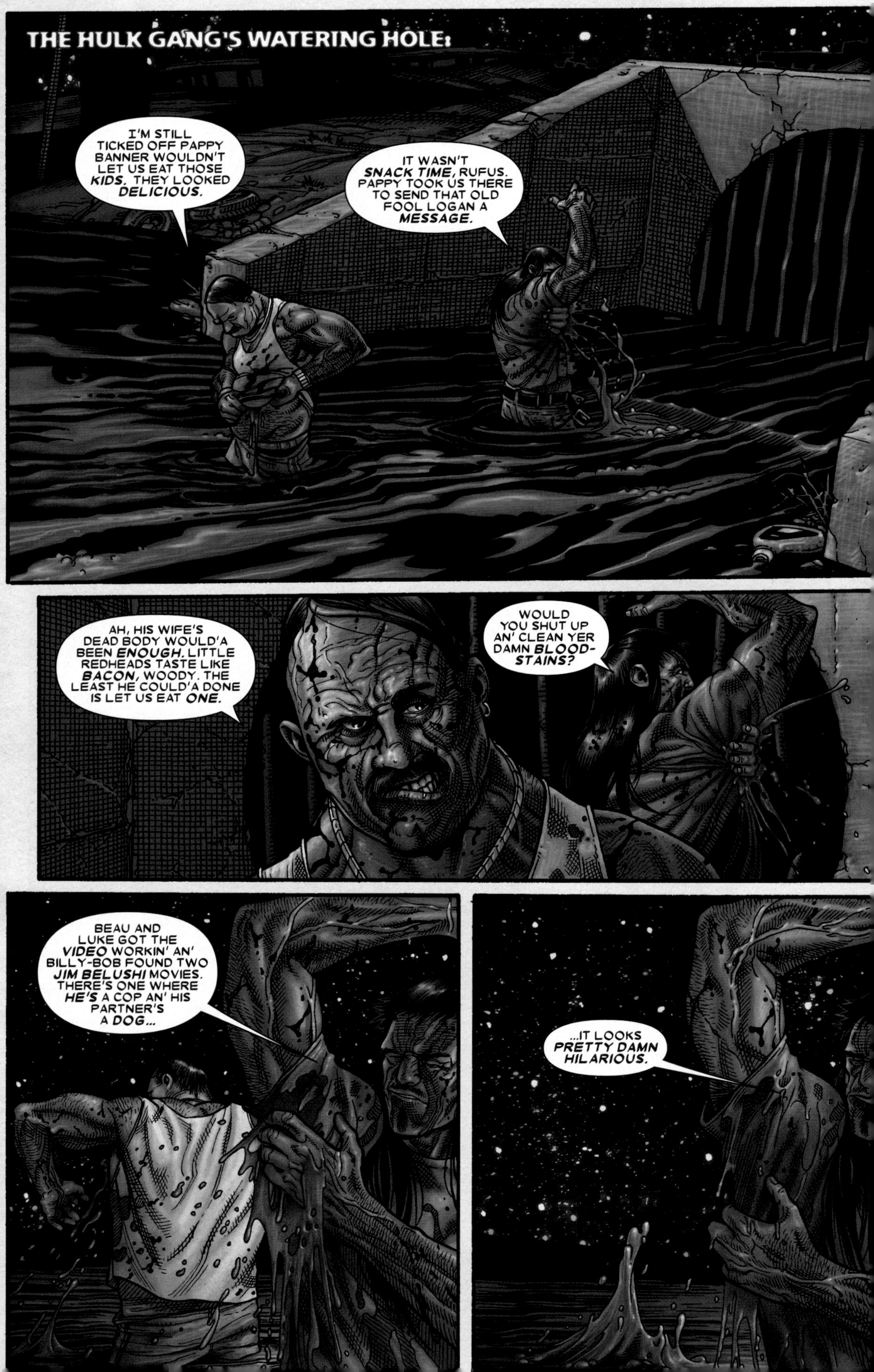
THE HULK GANG'S WATERING HOLE:
I'M STILL TICKED OFF PAPPY BANNER WOULDN'T LET US EAT THOSE KIDS. THEY LOOKED DELICIOUS.
IT WASN'T SNACK TIME, RUFUS. PAPPY TOOK US THERE TO SEND THAT OLD FOOL LOGAN A MESSAGE.
AH, HIS WIFE'S DEAD BODY WOULD'A BEEN ENOUGH. LITTLE REDHEADS TASTE LIKE BACON, WOODY. THE LEAST HE COULD'A DONE IS LET US EAT ONE.
WOULD YOU SHUT UP AN' CLEAN YER DAMN BLOOD-STAINS?
BEAU AND LUKE GOT THE VIDEO WORKIN' AN' BILLY-BOB FOUND TWO JIM BELUSHI MOVIES. THERE'S ONE WHERE HE'S A COP AN' HIS PARTNER'S A DOG...
...IT LOOKS PRETTY DAMN HILARIOUS.

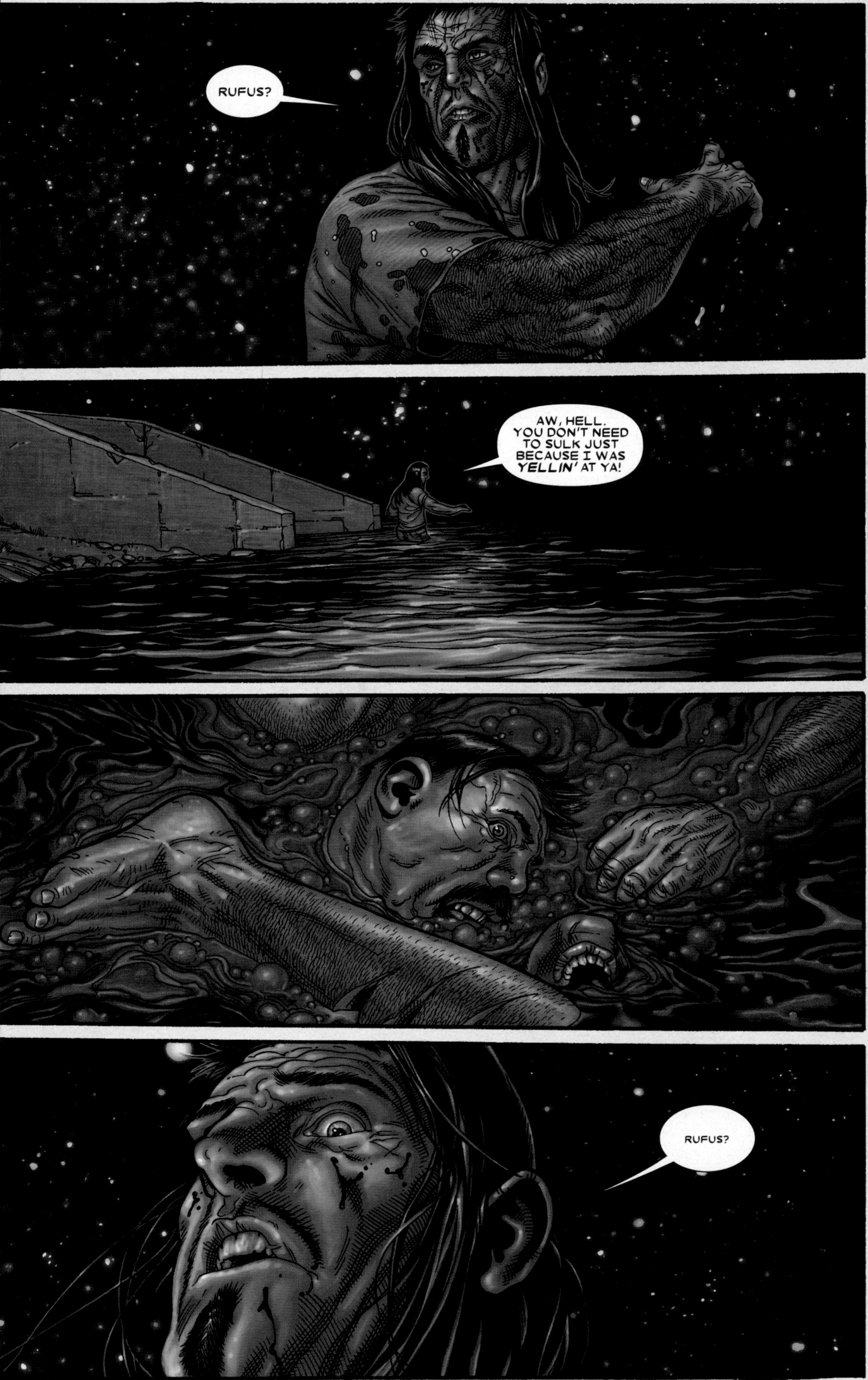
RUFUS?
AW, HELL. YOU DON'T NEED TO SULK JUST BECAUSE I WAS *YELLIN'* AT YA!
RUFUS?

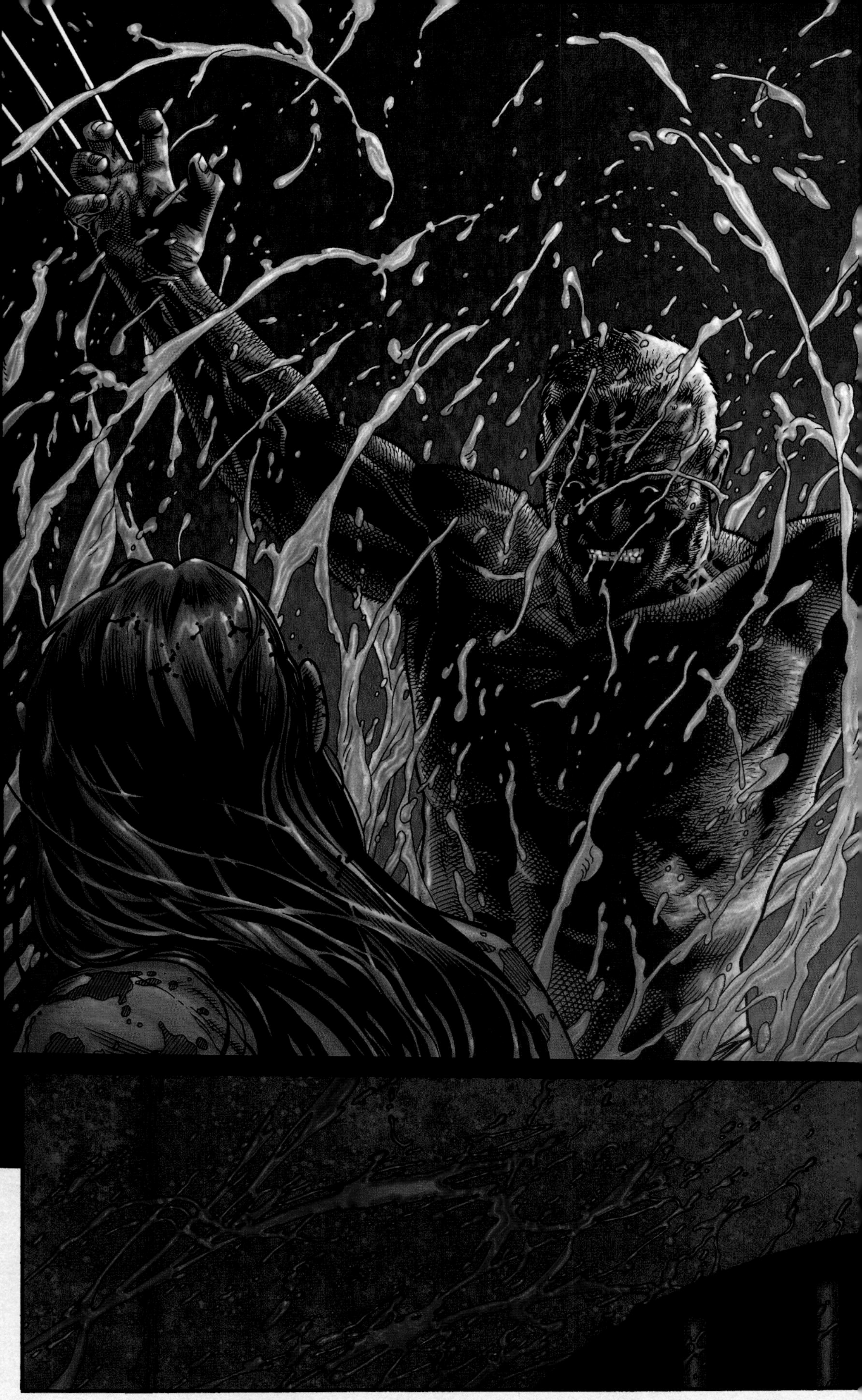

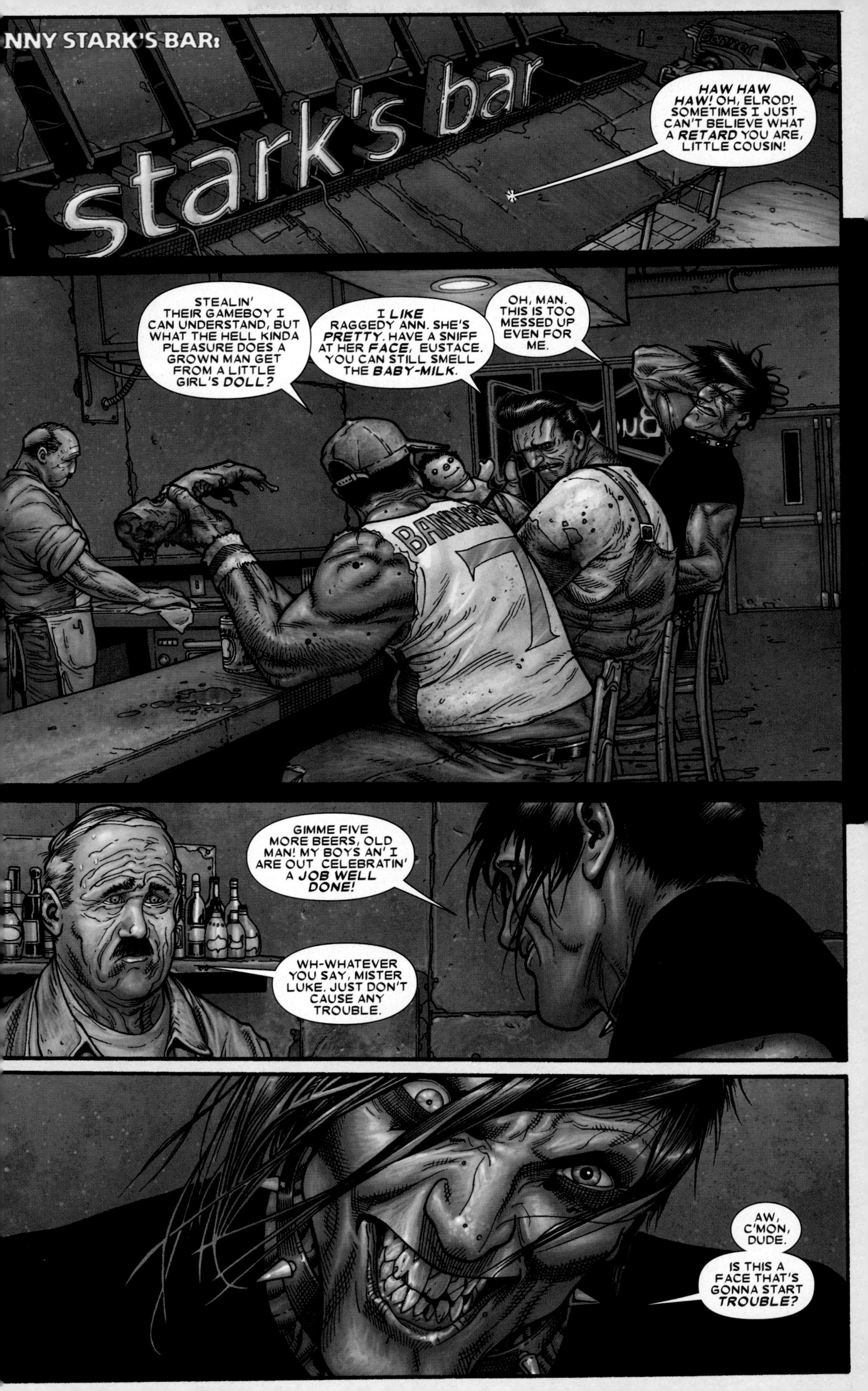
NNY STARK'S BAR:
stark's bar
HAW HAW HAW! OH, ELROD! SOMETIMES I JUST CAN'T BELIEVE WHAT A RETARD YOU ARE, LITTLE COUSIN!
STEALIN' THEIR GAMEBOY I CAN UNDERSTAND, BUT WHAT THE HELL KINDA PLEASURE DOES A GROWN MAN GET FROM A LITTLE GIRL'S DOLL?
I LIKE RAGGEDY ANN. SHE'S PRETTY. HAVE A SNIFF AT HER FACE, EUSTACE. YOU CAN STILL SMELL THE BABY-MILK.
OH, MAN. THIS IS TOO MESSED UP EVEN FOR ME.
BANNER
7
GIMME FIVE MORE BEERS, OLD MAN! MY BOYS AN' I ARE OUT CELEBRATIN' A JOB WELL DONE!
WH-WHATEVER YOU SAY, MISTER LUKE. JUST DON'T CAUSE ANY TROUBLE.
AW, C'MON, DUDE.
IS THIS A FACE THAT'S GONNA START TROUBLE?

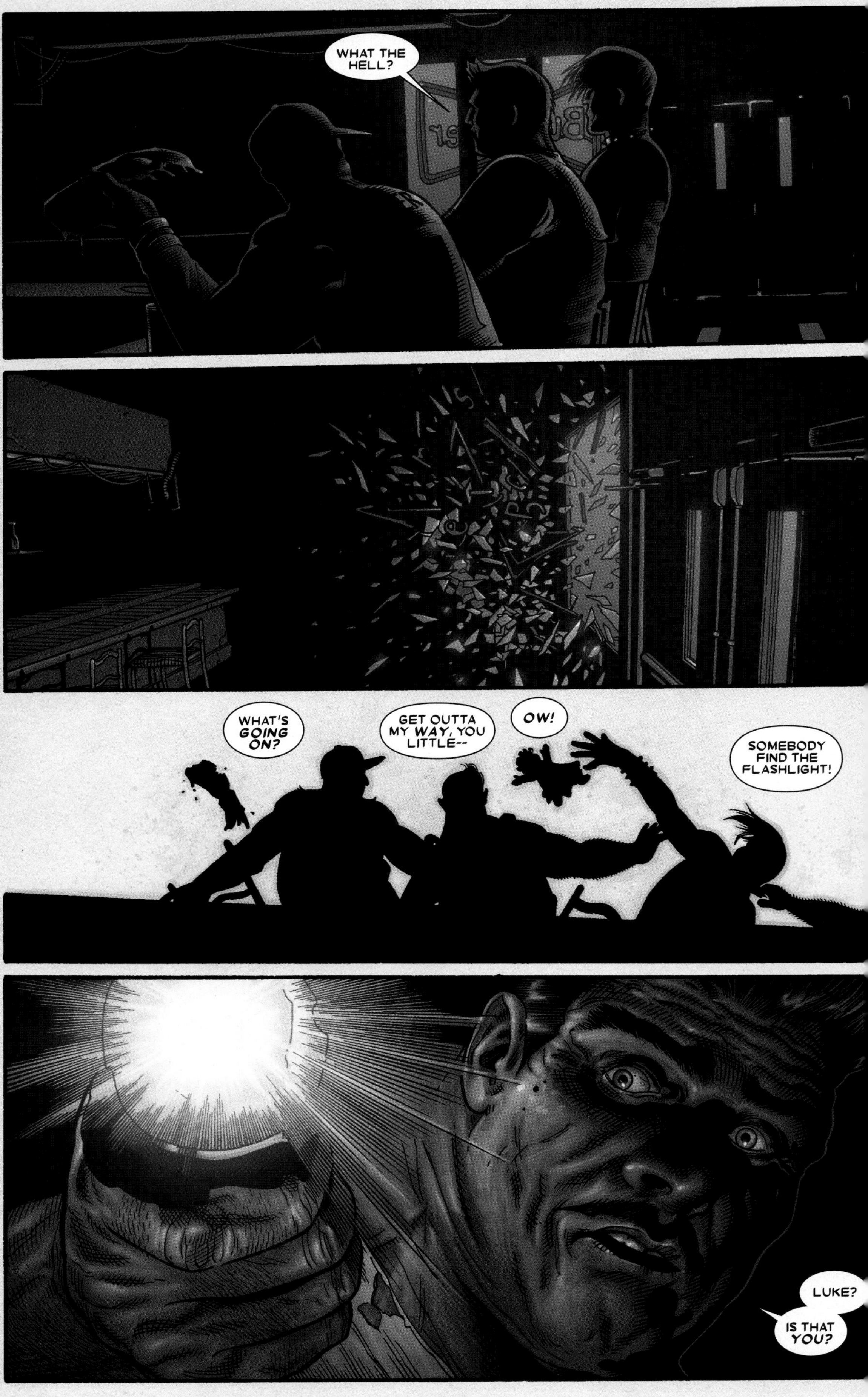
WHAT THE HELL?
WHAT'S GOING ON?
GET OUTTA MY WAY, YOU LITTLE--
OW!
SOMEBODY FIND THE FLASHLIGHT!
LUKE?
IS THAT YOU?

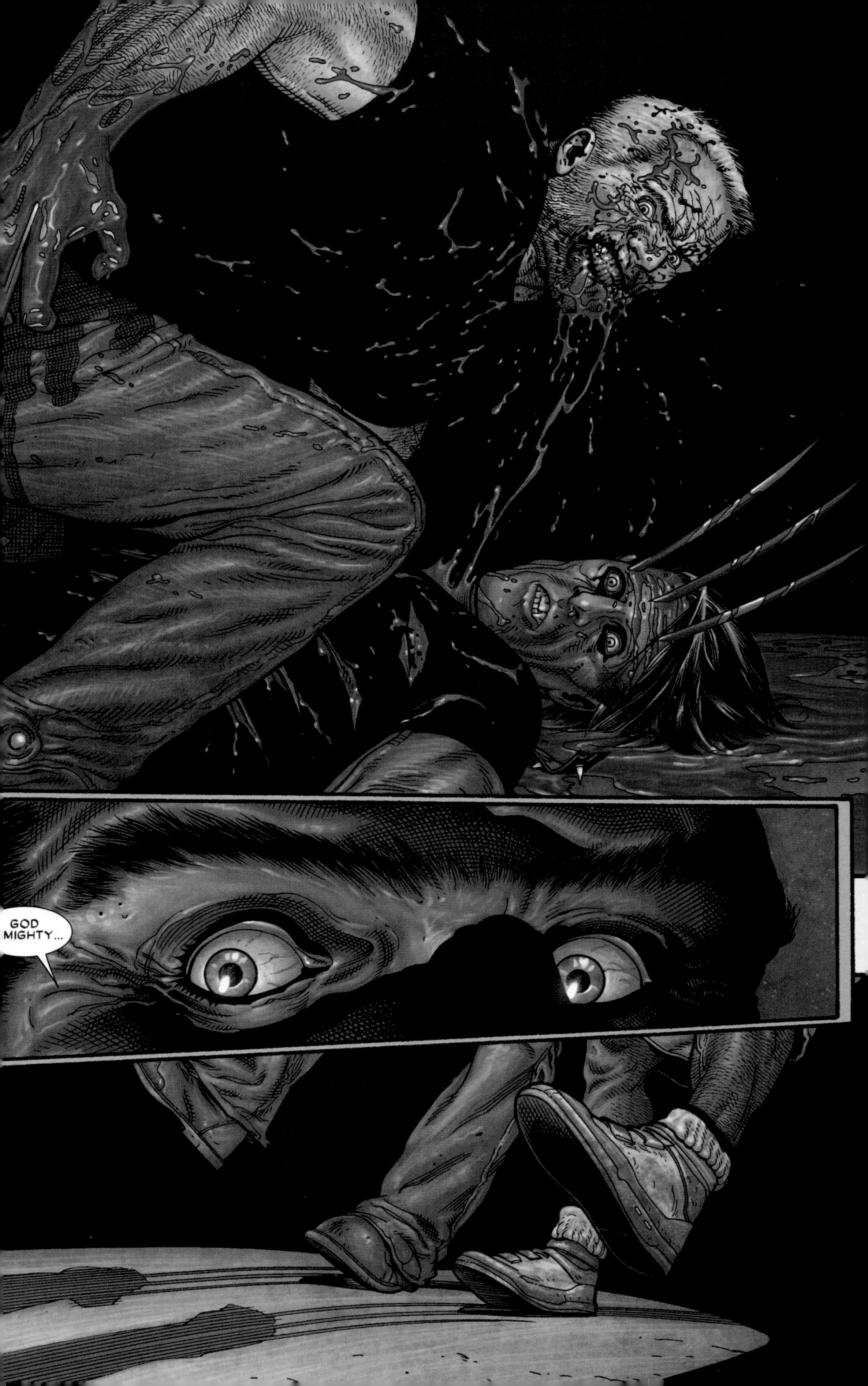
GOD MIGHTY...

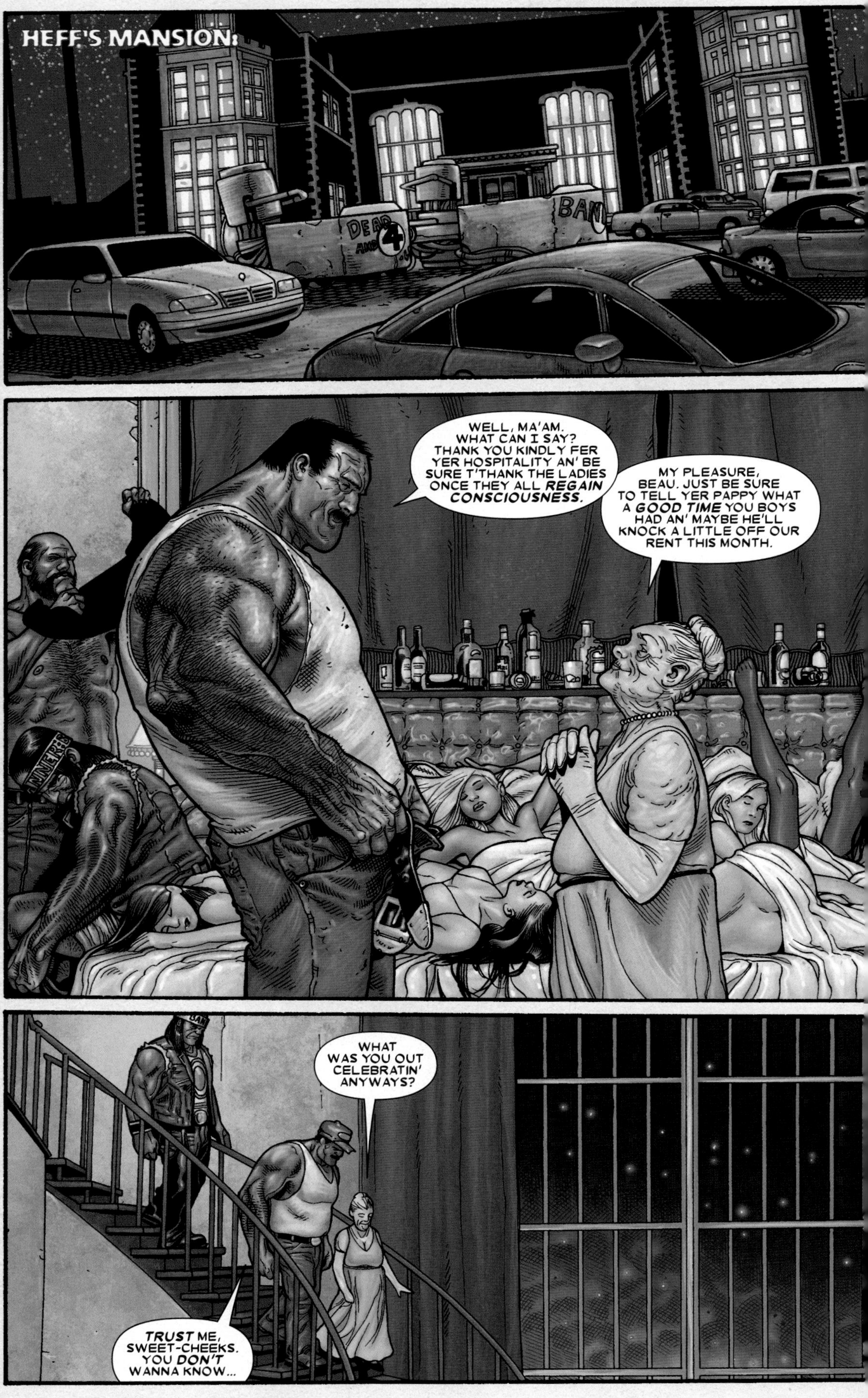
HEFF'S MANSION:
WELL, MA'AM. WHAT CAN I SAY? THANK YOU KINDLY FER YER HOSPITALITY AN' BE SURE T'THANK THE LADIES ONCE THEY ALL *REGAIN CONSCIOUSNESS.*
MY PLEASURE, BEAU. JUST BE SURE TO TELL YER PAPPY WHAT A *GOOD TIME* YOU BOYS HAD AN' MAYBE HE'LL KNOCK A LITTLE OFF OUR RENT THIS MONTH.
WHAT WAS YOU OUT CELEBRATIN' ANYWAYS?
TRUST ME, SWEET-CHEEKS. YOU *DON'T* WANNA KNOW...

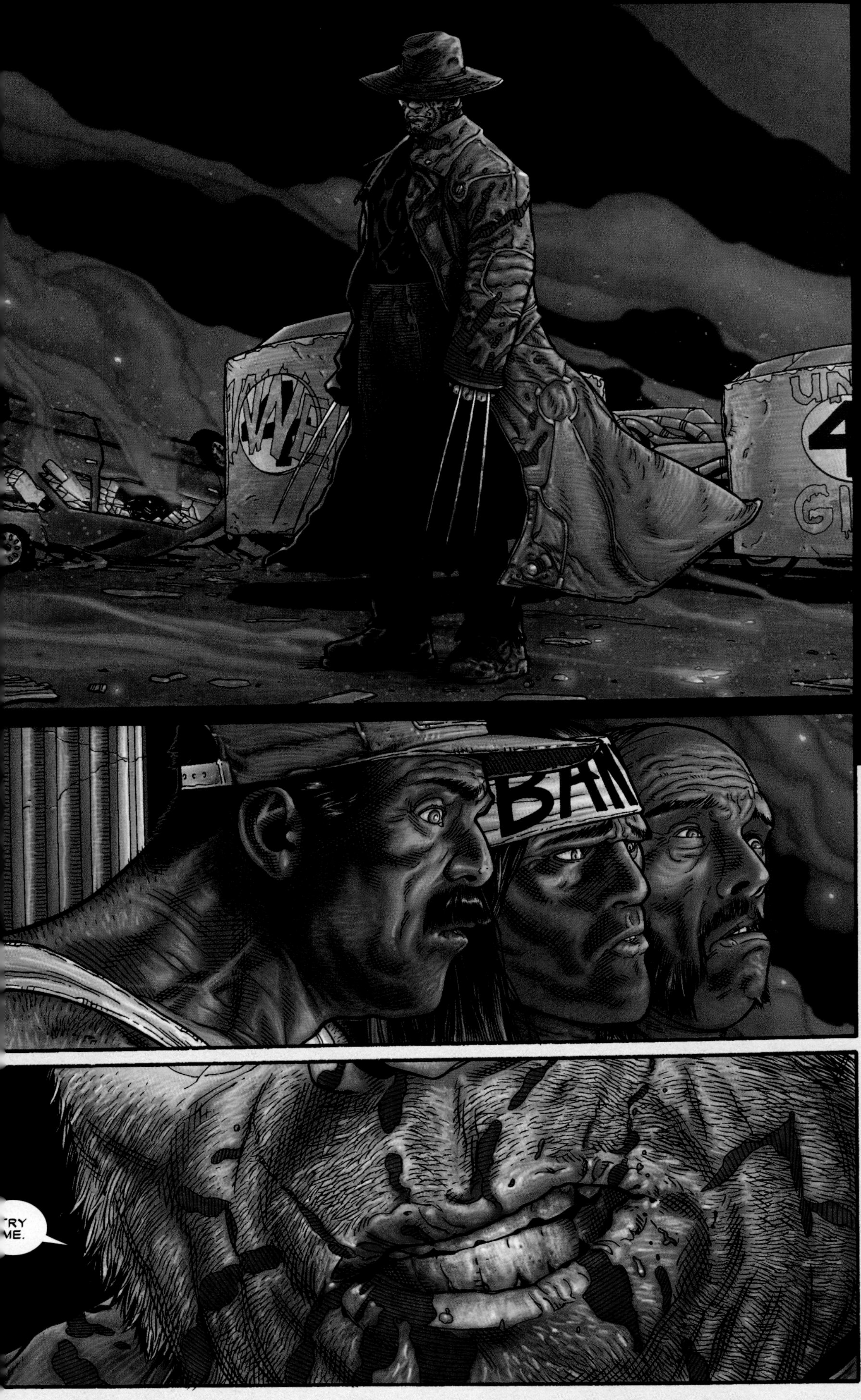
TRY
ME.

BANNER'S LAIR:

YOU THINK HE'S GONNA *COME HERE*, PAPPY?

EVEN THOUGH THERE'S *SO MANY* OF US? YOU THINK HE'S GONNA COME HERE LOOKIN' FOR *REVENGE*?

WE KILLED HIS *WIFE AND CHILDREN*, BOBBI-JO. LAID THEM OUT LIKE THEY WAS A DAMN *FINGER-BUFFET.*

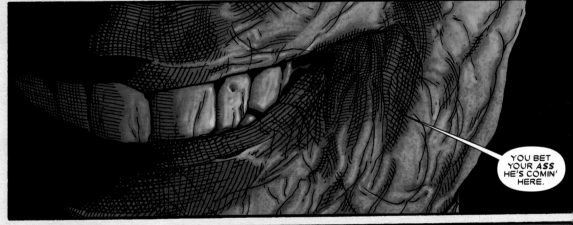

YOU BET YOUR *ASS* HE'S COMIN' HERE.

SWEET JEEZUS...

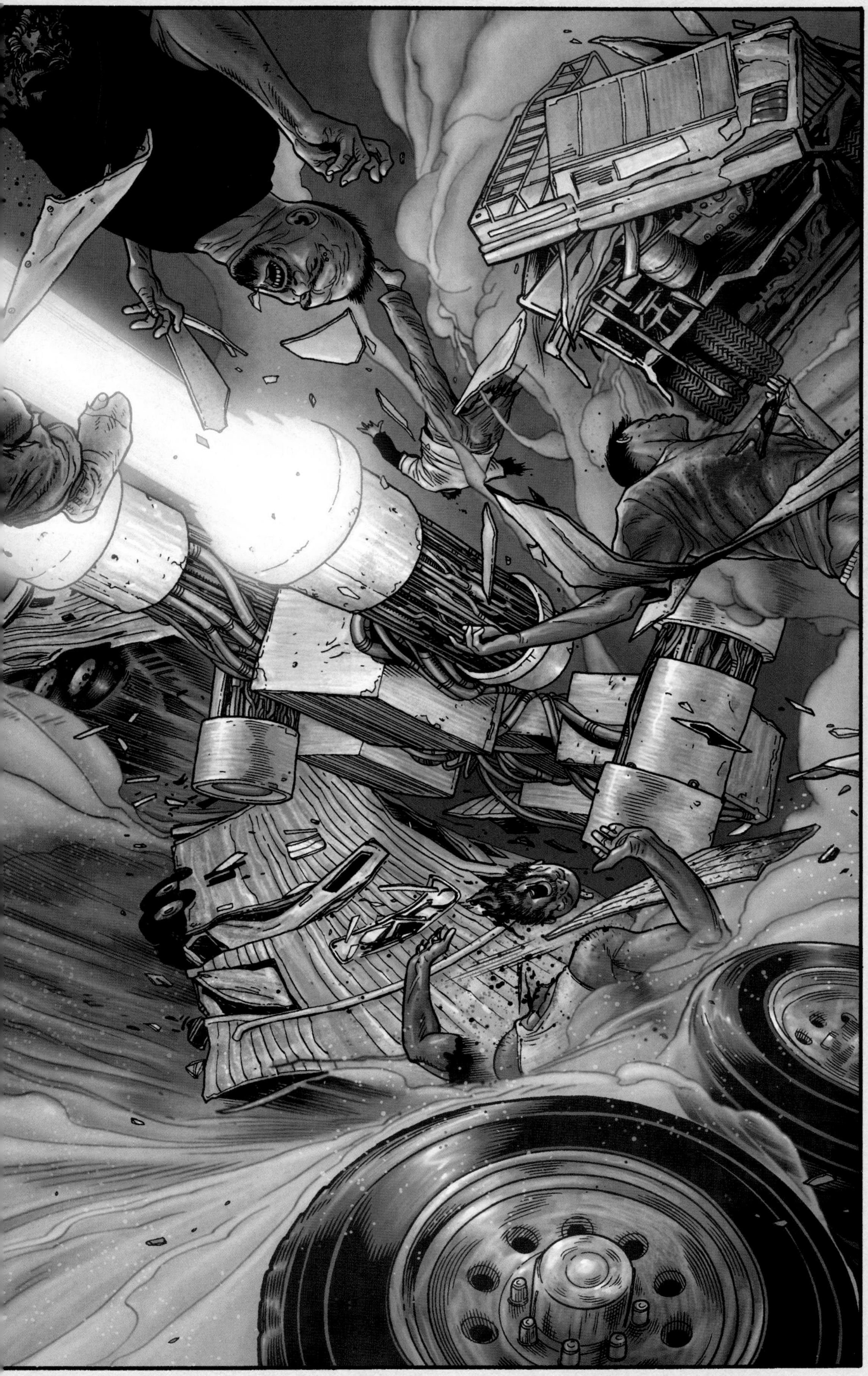

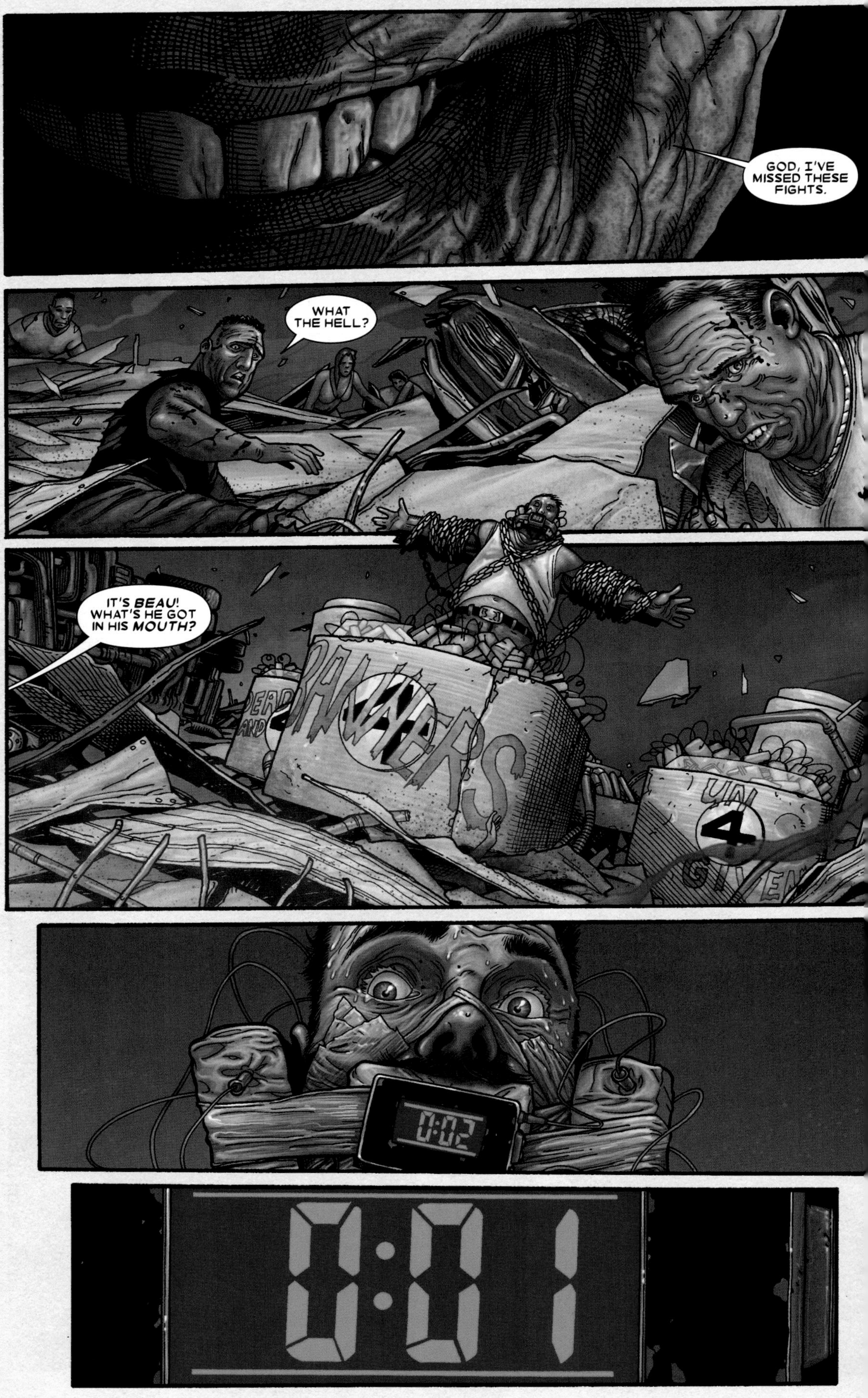
GOD, I'VE MISSED THESE FIGHTS.
WHAT THE HELL?
IT'S *BEAU*! WHAT'S HE GOT IN HIS *MOUTH*?
0:02
0:01

OH
%&$#.

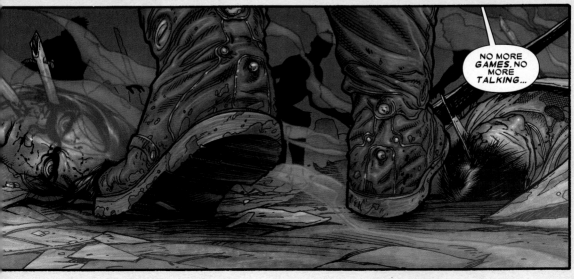

NO MORE
GAMES. NO
MORE
TALKING...

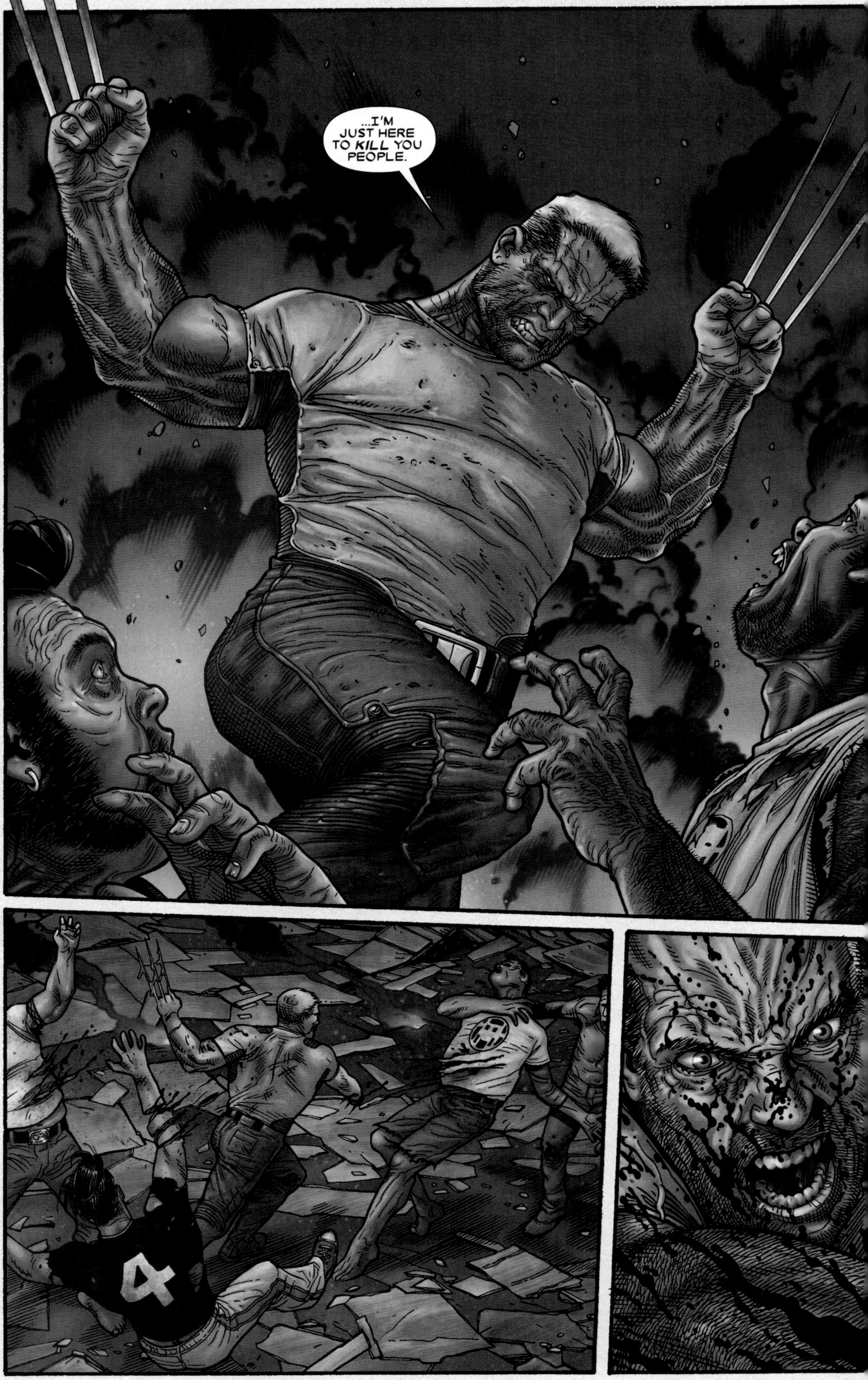
...I'M JUST HERE TO KILL YOU PEOPLE.

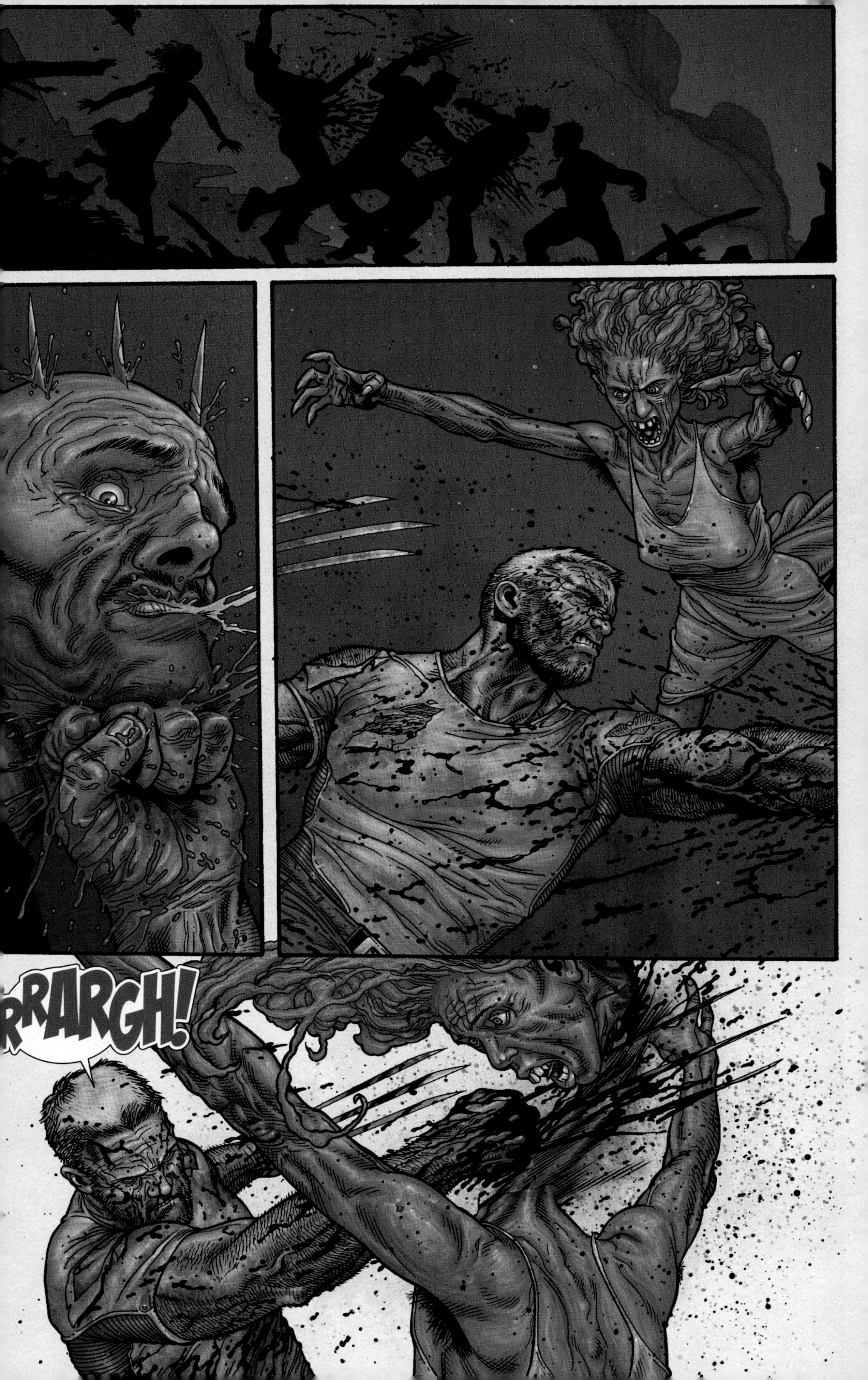
RRARGH!

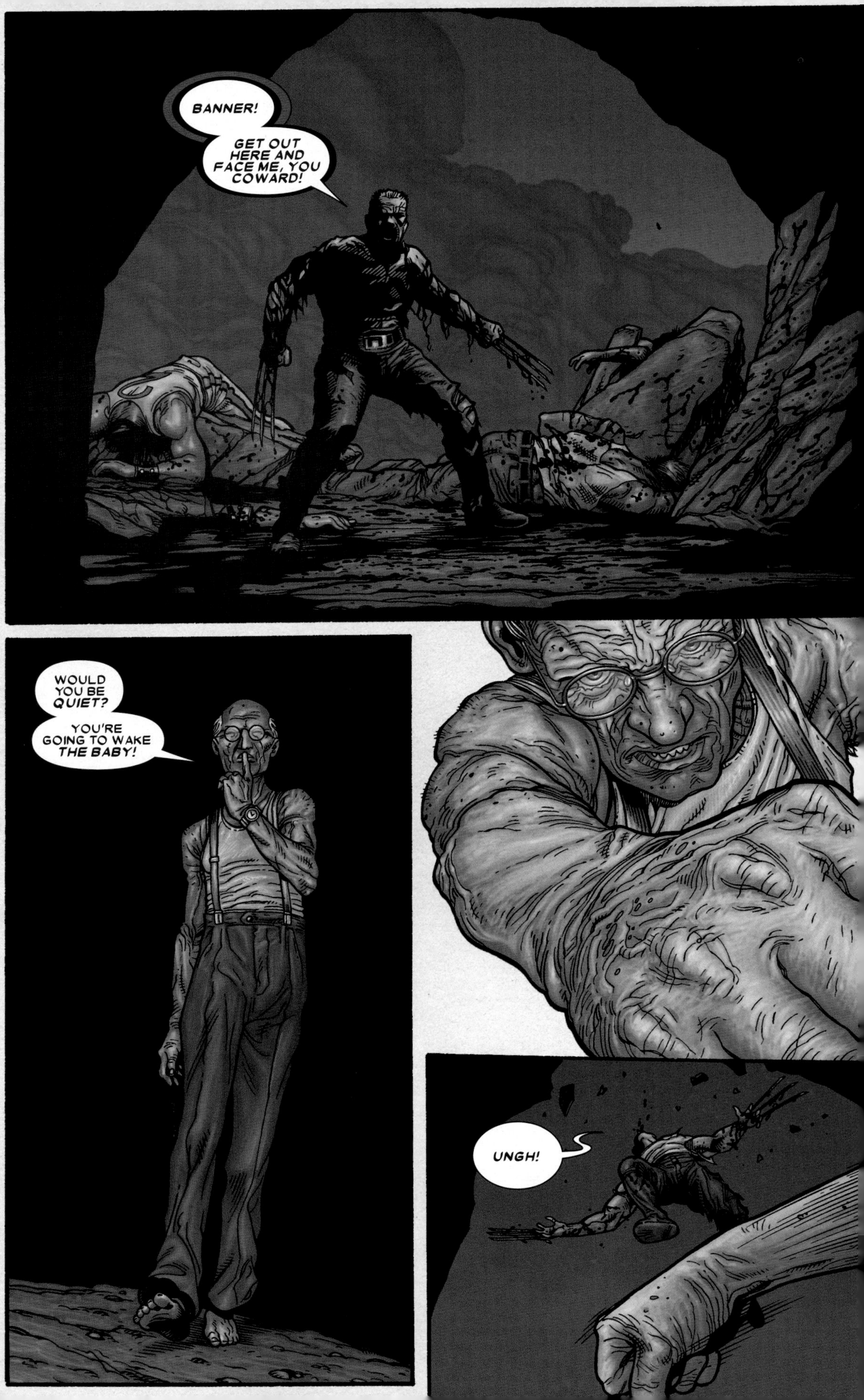
BANNER!
GET OUT HERE AND FACE ME, YOU COWARD!
WOULD YOU BE QUIET?
YOU'RE GOING TO WAKE THE BABY!
UNGH!

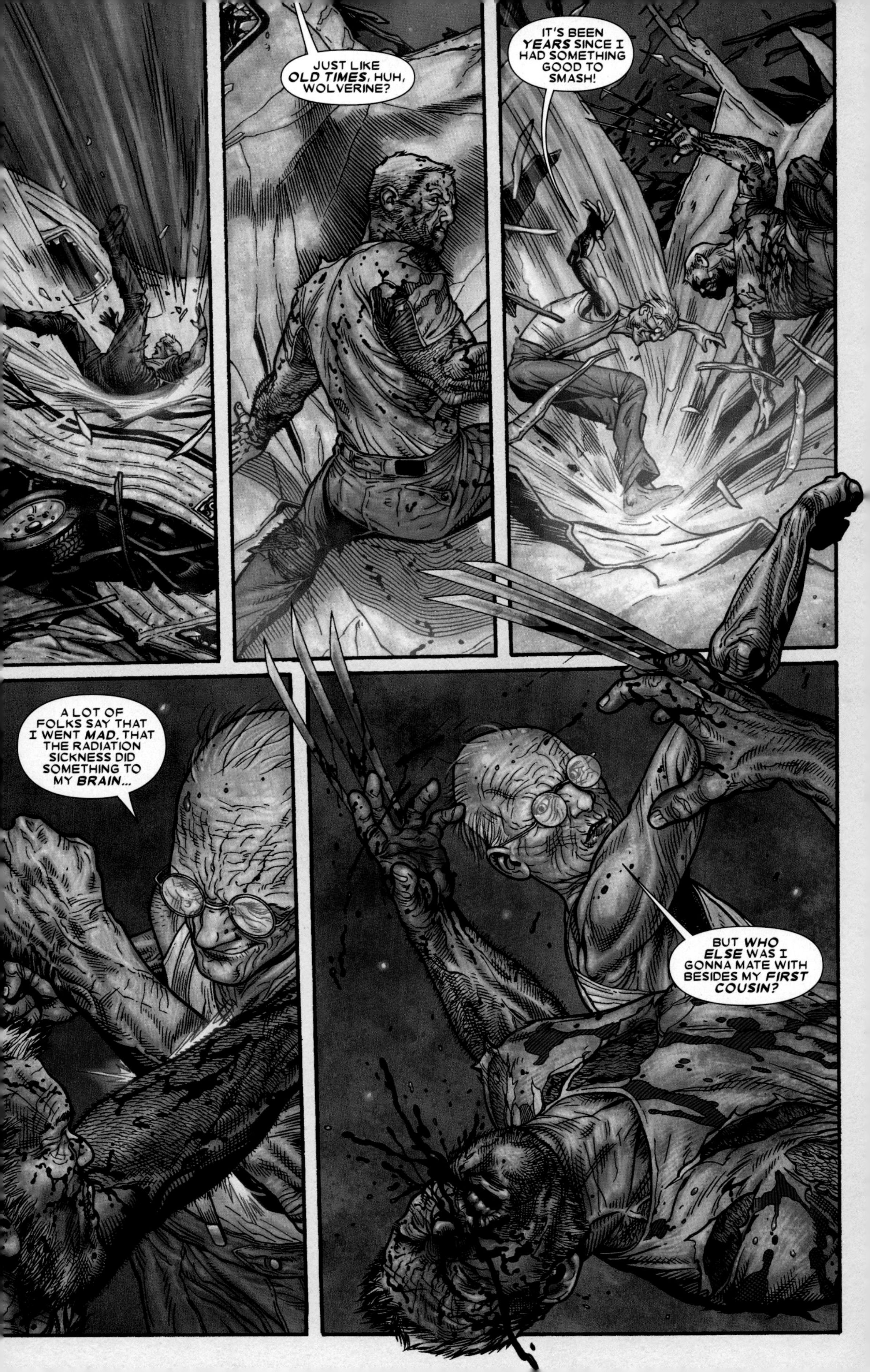
JUST LIKE OLD TIMES, HUH, WOLVERINE?
IT'S BEEN YEARS SINCE I HAD SOMETHING GOOD TO SMASH!
A LOT OF FOLKS SAY THAT I WENT MAD, THAT THE RADIATION SICKNESS DID SOMETHING TO MY BRAIN...
BUT WHO ELSE WAS I GONNA MATE WITH BESIDES MY FIRST COUSIN?

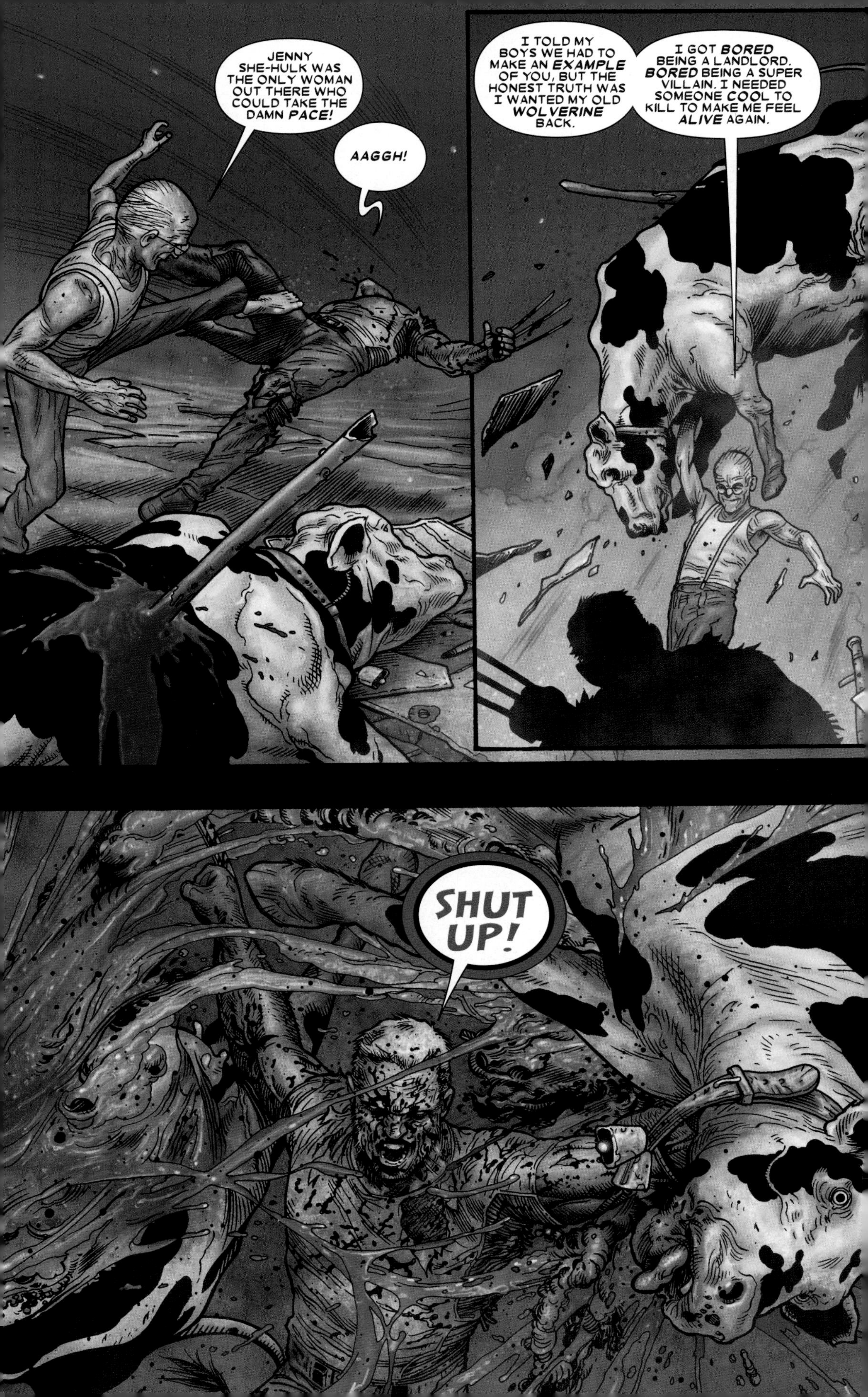
JENNY SHE-HULK WAS THE ONLY WOMAN OUT THERE WHO COULD TAKE THE DAMN *PACE!*
AAGGH!
I TOLD MY BOYS WE HAD TO MAKE AN *EXAMPLE* OF YOU, BUT THE HONEST TRUTH WAS I WANTED MY OLD *WOLVERINE* BACK.
I GOT *BORED* BEING A LANDLORD. *BORED* BEING A SUPER VILLAIN. I NEEDED SOMEONE *COOL* TO KILL TO MAKE ME FEEL *ALIVE* AGAIN.
SHUT UP!

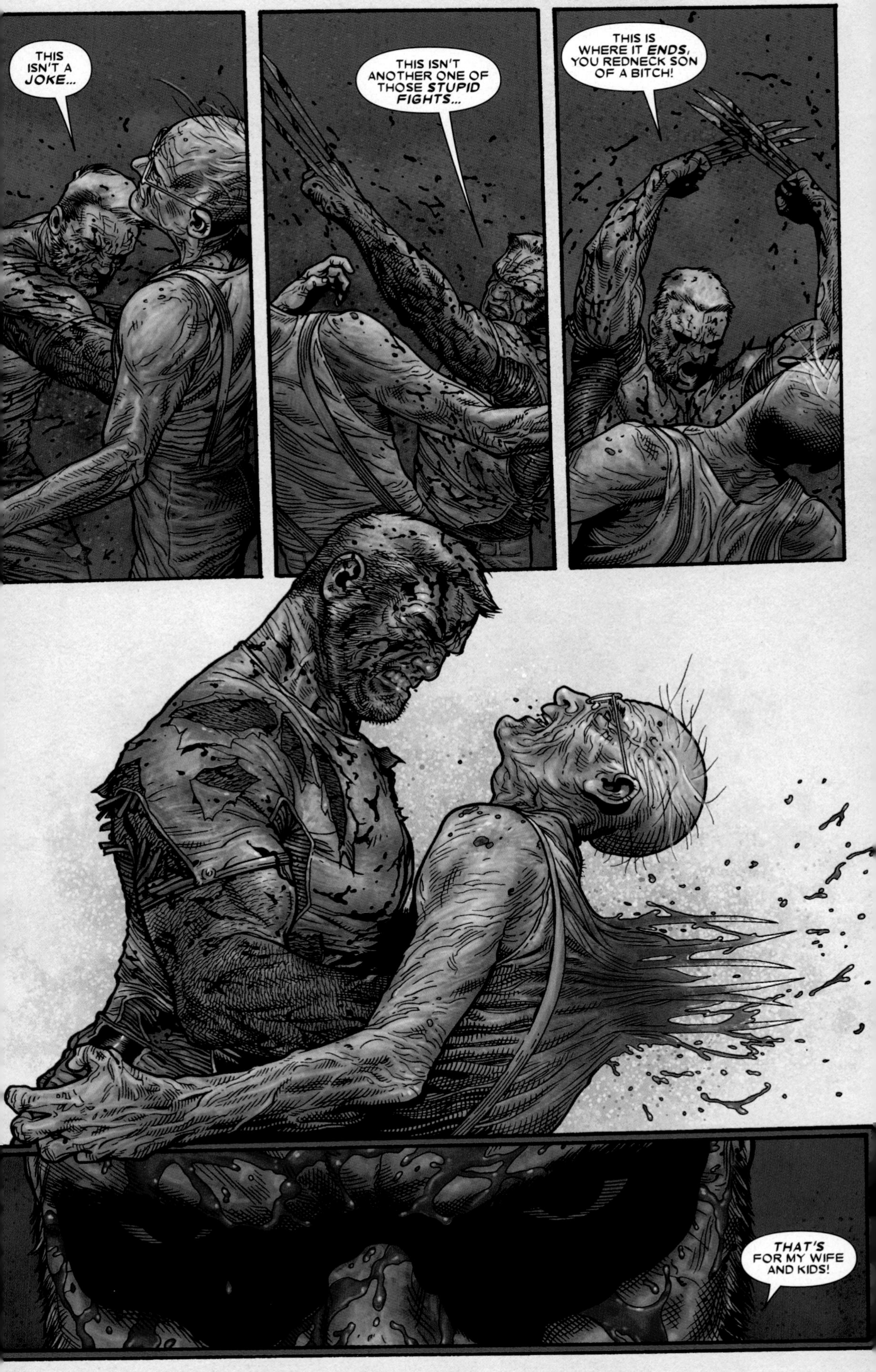
THIS ISN'T A JOKE...
THIS ISN'T ANOTHER ONE OF THOSE STUPID FIGHTS...
THIS IS WHERE IT ENDS, YOU REDNECK SON OF A BITCH!
THAT'S FOR MY WIFE AND KIDS!

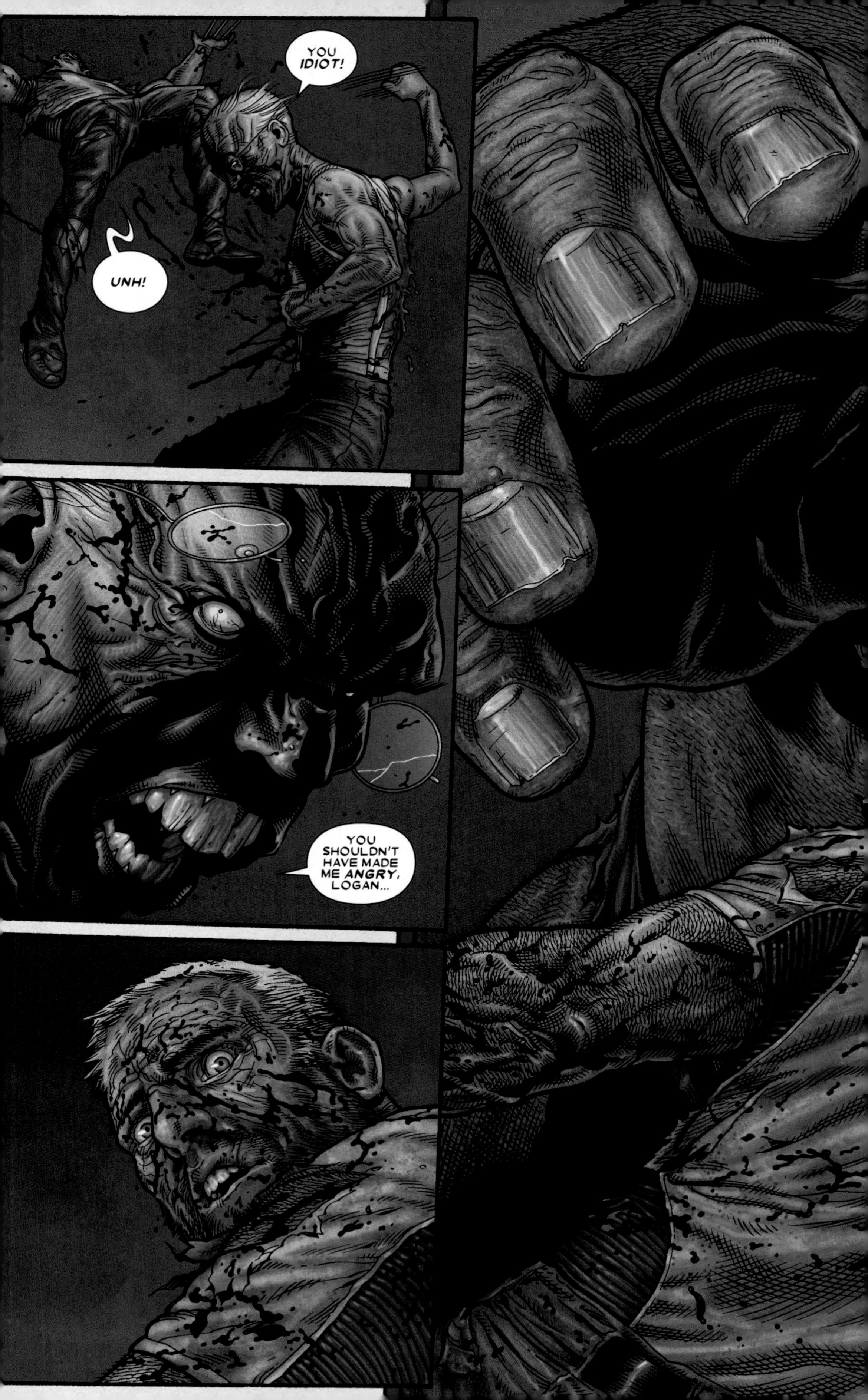
YOU IDIOT!
UNH!
YOU SHOULDN'T HAVE MADE ME ANGRY, LOGAN...

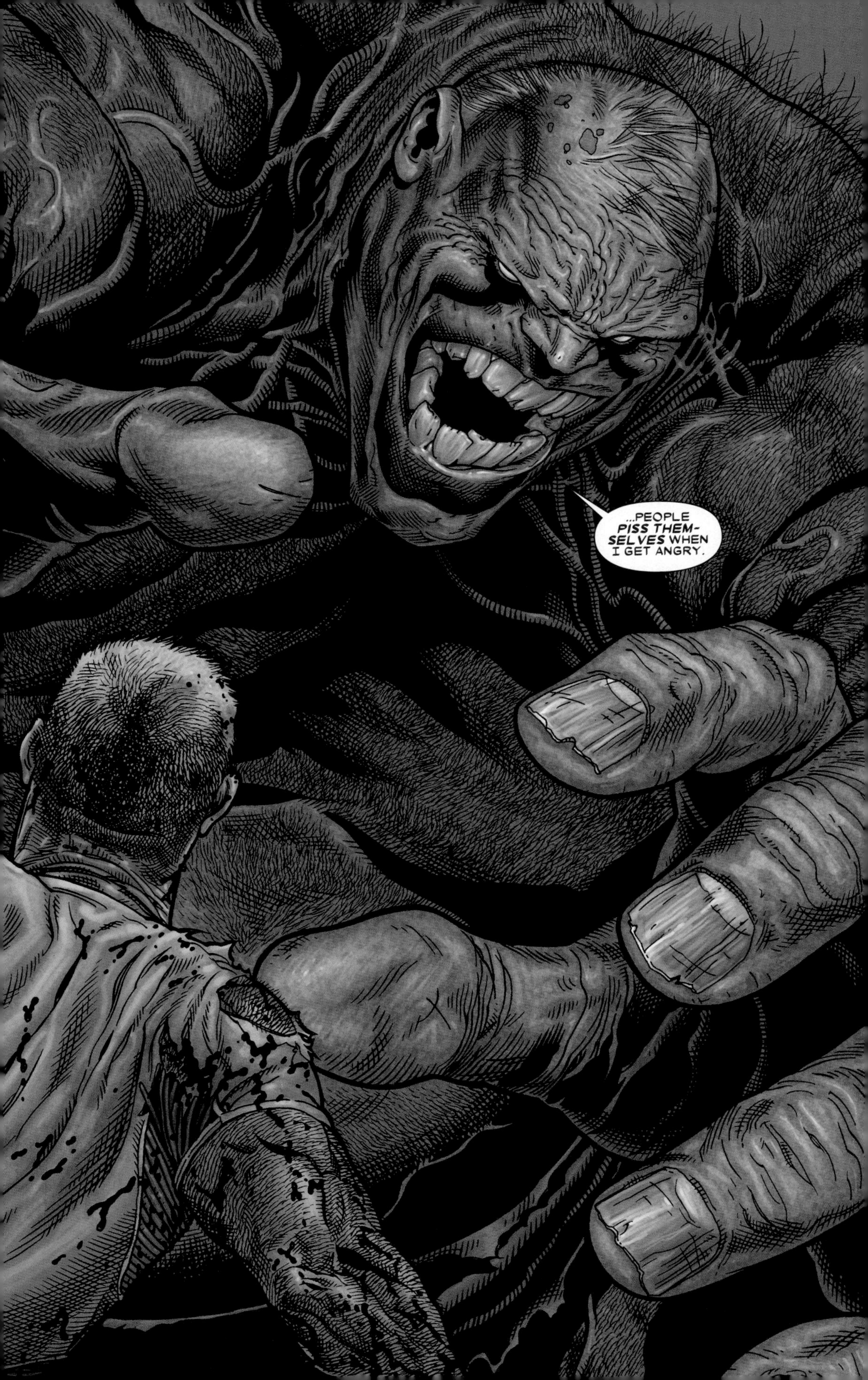
...PEOPLE PISS THEM-SELVES WHEN I GET ANGRY.

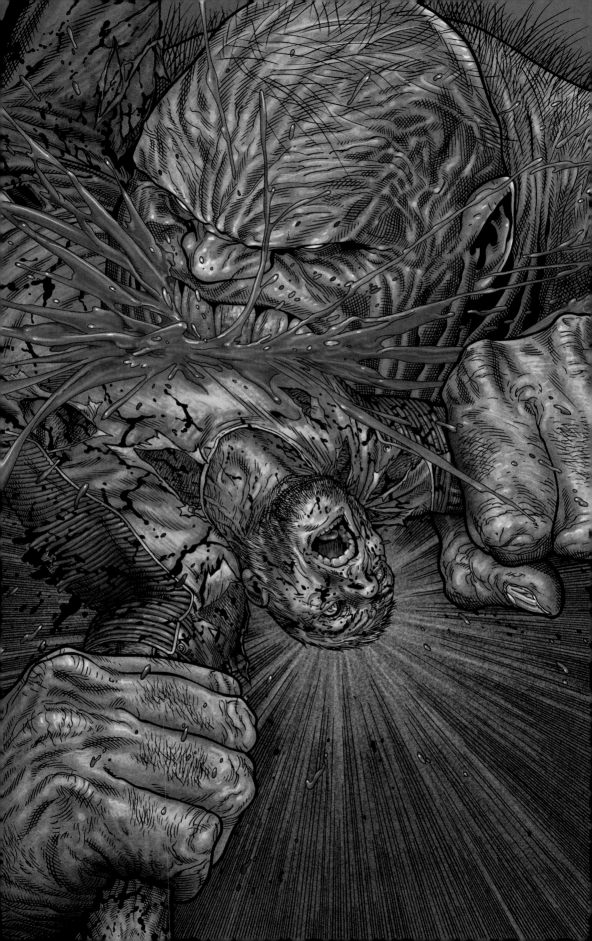

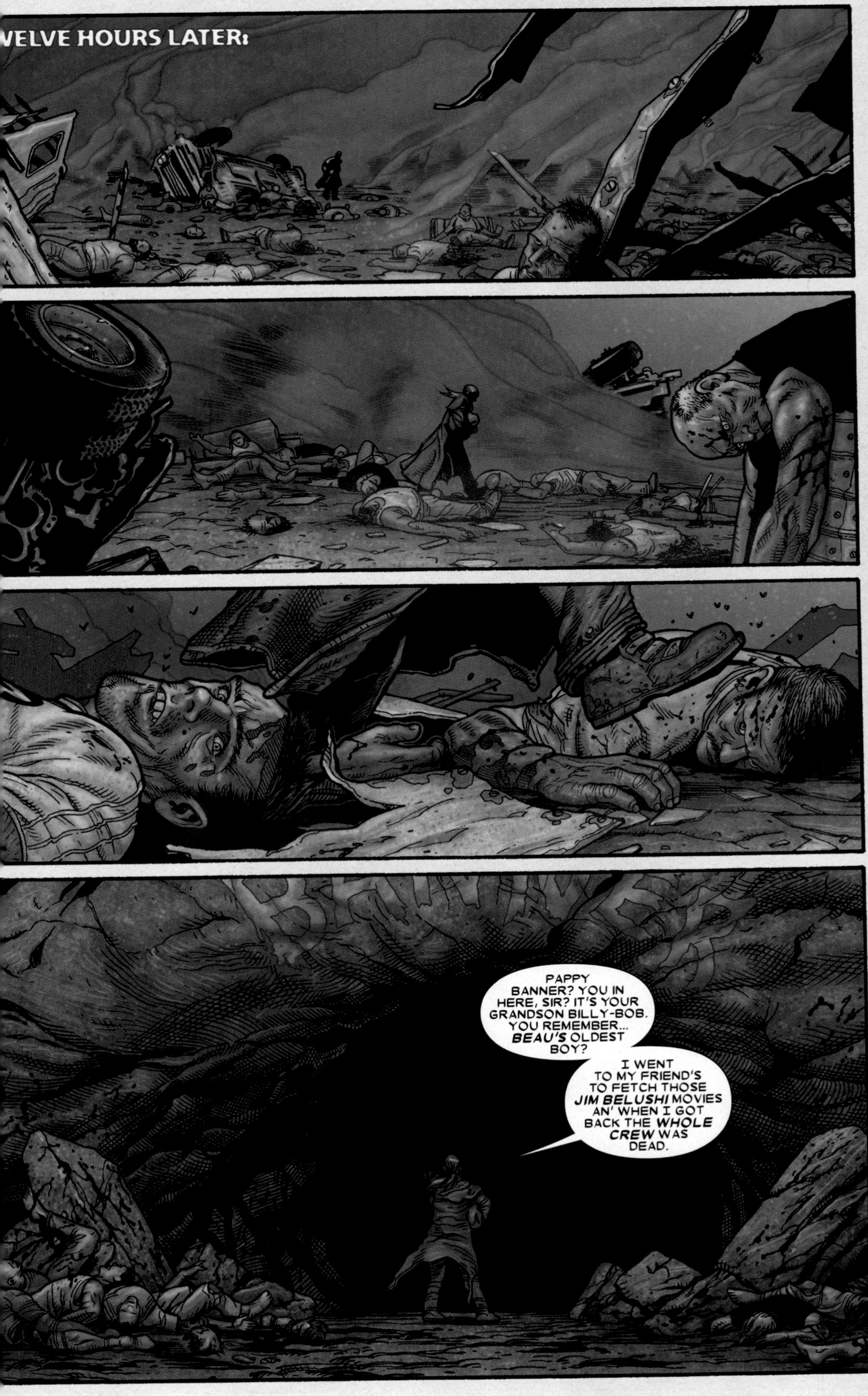
WELVE HOURS LATER:
PAPPY BANNER? YOU IN HERE, SIR? IT'S YOUR GRANDSON BILLY-BOB. YOU REMEMBER... BEAU'S OLDEST BOY?
I WENT TO MY FRIEND'S TO FETCH THOSE JIM BELUSHI MOVIES AN' WHEN I GOT BACK THE WHOLE CREW WAS DEAD.

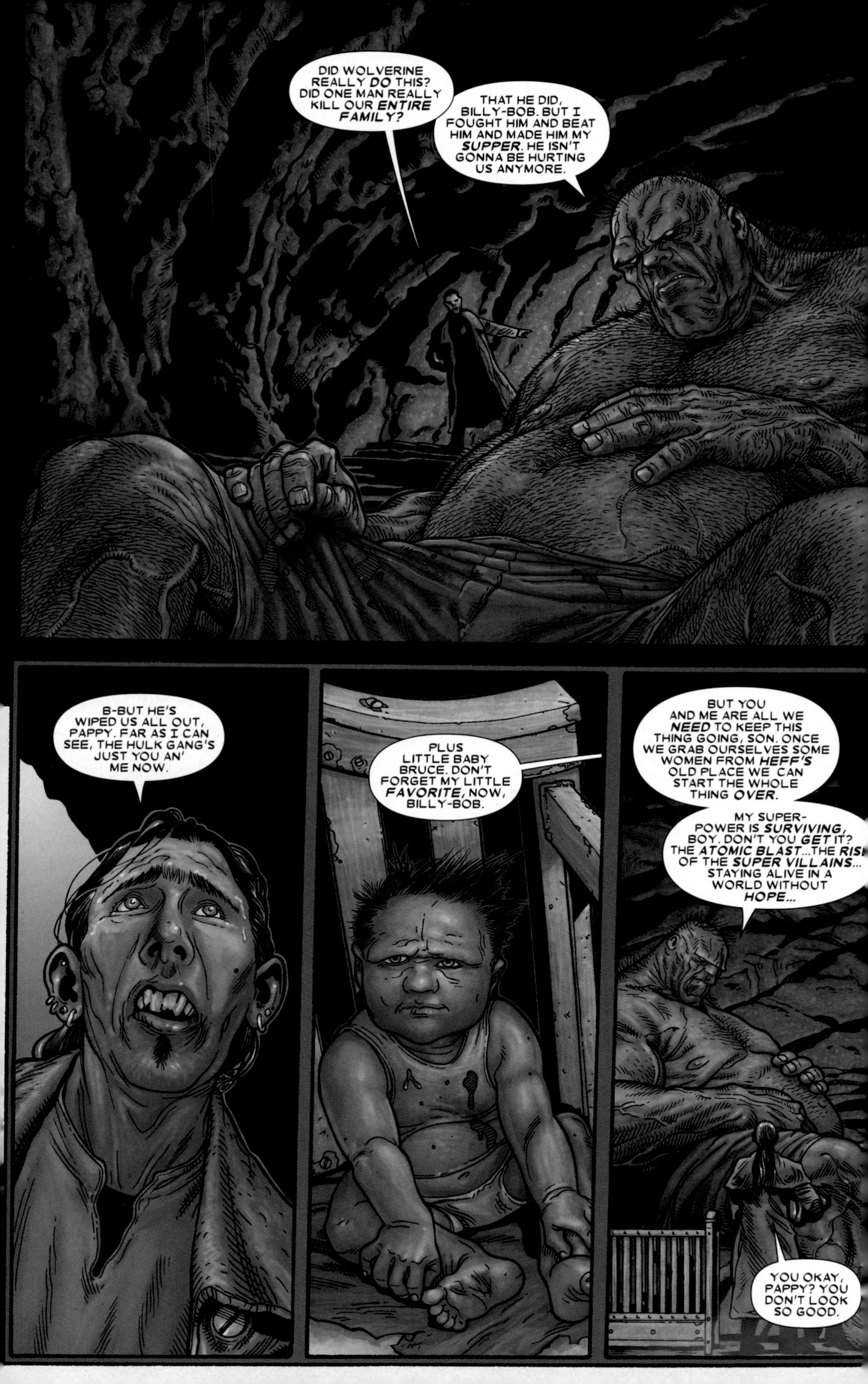
DID WOLVERINE REALLY DO THIS? DID ONE MAN REALLY KILL OUR ENTIRE FAMILY?
THAT HE DID, BILLY-BOB. BUT I FOUGHT HIM AND BEAT HIM AND MADE HIM MY SUPPER. HE ISN'T GONNA BE HURTING US ANYMORE.
B-BUT HE'S WIPED US ALL OUT, PAPPY. FAR AS I CAN SEE, THE HULK GANG'S JUST YOU AN' ME NOW.
PLUS LITTLE BABY BRUCE. DON'T FORGET MY LITTLE FAVORITE, NOW, BILLY-BOB.
BUT YOU AND ME ARE ALL WE NEED TO KEEP THIS THING GOING, SON. ONCE WE GRAB OURSELVES SOME WOMEN FROM HEFF'S OLD PLACE WE CAN START THE WHOLE THING OVER.
MY SUPER-POWER IS SURVIVING, BOY. DON'T YOU GET IT? THE ATOMIC BLAST...THE RIS OF THE SUPER VILLAINS... STAYING ALIVE IN A WORLD WITHOUT HOPE...
YOU OKAY, PAPPY? YOU DON'T LOOK SO GOOD.

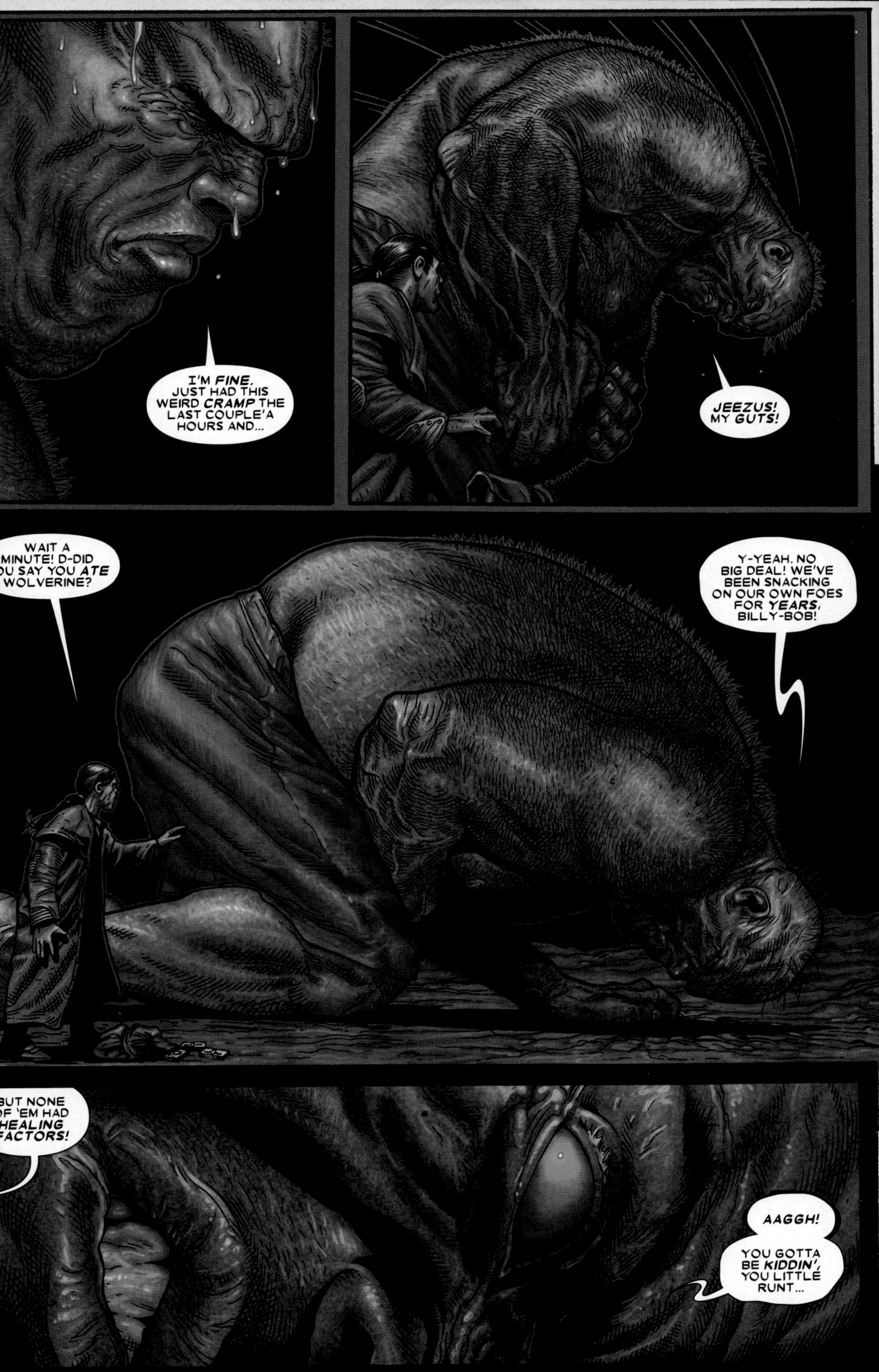

I'M FINE. JUST HAD THIS WEIRD CRAMP THE LAST COUPLE'A HOURS AND...
JEEZUS! MY GUTS!
WAIT A MINUTE! D-DID YOU SAY YOU ATE WOLVERINE?
Y-YEAH. NO BIG DEAL! WE'VE BEEN SNACKING ON OUR OWN FOES FOR YEARS, BILLY-BOB!
BUT NONE OF 'EM HAD HEALING FACTORS!
AAGGH!
YOU GOTTA BE KIDDIN', YOU LITTLE RUNT...

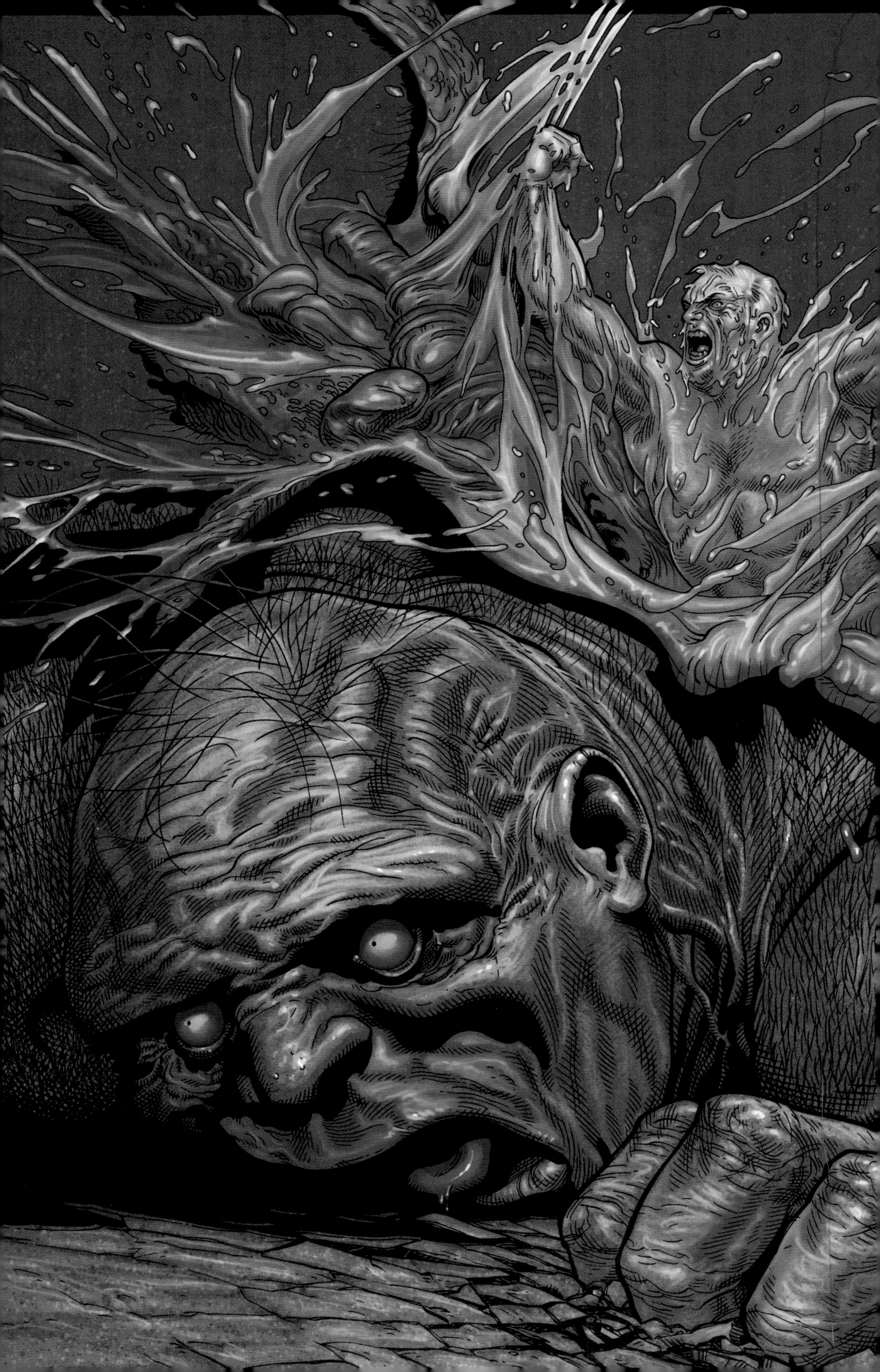

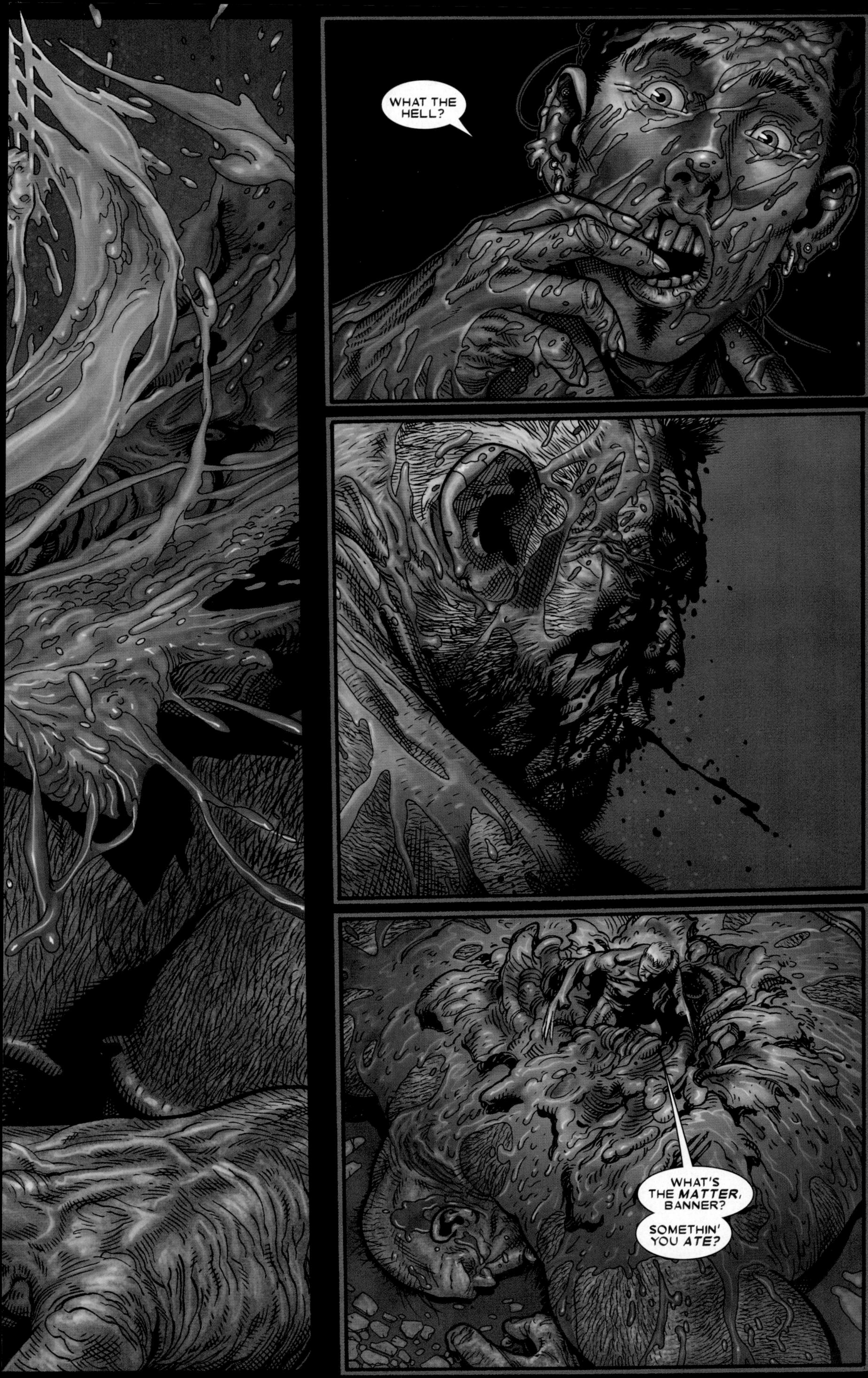
WHAT THE HELL?
WHAT'S THE *MATTER*, BANNER?
SOMETHIN' YOU *ATE*?

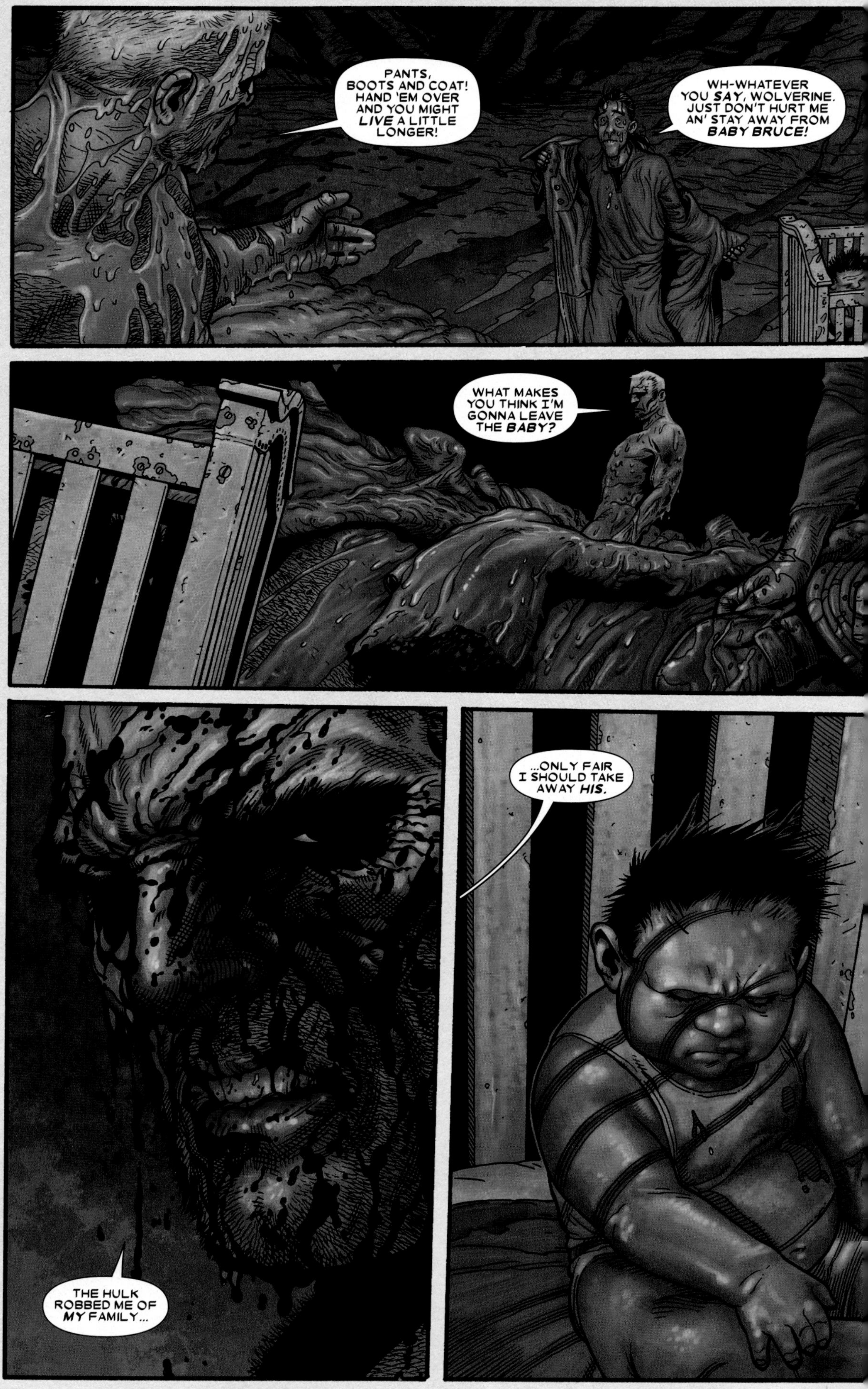
PANTS, BOOTS AND COAT! HAND 'EM OVER AND YOU MIGHT LIVE A LITTLE LONGER!
WH-WHATEVER YOU SAY, WOLVERINE. JUST DON'T HURT ME AN' STAY AWAY FROM BABY BRUCE!
WHAT MAKES YOU THINK I'M GONNA LEAVE THE BABY?
THE HULK ROBBED ME OF MY FAMILY...
...ONLY FAIR I SHOULD TAKE AWAY HIS.

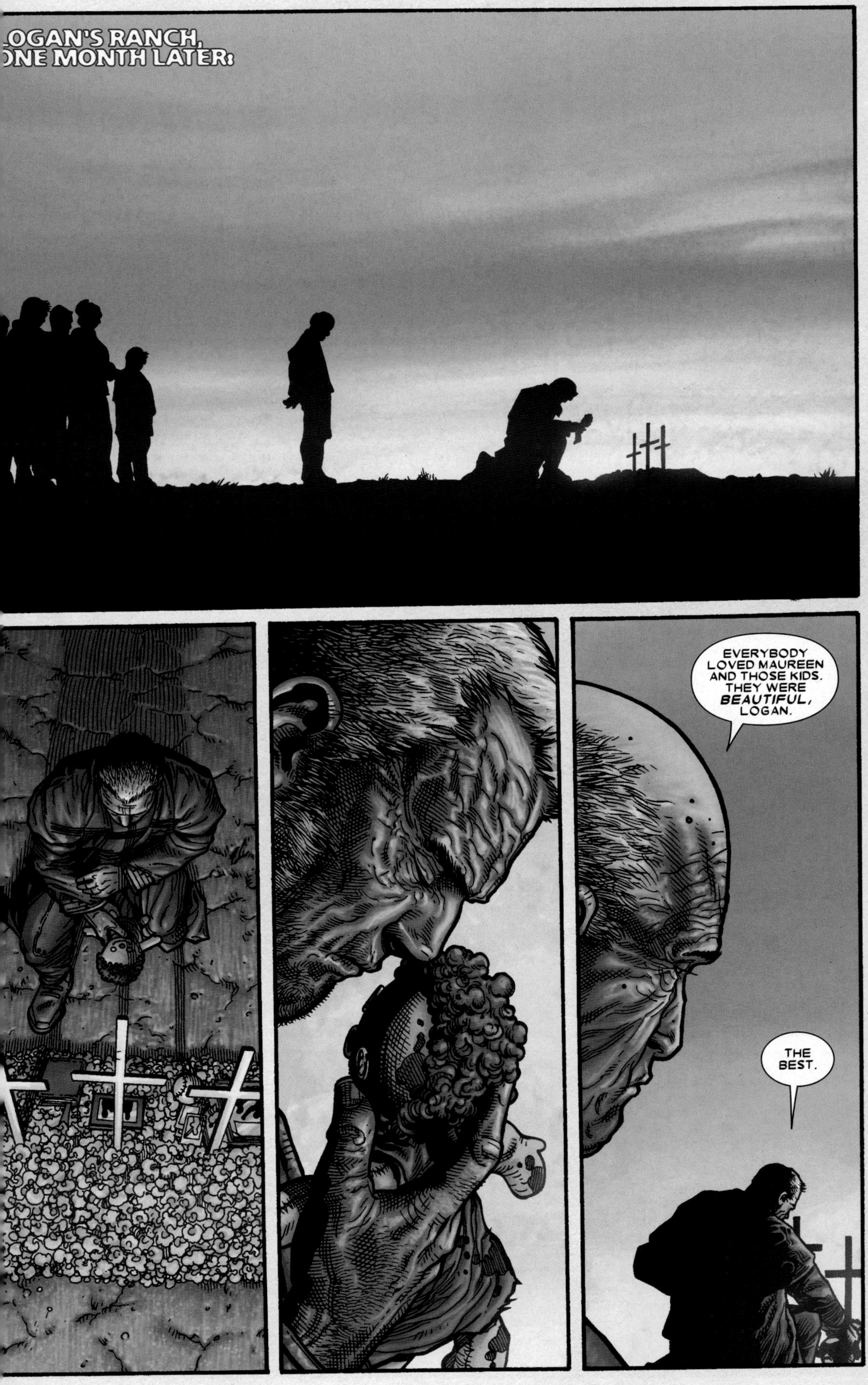
LOGAN'S RANCH, ONE MONTH LATER:
EVERYBODY LOVED MAUREEN AND THOSE KIDS. THEY WERE BEAUTIFUL, LOGAN.
THE BEST.

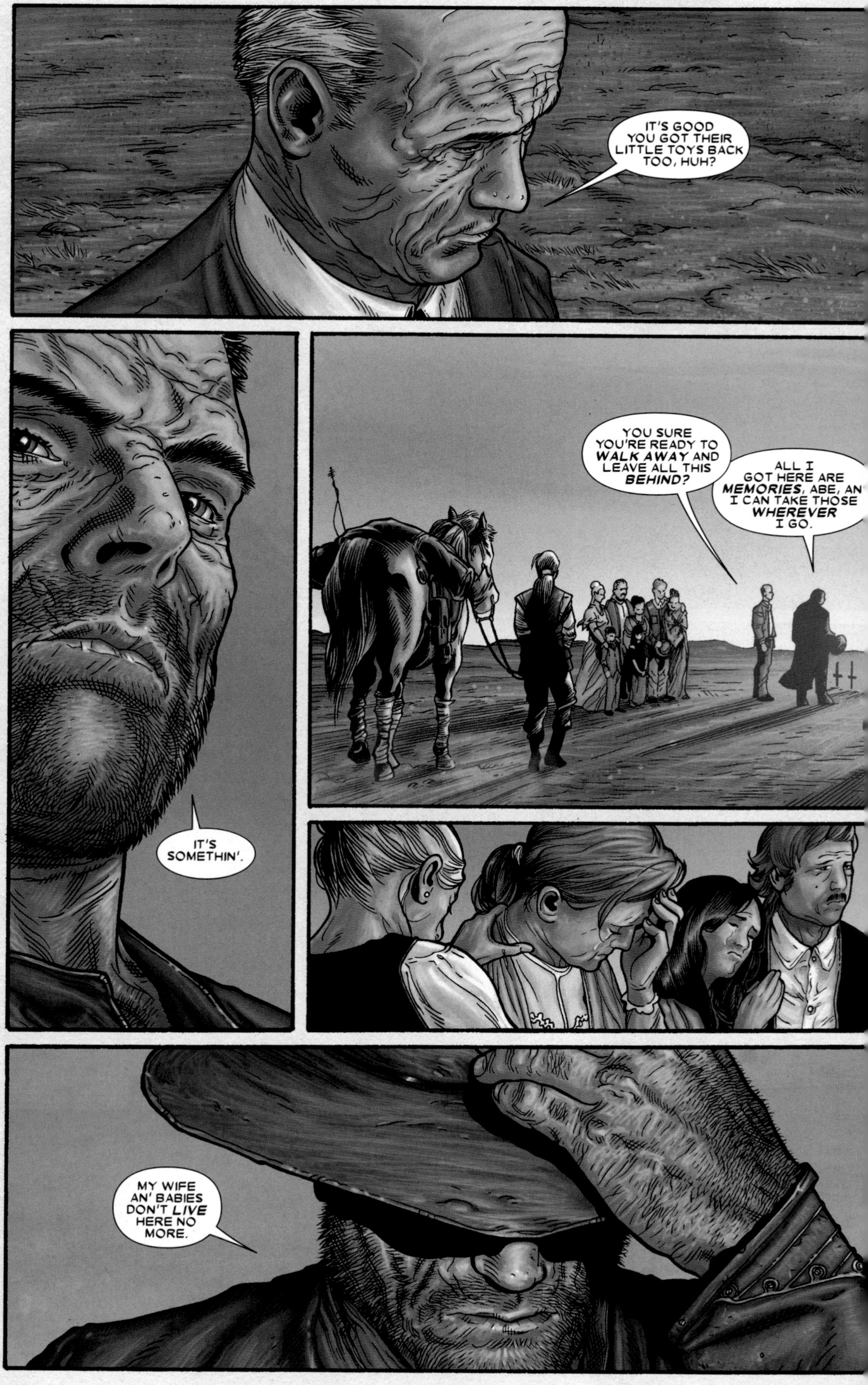
IT'S GOOD YOU GOT THEIR LITTLE TOYS BACK TOO, HUH?
IT'S SOMETHIN'.
YOU SURE YOU'RE READY TO WALK AWAY AND LEAVE ALL THIS BEHIND?
ALL I GOT HERE ARE MEMORIES, ABE, AN' I CAN TAKE THOSE WHEREVER I GO.
MY WIFE AN' BABIES DON'T LIVE HERE NO MORE.

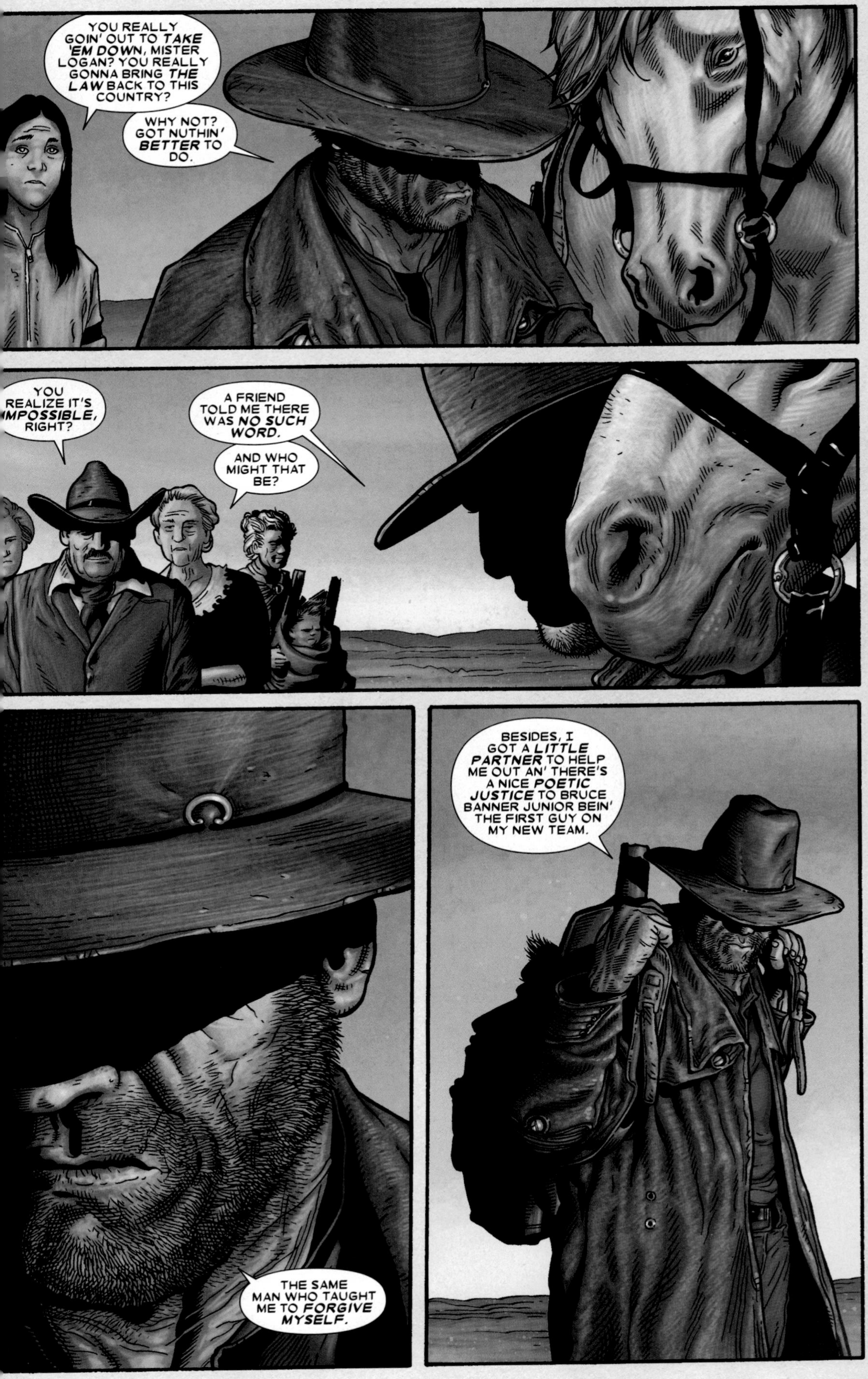

YOU REALLY GOIN' OUT TO TAKE 'EM DOWN, MISTER LOGAN? YOU REALLY GONNA BRING THE LAW BACK TO THIS COUNTRY?
WHY NOT? GOT NUTHIN' BETTER TO DO.
YOU REALIZE IT'S IMPOSSIBLE, RIGHT?
A FRIEND TOLD ME THERE WAS NO SUCH WORD.
AND WHO MIGHT THAT BE?
THE SAME MAN WHO TAUGHT ME TO FORGIVE MYSELF.
BESIDES, I GOT A LITTLE PARTNER TO HELP ME OUT AN' THERE'S A NICE POETIC JUSTICE TO BRUCE BANNER JUNIOR BEIN' THE FIRST GUY ON MY NEW TEAM.

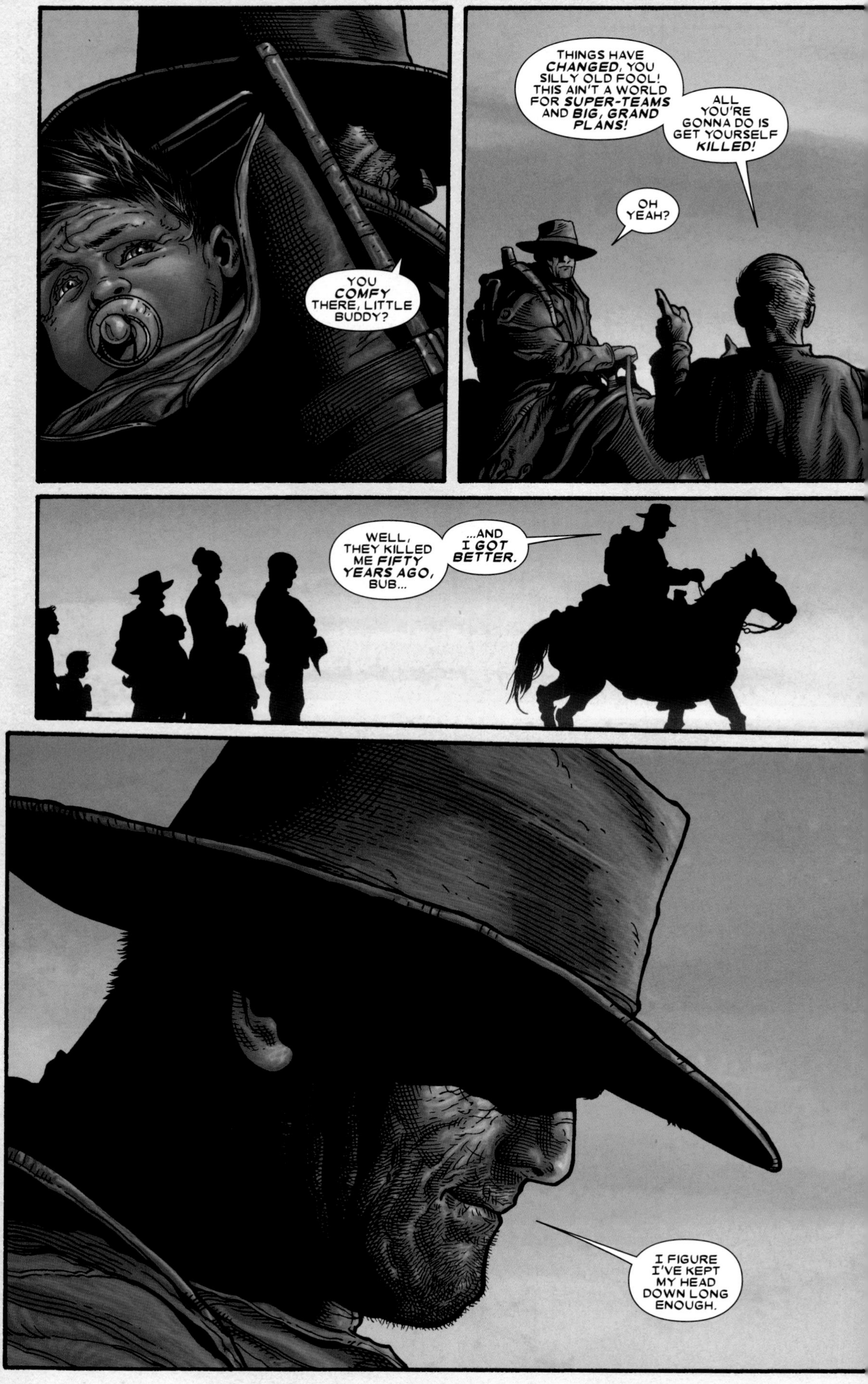
YOU COMFY THERE, LITTLE BUDDY?
THINGS HAVE CHANGED, YOU SILLY OLD FOOL! THIS AIN'T A WORLD FOR SUPER-TEAMS AND BIG, GRAND PLANS!
ALL YOU'RE GONNA DO IS GET YOURSELF KILLED!
OH YEAH?
WELL, THEY KILLED ME FIFTY YEARS AGO, BUB...
...AND I GOT BETTER.
I FIGURE I'VE KEPT MY HEAD DOWN LONG ENOUGH.

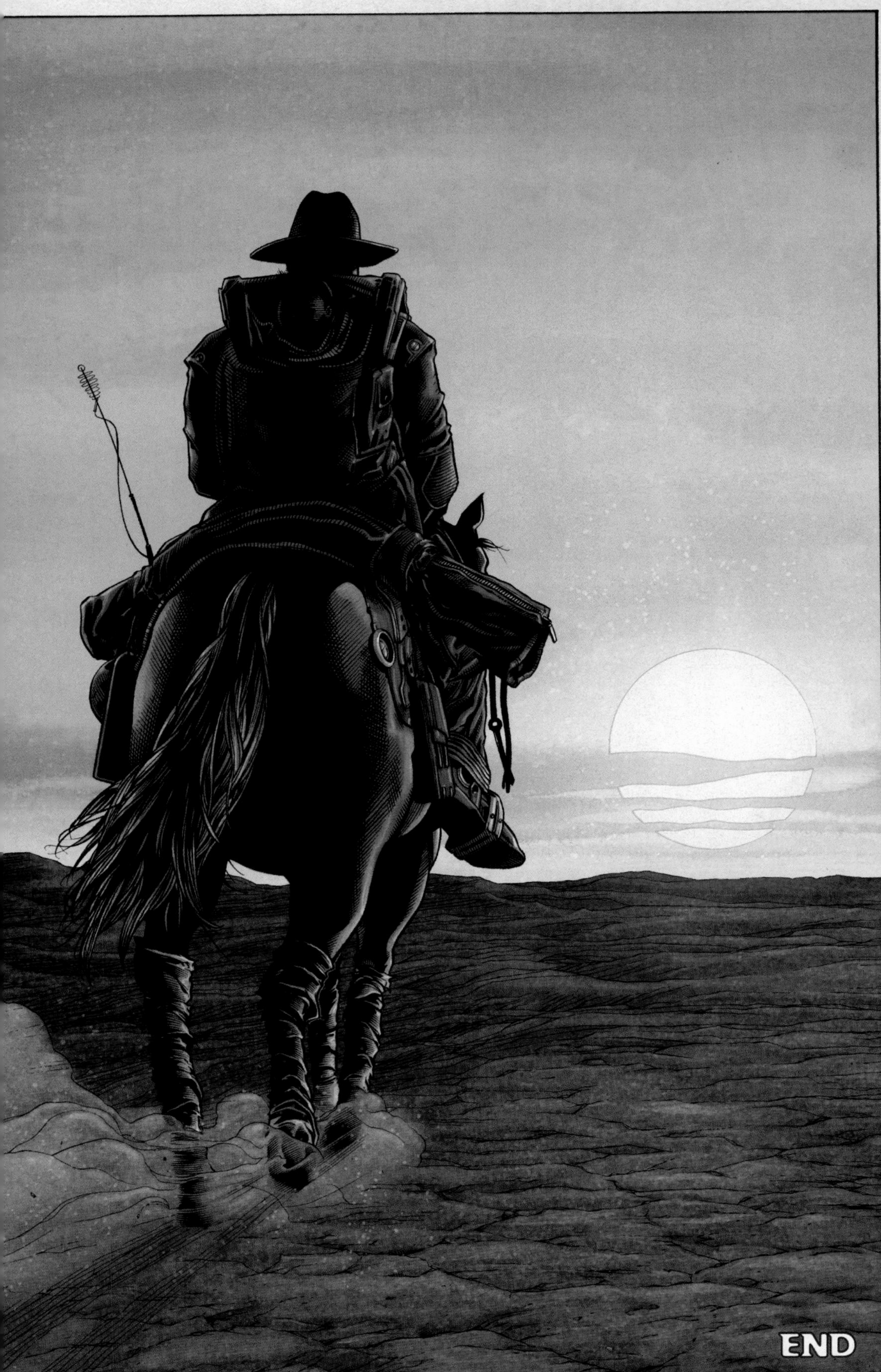
END

PINUP BY MORRY HOLLOWELL

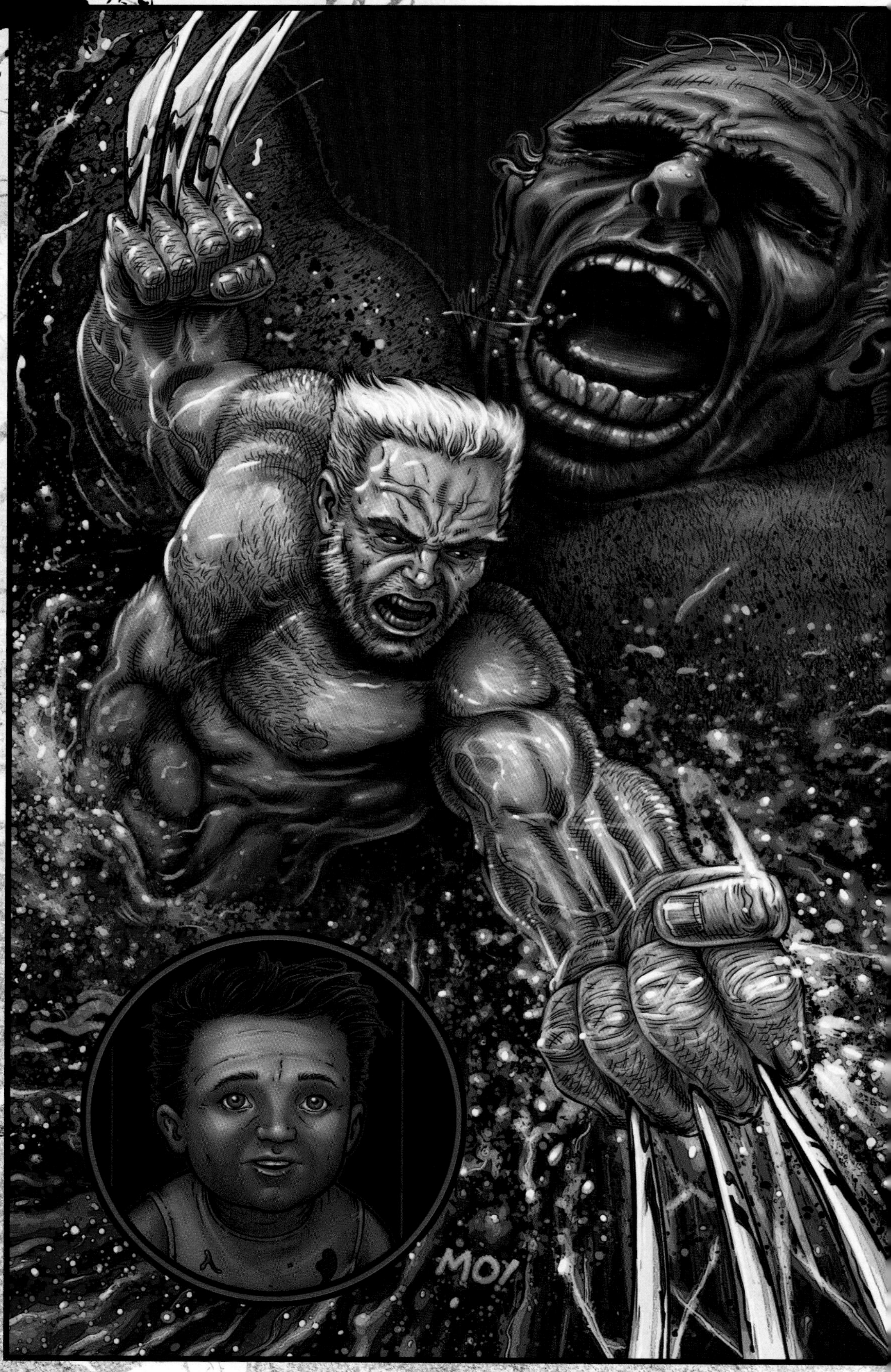

MOI

CHAPTER ONE DYNAMIC FORCES HERB TRIMPE VARIANT COVER

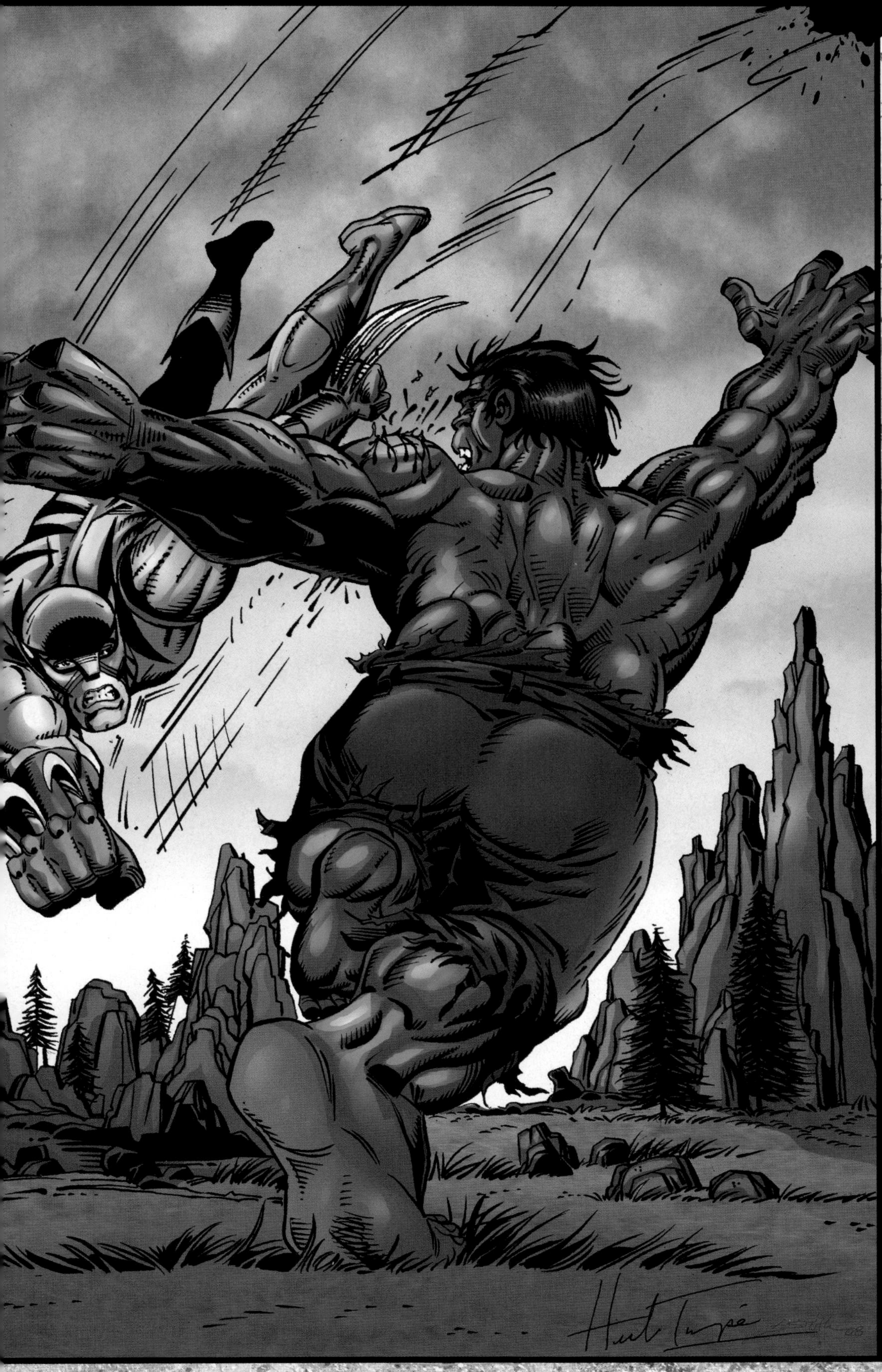

UNUSED COVER FOR CHAPTER ONE

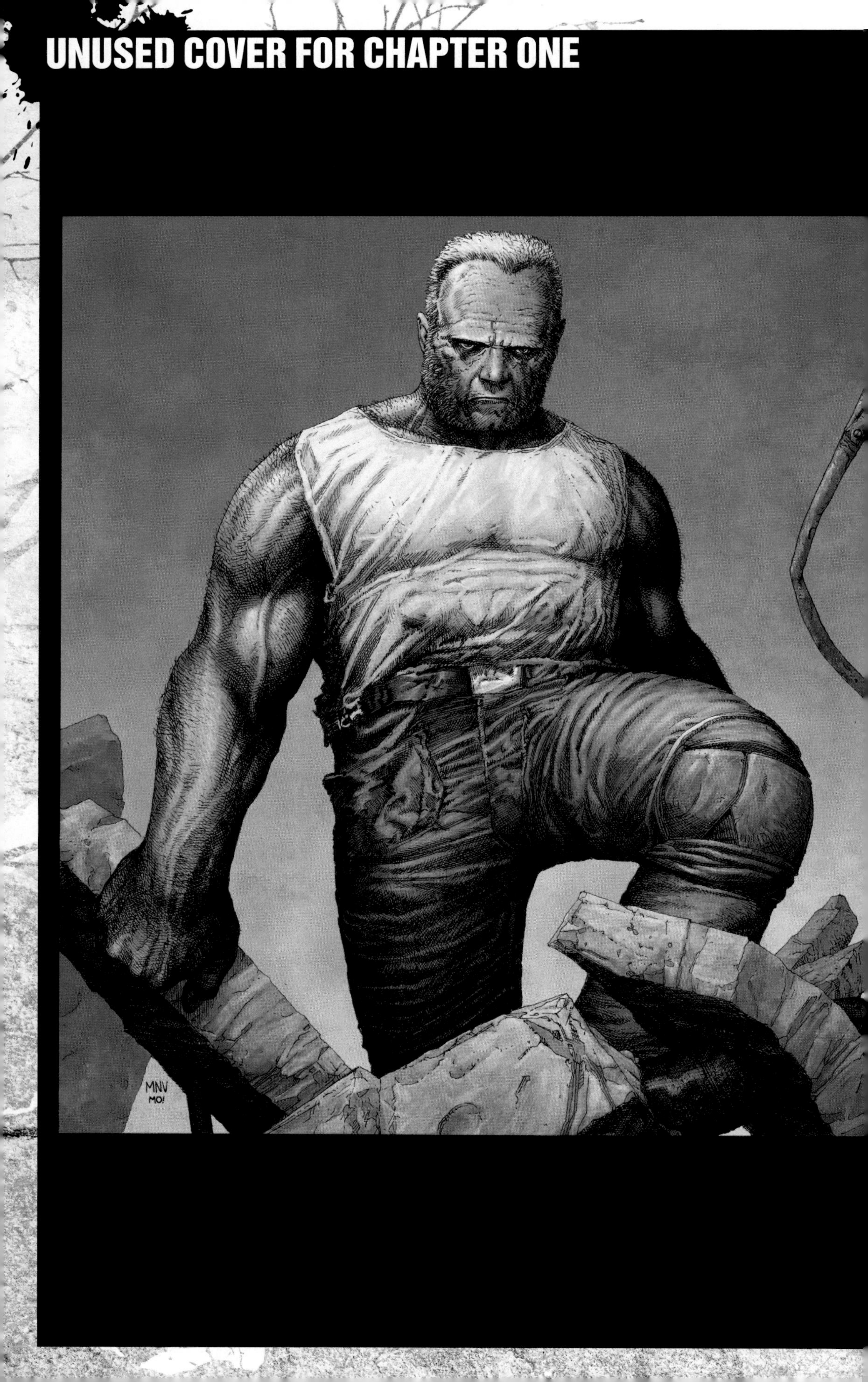
MNV
MO!

WIZARD #202 COVER

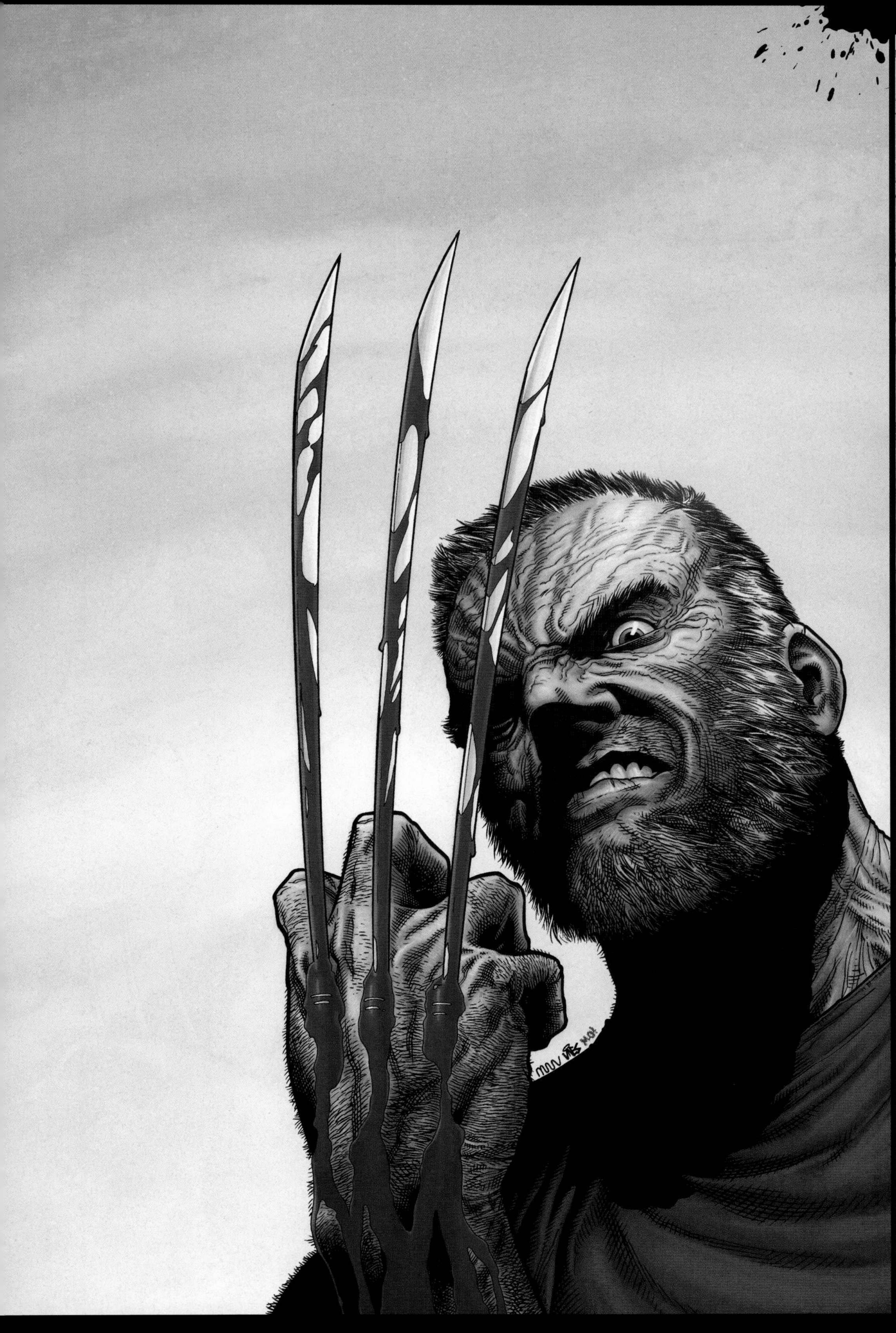

FINAL CHAPTER ED MCGUINNESS VARIANT COVER

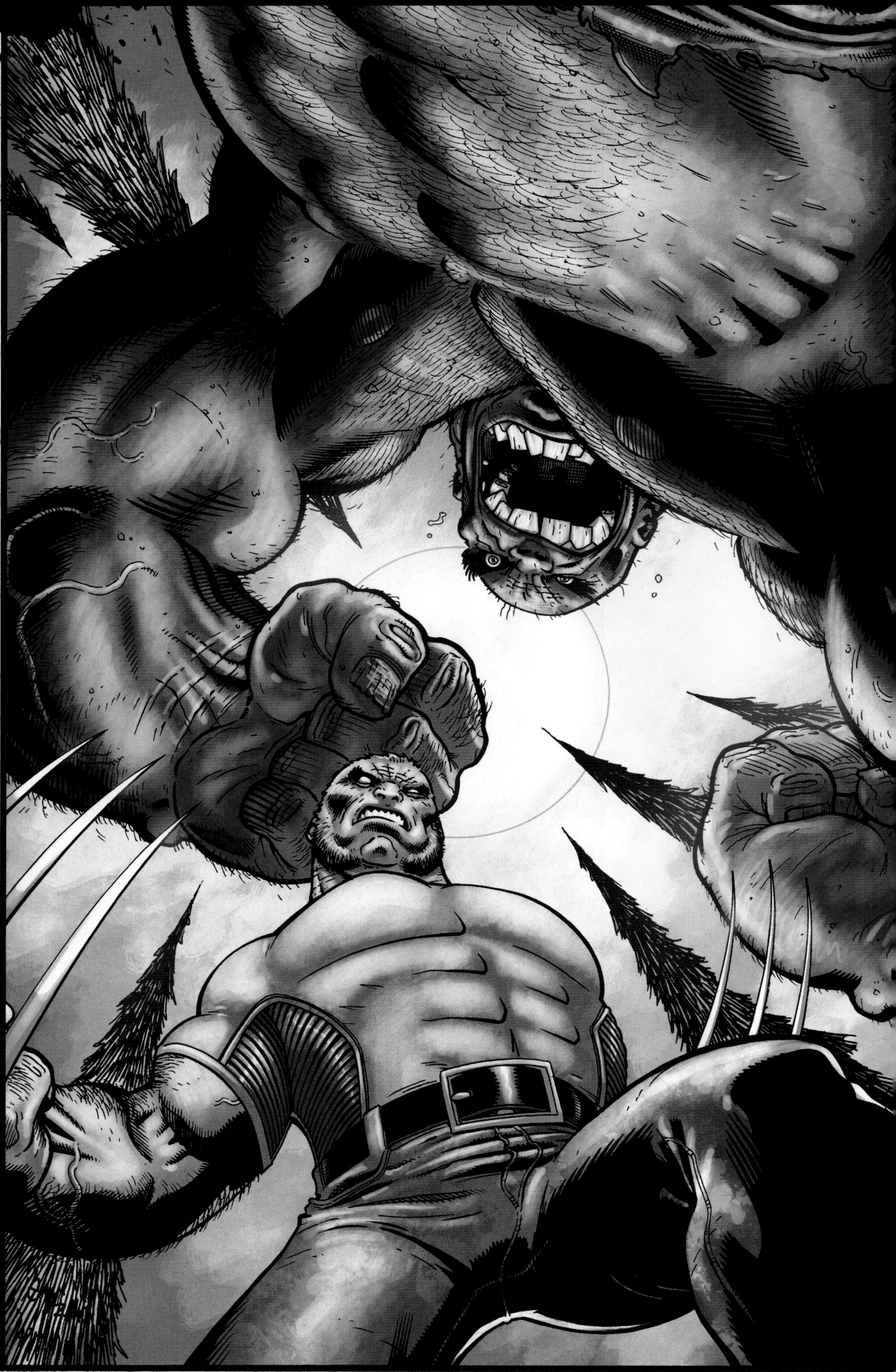

FINAL CHAPTER PAOLO RIVERA VARIANT COVER

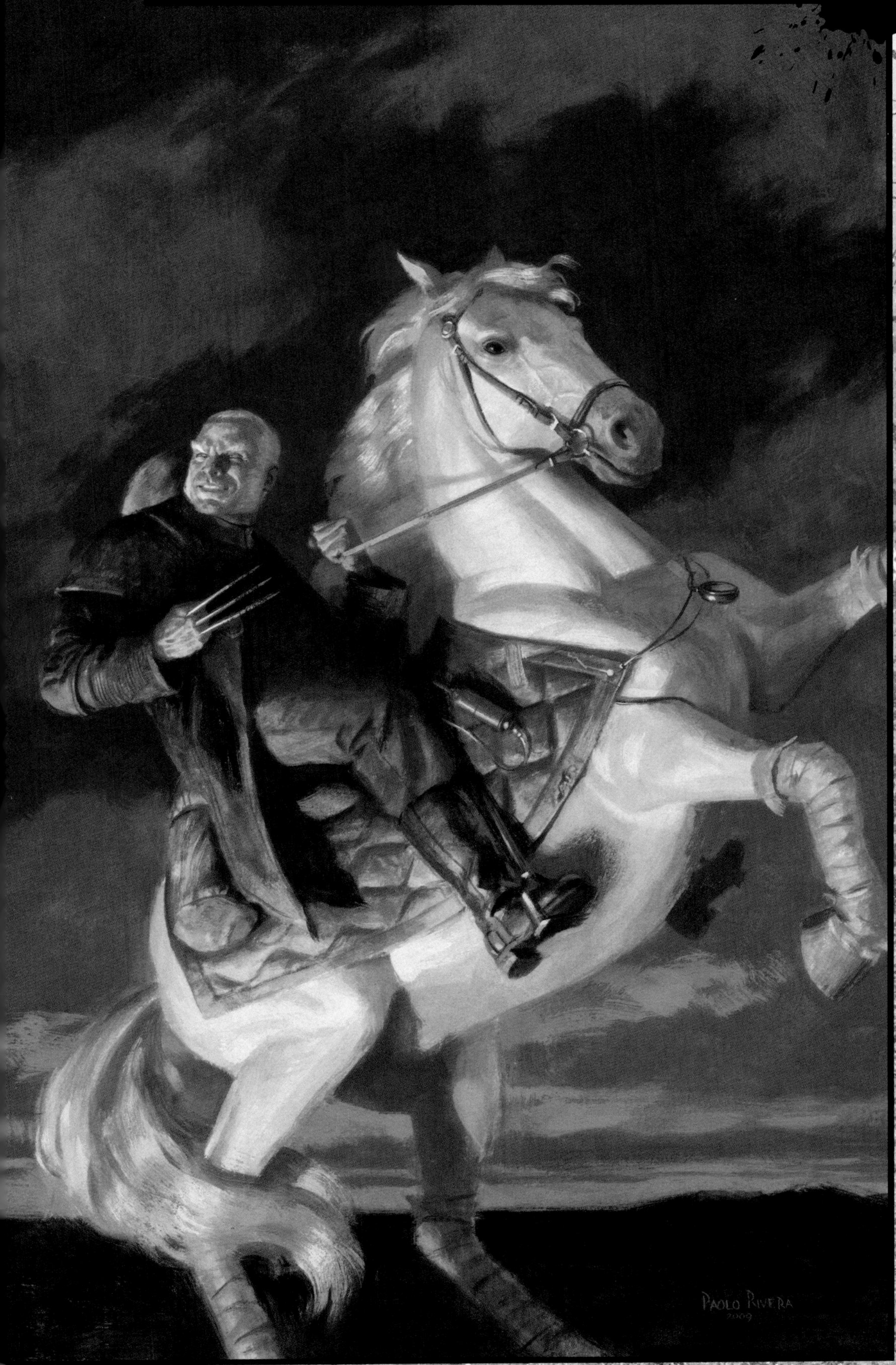
PAOLO RIVERA
2009

OLD MAN LOGAN CONCEPTS BY STEVE McNIVEN

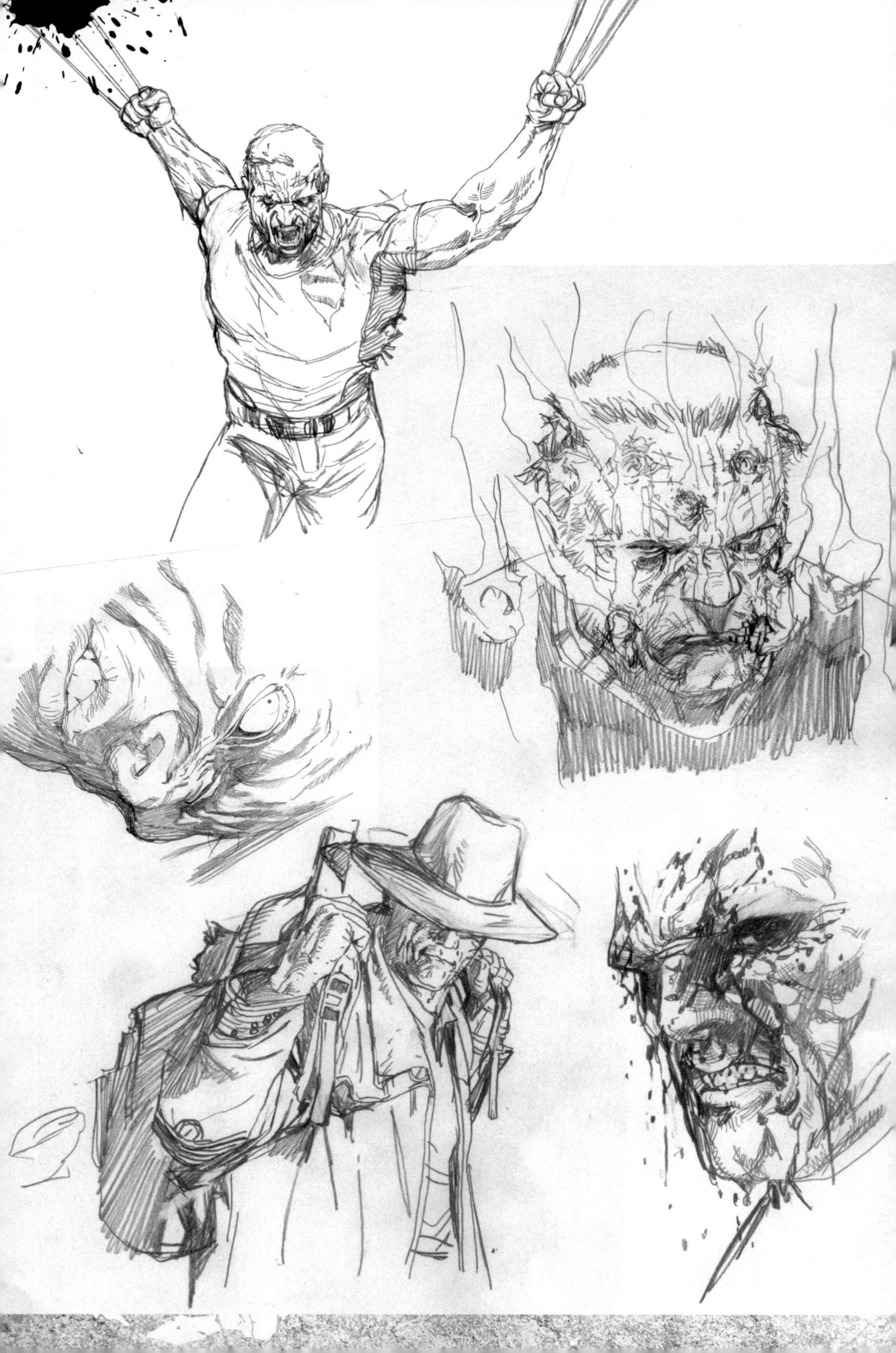

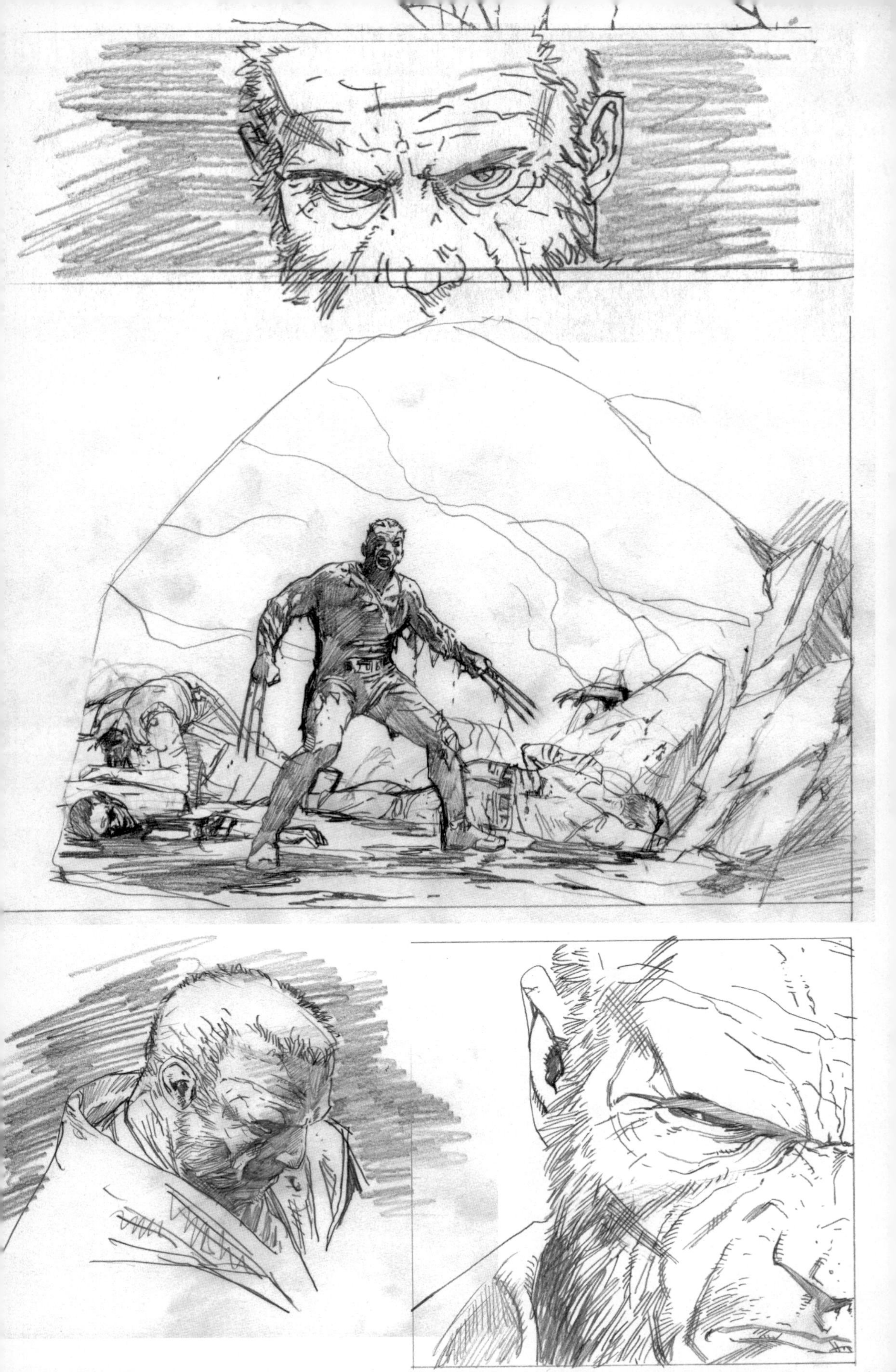

PRELIMINARY PENCILS FOR PAGES TWO AND THREE OF CHAPTER ON

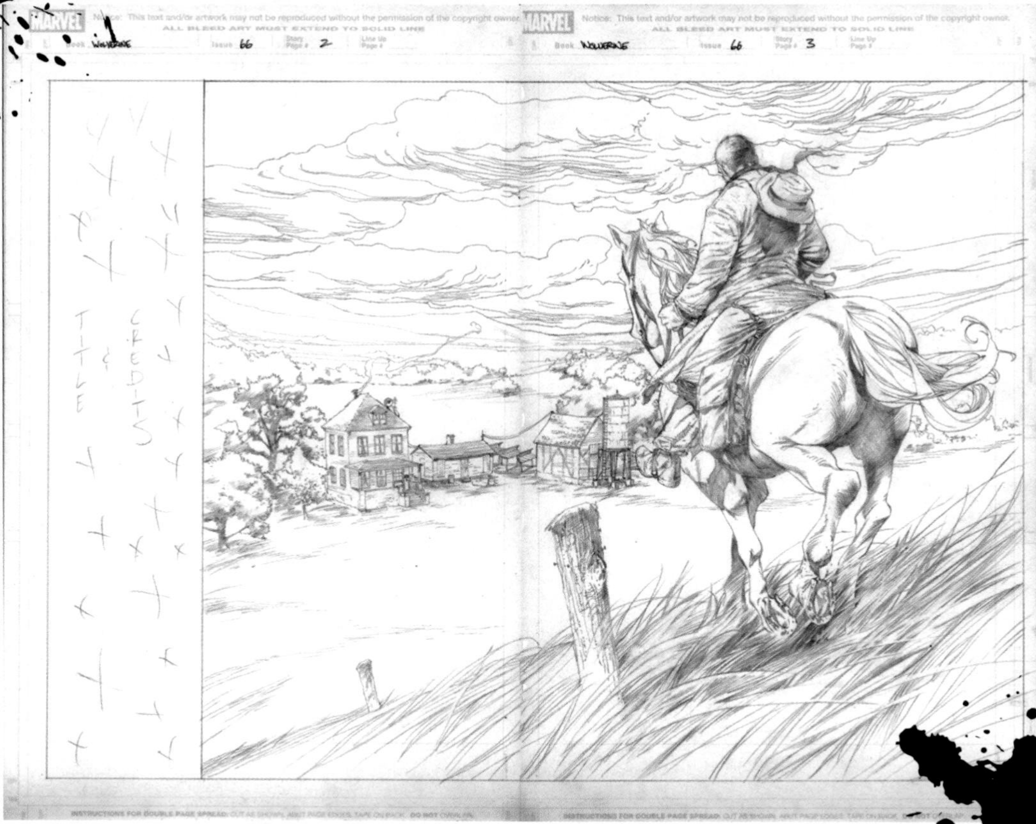

MARVEL
Notice: This text and/or artwork may not be reproduced without the permission of the copyright owner.
ALL BLEED ART MUST EXTEND TO SOLID LINE
Book WOLVERINE
Issue 66
Story Page # 2
MARVEL
Notice: This text and/or artwork may not be reproduced without the permission of the copyright owner.
ALL BLEED ART MUST EXTEND TO SOLID LINE
Book WOLVERINE
Issue 66
Story Page # 3
TITLE & CREDITS
INSTRUCTIONS FOR DOUBLE PAGE SPREAD: CUT AS SHOWN, ABUT PAGE EDGES, TAPE ON BACK. DO NOT OVERLAP.

FINAL PENCIL

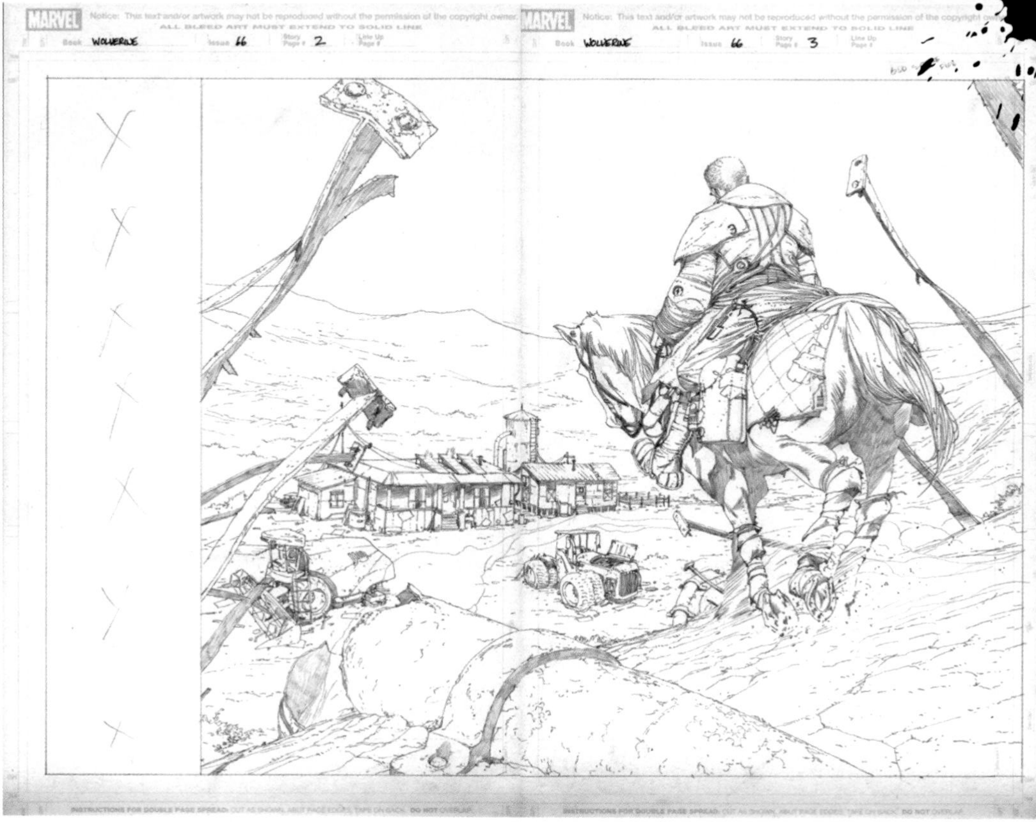

MARVEL
Notice: This text and/or artwork may not be reproduced without the permission of the copyright owner.
ALL BLEED ART MUST EXTEND TO SOLID LINE
Book WOLVERINE
Issue 66
Story Page # 2
MARVEL
Book WOLVERINE
Issue 66
Story Page # 3
INSTRUCTIONS FOR DOUBLE PAGE SPREAD: CUT AS SHOWN, ABUT PAGE EDGES, TAPE ON BACK. DO NOT OVERLAP.